the

19th Edition

A to Z

of careers
and jobs

THE ⚜ TIMES

the

19th Edition

A to Z

of careers and jobs

Edited by **Susan Hodgson**

KoganPage

LONDON PHILADELPHIA NEW DELHI

First published in Great Britain in 1984 by Kogan Page Limited
Nineteenth edition 2012

Kogan Page Limited
120 Pentonville Road
London N1 9JN
www.koganpage.com

British Library Cataloguing in Publication Data

A CIP record for this book is available from the British Library.

ISBN 978 0 7494 6429 5
E-ISBN 978 0 7494 6430 1

Preface

W hy use a book when there is so much information on the internet? Why browse a book about careers and jobs when the employment market is going through such troubled times? If these are questions in your mind, read on! This book is a quick and informative way to find about all the major types of work available in the United Kingdom. It gives you quick access to information that tells you how you can qualify for something, whether you are already qualified for something and how useful the attributes you already possess might be in different parts of the job market. The 'Earnings' sections are a guide, but remember that where very high salaries are mentioned, this is only likely to be for the few, most successful people in any particular career. Each entry points you in the direction of further information, so that if a job does grab your attention you know where you can start to delve more deeply.

Yes, the job market continues to be very tough indeed. It would be patronising and unrealistic to suggest that any one source of information is going to solve the problems of someone who has just been made redundant or is struggling to get a foothold in the job market after completing studies at school or college. Information, however, is a gateway to understanding and knowledge and to being able to maximise your chances of success when choosing a career or applying for a job. You could use this book in many ways: to confirm ideas that you have already started to work on; to explore the possibilities of a career change; to check which kinds of work fit your personal strengths; to ensure that when you are drawing up a CV for a particular career you press the right buttons; or to be well informed at a job interview.

In a competitive and changing job market, the more informed you can be, the better position you can put yourself in. I do hope you find the book useful and interesting.

Susan Hodgson, Careers consultant

Abbreviations

A level	Advanced level
AS level	Advanced Special level
Edexcel	Edexcel Foundation
GCSE	General Certificate of Secondary Education
GSVQ	General Scottish Vocational Qualification
H grade	Higher grade (SCE)
HNC/HND	Higher National Certificate/Higher National Diploma
HTC	Higher Technical Certificate
LSC	Learning and Skills Council
NC/ND	National Certificate/National Diploma
NVQ	National Vocational Qualification
QCA	Qualifications and Curriculum Authority
SCE	Scottish Certificate of Education (equivalent to GCSE)
SNC/SND	Scottish National Certificate/Scottish National Diploma
SQA	Scottish Qualifications Authority
SVQ	Scottish Vocational Qualification
TEC	Training and Enterprise Council
UCAS	Universities and Colleges Admissions System

Qualifications

S cottish readers should be aware that, in order to simplify the text, the editor has referred to qualifications required in terms of GCSEs, A levels and NVQs or equivalent. NVQs are directly equivalent to SVQs but Scottish National and Higher Qualifications are not equivalent to GCSEs and A levels. A new qualification, the Advanced Higher, does equate to A level but most universities still express their entry requirements in terms of the Higher. Full details of all Scottish qualifications can be found on the SQA website. The easiest way to compare the points awarded for A levels and Highers is to use the Universities and Colleges Admissions Service (UCAS) tariff calculator. Relevant Scottish sources of further information have been included where appropriate.

Overseas international qualifications

The National Recognition Centre (comparability of international qualifications) (NARIC) can provide a letter outlining how your overseas qualifications equate to UK qualifications. There is a charge for this service: £55.20 for paper applications; £46.00 if you apply online. Large organisations that deal with many overseas applicants may be able to give you some guidance too. You can contact NARIC at: Oriel House, Oriel Road, Cheltenham, Gloucestershire GL50 1XP; 0871 330 7033; **www.naric.org.uk.**

Useful points of contact

www.ucas.ac.uk
This is the central organisation which provides information about – and processes – applications for higher education courses. UCAS also offers advice on funding your studies.

www.ukpass.ac.uk
A new online service that enables you to research thousands of taught postgraduate courses.

www.cityandguilds.com
City & Guilds awards a wide range of qualifications across nearly 30 industries in the United Kingdom. You can find information on courses for 14–19-year-olds, adult learners and people looking for professional development opportunities.

www.crb.gov.uk
The Criminal Records Bureau (CRB) is the organisation which carries out the checks on anyone who has applied to work with children, young people or vulnerable adults. The website gives details about the procedure and includes an online application facility.

The National Minimum Wage

The current hourly rates are £6.08 if you are aged 21 or over, £4.98 if you are aged 18 to 20 and £3.68 if you are 16 or 17.

ACCOUNTANCY

Members of the accountancy profession are involved in the financial transactions of businesses, including the preparation and verification of accounts, auditing and analysis.

Accountant

Accountants work with, and have expert understanding of, a wide range of financial questions, issues and procedures. They work in many different settings, including small high street accounting firms, local and central government departments, management consultants and for the finance departments of commercial and industrial organisations, from small businesses to huge multinationals. They deal with such questions as taxation, business forecasting, monitoring financial performance, advising on investments, acquisitions and mergers, and good daily financial management. They also audit the paperwork and computer records of organisations to make sure that all financial transactions are accounted for and comply with the law.

Because accountants cover such a wide area of expertise, there are several different specialist branches within the profession. They work in one of the following three areas.

Management accountant

Chartered management accountants, usually referred to as management accountants, work in commerce and industry. They work with a company or organisation monitoring and planning budgets, preparing information for external auditors, overseeing credit control, monitoring financial performance and making suggestions about future business development. They work closely with other members of the management team. They may be qualified Chartered Accountants, Chartered Certified Accountants or Management Accountants.

ADVANCE YOUR CAREER

KNOWLEDGE FOR TODAY'S BUSINESS ENVIRONMENT

The Certificate in Finance, Accounting and Business (CFAB) will give you the key business skills to get ahead in your career. CFAB will provide you with the practical knowledge and essential tools in business, finance and accounting that can be used in any industry or organisation.

Choose what works for you. Flexible study options and no fixed exam dates allow you to fit CFAB around your existing commitments.

Find out more about CFAB today.

ICAEW

+44 (0)1908 248 250   icaew.com/careers

Your route to success

Have you considered where your future career lies? Do you want to work in a varied and dynamic business? Are you looking to enhance your CV? A professional business and accountancy qualification from ICAEW could be your route to success.

ICAEW is a world leader in the accountancy and finance profession. We have a range of qualifications which are recognised and respected around the world.

The Certificate in Finance, Accounting and Business

The Certificate in Finance, Accounting and Business (CFAB) will help you build key knowledge and skills that are transferable to any industry.

- Learn the fundamentals of finance, accounting and business.
- CFAB can give you a competitive advantage in the job market, showing employers you are intelligent, dedicated and business aware.
- You can study for CFAB regardless of your academic background or experience.
- Flexible study options and no fixed exam dates allow you to study for CFAB around your existing commitments.
- CFAB is achievable in less than 12 months.
- On completion, you'll be awarded a certificate which could help boost your CV.

If you're considering a career in finance or accountancy, CFAB covers the first six modules of the ACA qualification, so it will give you an introduction to becoming an ICAEW Chartered Accountant and what the profession is really like.

The ACA qualification

If you are looking for opportunity, variety and a highly rewarding career as a business leader – choose the internationally recognised chartered accountancy qualification – the ACA from ICAEW. It will give you the opportunity to work in any industry you choose. Many of the world's top business leaders are ICAEW Chartered Accountants.

Earn while you learn with the ACA

Along with some amazing career opportunities, you'll find that salaries for trainee and qualified ACAs are extremely competitive.

Routes to ACA training

There are several ways to qualify as an ICAEW Chartered Accountant. You don't need a background in accountancy, a business-related degree or even maths A-level, to start training towards the ACA straight after completing your A-levels. You can also complete the Certificate in Finance, Accounting and Business (CFAB) or join one of our university partnerships. The ACA gives you the opportunity to learn while in full-time employment, combining business and professional experience, study and exams. It is a challenging qualification which will start you on a successful and exciting career path allowing you to work in any industry anywhere in the world.

Find out more about your routes to success.

Visit **icaew.com/careers** or email **careers@icaew.com** or find us on **Facebook.com/icaewstartingpoint**

Accountant in private practice

Accountants working in private practice assess, monitor and advise on the financial status of private businesses. They work for freelances, for small firms or for large practices offering their services to fee-paying clients.

Practitioners are qualified as Associate Members of the Institute of Chartered Accountants in England and Wales (ICAEW), the Institute of Chartered Accountants in Scotland (ICAS), the Institute of Chartered Accountants in Ireland (ICAI), or the Association of Chartered Certified Accountants (ACCA). Members of the Association of International Accountants (AIA) also do private practice work.

One specific role within accountancy is that of the auditor. Auditors are responsible for checking the financial records of every kind of business and organisation and they are not employees of that organisation. External auditors must be qualified Chartered Accountants or international accountants.

Accountant in the public sector

Chartered public finance accountants (public sector accountants) control and assess the efficiency of public spending. Working for example in health trusts, local authorities, universities and central government departments, they examine the cost-effectiveness of policies, manage budgets, conduct internal audits and advise on policy.

Knowing in what kind of environment you would work and what specialist knowledge you wish to apply will help you choose which of the branches of accountancy is most appropriate for you.

Entry, qualifications and training

Each professional body offering training has slightly different entry requirements, but with much similarity. As an applicant you not only have to satisfy your prospective employer, but ensure that you meet the entry requirements of the accountancy body with which you wish to train.

With the exception of a few people with three good A levels, most trainees are graduates. A good honours degree in any subject is fine, although business, mathematics and technical subjects are strongly represented in the profession. If your degree includes a lot of maths, you may be exempt from some of the professional exams. Many employers set numeracy tests as part of their selection process.

You should have five GCSEs grades A or B and two A levels. Many accountancy firms require you to have 280 to 300 UCAS points if you wish to become a Chartered Accountant. All the accounting professional bodies offer alternative entry routes for mature students and for applicants who are already qualified accounting technicians.

Management accountants do not have to be graduates, but a good honours degree in a mathematical or business subject may offer exemptions from some of the professional examinations.

Accountants qualified with any of the professional accountancy bodies can work in the public sector, but the most relevant organisation is the Chartered Institute of Public Finance and Accountancy (CIPFA). If you don't have another accountancy qualification you must have three GCSEs grades A–C and two A levels and you must have maths and English at either GCSE or A level.

All the accountancy professions offer similar training routes where you have to complete three years' supervised work and take professional exams at two levels.

Training contracts are popular and you face a lot of competition for every opening. Some firms offer work experience during summer vacations and if you can obtain one of these positions this will also help your cause.

Personal attributes

Accountants have to be good at working with numbers but they must also be very good communicators. They have to be able to understand complex information and also to explain complicated information to people who don't have detailed financial knowledge. They must be persistent, and assertiveness is as important as tact and discretion.

Earnings

Starting salaries vary depending on location, size of firm and field of accountancy, but are around £25,000 to £28,000 for trainees in London and the South East; £17,000 to £24,000 is more typical elsewhere. On qualifying, salaries increase significantly – £40,000 to £55,000 with a few years' experience. Salary packages often include benefits such as pay bonuses, share options, and pension and private health plans. The professional bodies conduct regular salary surveys and you can obtain further information from them.

Info

Chartered Institute of Management Accountants (CIMA)
020 8849 2251
www.cimaglobal.com

Chartered Institute of Public Finance and Accountancy (CIPFA)
020 7543 5600
www.cipfa.org.uk

Association of Chartered Certified Accountants (ACCA)
020 7059 5000
www.accaglobal.com

Financial Skills Partnership
0845 257 3772
www.directions.org.uk

Accounting technician

Accounting technicians work in a variety of roles, often alongside professionally qualified Chartered Accountants. They are involved in the day-to-day practical work of accountancy and finance, including the preparation of information and accounts and the interpretation of computer information, such as audit, tax and payroll. Accounting technicians are widely employed in public finance, industry and commerce, and in private practice. Their roles range from accounts clerks to finance managers. A growing number of accounting technicians provide a range of services direct to the public and manage their own practice. Many go on to qualify with the senior chartered accountancy bodies.

Entry, qualifications and training

There are no set entry qualifications, but you must be confident with maths. Some employers may prefer you to have GCSEs (A–C) or equivalent in English and maths. Previous experience of office work and good IT skills, especially in creating spreadsheets, are also valuable.

You can start as an accounts clerk doing basic duties, and take work-based training or a part-time college course to qualify as a technician with the Association of Accounting Technicians (AAT) or Association of Chartered Certified Accountants (ACCA). You may not have to do the first stages of accounting technician training if you already have an A level or equivalent in accounting, previous relevant work experience or a basic bookkeeping qualification. AAT and ACCA qualifications comprise a foundation, an intermediate and a technician stage. The AAT or the ACCA can advise you about where to find a training place. It is also sometimes possible to do an apprenticeship as an accounting technician.

Personal attributes

You must be thorough and methodical and enjoy working with figures. Good IT skills and the ability to work as part of a team are also very important. Some positions involve considerable responsibility and/or the pressure of deadlines.

Earnings

Salaries are highest in London and the South East. Starting salaries for trainees are between £16,000 and £20,000. Qualified technicians earn from £18,000 to £27,000. Accounting technicians with other management responsibilities can earn far more.

Info

Financial Skills Partnership
0845 257 3772
www.directions.org.uk

Association of Chartered Certified Accountants (ACCA)
020 7059 5000
www.accaglobal.com

Association of Accounting Technicians (AAT)
0845 863 0800
www.aat.org.uk

ACTOR

(see Performing Arts)

ACTUARY

Actuaries use their knowledge of mathematics, statistics, economics and business to assess financial risks and probabilities. Traditionally their work is mainly concerned with the topical issue of pensions, plus life assurance and other types of insurance, but they may also work in investment and other business areas where major financial risks are involved.

They create statistical and mathematical models to analyse past events and predict the financial outcome of different situations. For example, in insurance they may study accident rates or medical data to develop and price new insurance policies, making sure that there are sufficient funds to cover liabilities but allow the company to remain profitable.

Around 45 per cent of actuaries work for consultancies, with the job title of actuarial consultant, providing specialist actuarial services to businesses of every kind. They advise on business recovery, acquisitions and employee benefit schemes. Central government also has its own actuarial departments, which provide actuarial support and information across central government, its agencies and the National Health Service.

Entry, qualifications and training

To qualify as an actuary you must become a student member of one of the professional bodies; either the Faculty or Institute of Actuaries – referred to collectively as the Actuarial Profession. Minimum entry qualifications are three GCSEs grades A–C including English and two A levels, one of which must be maths at grade B. If you have a second class honours degree in any subject, A level maths grade C is acceptable. If you have a degree in maths or actuarial science you do not need a maths A level. If your degree is in maths or a highly numerate discipline a third class honours degree may be accepted. In practice, entry to the profession is competitive, so the majority of entrants are graduates with good degrees.

Once you have completed your professional training, study and examinations you become a Fellow of either the Institute or Faculty. To qualify as a Fellow of the Faculty or Institute of Actuaries, you must pass 15 professional examinations. After one year's work experience and appropriate examinations you should reach associate membership and after three years' work experience and appropriate exams you should reach fellowship.

If you have a degree or postgraduate qualification in actuarial science, statistics or economics, you may be exempt from some or all of the exams at the Core Technical Stage and some at the next stage. Please contact the Institute of Actuaries for further details of exemptions.

Personal attributes

You need excellent maths and statistical skills and must be able to understand and explain complex information. You should have a thorough understanding of business and economics, be a great communicator and be aware of the bigger picture while paying attention to fine detail.

Earnings

Trainee actuaries start on around £30,000. This rises to between £35,000 and £45,000 for part-qualified associate actuaries. Qualified actuaries with at least five years' experience can earn between £55,000 and £75,000 and some salaries in the profession reach more than £150,000.

Info

The Actuarial Education Company
01235 550005
www.acted.co.uk

The Actuarial Profession
01865 268200
www.actuaries.org.uk

The Association of Consulting Actuaries
020 7382 4954
www.aca.org.uk

Faculty of Actuaries
0131 240 1300
www.actuaries.org.uk

Financial Skills Partnership
020 7367 9542
www.directions.org.uk

Government Actuary's Department (GAD)
020 7211 2601
www.gad.gov.uk

Discover Risk
www.discoverrisk.co.uk

ADVERTISING

Communication is the heart of this complex industry. Advertising agencies plan, organise and run advertising campaigns for clients from the worlds of business, government, charities, pressure groups and other organisations. They aim to maximise exposure of a product, service or idea to its potential market. They advise clients on which media to use – the internet, radio, newspapers, television, posters or direct marketing – then develop the appropriate material. In addition to the job titles mentioned here, advertising agencies also employ artists, designers and photographers, either in-house or on a freelance basis.

Account executive

Account executives are responsible within the agency for a particular client or group of clients. They interpret the client's wishes; coordinate and supervise the work of others within the agency, such as creatives, account planners, copywriters and scriptwriters; seek advice from other experts such as media executives; and then present the ideas most likely to meet with the client's approval.

Account planner

Account planners consider the client's brief and work to identify the ideal audience and optimum method of getting the client's message across. They analyse market research and other data and provide the creative team with the information that will help them develop the most effective campaign. They may also work on forward planning for the agency, identifying likely future clients based on market data they have researched.

Art editor/executive director

This position involves coordinating the work of the creative department, which converts the client's original intentions into a visual form for approval. Others, including copywriters, may elaborate upon this.

Copywriter and scriptwriter

The writers in the agency produce headings, text, jingles and copy for articles in journals, and scripts for films and commercials. Copywriters often work closely with the other professionals who have developed the basic ideas on which the copy- and scriptwriters are working.

Media executive

Media executives work as media buyers and media planners to ensure that advertising campaigns reach their target audiences. Media planners work out where advertising will be most effective – television, radio, posters, newspapers, magazines and of course the internet. They must keep abreast of the changing market; the growth in internet advertising is a prime example of this. Media buyers try to get the best possible deals for their clients when placing advertising with this wide variety of media.

Entry, qualifications and training

Advertising is a fiercely competitive sector, especially in the current economic climate. Most entrants to jobs in advertising have either a degree or an HND. Any subject is acceptable, but some employers prefer related subjects, including advertising, business studies, marketing, English or consumer science. Smaller agencies may take you without a degree, particularly if you have some relevant work experience. Work experience is extremely valuable: it shows you how agencies work and makes you a stronger applicant, but this experience is hard to come by. You may want to consider doing voluntary work for an agency. Some agencies offer formal work experience schemes and details of these appear on the Institute of Practitioners in Advertising (IPA) website. There are many courses in marketing, communications and media studies at many levels. These may provide useful background, but they won't necessarily make you more employable. There are a few highly respected postgraduate courses in advertising, including a diploma in copywriting at West Herts College and a postgraduate diploma in advertising at Falmouth College of Art and Design.

Most training is on the job, learning from colleagues, and you are usually considered to be a trainee for about two years. The IPA offers induction courses and continuing professional development courses, and the Chartered Institute of Marketing (CIM) offers a range of part-time and distance-learning courses for those who are already working in the sector.

A few schools and colleges have introduced new vocational diplomas in creative and media studies. These can be taken at foundation, higher or advanced level. These courses combine academic study and training with an employer.

Personal attributes

Excellent communication skills at every level are extremely important. Being able to deal with people, write clearly and work creatively are all essential skills. Many roles require you to be persuasive and tactful, and to be a media planner you need to be highly numerate. Advertising is a highly pressured business so you have to be thick-skinned and keep calm when chasing deadlines.

Earnings

Starting salaries range from £18,000 to £25,000 depending on your role. Trainee account executives often earn more than trainee media planners and buyers. Salary also depends on size of the agency. Many agencies are based in London and the South East. In the regions, starting salaries range from £15,000 to £20,000. Senior account executives can earn £100,000, but averages are closer to £43,000 to £50,000. Advertising has suffered in the current recession and salaries have not risen as fast in the past 18 months.

Info

Account Planning Group
020 8444 3692
www.apg.org.uk

The Advertising Association (AA)
0107 340 1100
www.adassoc.org.uk

British Interactive Media
Association (BIMA)
www.bima.co.uk

Chartered Institute of Marketing
(CIM)
01628 427500
www.cim.co.uk

Communication, Advertising and
Marketing Education Foundation
(CAM)
01628 427 120
www.camfoundation.com

Creative and Cultural Skills (The
Sector Skills Council for Craft,
Cultural Heritage, Design, Literature,
Music, Performing, and Visual Arts)
0207 015 1800
www.ccskills.org.uk

Institute of Practitioners in
Advertising (IPA)
http://www.ipa.co.uk/

AGRICULTURE

(see Farming and Gardening)

AMBULANCE SERVICE

Most of the work in the ambulance service is with patients, providing pre-hospital care and transport in response to emergency and urgent calls, or providing transport for those unable, for medical reasons, to make their own way to hospital. There are two distinct areas of front-line work: accident and emergency, and patient transport services.

Ambulance care assistant

Ambulance care assistants usually work in the patient transport service of an ambulance trust, where they drive disabled, elderly and vulnerable people to and from outpatient clinics, day-care centres and to routine hospital admissions. They are sometimes called PTS drivers. They may have to lift or assist patients in and out of vehicles and they have to ensure that their patients are comfortable and safe.

Ambulance technician

Ambulance technicians normally work alongside a paramedic, attending scenes of accidents and other emergencies. Supervised by a paramedic, an ambulance technician carries out a wide range of emergency treatments, treating burns, wounds, fractures and heart attacks. As well as treating patients, ambulance technicians have to liaise with patients' relatives, with members of the public and with staff from other emergency services.

Emergency medical dispatcher

Emergency medical dispatchers handle emergency 999 calls from the public and from GPs. Some ambulance services split this role into call takers and dispatchers. Where this is the case, call handlers take down details accurately, quickly and calmly. Dispatchers then decide how best to deal with this situation – how many vehicles to send, for example. In some ambulance services, the same person is responsible for taking down details, logging them onto a computer and sending out the ambulances.

Paramedic

Paramedics are the senior ambulance service healthcare professionals at an accident or a medical emergency. They assess a patient's condition and give essential and often lifesaving treatment. They use a range of sophisticated equipment and can administer drugs, drips and oxygen. They are trained to resuscitate and stabilise patients and they may also drive ambulances, since they usually work in teams of two to a vehicle.

PTS call handler

PTS (Patient Transport Service) call handlers work in the non-emergency part of ambulance services, organising routine transport to take patients to and from hospital appointments and home after discharge. They deal with requests for appointments and ensure the most efficient use of the available vehicles.

Entry, qualifications and training

Entry qualifications for ambulance care assistants and for emergency medical dispatchers vary between ambulance trusts – many require GCSEs, NVQs and/or relevant work experience. PTS call handlers don't need academic qualifications, though each ambulance service sets its own entry requirements. Training is on the job and covers how to use communications equipment and customer care skills. Drivers of non-emergency and emergency vehicles must hold a full, clean, manual driving licence.

Ambulance technicians have often worked as ambulance care assistants first. An alternative route is to obtain a post as a trainee ambulance technician. Academic requirements for this vary between different ambulance services, but GCSEs grades A–C are often required. Paramedics qualify either by training first as an ambulance technician or by doing a diploma, Foundation degree or degree course in paramedic science. Appropriate courses are approved by the Health Professions Council (HPC).

Training relevant to particular roles is given on the job and through special training courses on lifting and handling patients, advanced driving, etc. Ambulance technicians and paramedics need regular training to keep them up to date with new equipment, drugs and knowledge of dealing with emergency situations.

Personal attributes

For all the roles in the ambulance service it is essential that you have very good communication skills and a calm and reassuring manner. All those roles where you are dealing with emergency situations require you to act quickly but carefully. Paramedics and technicians dealing with emergencies have to be able to cope with distressing and sometimes frightening situations. They have to have good practical skills for handling complex and sensitive equipment and they have to be able to think quickly and take appropriate decisions.

Earnings

NHS pay is calculated on a detailed, graded structure. The NHS Careers website provides full details for every job title, showing which pay bands a particular job falls within. The pay structure is based on skills and responsibilities attached to each job. Here is a general guide.

An ambulance care assistant working in the NHS earns from £13,700 to just under £17,000. A paramedic earns between £19,500 and £26,000 a year. A fully qualified ambulance technician earns around £20,000 a year. Many ambulance jobs also attract antisocial working hours payments. There are additional allowances paid for working in Inner London, Outer London and the fringes of London.

Info

NHS Careers
0845 606 0655
www.nhscareers.nhs.uk

Ambulance Service Association
020 7928 9620
www.asa.uk.net

College of Paramedics
01278 420014
www.collegeofparamedics.co.uk

Health Professions Council (HPC)
0207 820 9684
www.hpc-uk.org

Skills for Health
0117 922 1155
www.skillsforhealth.org.uk

ANIMALS

(see also Veterinary Science)

While there are many different occupations working with animals, most of these employ relatively few people, so competition is strong for these popular jobs.

Animal care worker

Animal care workers feed, groom, clean, exercise and generally care for small animals of many kinds. They may also have to keep records and to deal with members of the public. They work in many settings, including kennels, catteries, animal rescue centres, open farms and animal sanctuaries. They also work as kennel assistants at quarantine centres and as auxiliaries at animal hospitals.

Entry, qualifications and training

The right attitude and some relevant experience – either paid or voluntary – are more important than qualifications. Some organisations may require you to have passed GCSEs, especially if you want to go on to part-time study. Work with animals is popular; a good way to improve your chances of success is to do some relevant voluntary work (see the Info panel to find out where to volunteer). There are Edexcel/BTEC certificate and diploma courses available in animal care; for these you will need three GCSEs grade A–C, including a science.

Personal attributes

You must be kind, gentle, calm and confident when handling animals. You need to be patient and you can't be squeamish. While being caring is essential, you must be resilient enough not to get too easily upset when dealing with badly treated or neglected animals. You need to be practical, you might need record-keeping skills and you should be good at dealing with humans as well as animals.

Earnings

Since much of the work is this field is for charities who want to minimise staff costs, pay is often close to minimum, but it can rise to £13,500 to £17,000 with experience and responsibility.

Info

Lantra
07426 696996
www.lantra.co.uk

People's Dispensary for Sick Animals (PDSA)
0800 917 2509
www.pdsa.org.uk

Royal Society for the Prevention of Cruelty to Animals (RSPCA)
www.rspca.org.uk

College of Animal Welfare
0844 372 9410
www.caw.ac.uk

Animal Care College
www.animalcarecollege.co.uk

Blue Cross
01993 822651
www.bluecross.org.uk

Animal groomer

If you work as an animal groomer you are most likely to be working with dogs, though occasionally you may find yourself working with cats, rabbits or other animals. The work involves shampooing, drying, brushing, combing, fur clipping and claw trimming, even claw polishing on some occasions. Many breeds of dog have to have their hair or fur cut in a very particular way, either for health or appearance reasons. As an animal groomer you must become familiar with all these requirements. Most businesses are small private establishments, though some are part of other establishments, including pet shops, garden centres, and boarding and breeding kennels. Some mobile groomers visit animals in their own home.

Entry, qualifications and training

You don't need formal qualifications, though good GCSE results are a plus. There are three ways to train: you can work with an experienced qualified groomer and learn your skills from them, you can do a college course or you can take an apprenticeship. Apprenticeships in this field are rather few and far between, so you may end up paying to qualify through a private college. A BTEC certificate or diploma may help you get a training place with a salon.

Personal attributes

You must be calm, kind and confident when handling animals – they don't always share their owners' enthusiasm for grooming. You must have good practical skills and take a pride in your work. You need to be able to communicate with pet owners and you may need business skills if you decide to run your own independent grooming salon or mobile grooming parlour.

Earnings

Dog groomers earn between £13,000 and £18,000 if working in a salon. Self-employed groomers charge from £25 to £90, depending on the breed of dog and what the grooming entails.

Info

Pet Care Trust
01234 273933
www.petcare.org.uk

Lantra
07426 696996
www.lantra.co.uk

Animal technician

(see Laboratory Technician)

RSPCA inspector

Inspectors for the Royal Society for the Prevention of Cruelty to Animals (RSPCA) deal with complaints from the general public about the alleged ill-treatment of animals and also perform more routine tasks. Inspectors have no power to take an animal from its owner unless the owner legally signs it over. They may caution people and, in some circumstances, the organisation will ensure that cases go before the courts. Inspectors also visit boarding kennels, pet shops and riding schools. They can be involved in physical rescues, often working unsociable hours and driving considerable distances.

Entry, qualifications and training

Anyone wishing to become an inspector must apply to join as an animal welfare officer. For this you need five GCSEs grades A–C, a UK driving licence, to be physically fit and able to swim 50 metres. Training is on the job and covers all aspects of the work – legal, practical and emotional. In Scotland, training starts at the headquarters in Edinburgh; in the rest of the UK it is at local offices. Animal welfare officers can also work towards NVQ level 3 qualifications in many aspects of animal care while undergoing training. There is great competition for jobs with the RSPCA and the Scottish Society for the Prevention of Cruelty to Animals (SSPCA) and working as a volunteer before you apply is one way to strengthen your application.

Personal attributes

Inspectors have to be very good at handling animals of all kinds. They must be calm, kind and authoritative. They need excellent interpersonal skills, must be able to be assertive, to deal with both sensitive and potentially confrontational situations. They must be able to speak in public, whether it is in court or in a classroom.

Earnings

In the RSPCA the starting salary is around £23,000 a year. Fully trained inspectors earn from £24,000 to £28,000. An accommodation allowance is included in the salary and there are additional allowances for officers working in or close to London.

Info

Volunteering England
www.volunteering.org.uk

Volunteering Scotland
www.volunteerscotland.info

Volunteer with Animals
www.vinspired.co.uk

Royal Society for the Prevention of Cruelty to Animals (RSPCA)
www.rspca.org.uk

Scottish Society for the Prevention of Cruelty to Animals (SSPCA)
0131 339 0222
www.scottishspca.org.uk

Zoo keeper

Keepers look after animals in zoos, mucking out their living quarters, preparing their food, feeding them and engaging in all other aspects of animal husbandry. There is increasing emphasis on education, public relations and research. Keepers work long hours – from 8 am to as late as 7 pm – much of the time outdoors, and the work is often physically demanding.

Entry, qualifications and training

You don't usually need academic qualifications, though some employers may ask for GCSEs grades A–C, including English and one science subject. Most zoos expect you to have experience of working with animals and the main way to acquire this is through volunteering. Most zoos have volunteer schemes, though these are popular and competitive. The British and Irish Association of Zoos and Aquariums website gives contact details for all zoos and wildlife parks. If you want to work in a safari or wildlife park you will need a driving licence. Your application may be strengthened by acquiring one of the following: a BTEC First Diploma and National Certificate/Diploma in Animal Care or Animal Management, a City & Guilds National Certificate and Advanced National Certificate in Animal Care, or NVQ levels 1 and 2 in Animal Care. Check individual colleges for entry requirements.

Some zoos may run apprenticeship schemes from time to time. Training is on the job and you may be able to work for some of the qualifications just listed on a day-release basis. Once you have worked as a zoo keeper for at least a year, you can do a two-year part-time block-release Foundation degree in zoo resource management at Sparsholt College in Hampshire. You can do Foundation degrees and degrees in animal management at some other colleges and universities.

Personal attributes

You must love animals and be good at assessing their condition and monitoring behaviour. You have to be practical, calm, confident, happy working in the open air and not squeamish about smells. You must be very alert and safety conscious, especially when working with dangerous animals. You should be able to work as part of a team, be interested in science and the environment, and be able to communicate with members of the public in a friendly and informative way.

Earnings

Salaries start from around £12,500 to £14,500. Experienced zoo keepers can earn from around £15,000 to over £21,000.

Info

British and Irish Association of Zoos and Aquariums (BIAZA)
www.biaza.org.uk

Sparsholt College
01962 776441
www.sparsholt.ac.uk

Lantra
02476 696996
www.lantra.co.uk

Dogs

Assistance dog trainer

Assistance dog trainers and instructors train dogs to help people with physical disabilities, hearing or sight impairments, or who are prone to seizures, to live independently. There are four types of assistance dogs. Guide Dogs for the Blind help people to avoid obstacles, find entrances, stairs, etc. Disability assistance dogs do such things as pick up a telephone, press an emergency button or load a washing machine. Hearing dogs alert people to sounds such as a doorbell or a telephone. Seizure alert dogs watch for tell-tale signs of an impending seizure, warn their owners and care for them if a seizure does occur. Most trainers are employed by the four relevant charities; they are listed in the Info panel. Trainers work closely with dogs to teach them the skills they need and then they work with the dog and the human with whom it is going to live to teach that person how to use the dog and also how to care for it properly.

Entry, qualifications and training

You must be at least 18 years old and have a full, clean driving licence. Academic and other requirements vary between the different employer organisations, so you should contact them for details. In general, you will need qualifications that are relevant to your client group, eg know British Sign Language if you are working with hearing impaired people and their assistance dogs. GCSEs grades A–C may be required and some employers prefer one of your subjects to be a science.

Personal attributes

You must have great patience and a real understanding of, and interest in, animal behaviour. You should also get on really well with people, who often need a lot of encouragement and support when they first acquire an assistance dog. You should be practical, well organised and good at thinking up solutions to problems.

Earnings

Starting salaries are around £12,500 a year, rising to £16,000 with experience. Salaries for trainers working with hearing dogs are a little bit higher.

Info

Guide Dogs for the Blind
0118 983 5555
www.guidedogs.org.uk

Hearing Dogs for Deaf People
01844 348100
www.hearingdogs.org.uk

Support Dogs
0870 609 3476
www.support-dogs.org.uk

Canine Partners
0845 658 0400
www.caninepartners.org.uk

Dogs for the Disabled
08700 776600
www.dogsforthedisabled.org

Dog handler

Dog handlers work for the police, the armed services, HM Revenue & Customs, fire and rescue services and private security firms. There are many examples of the kinds of work in which dogs and dog handlers are involved. Police dogs track missing people, help control crowds or guard prisoners. In the Army dogs are used to find injured people, guard premises and equipment and even search for landmines. Doing customs work, handlers get their dogs to sniff out drugs, tobacco and food. In the prison service dogs are mainly used for guarding activities. The fire service sometimes uses dogs to search for survivors after fires and other disasters. Private security firms mainly use dogs to patrol and guard premises and equipment.

Entry, qualifications and training

In most organisations you are not taken on as a dog handler. You start like any other recruit and dog handling is a specialist area for which you may then get the opportunity to train. You need to check the entry requirements of the other different career paths, but many will require you to have at least four GCSEs grades A–C, including maths and English. Private security firms often want you to have experience of dog handling before you work for them as a dog handler.

Personal attributes

It is essential that you love working with dogs, that you are confident and sure of yourself when handling them. The bond that builds up between handler and dog is often very strong and you may have to spend a lot of time working on your own, just with your dog. Depending on the organisation you are working for, you may have to work in stressful or dangerous situations, or in uncomfortable and unpleasant conditions. You also need to be good at communicating with people.

Earnings

Starting salaries vary according to who employs you, but are around £15,000 for new dog handlers and up to £25,000 or more for handlers with experience and other management responsibilities.

Info

Police Service Portal
www.police.uk

Security Industry Authority (SIA)
0844 892 1025
www.the-sia.org.uk

RAF Careers
0845 605 5555
www.rafcareers.com

National Search and Rescue Dog Association
www.nsarda.org.uk

Army Careers
08457 300111
www.army.mod.uk

HM Revenue & Customs
www.hmrc.gov.uk

National Association of Security Dog Users
www.nasdu.co.uk

Kennel worker

Kennel staff care for dogs in kennels, feeding, grooming and exercising the dogs and keeping their kennels and exercise areas clean. Where animals are sick or recovering from an operation, the kennel staff must also be able to provide adequate nursing care.

The balance of your work depends on what type of kennel you work in. If you are working in a greyhound training kennel you will spend a lot of time training and exercising your dogs. If you work at a boarding kennel you may spend more time reassuring your dogs. There are also quarantine kennels and breeding kennels where duties include weaning and training puppies, preparing dogs for shows and possibly handling them.

Entry, qualifications and training

No formal qualifications are needed to work in kennels and most employers prefer school leavers to train on the job. The NVQ level 2 in Animal Care and the National Small Animal Care Certificate are nationally recognised by the industry and provide a good base for further study. Many training organisations and agricultural colleges throughout the country offer these qualifications. Entry requirements vary depending on the institution.

Personal attributes

Good health, general fitness and stamina are required for this manual, physically demanding, outdoor work. Kennel staff must be unsentimental about animals but at the same time have a genuine concern for their well-being; they require patience and a placid but firm nature. A willingness to work long days, weekends and public holidays is also required.

Earnings

Kennel workers earn around £10,000 to start with. Experienced kennel workers earn between £12,000 and £15,000.

Info

Lantra
02476 696996
www.lantra.co.uk

Animal Care College
01344 636436
www.animalcarecollege.co.uk

College of Animal Welfare
0844 372 9410
www.caw.ac.uk

Horses

Farrier

If a horse needs new shoes a farrier is the person who makes and fits these shoes. Working mainly with metal, though some shoes are made from plastic and other modern materials, farriers measure, shape and fit shoes to every kind of horse and pony. While there are not large numbers of opportunities in this work, riding and keeping horses has become increasingly popular over the past decade, so there are some opportunities in this highly specialised work.

Entry, qualifications and training

To practise as a farrier you have to register with the Farriery Council and the only training route is a four-year apprenticeship which you must serve with a qualified farrier who is also registered to provide training. There are usually around 100 apprenticeships offered each year and the Farriery Training Agency may be able to help you find one of them. During your apprenticeship you also spend 23 weeks on block release at one of four approved colleges. Your apprenticeship leads to an NVQ level 3 in Farriery. You need four GCSEs grades A–C to start an apprenticeship and you also have to pass a medical. You have to pay for this medical yourself.

Personal attributes

You have to be confident handling and enjoy working closely with horses of all sizes and temperaments. You have to have good practical skills and be able to work quickly and accurately. You have to have good people skills too. You may have to point out a health problem with a horse's leg or foot that the owner has not noticed. Since almost all farriers are self-employed you also have to be able to run your own business.

Earnings

Apprenticeship pay rates are set annually by the Farriery Training Council and are linked to the National Minimum Wage. First-year apprentices aged 16 earn £3.00 an hour, fourth-year apprentices earn £5.50 an hour. There are also differences according to how old you are when you start your apprenticeship. Qualified farriers are self-employed and earn between £19,000 and £31,000.

Info

National Farrier Training Agency
01733 319770
www.farrierytraining.co.uk

Horse groom

Grooms look after all aspects of the horse's welfare. Their duties include grooming and strapping, mucking out, feeding, cleaning tack, saddling up, exercising and leading both mounted and dismounted, elementary veterinary care and sick nursing, preparation for and travelling with horses by road, sea and air, and care of the horse when at grass. Grooms work in racing stables, hunting establishments, private stables, studs and breeding concerns, riding schools, occasionally (seasonally) with polo ponies and at trekking centres.

Entry, qualifications and training

No formal qualifications are necessary but it is recommended that grooms take the British Horse Society (BHS) examinations stages 1, 2 and 3 in Horse Knowledge and Care, which comprise the Grooms Certificate. Alternative options are NVQs in Horse Care, levels 1, 2 and 3.

Training is usually on the job and should be sufficient to prepare students for exams. There are also courses of varying lengths to prepare students for particular exams; however, the fees are often high. Funding may be available for the achievement of BHS qualifications provided the applicant is not eligible for any other type of funding.

Personal attributes

A love of horses is essential, plus patience and the willingness to work long hours and perform many routine tasks. A heavy goods vehicle driving licence may be an advantage.

Earnings

Stable staff generally earn the national minimum wage. In some cases food and accommodation may be free, in others they may be deducted from the wage. The hours may be long. The BHS issues guidelines on salaries for those with BHS qualifications; details are on its website.

Info

Lantra
02476 696996
www.lantra.co.uk

British Racing School (BRS)
01638 665103
www.brs.org.uk

Thoroughbred Breeding Association
01638 661321
www.thoroughbredbreedersassociation.co.uk

Association of British Riding Schools (ABRS)
01736 369440
www.abrs-info.org

British Horseracing Authority
www.careersinracing.com

British Horse Society (BHS)
0844 848 1666
www.bhs.org.uk

Jockey

Jockeys ride racehorses in competitions on flat ground or over jumps (National Hunt). They may ride for one racehorse trainer or for several, and owners and trainers are interested in getting the best jockeys for their horses. Jockeys are also involved in preparing the horses for races, exercising them to bring them to best possible racing condition. Jockeys have to build up knowledge of individual horses, understand racing conditions, how the ground will affect performance and work out the most effective racing strategy.

Entry, qualifications and training

Most jockeys start as stable hands working for trainers in racing yards. There are no specific academic requirements to become a stable hand; if you want to become a jockey there are strict weight limits, about 9 stone 7~lb for a jump jockey and 8 stone for flat racing. You then have to persuade a trainer to take you on as either an apprentice jockey for flat racing, or a conditional jockey if you plan to become a jump jockey.

You can prepare for work in a racing yard by doing the NVQ level 1 and 2 Racehorse Care Residential Course. This course is free if you are aged between 16 and 25. There are NVQs levels 1 and 2 available in Racehorse Care. You can do these at a residential course at the British Racing School or the Northern Racing

College. Places on these courses are highly sought after and are free if you are aged between 16 and 25. Day-release courses in racehorse care are also available at some local colleges. Details of these are given on the British Horseracing Authority website.

The key to being taken on to train as a jockey is that you must have exceptional riding skills in order to get yourself noticed by a trainer. As an apprentice or conditional jockey, you train on the job. The trainer takes responsibility for where and what horses you ride and decides when you are competent and ready to race-ride (usually after about two years). You can then apply to the Horseracing Regulatory Authority for a licence to ride.

Personal attributes

You must have a love of horses as well as of riding, since in your early days you will be involved in a lot of horse care, and for good riding you need to be able to build up a real bond with your animals. You must be confident, physically brave, determined and able to handle disappointment. Your people skills need to be nearly as good as your horse skills.

Earnings

As a stable hand you earn around £8,000 and if you decide to become a groom rather than a jockey your earnings rise to between £10,000 and £16,000. Jockeys' earnings include a percentage of prize money and a fee for each ride. Experienced and successful jockeys can also earn money through sponsorship. Many jobs in racing yards provide free or subsidised accommodation.

Info

Lantra
02476 696996
www.lantra.co.uk

Horseracing Regulatory Authority (HRA)
020 7189 3800
www.thehra.org

Jockeys Employment and Training Scheme (JETS)
01635 230410
www.jets-uk.org

Northern Racing College (NRC)
01302 861000
www.northernracingcollege.co.uk

British Horseracing Authority
020 7152 0000
www.careersinracing.com

British Racing School (BRS)
01638 665103
www.brs.org.uk

Horse riding instructor

Riding instructors teach people – individuals or groups – how to ride horses. They may also accompany riders who hire horses by the hour, and be required to help train horses and look after them, cleaning tack and stables. The work includes teaching in riding schools and clubs and in summer camps, training competition riders and occasionally sitting as a judge or examiner.

Entry, qualifications and training

While you may not need formal qualifications to train you do need to work towards a series of certificated examinations offered by either the British Horse Society (BHS) or the Association of British Riding Schools (ABRS). Both offer several levels of qualification from preliminary to assistant instructor and instructor. There are three routes to working for these examinations: you may be able to get an apprenticeship; you could train as a private fee-paying student at riding stables; or you could attend a college course that includes BHS or ABRS qualifications. If you do opt for a college course or manage to obtain an apprenticeship you may need three or four GCSEs. However you choose to train and qualify, you will need to have a strong background in riding and in handling and caring for horses.

You can opt for further specialist training in work with riding for the disabled or riding holiday leadership.

Personal attributes

A love for and understanding of horses and good confident riding ability are essential. You also need to be good at communicating with people of all ages and different levels of ability. You should be observant, encouraging and sensitive. You must have a good awareness of safety issues.

Earnings

Trainees and assistant instructors earn between £12,000 and £16,000 and qualified instructors earn £16,000 to £25,000. Earnings vary according to whether accommodation and meals are provided. Some experienced instructors are self-employed and with experience and a good reputation can earn more than £35,000.

Info

Lantra
02476 696996
www.lantra.co.uk

British Equestrian Federation (BEF)
www.bef.co.uk

Riding for the Disabled Association
0845 658 1082
www.riding-for-disabled.org.uk

Association of British Riding Schools (ABRS)
01736 369440
www.abrs-info.org

British Horse Society (BHS)
0844 848 1666
www.bhs.org.uk

Stable hand

Stable hands (formerly known as 'stable lads') do a lot of labouring work, mucking out, fetching straw, filling haynets and sweeping. They must also learn to groom and exercise the horses, and usually become responsible for a certain number of their 'own'. On race days, a stable hand will accompany a horse, groom it, walk it round before the race and lead it into the winner's enclosure if it wins.

Entry, qualifications and training

Most jockeys start as stable hands working for trainers in racing yards. There are no specific academic requirements to become a stable hand. If you want to become a jockey there are strict weight limits, about 9 stone 7~lb for a jump jockey and 8 stone for flat racing. You then have to persuade a trainer to take you on as either an apprentice jockey for flat racing, or a conditional jockey if you plan to become a jump jockey.

You can prepare for work in a racing yard by doing the NVQ level 1 and 2 Racehorse Care Residential Course. You can do these at the British Racing School or the Northern Racing College. Places on these courses are highly sought after and are free if you are aged between 16 and 25. Day-release courses in racehorse care are also available at some local colleges. Details of these are given on the British Horseracing Authority website.

Personal attributes

You must have a love of horses as well as of riding, since in your early days you will be involved in a lot of horse care and for good riding you need to be able to build up a real bond with your animals. You must be confident, physically brave, determined and able to cope with disappointment, and good at dealing with people as well as with horses.

Earnings

As a stable hand you earn around £9,000 and if you decide to become a groom rather than a jockey your earnings rise to between £10,000 and £16,000. Many jobs include free or subsidised accommodation.

Info

Lantra
02476 696996
www.lantra.co.uk

Horseracing Regulatory Authority (HRA)
020 7189 3800
www.thehra.org

Northern Racing College (NRC)
01302 861000
www.northernracingcollege.co.uk

British Horseracing Authority
020 7152 0000
www.careersinracing.com

British Racing School (BRS)
01638 665103
www.brs.org.uk

ANTHROPOLOGIST

Anthropologists study the development of human societies, making comparisons between different communities and cultures. This academic discipline is linked with the other social sciences and with evolutionary biology. Much of the work still concerns non-industrial, 'primitive' or rural cultures, but changes brought about by contact with more sophisticated outside influences and pressures from 'modern' societies are an important aspect of study, and many anthropologists now undertake research in urban or industrial societies. The career involves a combination of research, teaching and finding out more about the people being studied by going to live with them over a period of time.

Increasingly, anthropologists are finding employment as consultants, for instance in the development, health and humanitarian fields and in such professions as journalism, human resource management, planning, tourism and heritage, museum curatorship and medicine.

Entry, qualifications and training

A good degree in anthropology. Postgraduate study is usually required.

Personal attributes

Those wishing to embark on this career must normally be committed to an academic way of life, although there is growing demand outside universities. Field researchers must be prepared to spend long spells abroad, often in basic conditions. Physical and mental stamina is required, as well as independence and resourcefulness. Anthropologists must be prepared to work on their own. However, as anthropology has diversified, so the ways of working have become more varied too and anthropologists now work in every imaginable setting, from offices and day-care centres to out in the field. Linguistic ability is useful.

Earnings

There is little salary data available, but many anthropologists would earn similar rates to research workers in universities – around £18,000 to £20,000 for junior staff and up to £23,000 with experience. On fieldwork overseas, earnings may include living and many other allowances.

Info

The Royal Anthropological Institute
020 7387 0455
www.therai.org.uk

ANTIQUE DEALER

To become a successful antique dealer, buying and selling old and valuable objects of many kinds, you need expert knowledge of the field combined with astute business sense. Many dealers specialise in particular types of antiques, such as paintings, ceramics, jewellery or furniture. One of the most specialised areas of the work is art valuing – where a highly detailed knowledge of painting or other art forms is essential. Dealers may sell from shops, antiques markets, antiques fairs and from home. An increasing number trade on the internet using auction sites such as eBay as well as their own websites.

Entry, qualifications and training

While there are no formal entry qualifications, experience in a saleroom or an antique shop is extremely useful. Some antique dealers have degrees in fine arts or applied arts and there are one or two specific postgraduate courses in understanding the arts and antiques market. Large dealers such as Christie's and Sotheby's offer a few training places to graduates. Training is on the job if you are employed by a large auction house, but otherwise it is mainly through your own study, persistence and research. You can start to learn by visiting as many antique fairs and markets as you can.

Personal attributes

A real interest in antiques in general or a particular category – books, ceramics, toys, etc – is essential. Many dealers are also collectors. You have to have a keen eye for detail or fraud, a professional, confident manner with people, and sound business sense.

Earnings

There is wide variation in earnings because so many antique dealers are self-employed and have to make earnings through commissions on what they sell. Starting in an antique shop or an auction house sales room, salaries are from £12,000 to £21,000. Successful dealers in good economic times may earn far more than this.

Info

**The British Antique Dealers'
Association**
020 7589 4128
www.bada.org

Sotheby's Institute of Art
www.sothebysinstitute.com

Christie's
www.christies.com

ARCHAEOLOGY

Archaeology is the examination of the human past through the study of buried remains and artefacts.

Archaeologist

Archaeology – building up a picture of the past – is both an art and a science. Archaeologists use highly technical and scientific methods of discovery, analysis and identification to reconstruct and study men and women from the past using their material remains. The evidence is collected through fieldwork, including excavations, where clues are sought in objects, their surroundings, the ground itself and the remains of living things. The evidence is then analysed, subjected to experiment, assessed, identified, catalogued, conserved and possibly exhibited. Archaeologists usually specialise in a particular period, technique or geographical area. Opportunities for full-time permanent positions are limited; consequently, competition is fierce for the few jobs available. These are to be found in central and local government, museums and universities, independent units and trusts, as well as a variety of positions in commercial operations. Job availability is closely related to building and development work. Some work includes the opportunity to spend time abroad.

Entry, qualifications and training

There are several degree courses in archaeology and most people who work as archaeologists will also have a postgraduate qualification and some work experience of volunteering on archaeological digs. There are also postgraduate courses in archaeological conservation.

Personal attributes

Archaeologists need to be practical, thorough and very careful and observant. They should be able to work well as part of a team, or as a team leader. They need to have a real passion for and commitment to their work.

Earnings

Starting salaries for excavators and site assistants are between £13,500 and £15,500. Supervisors earn from £15,500 to £17,500. Senior archaeologists managing site projects earn £27,000 to £30,000. Archaeologists working in museums or in universities are paid according to local authority or lecturer pay scales.

Info

Council for British Archaeology
01904 671417
www.britarch.ac.uk

Training Online Resource Centre for Archaeology (TORC)
www.torc.org.uk

British Archaeological Jobs Resource
www.bajr.org

English Heritage
www.english-heritage.org.uk

Environment and Heritage Service
028 9054 3034
www.doeni.gov.uk

ARCHITECTURE

Architecture is a profession requiring the practical combination of imaginative design with scientific and technological principles, to produce designs for new buildings and for the extension or renovation of those already existing.

Architect

Architects are professional experts in building design and construction. They advise individuals, developers, local authorities and commercial organisations on the design and construction of new buildings and the area around them. They have to take account of the environmental impact of construction and consider issues such as how energy efficient they can design a building to be. Architects are also involved in the restoration and conservation of historic and existing buildings.

Architects create designs through drawings, usually produced with computer-aided design (CAD). Drawings are based on information supplied by the client on the function of the building, the proposed budget and the site. An architect needs to have an understanding of structure, building materials, finance, planning law and creative design, and in many building projects acts as the coordinator in a team of specialist consultants such as engineers, builders and interior designers.

Opportunities exist for employment in private practice, with local authorities, in research, teaching, central government and some industrial organisations. Increasingly, interior design and companies working in associated fields employ architects as part of their team. Specialist areas can include domestic, public building and retail architecture. The use of CAD packages plays a significant part in the work of architects.

Entry, qualifications and training

Architecture is a graduate-level profession, unless you have considerable experience as a building surveyor, architectural technician or architectural technologist. The usual route to qualifying as an architect is to do a three-year degree course in architecture, ensuring that the course is registered with the Architects Registration Board (ARB). You then have to undertake at least two years' work in an architect's office. Having done this you have completed what is known as Part 1. You then take a two-year diploma or Master's in architecture; this is referred to as Part 2. Having completed these stages you sit an examination to achieve Part 3 and you can then apply to become a chartered architect. To gain a place on an architecture degree course you need five GCSEs grades A–C, including maths, English and either physics or chemistry. You need three good A levels and many universities require one of these to be in a science subject.

Personal attributes

You need a broad range of skills as an architect: you must have good scientific and mathematical ability, but you also need imagination, creativity and a flair for design. You need good IT skills, sound business awareness and an ability to communicate technical information and ideas to people without a technical background.

Earnings

Salaries vary according to the size of practice you work for. The Royal Institute of British Architects (RIBA) provides a rough guide to what you can expect to earn during the various stages of training; the rates for first-year trainees are £21,000 to £24,000; after completing your diploma you can earn £25,000 to £50,000. Salaries in this sector can suffer when the financial and property markets are not doing very well.

Info

Royal Institute of British Architects (RIBA)	Architectural Registration Board (ARB)
020 7580 5533	020 7580 5861
www.architecture.com	www.arb.org.uk

Architectural technologist

Architectural technologists work alongside architects and other professionals as part of the building design and construction team. Technologists can negotiate the construction project from inception to completion. Specific specialist skills could include surveying land and buildings, preparing and undertaking feasibility studies, presenting design solutions, analysing and detailing drawings, and managing and applying computer-aided design (CAD) techniques.

Entry, qualifications and training

A degree in architectural technology, an HNC/HND in Building Studies (with specific additional units) or an NVQ level 4 in Architectural Technology leads to Associate Membership of the British Institute of Architectural Technologists (BIAT) and the designation ABIAT.

Personal attributes

Architectural technologists should be able to work both as part of a team and on their own initiative. Attention to detail is necessary, as is the ability to take account of other professionals' needs. Effective communication skills are necessary when working as part of the team, liaising with clients or tendering for contracts, and they should feel comfortable with new technology and innovative concepts.

Earnings

Salaries start at between £15,000 and £20,000, possibly more in London. With experience salaries rise to between £30,000 and £45,000. This sector has suffered in the current economic climate, so salaries have not risen much in the past two years.

Info

Chartered Institute of Architectural
Technologists
020 7278 2206
www.ciat.org.uk

Asset Skills
01392 423 399/0845 6782 888
www.assetskills.org

ARCHIVIST

(see Information Science)

ARMED FORCES

The UK armed forces are comprised of the Army, the Royal Air Force and the Royal Navy. The Royal Marines are part of the Royal Navy. While their main roles are warfare and defence, the armed services take on many other roles. They can be involved in peacekeeping, holding a line in areas of conflict. They may be involved in search and rescue after natural disasters such as earthquakes overseas. In the UK they may provide help after a natural disaster such as a flood.

While the three armed services employ many civilian staff, most of their work is done by serving forces members, whether this work is catering, IT support, mechanical repairs to equipment, medical treatment or training and educating its own members.

Army careers

While there are many army careers, opportunities can be split into these main areas: combat, engineering logistics, intelligence, music and ceremony, IT, medicine, human resources and finance.

There are two basic levels at which you can join the British Army either as a private or as an officer. As a private you may be called a gunner or a signaller according to the regiment you belong to and the work you do. As an officer you start as an officer cadet. In either case there is a clear career structure through which you can climb, to regimental sergeant major as a private, and to lieutenant colonel as an officer.

Rank is the backbone of Army structure and defines your role and degree of responsibility. Soldiers and officers have different terms of rank and, broadly speaking, it is officers who have more leadership duties. Many officers are drawn from the ranks – if you show potential in the Army, your efforts will not go unrewarded.

Entry, qualifications and training

To join as a soldier you must be aged 16 to 33, pass a medical and meet nationality requirements. You don't normally need formal qualifications, though in some technical and engineering jobs you may. Your local Armed Forces Careers Office

(AFCO) will be happy to talk to you in detail. They can also give you a multiple-choice test, sometimes referred to as the BARB test, which can indicate which particular roles you might be most suited to and find most satisfactory. If you are interested in joining, you have to attend a two-day series of selection tests and if you pass these you can then join up. Initial training, referred to as basic training, takes 12 to 14 weeks. After this you will receive further training connected with your specific role and duties and the kinds of activities in which your unit is engaged.

If you are applying to join as an officer, you must be aged 17 to 28 and must also pass a medical and meet nationality criteria. You need five GCSEs grades A–C, including English, maths and either a science or a foreign language. This requirement is sometimes referred to as needing 35 ALIS points. You also need two A levels or equivalent equal to 120 UCAS points. The Army also runs graduate-entry training for officers. You then have to pass a three-day Army Officer Selection Board. If you are successful, you begin training as an Officer Cadet on the 44-week Commissioning Course (CC) at the Royal Military Academy, Sandhurst (RMAS). The course includes training in leadership and management, tactics, weapons and physical fitness. If you join as a professional officer already qualified as a nurse, doctor, vet, engineer, etc, you take a shortened course.

Personal attributes

For soldiers and officers self-discipline, confidence and initiative are important. You have to be physically fit, quick at reacting to situations and willing to work in highly dangerous or frightening situations. It is essential that you can work as part of a team. Officers and other ranks with leadership roles have to be able to motivate, lead and organise, encourage and discipline colleagues.

Earnings

Pay is linked to rank, length of service and responsibilities. A soldier in training earns around £14,500. Once training is complete earnings are between £17,000 and £28,000. Some higher ranks earn up to £46,000. Non-graduate officer cadets start on £15,000, graduate officer cadets on £23,000. After training, salaries rise to £28,000 to £33,000. The highest ranks earn up to £100,000. There are also additional allowances for working overseas and subsidised accommodation may be provided.

Royal Air Force careers

Like the Army, the Royal Air Force (RAF) is engaged in many different operations, but of course one of its main tasks is flying fixed-wing aircraft and helicopters over UK airspace and in actions all around the world, whether these are under the auspices of NATO, the UN or other situations. Much of the work involves flying and maintaining combat, reconnaissance and transport aircraft. As well as roles associated directly with flying the RAF employs catering staff, engineers, IT specialists, medical staff and administrators. While there are many different opportunities, the two basic levels of recruitment are RAF airman or woman (aircrew) and RAF officer. As an RAF airman or airwoman, you would provide specialist support in one of the following areas: aircrew – which includes non-commissioned aircrew and weapon systems operators; engineering and technical – including roles like aircraft technician; catering and hospitality – which includes roles such as catering officer; security and defence – with jobs in fire-fighting and the RAF police; medical and medical support – dental, nursing, medical and laboratory roles; air operations support – for example air traffic controllers; and communications and intelligence – such as photographers and intelligence analysts. RAF officers work in more than 20 roles, but some of the main ones are pilots, air traffic controllers and engineers. The RAF also employs non-commissioned officers in many flight and technical roles and as linguists.

Entry, qualifications and training

To join as an airman or airwoman you do not need formal qualifications. You must be over the age of 16. Upper age limits for joining vary according to the role in which you will be working. You also have to be a UK citizen and you have to pass a medical. Your local Armed Forces Careers Office will be able to provide you with more detailed information. The requirements to join as an officer vary and many applicants are graduates. You will have to pass a series of rigorous selection tests including medical, psychological and intelligence tests. For some roles, eg linguists, you will need relevant qualifications. Initial training for airmen and airwomen is 14 weeks, 33 weeks for officers. There is continuing training depending on your role and the operations and activities in which you are involved. There are very often opportunities to gain professional and technical qualifications once you have joined up.

Personal attributes

A real interest in the RAF is a good starting point. All RAF personnel have to be physically fit, well disciplined, be able to follow or give orders and be good at working as part of a team. Many posts will demand technical or practical skills. Officers will need good leadership skills, be able to motivate and keep other people working together. They will also have to be good at taking responsibility and making quick decisions. All RAF personnel will have to be prepared to work in difficult and dangerous situations.

Earnings

Airmen and airwomen start training on a little over £14,000; £17,000 when training is complete. Senior airmen and women at warrant officer level, the highest non-commissioned rank, can earn up to £44,000. New pilot officers earn £23,500, flying officers earn between £28,300 and £31,500, and squadron leaders earn up to £54,500.

Royal Navy careers

The Royal Navy has operations on the sea (the surface fleet), in the air (the air corps) and in submarines under the water. There are two basic entry levels, either as a rating or as an officer. Like the other armed services the Royal Navy employs personnel in catering, medicine, dentistry, engineering, logistics, finance and information technology.

Entry, qualifications and training

You don't need formal qualifications to join as a rating, but good GCSEs may increase the variety of roles you can take on. For most ratings you have to be aged 16, but to train as a diver you must be 18. Some other posts have higher age limits. All new naval ratings undergo nine weeks of introductory training at HMS Raleigh in Cornwall. Officers need five GCSEs and 180 UCAS points or their equivalent. Some posts have a height requirement. Ratings have to be aged 16 to join and officers must be 17. For some officer posts you need to be older.

Personal attributes

All Royal Navy personnel must be good at working as part of a team. They must be physically fit and emotionally resilient – capable of living in fairly confined conditions close to other people. They must be good at taking orders and giving instructions, quick to react and have good practical skills. They must be capable of working in difficult and dangerous situations. Officers have to have all of these qualities combined with the ability to lead, encourage, motivate and organise others.

Earnings

Starting salaries are from around £13,500 a year for ratings. Able ratings (the next rank) earn between close to £17,000 and £28,500 a year. Warrant officers earn up to £46,000.

Royal Marines careers

Royal Marines are part of the Royal Navy. They take part in front-line combat (on land and at sea) and are sent at short notice to deal with emergency situations, which may include military operations or natural disasters. The basic entry level is as a commando. As a newly trained recruit, you would usually start as a rifleman. You might be based in a unit responding to emergencies around the world as part of the Joint Rapid Reaction Force, the Fleet Protection Group, guarding UK nuclear weapons or a Fleet Standby Rifle Troop, trained to board ships at sea. The Royal Marines recruits officers as well as commandos. Officers are responsible for leading units in all the activities mentioned above. They are also responsible for training and discipline. Many officers will be qualified professionals – engineers or doctors for example.

Entry, qualifications and training

To join as a commando you must be aged 17, male and a British citizen. You do not need any formal qualifications, but you do have to pass a series of selection tests, including a medical and a rigorous physical fitness test. Your initial training lasts 32 weeks and covers teamwork, survival, assault course and weapons training. To apply to become a Royal Marines officer you must pass the rigorous three-day selection process, you must be aged at least 17, a British citizen and at least 1.51 metres tall. You also need three GCSEs grades A–C. There is also a graduate officer training programme operating in the Royal Marines. Training for officers consists of five stages, from basic training to amphibious craft training. At the end of your training period you will command a troop or unit.

Personal attributes

All Royal Marines personnel must be resilient, resourceful and determined. You need to be very good at working as part of a team, following or giving orders as appropriate. You must be physically very fit and able to cope with tough conditions. You need to be practical, quick to think and quick to react. Officers must be good leaders, able to keep a team working well together and able to motivate colleagues in challenging situations.

Earnings

On entry, commandos earn around £14,000 a year, rising to between £16,500 and £28,000 a year after training. The most senior non-commissioned ranks can earn up to £45,000. Officers in training earn between £13,200 and £17,100 a year. Captains earn between £36,160 and £43,002. Colonels can earn up to £85,268.

Info

British Army
0845
www.army.mod.uk

Royal Air Force Careers
0845 605 5555
www.rafcareers.com

Royal Navy Careers
Careers Enquiries: 0845 607 5555
www.royalnavy.mod.uk

Armed Forces Careers Office (NI)
028 9042 7040

Visit your local Armed Forces Careers Office (AFCO) for information on all the armed services and the career opportunities in each.

ART AND DESIGN

There are many options in art and design, though they are all competitive. Artists work with many different media and materials in a range of creative and commercial applications. Popular areas include fashion and textiles, jewellery, furniture, interior design, graphic design, industrial design and photography. Less commercial applications include painting and sculpture.

Artist

Artists communicate ideas, emotions and thoughts through visual media such as painting, print making, digital fine art or sculpture. They work with a wide range of materials, though most artists develop a preference for working with particular materials and in particular styles. They earn money by selling work which they produce either independently or by undertaking commissioned work. A few artists may be employed as artist in residence at a gallery or for some other organisation. Some work on community arts projects or as art teachers. As an artist, your work may also involve liaising with galleries, sourcing materials, coming up with new ideas, managing, marketing your work and building up a business.

Entry, qualifications and training

While some artists have no formal qualifications and may simply be self-taught and have a rare talent, the majority of artists will have a degree in an arts-related subject. There are many fine arts degrees in subjects including painting, digital fine art, print making, sculpture and photography. There are also degrees in art criticism and contextual art. To get onto an arts degree course you normally have to have completed a foundation year and prepare a portfolio of your work to demonstrate your artistic ability.

Personal attributes

You must have flair and imagination and a really strong desire to work with your chosen subjects and media. You have to be resilient, good at building up relationships with people, flexible and able to handle disappointment. You also need to be able to work on your own and sometimes to work long hours.

Earnings

As an artist trying to make your way into the creative world it is very difficult to make a living entirely from your art. You can get advice on how to price your work, but many new artists assist more experienced artists and this work pays between £8 and £10 per hour. Salaries in teaching are between £23,000 and £35,000 depending on your level of experience and geographical location.

Info

Creative and Cultural Skills
(The Sector Skills Council for Craft,
Cultural Heritage, Design,
Literature, Music, Performing, and
Visual Arts)
020 7015 1800
www.ccskills.org.uk

The Artists' Information Company
www.a-n.co.uk

Graphic designer

A number of different disciplines come under the umbrella heading of graphic design. These include design studies, film and animation work, typography and lettering, illustration, printing processes, display and exhibition work, technical graphics for engineering, calligraphy, packaging and design for advertising, corporate identity and multimedia. Graphic design incorporates drawing and presentation skills and requires an understanding of colour, lettering and patterns. Many graphic designers work in three dimensions using specialist computer software; a high level of technical skills is therefore expected along with design ability. A rapidly growing area in graphic design is the field of new media, with new opportunities in multimedia, digital imagery and computer-aided design/manufacture.

Entry, qualifications and training

It is sometimes possible to get work as a graphic designer without formal qualifications, provided you have relevant experience and a really impressive portfolio of your design work – this is a highly competitive field. In practice, most graphic designers have a degree either in graphic design or in another art and design-related subject. To be accepted on many art and design degrees you also need a recognised foundation course. You will need to have or to get training in a number of relevant computer graphics packages including QuarkXpress, Photoshop, Illustrator, Freehand and Dreamweaver. Local colleges offer courses in many of these, and the Chartered Society of Designers funds a programme of continuing professional development for designers who want to keep their skills and knowledge current.

Personal attributes

You must be creative and imaginative with drawing as well as computer graphics skills. You should have some knowledge of printing technology, be able to work to a budget and to deadlines, and be an excellent communicator.

Earnings

Newly qualified designers earn between £14,000 and £22,000. Experienced designers earn between £22,000 and £50,000. Someone with exceptional talent and a good reputation can earn more than this and many graphic designers are self-employed, working freelance.

Info

Chartered Society of Designers
(CSD)
020 7357 8088
www.csd.org.uk

Creative and Cultural Skills
(The Sector Skills Council for Craft,
Cultural Heritage, Design, Literature,
Music, Performing, and Visual Arts)
020 7015 1800
www.ccskills.org.uk

Illustrator

]Illustrators use painting, drawing and multimedia technology to provide illustrations in a whole variety of media and for a wide range of clients. They might illustrate children's books, work for magazines, or create artwork for posters and storyboards for advertising clients. They may design greetings cards or designs to appear on ceramics. They may work on corporate brochures and increasingly they work on multimedia materials. The aim of an illustration can be to entertain, inform or persuade. Many illustrators become specialists in a particular area such as scientific or technical illustrating.

Entry, qualifications and training

To be successful as an illustrator, your portfolio of work is more important than formal qualifications. Many entrants have degrees in graphic design, fine art, fashion or similar, but this is not essential. Your portfolio and your ability to promote yourself and your work are very important. Illustrations don't just have to be creatively good: you have to be clear about the message or idea that they are conveying. This ability to translate an idea or a thought into a design is what clients look for.

Personal attributes

Design and artistic skills. Ability to develop good client relationships and to interpret client briefs. Ability to work in a variety of styles. Self-motivation and marketing skills.

Earnings

Since illustrators work freelance it is hard to give typical salary details, but the Association of Illustrators can give help and advice on how to charge and how to price your work.

Info

The Artists' Information Company
www.a-n.co.uk

The Association of Illustrators
020 7613 4328
www.theaoi.com

Creative and Cultural Skills
(The Sector Skills Council for Craft, Cultural Heritage, Design, Literature, Music, Performing, and Visual Arts)
020 7015 1800
www.ccskills.org.uk

Industrial product designer

Trained designers work within industry with engineers who have created products. These range from household goods and furniture to specialised equipment for science, industry and commerce. Designers are concerned with creating products that both look attractive and are efficient and convenient in use. The competition for the sale of new goods, from suitcases or spectacles to CD players or cars, has resulted in an increased demand for the services of industrial designers.

Entry, qualifications and training

Employers recruit from those with an HND or degree in a design-related subject; some courses offer specialist modules in industrial design. Entry to such courses is normally via a National Diploma course after GCSEs or a foundation course at an art college after A levels. Applicants for art and design courses are expected to have a portfolio of their artwork when interviewed.

Personal attributes

As well as artistic ability, an understanding of mass-production processes is necessary; the industrial designer should also be able to work as part of a team, to schedule and recognise the needs of the consumer.

Earnings

Salaries start at between £20,000 and £27,000, rising to £30,000 to £35,000 with a few years' experience.

Info

Chartered Society of Designers (CSD)	SEMTA (The Sector Skills Council for Science, Engineering and Manufacturing Technologies)
020 7357 8088	0845 643 9001
www.csd.org.uk	www.semta.org.uk

Interactive media designer

(see also Information and Communication Technology)

Interactive media design is a new and highly popular area within art and design. There are now over 500 multimedia courses in the UK. Multimedia design draws on both technical and design skills, and is used in designs for interactive media products such as websites, CD ROMs, interactive TV and computer games. Career opportunities exist in a wide variety of organisations, from corporations with websites to specialist producers of computer games.

Entry, qualifications and training

Technical and design skills are essential. Many general courses in Art and Design also have a multimedia option, though there are now specialist multimedia and interactive design courses available. The majority of employers expect an HND or degree.

Personal attributes

Strong design and IT abilities are essential, as are the ability to work within a team and to understand the requirements of the organisation if employed on a company website. The development of new multimedia products such as computer games and CD ROMs also requires an understanding of business and marketing principles.

Earnings

Pay starts at around £20,000, although experienced designers can earn £40,000+.

Info

Chartered Society of Designers
(CSD)
020 7357 8088
www.csd.org.uk

Design Business Association (DBA)
020 7251 9229
www.dba.org.uk

British Interactive Multimedia
Association
www.bima.co.uk

Skillset (The Sector Skills Council
for the Creative Industries)
0808 100 80994
www.skillset.org

Interior designer

Interior designers work for commercial organisations as well as undertaking private commissions. They are responsible for the interiors of buildings (whereas an architect is responsible for its shell). Interior design can cover materials for floors and ceilings, fitments and fittings, and colour schemes, along with electrical and spatial planning. The commercial organisations may be offices, hotels, pubs, stores or banks. Interior designers may work with architects, have their own consultancies, or work in design units within large organisations.

Entry, qualifications and training

Entry to art school and college via a foundation course is the same as for an industrial product designer (see page 38). Once at art college, the student may specialise in interior design.

Personal attributes

A natural aptitude for art and the ability to work as part of a design team and to present work to customers are necessary.

Earnings

Junior designers earn from £15,000 to £23,000. With experience this range is £25,000 to £45,000, though few achieve the top of the range. Interior designers working freelance set their own hourly rates or fees per job.

Info

Chartered Society of Designers
(CSD)
020 7357 8088
www.csd.org.uk

British Institute of Interior Design
(BIID)
www.biid.org.uk

Creative and Cultural Skills
(The Sector Skills Council for Craft,
Cultural Heritage, Design, Literature,
Music, Performing, and Visual Arts)
020 7015 1800
www.ccskills.org.uk

Sign-writer

Sign-writers design and paint company names and logos on to shop fronts and the sides of vans and lorries; they may also paint estate agents' signboards and a wide variety of other temporary signs and notices. Sign-writers increasingly use a range of materials and techniques, including computer technology, to create signs. The letters are often formed from plastics, metal or wood and stuck on to the background.

Some sign-writers are in business on their own; others work for commercial sign-writing companies.

Entry, qualifications and training

There are no formal academic entry requirements for this type of work, but artistic talent combined with an interest in lettering is important. Some graphic design courses include typography and sign-writing and provide wider training. Some commercial sign-writing firms take on trainees, and NVQs in Assembly, Fabrication and Manufacturing Processes and Sign making are available at level 2.

Personal attributes

You have to be practical, creative and imaginative. As well as artistic flair you must be a good speller and an accurate worker. You need excellent communication skills and a good grasp of running your own business.

Earnings

Earnings are between £13,000 and £18,000 at the start of your career. The highest salaries are around £21,000 to £24,000.

Info

British Sign and Graphics Association
01733 230033
www.bsga.co.uk

Cogent (Skills for Science Based Industries)
01925 515200
www.cogent-ssc.com

Creative and Cultural Skills (The Sector Skills Council for Craft, Cultural Heritage, Design, Literature, Music, Performing, and Visual Arts)
020 7015 1800
www.ccskills.org.uk

Art therapist

(see Therapy)

Arts administration

Arts administration in its broadest sense covers a range of work for many different organisations, such as national or regional arts bodies, local authorities, theatres, orchestras, ballet companies, art galleries, arts centre and community arts projects.

Art gallery curator

What your day-to-day work involves as an art gallery manager depends very much on the size of the gallery you manage. Your work could include choosing art work to be displayed, arranging for conservation of existing items, ensuring that items remain secure, and commissioning work. The gallery may sell work, in which case you will need to work with artists and help to bring likely buyers into the gallery. In a small gallery you may be involved in some of the basic daily administration as well, hiring staff, talking to visitors and producing publicity materials.

Arts administrator

Your work could include any combination of the following: choosing venues, managing venues, arranging sponsorship, managing budgets, hiring staff, developing future strategies, putting on cultural events, building links with local communities, organising marketing and publicity and sorting out appropriate security arrangements for events. Working in a small arts centre, you are likely to be involved in all the daily administrative tasks. Working for a large organisation, you may specialise in aspects such as marketing, finance or planning.

Community arts worker

Through projects and support, community arts workers help local communities to participate in and develop arts activities of all kinds, including music, dance, drama, filmmaking, creative writing, photography and mural painting. As a community arts worker you help people to develop not just their artistic, but also their organisational skills. You may have to attend meetings, argue your case for funding and help find sponsorship.

It is impossible to say what a typical role would be, but you could, for example, be working with a local youth group encouraging them to do mural painting rather than spray graffiti. You might work with local care home residents to encourage creative writing about local history. The range is very wide.

Entry, qualifications and training

There are two main ways to get into gallery management or arts administration. It is possible to work your way up from a junior administrative position, but many arts administrators are graduates with a relevant degree, in arts, arts administration, business or marketing. Even more important than any formal qualification is relevant experience. Community arts workers usually have a background of experience and qualifications in one of the performing or creative arts and may also have a background in arts administration, community work or teaching. For both arts administration and community arts work, voluntary or temporary experience is of enormous value.

Personal attributes

Whatever aspects of arts administration appeals to you, you need to be passionately committed, enthusiastic and really interested in your chosen field. For some of the more senior jobs a great deal of self-confidence is needed if you are to negotiate sponsorship deals or organise major cultural events. Many roles also require you to work closely with members of the public, so you need to be an excellent communicator. Many roles also require good financial acumen.

Earnings

Trainee administrators earn between £15,000 and £20,000. Gallery curators earn from £18,000 to £28.000. Curators of well-known city-centre galleries can earn up to £40,000. Community arts workers earn £17,000 to £26,000. This particular sector is under extreme financial pressure at present.

Info

Arts Council England
0845 300 6200
www.artscouncil.org.uk

Arts Marketing Association (AMA)
01223 578 078
www.a-m-a.co.uk

Voluntary Arts Network
www.voluntaryarts.org

**Creative and Cultural Skills
(The Sector Skills Council for Craft,
Cultural Heritage, Design, Literature,
Music, Performing, and Visual Arts)**
020 7015 1800
www.ccskills.org.uk

National Campaign for the Arts
020 7287 3777
www.artscampaign.org.uk

Museums Association
www.museumsassociation.org

ASTRONOMER

Astronomers study the sun, planets, stars, galaxies and other objects in the sky, analysing the radio, infrared, optical, ultraviolet, X and gamma radiations they emit, to find out how they work. Some of these radiations do not penetrate the earth's atmosphere, so observations by satellite as well as from the ground are necessary. Modern astronomical detectors are usually based on electronic methods and give results that can be analysed by computer.

Entry, qualifications and training

To become a research astronomer, a good degree in physics or maths is necessary and it is possible to do degrees in astronomy or astrophysics. This is normally followed by postgraduate study and research. Various grants are available to support students undertaking such courses.

Astronomy-related careers at an engineering or technical level are also open to those with skills in applied physics, electronics, computer hardware and software, optics and mechanical engineering.

Personal attributes

Astronomers need curiosity and imagination; they must be able to make logical deductions from the available observations. Working long and unusual hours and travelling to remote observatories may also be involved.

Earnings

A junior researcher in astronomy earns between £20,000 and £25,000. Senior researchers earn more than £35,000. Senior lecturers and astronomers associated with prestigious research projects or working with technical organisations may earn far more than this.

Info

Science and Technology Facilities Council
01793 442000
www.scitech.ac.uk

Royal Astronomical Society
020 7734 4582
www.ras.org.uk

AUCTIONEER

The auctioneer's work involves the sale by auction of property of all kinds, including buildings (houses, farms and estates), livestock, and goods such as furniture, antiques, paintings, glass, toys, carpets and china. The work also entails valuations for various purposes, including investment and insurance.

Entry, qualifications and training

An auctioneer's work involves the valuation of land and property, so surveying or valuation qualifications are necessary. There are two components to qualifying as a chartered surveyor or valuer. First is successful completion of a Royal Institution of Chartered Surveyors (RICS) accredited degree or diploma, followed by enrolment onto the Assessment of Professional Competence (APC). The latter is two years' practical training while in employment, finishing with an RICS professional assessment interview. One-year full-time and two-year part-time postgraduate conversion courses are also available.

Personal attributes

Attention to detail is important for this job, together with a practical attitude and an aptitude for figures. In fine art auctioneering, a certain flair and the ability to distinguish a fake from the genuine article are essential.

Earnings

Salaries for newly qualified valuers are around £20,000. Experienced valuers and auctioneers earn from £25,000 to £40,000. Any earnings linked to the property market and where commission is part of the package will be affected by the current economic climate.

Info

Arts Marketing Association (AMA)
01223 578 078
www.a-m-a.co.uk

**Creative and Cultural Skills
(The Sector Skills Council for Craft,
Cultural Heritage, Design,
Literature, Music, Performing, and
Visual Arts)**
020 7015 1800
www.ccskills.org.uk

**Royal Institute of Chartered
Surveyors**
0870 333 1600
www.rics.org

**Institute of Revenues, Rating and
Valuation**
020 7691 898
www.irrv.net

AUDIOLOGIST

Audiologists work with patients as part of a multidisciplinary team of professionals. They identify, assess and treat hearing and/or balance disorders, recommending and providing appropriate rehabilitation and management. Most audiologists work in hospitals. Many choose to specialise in particular client groups such as babies, young children or older people. They may choose to specialise in particular conditions such as tinnitus or balance problems.

Entry, qualifications and training

There are three main routes to qualifying as an audiologist: a BSc in Audiology, an MSc in Audiology or a Postgraduate Diploma in Audiology. To gain a place on either the MSc or postgraduate diploma courses you normally need a good degree, first or upper-second class, in a science subject. The BSc in Audiology takes four years, of which the third year is a clinical placement in an audiology department.

It is also possible for graduates with an appropriate science degree at first or upper-second class level to apply for training as a clinical scientist in audiology through the Association of Clinical Science. Training takes four years and leads to the MSc or postgraduate diploma.

Clinical scientists in audiology who have successfully completed their training must register with the Health Professions Council (HPC) in order to practise.

Personal attributes

Audiologists need to be able to communicate with people of all ages. They need to be able to think logically and adopt a scientific approach combined with caring and patience.

Earnings

Salaries for trainees are around £21,400, rising to £27,000. Qualified audiologists post-registration are paid £30,00 to £40,000.

The British Academy of Audiology
01625 504066
www.baaudiology.org

British Society of Audiology
www.thebsa.org.uk

Health Professions Council (HPC)
0845 3004 472
www.hpc-uk.org

NHS Careers
0845 60 60 655
www.nhscareers.nhs.uk

Association of Clinical Scientists
www.assclinsci.org

BAKER

All the bread, cakes, pastries, biscuits, pies and confectionery are made by bakers working in three types of bakery – plant, in-store or craft. Plant bakeries are large food manufacturers, where most of the work is done by automated processes; it is the baker's job to oversee these processes. In-store bakers working in the bakery departments of supermarkets use some automated processes, but do more hand preparation and finishing of some products. Craft bakers make products for local bakers' shops, delicatessens and farmers' markets. Craft bakers do more work by hand, though with the assistance of machines, and they may be closely involved in developing new products and trying out new recipes.

Entry, qualifications and training

You may not need any formal qualifications to train as a baker. If you start this work through an apprenticeship, individual employers may ask for three or four GCSEs. Training is on the job, but you can also work towards NVQ levels 1, 2 and 3 in baking skills.

Personal attributes

In all areas of baking you must have a good appreciation of food hygiene and public health. You need good practical skills and good manual dexterity for some of the more fiddly processes in craft baking. In plant bakeries you need to be able to cope with hot, noisy conditions. In all cases you are likely to have to work as part of a team and you may sell products to customers if you work in a supermarket or a local shop.

Earnings

Trainees earn around £11,500 to £12,000. Good craft bakers or supervisors in plant bakery production can earn £16,000 to £20,000.

Info

Improve Ltd	Federation of Bakers
0845 6554 0448	020 7420 7190
www.improveltd.co.uk	www.bakersfederation.org.uk

BANKING AND FINANCE

There are several different types of bank. Retail or high street banks are the local banks with branches all over the country; all of these now have large call centre operations too. Retail banks serve individual customers, helping with all their personal banking needs. Investment or corporate banks provide financial services to large companies and other organisations.

Bank customer service adviser

Bank cashiers, more often called customer service advisers, deal with all the daily enquiries made by customers in person, by telephone or via the internet. They work either in high street branches or at call centres. They are responsible for processing cash and cheques, entering account details onto computer systems and issuing foreign currency. They also book appointments for customers who need more specialised advice. Senior cashiers handle more complex enquiries and also supervise small teams of cashiers.

Entry, qualifications and training

Each bank sets its own entry requirements. Some do not ask for specific qualifications, but they set entry tests which assess maths, English and computer skills. Many banks require four or five GCSEs grades A–C, including English and maths. Training is on the job and often includes options to study for NVQ levels 2 and 3 in Retail Financial Services, NVQ levels 1 and 2 in Contact Centre Operations, or levels 3, 4 and 5 for contact centre professionals (if you work in a call centre) or NVQ levels 2 and 3 in Customer Service. Anyone interested in management may be able to study for one of the diploma courses listed in the 'Bank manager' entry below.

Bank manager

Bank managers plan and deliver effective sales strategies and monitor the performance of new and existing financial products. Bank managers work either in high street branches, taking responsibility for day-to-day management, or in more specialised posts in corporate or commercial departments at regional or head office level. Their work involves talking to customers, offering advice and planning the workload of other staff in their branch or department. The financial services sector is now extremely competitive, so product sales are a key part of the manager's role.

Entry, qualifications and training

There are two routes to management – either joining a training scheme run by a bank, or gaining promotion after joining the bank as a cashier/customer services adviser. Most banks expect management trainees to have a good honours degree in a business- or finance-related subject, but it is worth checking individual requirements. Some banks will accept A level entrants or applicants with HNDs. For anyone already working for a bank and wishing to get into management, being good at dealing with customers and having some supervisory experience are very important.

There are several professional qualifications you can work towards on a part-time basis. These include the Professional Diploma in Financial Services Management (Professional DFSM), the Applied Diploma in Corporate Banking and the Applied Diploma in Retailing Financial Services. Management training programmes in banks are normally quite structured and often include the requirement to study for one of the above qualifications.

Personal attributes

All bank staff need very good communication skills. You must be able to explain complex information and be assertive enough to disappoint people sometimes. You must have good IT skills and the ability to interpret figures and other financial information. In management you have to be able to take responsibility for motivating other staff and for implementing sales policies. As a cashier, you may well want to develop some supervisory and management skills by working towards becoming a senior cashier or a customer services adviser in a specialised area such as mortgages or personal investment.

Earnings

Customer service advisers start on between £14,000 and £17,000, rising to £19,000 to £25,000 with experience. Earnings often include bonuses or commission for selling financial products to customers. Management trainees earn between £21,000 and £26,000. Some banks pay a joining bonus of between £3,000 and £5,000 to their graduate trainees. Experienced managers earn between £25,000 and £40,000. Bank staff in senior positions can earn up to £100,000. Many roles include the payment of bonuses.

Info

British Bankers Association (BBA)
020 7216 8800
www.bba.org.uk

Financial Skills partnership
0845 257 3772
www.directions.org.uk

ifs School of Finance, Institute of Financial Services
01227 818609
www.ifslearning.ac.uk

Building society customer service adviser

Building society customer service advisers (sometimes called cashiers) undertake very similar work to that of banking cashiers. They deal with all the daily enquiries made by customers in person or by telephone. They work either in high street branches or at regional offices. They are responsible for processing cash and cheques, entering account details onto computer systems and issuing foreign currency. They also book appointments for customers who need more specialised advice. Senior cashiers handle more complex enquiries and also supervise small teams of customer service advisers.

Despite the current similarity between banks and building societies, there are still more customers who apply for mortgages through building societies and who use building societies for longer-term investments.

Entry, qualifications and training

Some building societies require applicants to have four GCSEs including English and maths. Others rely on their own selection tests. Experience of customer service work and handling cash is a big advantage, so having worked in any form of retail is very beneficial. Most training is on the job and well structured.

You often have the chance to combine your training with studying for a financial services qualification such as NVQ levels 2 and 3 in Retail Financial Services, NVQ/SVQ levels 2 and 3 in Customer Service or the ifs School of Finance Customer Service Professional (CSP) award. As you gain qualifications, and with increased experience, there are often opportunities to train and specialise in financial or mortgage advice.

Building society manager

Building society managers are responsible for running one or more branches of a high street building society. As well as the day-to-day management of their branch or branches they have to ensure that existing customers are happy, that new customers are acquired and that sales of new financial products are increased. They work with individual customers and develop business plans. They have to motivate staff and monitor sales performance.

Entry, qualifications and training

Most building societies run management training schemes, but it is also possible to gain promotion to a management role if you are already working as a customer services adviser/cashier. Most management training schemes are only open to applicants with a good honours degree in a business- or finance-related subject. Check individual company requirements though, because some will accept management trainees with degrees in other subjects or with good A levels or HNDs.

Training is on the job and well structured, with opportunities to learn about different aspects of the role. Most trainee managers are either required or encouraged to study for one of the following qualifications: the Professional Diploma in Financial Services Management (Professional DFSM), the Applied Diploma in Corporate Banking or the Applied Diploma in Retailing Financial Services.

Personal attributes

All building society staff need good interpersonal skills for dealing with enquiries. You have to be able to convey complex financial information so that it is easily understood. Good computer skills are important and an ability to work accurately and carefully is necessary. Customer service staff aiming towards management roles and managers need to be able to take responsibility for leading and motivating staff teams.

Earnings

Customer service staff start on between £14,000 and £17,000 rising to £19,000 to £25,000 with experience. Salaries are higher in London. Management trainees earn between £22,000 and £25,000 while experienced managers earn up to £50,000. Senior managers in the organisation can earn up to £100,000. Benefits often include bonus sharing schemes, subsidised mortgages and share options. Earnings often include commission on financial products sold.

Info

Financial Skills Partnership
0845 257 3772
www.directions.org.uk

Building Societies Association
020 7520 5900
www.bsa.org.uk

ifs School of Finance, Institute of
Financial Services
01227 818609
www.ifslearning.ac.uk

Commodity broker

Commodity brokers buy and sell commodities, including tea, coffee, grain, oil, gas and metals. They work either for companies that specialise in dealing in commodities trading or for companies that produce and/or grow the commodities. As well as trading in the actual products, they trade in futures (commodities that will be produced or grown in the future). They have to monitor world markets, possibly visiting sites and countries where commodities are produced. They have to advise clients when to buy, when to sell and where to place themselves in the market. They also have to work closely with shipping, transport and insurance organisations. When much of the financial services sector faces difficulties, commodities trading becomes very busy as commodities are seen as (though they are not necessarily) more reliable.

Entry, qualifications and training

While there are no specific entry qualifications, most successful applicants have a 2.1 degree in a relevant subject such as economics, maths, science, business or finance. The recruitment process can be very demanding, including several interviews and psychometric tests.

Personal attributes

You must be highly numerate and an excellent communicator. You have to be able to take decisions under pressure, accept responsibility and work as part of a team. Being able to live with job insecurity is also important; opportunities in this work fluctuate widely.

Earnings

New entrants earn between £35,000 and £50,000 and experienced brokers with a successful trading record can earn extremely high salaries. It is a volatile market, though, with a lot of associated risk.

Info

eFinancialCareers Ltd	Intercontinental Exchange (ICE)
020 7997 7900	020 7481 0643
www.efinancialcareers.co.uk	www.theice.com
Financial Skills Partnership	The London Metal Exchange
0845 257 3772	020 7264 5555
www.directions.org.uk	www.lme.co.uk

Corporate treasurer

Treasury in a company is key in determining the firm's financial strategy and financial policy – advising on what businesses to invest in, organising the appropriate funding for this, and controlling the risk in the organisation. A treasurer works in a team to protect a company's financial assets and to ensure the company has the necessary cash available to run its business. The treasury team will deal with banking requirements and funding for the business and manage financial risk. Treasury therefore incorporates raising and managing money; currency; commodity and interest rate risk management and dealing; and, in some organisations, the related areas of insurance, pensions, property and taxation. The size of a treasury team is dependent on an organisation's size and capabilities. Even where no dedicated role exists, someone in the organisation will almost certainly be taking on the treasury role as part of their job.

Entry, qualifications and training

Any degree discipline is acceptable, although accountancy, finance, economics or mathematics is useful. As with many roles, training will be largely on the job. Some large companies offer training programmes for finance/accounting graduates from which it may be possible to request a secondment within the treasury function. You can also enter through the tax, corporate, finance, legal or accounting functions. The professional body for corporate treasury is the Association of Corporate Treasurers (ACT). It provides a range of well-respected industry qualifications and training courses, including the AMCT Diploma, the core treasury qualification.

Personal attributes

A career in treasury requires you to work in a fast-paced environment. A key part of the role involves handling relationships with shareholders, banks and other lenders, so strong communication skills are essential. An effective treasurer needs to be able to analyse and absorb information quickly, be numerate, accurate and pay close attention to detail, but you need to be innovative too. You will almost certainly be dealing with sums of money running into the millions, even billions, which requires a strong nerve. It is a demanding but extremely rewarding career.

Earnings

You can expect a minimum starting salary of £25,000. Qualified treasurers with experience can expect a salary of £100,000+, with additional higher earning opportunities.

Info

Association of Corporate
Treasurers (ACT)
020 7847 2540
www.treasurers.org

Economist

(see Economist)

Financial adviser

Financial advisers provide advice on all aspects of financial planning to a wide range of clients. They provide advice to individuals, corporate clients and other groups of people such as societies or charities. They offer advice on such diverse matters as loans, mortgages, pensions, investments and other financial products and services.

Their work involves meeting clients and explaining financial products and services to them clearly and carefully. They have to assess people's different financial circumstances in order to advise on the most suitable products. They conduct in-depth research into different products and liaise closely with banks, building societies, insurance companies, etc – the financial product suppliers. They are often self-employed, so they also have to be good at marketing and promoting themselves and seeking out new clients.

Half the financial advisers working in the UK class themselves as independent rather than tied advisers. Being independent, however, does not necessarily mean being self-employed. Both tied and independent financial advisers may work for an organisation or may be self-employed. Many independent advisers work for firms which themselves are known as independent financial advisers.

Tied advisers work for financial services companies, insurance companies, investment firms, banks and building societies. Some are employed by estate agencies, law firms and by retailers that have developed financial services as a part of their business.

Entry, qualifications and training

You don't have to be a graduate, though a degree in business studies, accountancy or financial services can give you an advantage. Many employers are happy to take people from a wide range of working backgrounds and do not require academic qualifications. You nearly always need a driving licence, and some employers set a lower age limit of 21 or older for trainees.

All entrants to the profession have to pass the Financial Planning Certificate examinations parts 1, 2 and 3 or the Certificate for Financial Advisers in order to be licensed by the Financial Services Authority. A lot of the training is provided on the job and when you start you often learn by shadowing a more experienced adviser. Advisers who work for financial organisations, rather than independently, can progress to management posts in the financial services sector.

Personal attributes

You need excellent communication skills, to be able to talk convincingly to corporate clients and sensitively to private individuals. You must be smart, well organised and highly motivated – this is a competitive sector. You need good numeracy and IT skills and the ability to deal with highly complex information.

Earnings

If you are employed by financial services companies your earnings are made up of a combination of a basic salary plus commission on products sold. Basic salaries are between £18,000 and £30,000. Achieving sales targets can boost earnings to between £30,000 and £60,000. In a difficult marketplace these commissions and target-related earnings are much harder to achieve. Some independent financial advisers charge a fee to clients rather than earning commission on products sold.

Info

Financial Skills Partnership	ifs School of Finance
0845 257 3772	01227 818609
www.directions.org.uk	www.ifslearning.ac.uk
Chartered Insurance Institute	Personal Finance Society
020 8989 8464	020 8530 0852
www.cii.co.uk	www.thepfs.org

Investment analyst

Investment analysts analyse the financial markets to advise on the best investments for clients. Investment managers rely on their information. There are two main types of investment analyst. First are those who work for stockbrokers and undertake their own analysis to provide information for fund manager clients. The aim is to generate 'buy and sell' orders for the stockbrokers for whom they work. This is known as the 'sell side'. Second, there are those who work for investment management institutions. They provide ideas and information to enable their in house fund managers to make the best decisions for their clients. This is known as the 'buy side'. The majority of investment analysts work on the 'sell side'.

Fund manager

Investment fund managers invest the funds of other people – private clients and institutions, such as insurance companies, charities, independent schools and specialised research institutions. Managers must keep their clients' interests continually under review, offering advice on how to retain their clients' income and when to change investments. Investment fund managers may be employed by the larger institutions or work in specialist firms that tend to serve smaller clients.

Entry, qualifications and training

Investment banks and stockbroking firms prefer to recruit graduates. A good honours degree in any subject is acceptable, but degrees in accountancy, business, economics or maths are especially relevant. Some investment analysts need in-depth knowledge of particular industry markets, so it may be useful to have experience in areas such as energy, engineering, mining or life sciences. Training is on the job and graduates are usually placed with a more experienced analyst and given other structured training. Initial training takes around three years.

Trainees are usually required or encouraged to study for relevant professional qualifications. Two of the most widely offered are the United Kingdom Society of Investment Professionals (UKSIP) Investment Management Certificate (IMC) and the Securities and Investments Institute (SII) Certificate in Securities and Financial Derivatives. Many analysts then carry on to study for more advanced diplomas.

Personal attributes

You must have an enquiring mind and be persistent and thorough in your research. A broad range of interests, including politics and economics as well as finance, is important. You have to be confident dealing with people, one-to-one or at meetings with senior representatives of companies. You should be able to write clear, concise summaries of statistical data and other research findings.

Earnings

Typical starting salaries are £27,000 to £40,000 in London, with bonuses of 20–100 per cent possible in the first three years, less in other parts of the UK. After five to eight years, salaries rise to £65,000–100,000, with bonuses of 40–100 per cent possible. Salaries vary according to the nature and size of the company and geographical location. Salaries are higher with investment banks.

Info

Financial Skills Partnership
0845 257 3772
www.directions.org.uk

Chartered Institute for Securities &
Investment (CISI)
020 7645 0680
www.cisi.org.uk

CFA Institute
020 7531 0751
www.cfainstitute.org

CFA Society of the UK
020 7796 3000
www.cfauk.org

Stockbroker

Stockbrokers buy and sell securities on the Stock Exchange on behalf of investors, who may be individuals but are increasingly institutions such as banks, insurance companies, pension funds or unit trusts. They also advise clients on shares they hold and suggest good times to sell or buy. Stockbrokers work from their offices using the phone and internet to keep in touch with financial markets and news.

Entry, qualifications and training

While there are no formal entry requirements, most investment banks will only consider you if you have a 2.1 degree and some employers require an MSc or an MBA. Relevant subjects such as economics or business are preferred and the selection procedure is tough. If you do not have a relevant degree, it is really important that you are able to demonstrate your understanding of how financial markets work. Some people move from investment analysis or investment administration into stockbroking. To practise as a stockbroker you must register with the Financial Services Authority (FSA). The Financial Services Skills Council can provide you with a full list of all the qualifications that allow you to register. Investment banks and other firms that take on trainee brokers offer in-house training.

Personal attributes

A great aptitude with numbers and excellent communication skills are essential. You must be calm under pressure, able to take decisions and happy working on your own or as part of a team.

Earnings

Trainees start on £26,000 to £35,000 rising to £50,000 to £80,000. Experienced and successful brokers can earn £150,000 but at the moment this profession is going through a difficult period and job insecurity may balance out the high salaries.

Info

CFA Society of the UK
020 7796 3000
www.cfauk.org

Financial Services Skills Council
0845 257 3772
www.financialskillspartnership.org.uk

Chartered Institute for Securities
& Investment (CISI)
020 7645 0680
www.cisi.org.uk

Trader/dealer

Traders or dealers fall into three categories, each working in different ways and/or for different client groups. Flow traders buy and sell such products as shares, bonds, commodities and foreign exchange on the financial markets. They buy and sell on behalf of banks or other financial institutions' clients. They try to minimise risk and maximise profits for their clients. Proprietary traders trade on behalf of a bank or financial institution rather than its clients. They try to buy at low prices and sell high. Flow and proprietary traders work mainly in dealing rooms, constantly tracking market performance and making decisions about when and what to buy and sell. Sales traders deal directly with clients, providing market information and promoting new financial ideas to clients. Their role includes preparing detailed reports based on market information – so is more research-based than the work of flow traders.

Entry, qualifications and training

This is now very much a graduate profession – you normally need a good degree, and while any subject is acceptable, business studies, economics, maths and politics are particularly useful. You may also get in if you have an HND or Foundation degree in one of these subjects. This has been a highly competitive area and you are likely to face a rigorous selection process. If you have not gone on to higher education, it may be possible to work your way in from an administrative job for a bank or other financial organisation, especially if you are able to build up a good network of contacts. Most training is on the job, combined with in-house short courses or work towards financial sector qualifications.

Personal attributes

All traders have to be able to develop a really good knowledge of financial markets and to apply that knowledge. In work other than sales, a good trader should be able to take risks, but in a balanced way – weighing up benefits and dangers realistically. Traders working in dealing rooms have to be resilient and able to think quickly and take decisions under pressure. Traders working in sales have to build up excellent relationships with their clients.

Earnings

Initial earnings are between £25,000 and £50,000 and with a few years' experience and a successful record some salaries are very high – £250,000 plus with large bonuses and other benefits.

Info

Financial Skills Partnership
0845 257 3772
www.directions.org.uk

Chartered Institute for Securities &
Investment (CISI)
020 7645 0680
www.cisi.org.uk

BEAUTY

(see also Hairdresser)

There are several occupations in the beauty sector, including therapists who provide body and face treatment, undertake body piercing, nail treatments or give advice on what colour to wear. There are make-up artists who work in film and television. The sector has grown in the past decade, with more salons, spa hotels and private practitioners.

Beauty sales consultant

Beauty sales consultants work on cosmetics counters in large department stores, or in individual stores owned by a particular brand of make-up and beauty products. Consultants advise customers on what products, colours or fragrances might suit them best. They may apply make-up on customers, so that the customer can see the results before making a purchase and they also demonstrate new products or gadgets.

Entry, qualifications and training

You don't need formal qualifications to start training – your employer normally provides an introductory course. There are several NVQ level 2 courses available in beauty consultancy for which you can study on a part-time basis. Previous experience in either retail or beauty therapy can also be very useful.

Personal attributes

You need to have excellent communication skills, to be able to talk to people, make them feel comfortable and encourage them to purchase products. You need to be practical and sensitive when applying make-up and other beauty products. You often have to organise your own product displays, so you must be imaginative and have good visual awareness. You need to be highly presentable yourself – a good advert for what you are selling.

Earnings

Trainees earn around £12,000 to £13,000, rising to £19,000 with experience. Consultants are often expected to meet sales targets and earn part of their salaries through sales commission on products sold.

Info

Vocational Training Charities Trust (VTCT)
023 8068 4500
www.vtct.org.uk

Hairdressing and Beauty Industry Authority (HABIA)
www.habia.org

Beauty therapist or beautician

Beauty therapists work in salons, health clubs and private homes and, at the glamorous end of the market, for film, television and fashion magazines. Beauty therapists offer a range of treatments to their clients, such as facials, massage, make-up, manicures, waxing and body toning and tanning treatments. Beauty therapists who visit clients in their own homes have to be good business people, keeping accounts, ordering stock and keeping up to date with the latest developments. The top end of the market is highly competitive, but it is a profession that gives you a lot of flexibility. UK hairdressers and beauty therapists are generally highly thought of.

Entry, qualifications and training

You normally need three or four GCSEs grades A–C and then there are several relevant qualifications, including the City & Guilds diploma in beauty therapy, City & Guilds level 3 diploma in specialist beauty therapy, Edexcel national certificate and diploma in beauty therapy sciences, Vocational Training Charities Trust (VTCT) advanced diploma in beauty therapy and NVQ level 3 in beauty therapy. You can either go to a further education or private college full-time, or work as an assistant at a beauty salon and attend college part-time. Private college courses may be shorter and more intensive, but they are also expensive.

Personal attributes

As a beauty therapist you have to look neat, presentable and well groomed. You must be friendly, welcoming and able to put clients at ease; you also need to be tactful and sensitive. You must be comfortable working in close physical proximity with your clients and you need reasonable stamina as you will be on your feet for most of the time. If you run your own business you need all the appropriate business skills too.

Earnings

Beauty therapists earn between £12,000 and £18,000 while salon managers earn between £20,000 and £25,000. Beauty therapists often receive tips and they may also make commission from selling cosmetics and beauty products. Some beauty therapists are self-employed, in which case earnings vary according to how much work they undertake.

Body artist/tattooist

Body artists/tattooists working in studios or parlours draw designs of words, patterns and pictures on the bodies of customers. This form of body adornment has grown increasingly popular over recent years. The body artist either draws the design freehand or works from a transfer placed on the customer's skin. He or she then follows the outline with an electrically operated needle that delivers permanent ink dyes just under the skin.

Entry, qualifications and training

No formal qualifications are required, but you will have to persuade a registered tattooist to take you on as an apprentice. It is illegal to tattoo if you are not registered with your local Environmental Health Department. This department should be able to provide you with names of local registered artists and the Tattoo Club of Great Britain can also help you with this. Training takes from one to three years, but it takes at least five years to become really competent.

Personal attributes

Body artists/tattooists must have a flair for design and also be very good at working with people. Customers may want a tattoo, but they are often a bit nervous about it. Body artists must be extremely careful about their art work, since the designs are permanent. They must also have scrupulous hygiene and health and safety awareness.

Earnings

Trainees earn around £12,000 rising to £17,000 with considerable experience. It is possible to earn more if you develop a really good reputation and have obvious talent, or if you work in a highly fashionable studio.

Make-up artist

Make-up artists prepare and work on make-up and hair styling for clients, including artists' models, singers, dancers, actors and others appearing on television and in films. Make-up artists also work in other settings – on cruise liners, in beauty salons in large hotels, stage shows, fashion shows or in the medical profession, where they provide make-up to camouflage clients' injuries following an accident or surgery.

An experienced make-up artist works on more versatile projects using elaborate make-up, wigs, prosthetics and other materials to change the shape of a face or create scars and wounds for television and film productions.

Entry, qualifications and training

While there are no set entry qualifications, many applicants have degrees or HNDs in art and design-related subjects and/or beauty therapy and hairdressing qualifications. There is a wide range of training courses available and Skillset gives useful advice on these. Examples of some relevant qualifications include the BTEC/SQA National Certificate/Diploma in Performing Arts (Make-up), Vocational Training Charitable Trust (VTCT) level 3 Diploma in Theatre and Media Make-up, and International Therapy Examinations Council (ITEC) level 3 Diploma in Fashion, Theatre and Media Make-up. The London College of Fashion offers a Foundation degree in make-up artistry. Most people start as a make-up assistant while doing one of the courses mentioned above.

Personal attributes

You need to have artistic flair and imagination. You must be practical, methodical and patient, but you must also be able to work quickly under pressure. You should be able to get on well with all sorts of people, and be confident and tactful, able to make suggestions and put people at ease. You may need good research skills if, for example, you are trying to create the look of a particular historical period.

Earnings

Many new entrants to the profession work for free to gain experience. After this there are recommended industry minimum pay rates for film and television work. Current rates are £250 per day for junior make-up/hair assistant and £350 for make-up designer prosthetics. Experienced artists working on major productions can earn as much as £3,000 per day – but it is only the rare few who achieve these incomes.

Info

Skillset Careers
08080 300 900 (England and
Northern Ireland)
0808 100 8094 (Scotland)
0800 121 815 (Wales)
www.skillset.org

National Association of Screen
Makeup and Hair Artists (NASMAH)
www.nasmah.co.uk

Vocational Training Charitable
Trust (VTCT)
023 8068 4500
www.vtct.org.uk

Get Into Theatre
www.getintotheatre.org

Hairdressing and Beauty Industry
Authority (HABIA)
www.habia.org

Broadcasting Entertainment
Cinematograph and Theatre Union
(BECTU)
www.bectu.org.uk

Producers Alliance for Cinema and
Television
www.pact.co.uk

Nail technician

As greater numbers of people are going to salons to have either regular manicures or false nails or nail extensions applied, so there has been a growth in this specialist area of beauty therapy. There are now many salons which specialise purely in nail care, treatment and decoration. Nail technicians do manicures, apply, maintain and repair false nails and extensions, and decorate both natural and gel nails with polish or with painted artistic designs.

Entry, qualifications and training

There are usually no formal qualifications required to get into this work, but some large salons may require you to have GCSEs in English, maths and a science. Many nail technicians are qualified beauty therapists who choose to specialise in nail technology. If this is not the case, then a good way to start is by working towards an NVQ level 1 in Beauty Therapy and then trying to gain work as an assistant in a salon. Once you have learnt the basics about nail care and nail treatments and decoration, there are further NVQs levels 2 and 3 in Nail Care and Nail Technology towards which you can work while employed.

Personal attributes

You have to be smart and presentable and have a friendly and pleasant manner. You should have good manual dexterity and an interest in colour and design. You should have a careful and patient approach to your work, and a good awareness of health and safety and hygiene issues.

Earnings

Earnings are usually £12,000 to £16,000. In some city centre salons with a really good reputation earnings can be up to £25,000. Many nail technicians are self-employed, as this is work that can be done from home or by visiting clients in their homes.

Info

Vocational Training Charities Trust
(VTCT)
023 8068 4500
www.vtct.org.uk

Hairdressing and Beauty Industry
Authority (HABIA)
www.habia.org

BIOLOGY

Biology is the study of living organisms, plants and animals in their natural habitats and in laboratory conditions.

Biologist

Biologists work in many fields, including medicine, food manufacture and the natural environment. As a biologist you would specialise in one of these areas and perhaps in a very specific aspect of that area. Biologists might study the marine environment, or work in the food industry to ensure that food is free of contamination and has a maximum shelf-life. They might work in medicine studying the human immune system or for an environmental protection organisation studying habitats and ascertaining how best to preserve them. Many people who graduate in biology also choose to teach the subject in school or university. The working day of a biologist will vary enormously depending upon the field in which he or she works. Scientific study, observation of results, solving problems and working as part of a team are always likely to be key aspects of the work.

Entry, qualifications and training

Most biologists have a degree in biology, biological science, marine biology, microbiology or conservation biology. It may be possible to start at technician level with 4 GCSEs, including maths, English and a science grades A–C, but many employers ask for A levels or a degree even for technician-level entry. For research work many applicants offer postgraduate qualifications too.

Personal attributes

You need an enquiring mind, a systematic approach and a rigorous attention to recording detail regardless of the field of biology in which you work. You must be able to solve problems, but also pose the questions to which it is worth finding an answer. Being able to work on your own, but also as part of a team sharing results and exchanging ideas, is very important.

Earnings

Salaries depend on who employs you as well as how much experience you have. A junior research biologist starts on £20,000 to £22,000 a year. In industry senior research biologists can earn £35,000 to £50,000.

Info

Society of Biology
www.societyofbiology.org

Biology4All
www.biology4all.com

Biochemist

Biochemistry is the study of chemical substances and processes in living cells and tissues. Most biochemists work in laboratories, although some make their careers in education or industry, in brewing, food technology, forestry, agriculture, dietetics, pharmaceuticals, management and planning.

Many biochemists are employed in hospitals; they are referred to as clinical biochemists. They manage and develop the service and carry out research into diseases. Pharmaceutical firms also employ biochemists to develop new drugs and study their effects on diseases and patients. Qualified biochemists are also employed in research institutions funded by the Medical Research Council, the National Institute for Medical Research and Biotechnology, and the Biological Sciences Research Council, as well as some funded by charities such as the Imperial Cancer Research Fund (ICRF).

Entry, qualifications and training

Most biochemists are graduates with a degree in biochemistry or chemistry. Increasingly, many applicants also have postgraduate qualifications in biochemistry or clinical chemistry. If you can get some work experience in a laboratory while studying for your degree, this is really useful. It is possible to work your way up by starting as a laboratory technician and doing a degree in biochemistry part-time.

If you choose to work for the NHS as a biochemist, you normally start training as a clinical biochemist and work for professional qualifications as a clinical scientist. In industry and research, once you are working as a trainee biochemist your employer may encourage or require you to take further postgraduate qualifications.

Personal attributes

You need all the skills of a good scientist. You must be a good problem solver and be able to think creatively. You need to pay great attention to detail, follow procedures carefully and be highly observant. You should be practical, with reasonable IT skills. You must be able to work as part of a team, or capable of working on your own. At senior level your work may involve management of other staff and various projects.

Earnings

Starting salaries range from £25,500 to £28,000. Experienced biochemists can earn £35,000 to £55,000. In the NHS, biochemists' salaries are linked to a clear graded structure. Research jobs in industry may offer higher salaries than those in the NHS and the public sector.

Info

NHS Careers
0345 60 60 655
www.nhscareers.nhs.uk

Society of Biology
www.societyofbiology.org

Institute of Biomedical Science
020 7713 0214
www.ibms.org

Association for Clinical Biochemistry
www.acb.org.uk

Biochemical Society
01206 796 351
www.biochemistry.org

Biomedical scientist

(see Medical and Healthcare Science)

Biotechnologist

Biotechnologists work in agriculture, the food industry, medicine and the environment. They apply their knowledge of biological systems and structure in plants and animals to solve problems and develop products and processes in all these sectors. Applications of biotechnology are wide, but examples include developing vaccines and hormones to help treat inherited diseases; the study of human genetics, plants, animals and other organisms to understand the nature of inherited disease; and the development of genetic modification to alter certain properties of plants and seeds. Other examples include manufacturing enzymes that can preserve food, developing dyes and detergents for the textiles industry and developing microorganisms and plants that will clean land.

Entry, qualifications and training

To work as a biotechnologist you need a degree in a subject such as biotechnology, bioscience, microbiology, biochemistry, chemical engineering or a related biological science. You should also consider which specific area of biotechnology interests you, eg food, agriculture or medicine, as some degree courses offer work placements in industry and having experience in the field that particularly interests you will be helpful when you come to apply for jobs. Since so much of the work is research-based, you may also need an MSc or a PhD plus several years working as a laboratory assistant or a research assistant before you can progress to becoming a biotechnologist.

Training is on the job. Pharmaceutical companies often have in-house training schemes. Your training covers working with advanced technical equipment, computing skills and project management. If you don't join this sector with a postgraduate qualification, it is often possible to study for this on a part-time basis. Many postgraduate biotechnology courses allow you to focus on one area of the work and so develop specialised expertise.

Personal attributes

An enquiring mind and an interest in biology and chemistry are essential. You need to be a good, imaginative problem solver, but also highly meticulous and accurate in the way you work. Good IT and writing skills are also important. You have to be able to work well as part of a team, but also be good at working on your own without supervision.

Earnings

Trainees earn between £21,000 and £27,000. You may start on less as a junior research assistant or laboratory assistant. Senior biotechnologists earn £30,000 to £45,000.

Info

Association of the British
Pharmaceutical Industry (ABPI)
020 7930 3477
www.abpi.org.uk

Biotechnology and Biological
Sciences Research Council
01793 413200
www.bbsrc.ac.uk

SEMTA (The Skills Sector Council
for Science, Engineering and
Manufacturing Technologies)
0800 282167
www.semta.org.uk

Royal Academy of Engineering
020 7227 0500
www.raeng.org.uk

Botanist

Botany is the study of plans of every kind – flowers, food crops, trees, fungi, algae, mosses and lichens. While this is not a large field of employment, there are opportunities in agriculture, horticulture, government departments, the food industry and environmental conservation. Botanists study all aspects of plant life, including anatomy, chemistry, molecular biology and habitat. Job roles vary, but can include monitoring the prevalence or decline of particular plant species, classifying plants (taxonomy), searching for and identifying new species, working out how to extract chemicals from plants and looking at the effects of pollution, urban development or leisure activities on plant species. Botanists work in laboratories but also out in the field collecting and recording specimens. Their work can also including presenting research information and teaching.

Entry, qualifications and training

Botanists are normally expected to have a degree in either botany (often referred to as plant biology) or a closely related science. The Field Studies Society and the Botanical Society of the British Isles run some training courses in species recording and monitoring.

Personal attributes

Your interest in plants, or a specific group of plants, such as trees, seaweed, roses, toadstools, etc, needs to be backed up with excellent observational skills, the ability to record information very carefully and to be able to draw logical conclusions and explain these to others. You also need good communication skills: working as part of a team, supervising other field workers or arguing a case for environmental protection of a specific piece of land, for example.

Earnings

Junior research botanists earn between £20,000 and £23,000. Senior researchers earn up to £30,000. Posts in industry may pay more, while some posts in environmental conservation may be on the low side.

Info

Field Studies Society
0845 3454071
www.field-studies-council.org

Society of Biology
www.societyofbiology.org

Biology4all
www.biology4all.com

Botanical Society of the British Isles
www.bsbi.org.uk

BOOKMAKER

As a bookmaker or in betting shop management, you work with people who are placing bets on everything from horse and greyhound racing results to whether or not there will be a white Christmas. The majority of betting shops are part of large chains, but there are a few small, independent operators. This sector has done a lot to improve its image and make its outlets more appealing to customers, especially since the advent of online gambling, and a bookmaker managing an outlet needs to work to create a pleasant retail environment.

Entry, qualifications and training

Many people start as cashiers in betting shops and don't need formal qualifications other than a good general education. However, many off-course bookmakers do take on management trainees who have HNDs, degrees or other qualifications. Business-related subjects are the most sought after. At any level, you are likely to have to take a maths test to check how well you deal with percentages and calculating odds. A background in retail or other customer service roles is useful and further training is available in marketing, business management and customer service.

Personal attributes

You need excellent customer service skills, a lot of common sense, good numerical skills and the ability to manage other people.

Earnings

Cashiers earn £12,000 to £14,000. Trainee managers earn between £14,000 and £19,000, while branch managers earn between £22,000 and £40,000.

Info

People 1st (The Retail Sector Skills Council)
0870 060 2550
www.people1st.co.uk

National Association of Bookmakers Ltd
01884 841859
www.nab-bookmakers.co.uk

Association of British Bookmakers Ltd
020 7434 2111
www.abb.uk.com

BOOKSELLER

Booksellers work in a variety of stores: bookselling chains, book sections in department stores, specialist bookshops selling books on a particular topic, academic bookshops on university or college campuses, or second-hand bookshops. The work involves dealing with customer enquiries, checking stock, dealing with publishers, ordering new material and marketing products. Bookshops have to compete with online booksellers that sell products more cheaply. Marketing is therefore an important aspect of the work. This also means that good booksellers have to be very effective in dealing with detailed customer enquiries, making helpful recommendations and sourcing products that are hard to track down. At a management level your work could also include managing staff, attending book fairs and organising publicity and promotional events.

Entry, qualifications and training

No formal qualifications are necessary, but in practice many staff working in bookshops have either a degree or a diploma; business-related disciplines are very popular with employers. Bookshop chains offering management training set their own entry requirements – normally five GCSEs grades A–C, A levels, or other academic qualifications. Most training is on the job, with an induction course to get you started.

Personal attributes

It helps to be interested in books and widely read. You must enjoy dealing with people and be happy to answer questions and offer advice. You need good IT skills both for ordering stock and for researching product queries for customers. A flair for organising window and counter displays and a talent for marketing are also very useful.

Earnings

Earnings are from £13,000 to £18,000 for trainees while store managers and senior staff working for large chains earn between £25,000 and £45,000. Some companies run bonus schemes for achieving high sales.

BREWING

Brewing and brewery work is the manufacture and production of beer and lager for the hospitality and retail sectors. Breweries can be large, supporting their own pub and hotel chains, or they can be small, independent local breweries that sell to free houses and other customers. They can also be micro breweries where members of the public brew their own batches of beer under supervision and guidance from brewing professionals. While breweries employ a range of staff, including marketing, finance and human resource professionals, the two groups of brewing specialists they employ are brewery workers and technical brewers.

Brewery worker

Brewery workers or brewery operatives work under the supervision of technical brewers helping with the manufacture and production of beer or lager. In small breweries they are often involved in all the different processes of manufacture. Working for larger companies, they may specialise in one process. The work could include weighing and mixing ingredients, monitoring quality, packing and labelling products, cleaning equipment, and loading and storing the beer ready for delivery to pubs, restaurants and shops.

Entry, qualifications and training

You do not need formal qualifications, but GCSEs including science or another technical subject could be useful, especially if you would like to progress to more technical and supervisory work. Training is on the job.

Personal attributes

You have to be good at following instructions, observant and careful in your work. You need to be able to cope with routine work while being prepared to be flexible as well. You are often working as part of a team and you may need to develop the skills of supervising others.

Technical brewer

Technical brewers or brewing technologists are responsible for developing and overseeing the production of beers and lagers. They have to decide on the right mix of ingredients, the temperatures at which processes should take place and the length of time that each part of the brewing process should take. It is their responsibility to ensure the quality and consistency of the product and to analyse and correct problems when they arise. They also have to source the right quality of raw materials and work within set budgets.

Entry, qualifications and training

Most trainee technical brewers have degrees in relevant subjects. Useful subjects include biological science, chemistry, chemical engineering and food technology. There are a few degrees available in brewing and distilling technology. You may get into this work with a BTEC or HND.

Personal attributes

You need a combination of good technical skills, being methodical, careful and good at problem solving, along with excellent management skills.

Earnings

Brewery workers start on £12,500 to £14,000 and technical brewers on £16,000 to £22,000. Senior technical brewers with management responsibility working for large breweries may earn £45,000 plus.

Info

Institute of Brewing and Distilling
020 7499 8144
www.ibd.org.uk

British Beer and Pub Association
020 7627 9191
www.beerandpub.com

Improve Ltd
0845 644 0448
www.improve-skills.co.uk

BROADCASTING

(see also Film and Television Production and Performing Arts)

This section covers the wide range of career opportunities available in radio broadcasting. You should also look at the section on Film and Television

Production as there are many similar roles in both sectors, eg sound recording, research and editing. Radio in the UK covers a diverse range of broadcasting outlets. The BBC is the largest and broadcasts national and local stations. There are several commercial radio stations, national and local, and there is also community radio: hospital radio, for example. There are also many independent production companies developing drama, documentaries and other programmes and they may produce work for public and commercial radio outlets. Broadcasts are many and varied, designed to inform, educate, update or entertain listeners, and the remit of each programme will be different. As well as the specific careers outlined below, you may also find openings in finance, administration, IT support and marketing – just as with any other organisation, large or small.

Broadcast editor

Editors work to ensure that the finished programme is of the highest quality. For anything that is pre-recorded, editors go through the material, making sure that the quality of sound is correct, that the programme fits exactly to time and that anything inappropriate is removed. If editing live programmes, they work with producers to ensure that everything runs smoothly and to time. Increasingly, even though radio is not a visual medium, editors work with other staff to put appropriate pictures, recordings and other material on a website associated with the radio broadcast.

Broadcast journalist

(see Journalism)

Broadcast engineer

Broadcast engineers or transmission engineers work to ensure that programmes go out at the right time and are of the best possible quality. You might be based in a studio or with an outside broadcasting unit. Your role could include testing equipment, setting up links between different studies or studios and outside broadcasts. You may be developing links between programmes and associated multimedia facilities. You would certain have to solve any problems like breaks in transmission as quickly as you can.

Broadcast sound engineer

Sound engineers are responsible for recording any radio station's output. This may be in a studio or on location, eg the seashore for a nature documentary or a concert hall for a live recording of an orchestral work. Engineers work to ensure that maximum quality of sound is produced and that there are no breaks in transmission. The work involves ensuring that all the technical equipment is functioning properly, solving problems the second they arise and working very closely with producers, presenters and other studio staff.

Broadcast sound technician

Sound technicians are part of the team that supports sound engineers. They help set up equipment and check and test that it is working properly. They may also work with the finished recording, cutting out unnecessary background noise, getting the levels right, or adding sound effects.

Broadcast presenter

Presenters work at the front line of radio and television, entertaining or informing the audience. They work on many different types of programme, including current affairs, documentaries, special interest and game shows. They work in all areas of broadcasting – national and regional television and radio, satellite and cable channels. Another version of presenting is the role of continuity announcer. They are the people who make announcements between scheduled broadcasts. Presenters and announcers have to do a great deal of preparatory work and liaise closely with their production staff, so it is not simply a matter of presenting a programme.

Broadcast researcher

Researchers work for producers, programme commissioners and presenters gathering all kind of background information required for a broadcast to be interesting, accurate or entertaining. This research may involve finding out more about potential interviewees, ascertaining who might be an ideal interviewee, and researching facts – historical, cultural or current affairs related.

Producer and assistant producer

Radio producers are responsible for the content of audio broadcasts on radio, and increasingly through internet versions of radio broadcasts. The producer takes responsibility for the whole process. This starts with generating ideas and entails liaising with presenters, DJs, engineers and broadcasting assistants throughout the planning and the actual output of the programme. They are also responsible for ensuring that audience feedback and responses to a particular programme are gathered and used to inform the planning of future programmes. Assistant producers help producers with all aspects of the work, but often carry out more of the basic administration and organisation. It is usual to start as an assistant producer before gaining promotion to producer.

Radio broadcast assistant

Broadcast assistants are referred to in the business as 'BAs'. Your work as a broadcast assistant would involve supporting all aspects of programme making and transmission. You would help presenters and producers with administration, technical support in the studio and generally help out wherever you can. You would often meet and greet guests and explain to them what to expect – especially if they are not familiar with studios and how they work.

Entry, qualifications and training

In this popular and highly competitive sector any experience you can gain in student broadcasting, volunteering to help on a hospital or other community station or any other relevant experience is tremendously helpful and undoubtedly strengthens your application. You also have to be able to convince potential employers that it really is radio that interests you, above TV or any other platform. Many people are prepared to work for free for a while to gain experience.

Broadcast journalist

You need either a relevant degree or postgraduate qualification, or a background in magazine or newspaper journalism. Some companies offer a very limited number of training schemes, and competition for these is fierce.

Broadcast engineer

Broadcast engineers are normally graduates with degrees in electronics, electronic engineering or broadcast engineering. It may be possible to get a traineeship with an HND or Foundation IT degree. It is sometimes possible for graduates of other disciplines to get into this work, but they need good A level maths and demonstrable technical/IT skills. Technician-level training or entry is sometimes possible with five GCSEs, grades A–C, including maths, English and a science.

Broadcast researcher

Broadcast researchers usually have a degree, though the subject does not particularly matter. It is more important that you can demonstrate that you have good research and communication skills. Like all broadcasting jobs, competition for this work is fierce, so some researchers start work in other administrative roles and move into research.

Radio broadcast assistant

While radio broadcast assistants don't necessarily need formal qualifications, this is such a competitive industry that many applicants do have A levels or degrees. Getting a job as a BA is a very useful first step on the ladder to working as an assistant producer and then producer.

Producer and editor

Producers, assistant producers and editors come from a variety of backgrounds. Many are graduate entrants, with degrees or postgraduate qualifications in broadcast journalism or broadcast production, simply because there is such great competition for this work. Good technical qualifications, A levels or an HND can be an advantage if you don't have a degree.

Personal attributes

You must be truly passionate about the medium. Listen to radio, learn about it and think about it. While there are some skills particular to specific roles, there are many skills and qualities essential to anyone working in radio. You have to have excellent communication skills and an ability to work well as part of a team. If you are in a front role such as announcer or presenter, you need self-confidence and an ability to think on your feet. If you are more behind the scenes, you need equally quick reactions – dealing with equipment failure or a guest who fails to arrive, for example. In all roles you have to be happy to cope with constant change and embrace changes in technology.

Earnings

Earnings vary widely depending on the job you do, your level of experience and the qualifications you have. Generally at the start of your career earnings may be relatively low. Salaries for assistant-level jobs are around £15,000 to £20,000 in London, £12,000 to £18,000 in other areas. Senior producers can earn £30,000 to £40,000. Presenters work on individually negotiated contracts.

Info

BBC
020 8752 5252
www.bbc.co.uk

Broadcast Journalism Training
Council
01778 440025
www.bjtc.org.uk

Broadcasting Entertainment
Cinematograph and Theatre Union
(BECTU)
www.bectu.org.uk

RadioCentre
020 7306 2603
www.radiocentre.org

Community Media Association
0114 279 5219
www.commedia.org.uk

Get Digital Radio
020 7306 2630
www.getdigitalradio.com

Hospital Broadcasting Association
www.hbauk.com

National Council for the Training of
Journalists
01799 544014
www.nctj.com

The Radio Academy
020 7927 9920
www.radioacademy.org

Skillset Careers
08080 300 900 (England and Northern Ireland)
0808 100 8094 (Scotland)
0800 121 815 (Wales)
www.skillset.org/careers

BUSINESS ADMINISTRATION

Business administration covers all those roles required to ensure the smooth day-to-day running of a business. 'Business' refers to any organisation in the public, private or charities sectors providing every kind of product and service. There are too many job titles to cover all of them here, but below are some of the most commonly found job titles, ranging from company secretary at director level to the day-to-day role of a receptionist.

Administrative assistant

Administrative assistants undertake a wide variety of routine and clerical tasks in every kind of office and organisation. The same job shares many different job titles, including clerical assistant, clerical worker, office assistant, office junior and administrative support worker. It is hard to describe a typical job because you may be working in such different settings and dealing with such different office procedures. You may be the only administrative worker in a very small company, or you could be working in a hospital, a local authority department, a charity or a multinational company. There are some common threads to the work. These include processing paperwork, entering data into computer files, dealing with telephone queries, arranging filing systems (electronic and paper), dealing with incoming post and sending out correspondence, checking and updating records, photocopying and gathering and disseminating information. Some jobs involve considerable responsibility, with the opportunity to supervise, train and manage other members of staff.

Entry, qualifications and training

Employers usually expect a good standard of general education and often require you to have four or five GCSEs grades A—C, including English and maths. A lot of the training is on the job because you will need to learn about an organisation's particular systems, procedures and structures. Administrative and clerical work can be a very good starting point for other careers in finance, human resources and many other fields. It is common to find people with A levels and degrees starting their careers in administration and clerical support, but this is by no means essential. College courses in administration leading to NVQ levels 1 and 2 awards may improve your chances.

Personal attributes

You need good written English skills, including good spelling and grammar. You may need to have good numeracy skills and you should have good basic IT skills. You need to be able to deal with people and cope with problems, but also concentrate on repetitive tasks.

Earnings

Reflecting the wide range of jobs with many different types of employer, salaries vary considerably. A typical range of starting salaries is £13,000 to £17,000 – more in London and other large cities. Experienced staff earn between £16,000 and £25,000.

Company secretary

All public limited companies must employ a qualified company secretary and many private companies and other organisations choose to do so. Company secretaries work for banks, insurance companies, trade unions, employer organisations, housing associations, charities and businesses of many kinds. The company secretary's duties include ensuring that the company complies with relevant legal and regulatory matters, administration of mergers and acquisitions, drafting contracts, advising the board of directors on company law and procedures and maintaining company records. Other duties can include pensions administration, personnel matters, shareholder issues, property management and finance.

Entry, qualifications and training

Most company secretaries have substantial business experience. Many have degrees or professional qualifications in business, law, accountancy or public administration. To be the secretary of a public limited company you must by law either qualify with the Institute of Chartered Secretaries and Administrators (ICSA) or be an accountant, solicitor or barrister. To qualify as a company secretary you must complete the ICSA International Qualifying Scheme (IQS). How much you will have to study depends on your previous qualifications, since law or accountancy qualifications will give you exemption from some papers. There are also some university postgraduate courses that meet the IQS requirements. The ICSA website lists these.

Personal attributes

You need excellent written and spoken English and very good presentation skills. You should be able to deal with highly complex information and be very well organised. You need to be a good problem solver who can employ sound judgement.

Earnings

Salaries start at around £30,000 – remember that this is normally a second career for most people. Salaries rise from £40,000 to £90,000 according to responsibilities and size and type of employer. A few company secretaries earn £130,000 plus.

Info

Institute of Chartered Secretaries
and Administrators (ICSA)
020 7580 4741
www.icsa.org.uk

Council for Administration (CfA)
020 7091 9620
www.cfa.uk.com

Personal assistant

(see also Secretary)

Personal assistants, also referred to as PAs, executive secretaries or executive assistants, work for every kind of commercial business, government, professional and charity organisation. As a personal assistant your role is to help ease your manager's workload by providing secretarial support and dealing with a range of administrative tasks.

Your duties are likely to be varied, but typical tasks include managing your manager's diary, booking appointments, screening and dealing with telephone calls, dealing with e-mails and paper correspondence, keeping records, collecting information for meetings or reports, writing letters and e-mails, taking minutes of meetings, making travel arrangements and arranging meetings. At a senior level you may stand in for your manager when he or she is away, handle accounts problems and act as office manager.

Entry, qualifications and training

A minimum of GCSEs in maths and English is usually required, but it is not uncommon for people with A levels or degrees to go into this work. Any relevant IT training courses on software packages for managing data or accounts are also useful. Some colleges run full- and part-time secretarial and administrative courses to GNVQ levels 2 and 3. Courses can also be taken through part-time study while working, through the London Chamber of Commerce and Industry Examination Board (LCCIEB), Oxford, Cambridge and RSA Examination Board (OCR) and Pitman Qualifications (City & Guilds), which offer relevant qualifications that take one to two years to complete. Personal assistant work spans everything from fairly junior jobs in small companies to extremely responsible roles working with directors of large organisations. The training courses available reflect this, and courses are offered at several different levels.

Personal attributes

You must be friendly but discreet and diplomatic. You need to be extremely well organised and calm when you are under pressure or working to deadlines. Knowing when to use your own initiative is also important.

Earnings

Salaries vary depending on the size, type and location of the organisation for which you work and the seniority of the person to whom you are personal assistant. £18,000 to £25,000 is a typical starting salary range, a little less outside London and the M25. A personal assistant to a senior manager can earn up to £40,000.

Info

Council for Administration
020 7091 9620
www.cfa.uk.com

Break Into Biz
www.breakinto.biz

Receptionist

As a receptionist, you are the one who welcomes visitors to an organisation. It is your job to direct them to the person or department they need to see, to confirm appointments and to provide information. You may also deal with telephone enquiries. Receptionists work in many settings: hotels, health centres, government offices and private businesses of many kinds. Where you work determines what your day-to-day tasks are likely to be. In a hotel you welcome guests, make bookings and prepare the final accounts. In a small company you may combine your reception role with other administrative work such as filing, photocopying, or dealing with correspondence

Entry, qualifications and training

While formal qualifications are not essential, many employers do require you to have GCSE grades A–C in English and maths; knowledge of other languages is important. Many further education colleges offer one-year full-time courses and a range of part-time courses in reception skills. A range of qualifications is available, including NVQs at levels 1, 2 and 3 and Modern Apprenticeships.

Personal attributes

Receptionists should be friendly and pleasant, with a good phone manner and neat appearance. They also need stamina as they are often expected to work shifts that include evenings and weekends. They should have a real liking for people and a good memory for faces. Computer literacy is also important.

Earnings

Receptionists earn between £13,000 and £19,500, more than this in London or if the work involves other duties and responsibilities. Hotel receptionists earn between £12,000 and £16,000. In large hotels with big reception teams, supervisory work can take earnings up to £22,000.

Info

Council for Administration
020 7091 9620
www.cfa.uk.com

Break Into Biz
www.breakinto.biz

Secretary

Secretaries work in all types of organisation. Sometimes they are assigned to one person, sometimes they provide support services for several people. Most secretaries need to have well-developed IT skills but there is still a demand for those with shorthand and audio typing. As well as producing documents, secretaries undertake a range of organisational tasks such as arranging travel and meetings. They may also work as receptionists and deal with callers and queries by phone or e-mail. Those in senior positions may make decisions on behalf of managers.

Bilingual secretary

Bilingual secretaries are fluent in a second (even a third) language and may work in commerce, overseas or as an employee of an international organisation. The work will include composing, reading and translating documents in the foreign language. They may use speaking/listening skills in their languages for telephone work, receiving visitors and Interpreting at meetings.

Farm secretary

In addition to normal secretarial work, farm secretaries will be responsible for completing complex forms, keeping records and accounts and calculating wages. A farm secretary may work for one employer, be freelance or be sent out by an agency to smaller farms.

Legal secretary

Accurate skills have always been paramount for legal paperwork, but word processors have made the job easier. Legal secretaries are employed by barristers and solicitors in professional practice and in large commercial organisations.

Medical secretary

Medical secretaries are good administrators, keep records, and handle correspondence and filing. They work in hospitals, for individual doctors/consultants and in health centres. Accuracy and confidentiality are essential, as is a thorough knowledge of medical terminology.

Entry, qualifications and training

There is a range of full- and part-time courses available. Courses usually include word processing, audio, shorthand and office procedures. There are training opportunities for young people leading to NVQ levels 1, 2 and 3 in Administration.

GCSEs are usually required to obtain a place on a full-time secretarial course. A good working knowledge of the English language is essential. Additional qualifications are needed to specialise as a legal, medical or farm secretary. There are a number of postgraduate diploma courses for graduates wishing to train as bilingual secretaries.

Personal attributes

Above all, secretaries have to be well organised, calm and pleasant. They have to be able to cope with working under pressure and producing work for deadlines. People skills are very important, especially when working in healthcare or other sensitive areas. Discretion and tact are also important.

Earnings

Outside London pay starts at £14,000 to £18,000, in London £19,000 to £25,000. Jobs in not-for-profit sectors are at the lower end of the pay scale; employment in banking, finance and law firms is at the upper end. With between 10 and 15 years' experience, salaries can rise to £30,000–40,000.

Info

Council for Administration (CfA)
020 7091 9620
www.cfa.uk.com

**The Institute of Legal Secretaries
and PAs**
0117 927 7007
www.institutelegalsecretaries.com/

**Institute of Professional
Administrators (IPA)**
0844 8000 182
www.ipa.org

CABINET MAKER

Cabinet makers make individually designed and produced pieces of wooden furniture such as chairs, tables, bookcases, chests of drawers and storage or display cabinets. They may also restore antiques or repair damaged furniture. Cabinet makers start by making a drawing, either by hand or on computer. They then choose the appropriate quantity and quality of wood to employ and using a range of tools they construct the item from scratch. If they are employed by a company, they may not be so involved in the drawing and planning stage. Many cabinet makers, however, are self-employed and their work would include discussing every aspect of the design and the cost with their customers.

Entry, qualifications and training

You don't need any specific qualifications, but some employers may like you to have GCSEs, particularly in maths or a technical subject. If you are aged between 16 and 24, you could train through an apprenticeship. If you are over 24, you need to have some relevant skills, experience or qualifications.

There are several college-based City & Guilds courses in furniture production – these are aimed at newcomers and current employees in the industry.

Personal attributes

You must be very practical and confident using machines and hand tools. You should be able to follow a technical drawing, adapt designs and do drawings of your own. You need good numeracy skills and if you become self-employed you also need some business awareness.

Earnings

Earnings start at around £12,500, rising to £15,000 with three or four years' experience. Cabinet makers who become really skilled and get a good reputation can earn £35,000 plus.

Info

Proskills UK (The Sector Skills
Council for the Process and
Manufacturing Sector)
01235 833 844
www.proskills.co.uk

CALL CENTRE OPERATOR

Call centre or contact centre operators work for many different business and service providers, dealing with customer queries on the telephone, by e-mail, text, fax or letter. Telephone work is the most likely and is what most people think of as call centre work. You might work for a mail order catalogue, a financial services advice line, a utilities provider, an IT support company or an organisation offering welfare, health or counselling advice of some kind. The type of employer you work for will determine the range of duties you undertake, but you are always likely to be involved in many of the following: answering queries, providing further information, referring callers to other agencies, updating computer records or selling products and services. As you gain experience, your work is likely to include supervising other staff and training new members of the team.

Many call/contact centres operate 24-hour services, so there are often opportunities to work as a shift supervisor and then to progress to a position with more management responsibility.

Call centre manager

Call centre managers ensure the smooth running of the centre. The work involves drawing up work rosters, training new recruits and dealing with those customers who have a more complicated query or who wish to complain.

Entry, qualifications and training

You don't always need formal qualifications – individual employers set their own entry requirements, which can include GCSEs grade A–C in maths and English. Job interviews often include practical tests to assess your telephone manner and your keyboard skills. Most employers offer training in call centre techniques and in any specialist knowledge that applies to its particular products or services. There are some college courses in call centre techniques; these include City & Guilds in Contact Centre Skills and a BTEC introduction to Contact Centre Skills. These courses cover general topics such as telephone manner, confidentiality, data management and other communication skills. In some areas you may be able to take an apprenticeship in call/contact centre skills. Having built up some experience in this work, and if you gain promotion to supervisory or management level, there are several further qualifications you could work towards. These include Telesales levels 2 and 3, Contact Centre Operations levels 1 and 2, and Contact Centre Professionals levels 3, 4 and 5. These NVQs cover areas such as developing customer relationships, IT skills, sales techniques, managing staff and resources, quality control and performance management.

There are sometimes openings for graduates to join call centres at management level.

Personal attributes

You must have excellent communication skills, primarily for speaking on the telephone. You may need to be persuasive, patient, sympathetic, thick-skinned, sensitive or calm. Clearly you need a different mix of skills to deal with someone who is placing a catalogue order compared to someone who is anxious that they cannot pay a utility bill, for example. You need good IT skills, the ability to work under pressure and to take responsibility if you want to progress to supervisory and management levels.

Earnings

New call centre staff earn £12,000 to £15,000, rising to £15,000 to £19,000 with experience. Managers earn £20,000 to £25,000. With some call centre work there are opportunities to earn bonuses or commissions on sales made or customers signed up.

Info

Institute for Customer Service
01206 571716
www.instituteofcustomerservice.com

e-skills UK (The Sector Skills Council
for Business and Information
Technology)
www.e-skills.com

Customer Contact Association (CCA)
0141 564 9010
www.cca.org.uk

CAREERS ADVISER

Who provides careers guidance services, how many staff are employed and what their role will be is likely to change from April 2012.

Careers advisers or personal advisers/careers provide information, advice and guidance to school and college students and to adults in the community. They work both inside and outside education. In England, careers advisers work mainly for local authorities as personal advisers (PAs), helping young people aged 13–19 make choices about employment and further study, and helping them overcome any difficulties they face in this area. The work involves one-to-one interviews with clients, presentations to groups of clients or parents, and marketing work with local and national employers.

Outside England, careers advisers work in Careers Scotland, Careers Wales and the Training and Employment Agency in Northern Ireland. Some careers advisers also work in higher education and are employed by individual universities and colleges.

Entry, qualifications and training

There are several ways to become a careers adviser/personal adviser. If you do not have a degree, HND or Foundation degree, but you do have NVQ level 3 qualifications and some experience of work with young people, you can start as a an employment training adviser or a Connexions assistant and work your way up to trainee personal adviser. Many entrants to this profession do have a degree, HND or Foundation degree. Relevant subjects include sociology, psychology, youth work and teaching.

Foundation degrees in working with young people and young people's services are now available, specifically with potential PAs and youth workers in mind. More details are available from the Universities and Colleges Admissions Service (UCAS).

Although postgraduate qualifications are not necessary for entry, the QCG (Qualification in Careers Guidance) and other qualifications in social work or youth work can reduce the training needed for full qualification. The QCG is available full-time, part-time and through distance learning, and the vast majority of people who take it go on to employment in careers work, mainly as PAs.

Personal attributes

Excellent communication skills are essential. You are dealing with young people, their parents, teachers, employers and other professionals. You have to be well organised, good at disseminating information, able to present material to individuals and groups, and have reasonable IT skills. You should be confident, persuasive, assertive and tactful and you must be a good listener.

Earnings

Pay for trainees ranges from £20,000 to £23,000. Part-qualified advisers earn between £21,000 and £27,000. There is no national agreed pay scale for careers or personal advisers. In the higher education sector, salaries used to be higher than for work with school leavers, but this is becoming less likely.

Info

Department for Education
0870 001 2345
www.education.gov.uk

Independent Schools Careers Organisation
01276 687525
www.isco.org.uk

Institute of Career Guidance (ICG)
01384 376 464
www.icg-uk.org

Association of Graduate Careers Advisors
0114 251 5750
www.agcas.org.uk

CARPENTRY

(see Cabinet Maker and Construction Trades)

CARPET FITTER/FLOOR LAYER

Carpet retailers, furniture stores and department stores all employ their own trained personnel who deliver and fit carpets and other floor coverings to customers' homes, shops, offices or hotels. Some fitters are also self-employed.

Entry, qualifications and training

GCSE English and maths or equivalents are usually required, especially if you train through an apprenticeship. Training is mainly given on the job, working with an experienced fitter, although in some firms there are possible opportunities for day-release courses leading to the examinations of the National Institute of Carpet and Floor Layers. Short one- to five-day and tailored courses are available through the Flooring Industry Training Association.

Personal attributes

Strength and fitness are important in order to handle heavy rolls of carpet. A good head for calculations and an eye for detail (such as matching patterns) are also essential. Generally, too, it is necessary to be able to drive.

Earnings

Trainees earn between £12,000 and £15,000. Experienced carpet fitters earn between £15,000 and £21,000, and senior supervisors, who are fitters with other management and training roles, earn up to £25,000. Some carpet fitters become self-employed.

Info

ConstructionSkills
01485 577577
www.cskills.org

Flooring Industries Training Association
0115950 6836
www.fita.co.uk

UK Flooring Academy
01283 711428
www.uk-flooring-academy.co.uk

CARTOGRAPHER

Cartographers make maps of every kind, from the map you might take on a walk to the maps that supply your satellite navigation. They make highly specialised maps for industry, eg mining or shipping. Some also make globes or other 3D models.

Cartographers are employed by several government departments – the Ordnance Survey, the Ministry of Defence, the Met Office and the Department of Transport, for example. Local authority planning departments may employ cartographers and in industry they may work for utilities companies, oil companies or the leisure industry.

Work varies and most cartographers become specialists in one type of mapping. Tasks could include updating current maps, checking maps and charts for accuracy or making maps for as yet uncharted regions (not so many of these now). It could involve carrying out land surveys and liaising closely with surveyors. Cartographers use desktop publishing, digital photography and sophisticated software to model and produce data and to collect information from remote sensors and satellites. They also work on geographical information systems (GIS) which link all kinds of data such as population statistics with maps.

Entry, qualifications and training

To train as a cartographer you normally need a degree in a relevant subject, such as geography, earth sciences, GIS, mapping science and surveying. There are no degrees that cover only cartography, so you need to look carefully at course details to ensure that relevant cartography elements are included in the courses you are considering. The British Cartography Society's website includes useful information on appropriate courses. Training is on the job and covers surveying and the use of specialised computer packages. The Ordnance Survey and other government departments provide structured training programmes.

Personal attributes

You must be interested in geography and the environment. You need to be able to work accurately, paying attention to detail, and you should have good spatial awareness and a good sense of design. Excellent computer skills are very important. As you progress to more senior roles, you also need to be able to take responsibility for managing projects and staff.

Earnings

Cartographers earn between £18,000 and £23,000; with experience salaries rise to between £25,000 and £37,000. You can earn more if you are a project leader or have other management responsibilities.

Info

The British Cartographic Society
www.cartography.org.uk

Society of Cartographers
www.soc.org.uk

Ordnance Survey (OS)
08456 05 05 05
www.ordnancesurvey.co.uk

The Survey Association (TSA)
01636 642840
www.tsa-uk.org.uk

Remote Sensing and
Photogrammetry Society
www.rspsoc.org

CATERING

(see Hospitality and Catering)

CHEMISTRY

Chemistry is the basis of a wide range of careers and is the science that deals with the composition, structure and uses of chemicals and substances.

Analyst

Analysts, referred to as analytical chemists, work in industry providing a service for research, development and production departments. They analyse the results of experiments and advise what a newly produced substance may be. An analyst may check the quality of raw materials bought in by a company and examine the quality of the company's own products. Public analysts are employed by local authorities to examine, for example, the state of the water supply; the adequacy of the sewage treatment system; toxic and suspect materials; and leaching from landfill sites. They may also be asked to examine food from a suspect restaurant. Public analysts are frequently required to give witness on their findings in courts of law, and should be familiar with the law relating to goods and services.

Chemist

Chemists study the structure and make-up of chemicals and other substances. They interpret the way substances interact and react under different physical conditions. They apply their knowledge in a variety of ways, eg to create new food products or materials such as plastics and artificial fibres. They work in many industries, developing new drugs for the pharmaceutical sector, analysing the impact of climate change on oceans, keeping water supplies safe and clean or developing products to improve the shelf-life of food and drink. They may also work in forensics, examining the substances at the scene of a crime.

Some professional chemists are referred to as analytical chemists and their work focuses specifically on analysing chemicals and other materials, but they can still work across several different industries and sectors. Some chemists also work in academic research.

The chemist's work involves planning and conducting experiments, analysing results and writing up and/or presenting the results he or she produces. The work often involves the management and supervision of other laboratory staff.

Entry, qualifications and training

To work as a chemist or analyst you need a degree in either chemistry or chemical science. Many employers prefer you to have a postgraduate qualification as well, or to have done a course that includes a placement in industry. Many graduate chemists may have to start work as a laboratory technician in a laboratory involved in the aspects of chemistry which interest them. Training is on the job, covering the use of technical equipment, computer packages, and health and safety. If you don't have a postgraduate qualification before you start work, you may be able to work towards this while you are employed.

Personal attributes

You must combine an interest in chemistry with an enquiring mind and a patient, persistent attitude to solving problems. You should be accurate and thorough in all your work, and highly observant. You need to be good at handling delicate equipment and confident with IT. If you are supervising other staff you need good management and the ability to motivate colleagues.

Earnings

New graduate chemists earn between £16,000 and £30,000, higher salaries being paid to entrants with PhDs and by pharmaceutical companies. With experience this range rises to £30,000 to £60,000.

Info

Analytical Science Network (ASN)
c/o Royal Society of Chemistry
020 7440 3326
www.chemsoc.org/networks/acn/
asn.htm

Royal Society of Chemistry (RSC)
020 7437 8656
www.rsc.org

Royal Pharmaceutical Society of
Great Britain (RPSGB)
020 7735 9141
www.rpsgb.org.uk

SEMTA (The Sector Skills Council
for Science, Engineering and
Manufacturing Technologies)
0800 282167
www.semta.org.uk

CHILDCARE

Working with and caring for children, especially pre-school aged children, offers a range of career options. The main ones are described here, but there are others such as school lunchtime supervisors (for part-time work) and childcare inspectors for people who already possess some background in childcare or other relevant experience.

Childminder

A registered childminder looks after children and provides a caring environment along with stimulating play and learning activities. Childminders need to be responsible, trustworthy and affectionate. Childminders look after babies and children under 5; there is a limit to the number of children of different age groups that can be cared for by a childminder.

A childminder's job needs good planning and organisation skills to arrange individual routines for children of different ages to include periods of play, exercise, naps and meals. It is important to keep records of payments, expenses and insurance. It is essential for the children's learning and development to include activities such as painting and drawing, reading stories and singing, and playing with natural materials and construction toys in- and outdoors.

A childminder is expected to provide food for the children, and with babies prepare bottles, feed the babies and change nappies. Older children will require physical care, such as washing hands and going to the toilet. It is important not to discriminate against children from different ethnic groups, religious backgrounds and family types.

Entry, qualifications and training

While you do not need formal qualifications to work as a childminder, you must be aged over 18. If you are caring for children under the age of 8 in England, you must be registered with the Office for Standards in Education, Children's Services and Skills (Ofsted).

In England your local authority's Children's Information Service (CIS) can provide you with information on how to register and send you an application pack. You have to be interviewed and your home is also inspected. If you are approved, you must take a registered training course. The Council for Awards in Care, Health and Education (CACHE) and the National Childminding Association have developed NVQ level 3 certificate and diploma courses in home-based childcare.

In Scotland you should contact the Care Commission, in Wales the Care Standards Inspectorate and in Northern Ireland your local Health and Social Care Services Trust.

Personal attributes

Of course, you have to really enjoy working with children and to be prepared to share your home with them. You should have an open-minded attitude about different ways of bringing up children and you should be quite comfortable with both you and your home being scrutinised. You have to be extremely responsible, sensitive and patient. You need to be practical, with a sense of humour, and keep calm if problems arise. You have to be able to communicate well with parents as well as with their children. You need to be imaginative, sympathetic and sensible. You need to be very alert, especially on matters of health and safety.

Earnings

Childminders charge between £3.20 and £6.00 per hour per child, more in some areas. What you earn depends on how many children you are caring for and for how long. As a childminder you are responsible for paying your own tax and insurance and you have to provide toys and the right environment for children from your earnings.

Info

National Childminding Association
0845 880 0044
www.ncma.org.uk

Office for Standards in Education Children's' Services and Skills (Ofsted)
0845 640 4045
www.ofsted.gov.uk

Scottish Childminding Association
01786 445377
www.childminding.org

Child Workforce Development Council
www.cwdcouncil.org.uk/early-years/childcare-careers

Council for Awards in Care, Health and Education (CACHE)
0845 347 2123
www.cache.org.uk

Nanny

Nannies work in private houses caring for babies and children of parents who are working or need help with childcare, for whatever reason. Your work depends very much on the ages of the children you care for. If you are looking after young babies you are likely to be bathing, feeding, changing nappies, dressing, etc. For older children, you may be meeting them from school, preparing meals, taking them to activities, helping them get ready for school, playing or just spending time with them. Some nannies live in with the families they work for – others come to work each day. In either case, working hours can be longer than a normal 9 to 5 day.

Entry, qualifications and training

While you may not need to have formal qualifications to work as a nanny, many employers will consider you far more favourably if you do. In September 2010 new Children's Workforce Development certificates and diplomas at NVQ levels 2 and 3 were introduced. These are offered at state and private colleges. A first-aid qualification can also help you gain employment as a nanny. Many nannies do have nursery nursing qualifications.

Personal attributes

You have to enjoy working with babies and children of all ages. You have to have a mature, calm and sensible attitude that inspires confidence in parents or other carers. You need to have a lively enthusiastic personality to help children play, learn and socialise. You have to be practical and may need to be able to cook basic meals for children and to hold a driving licence.

Earnings

Nannies earn from £12,000 to £18,000 – sometimes much more in some geographical locations. Some posts also include board and lodging and other benefits.

Info

Council for Awards in Care, Health
and Education (CACHE)
0845 347 2123
www.cache.org.uk

Nursery nurse

A nursery nurse works with babies and children under 8 in the public, private and voluntary sectors. This can include schools, nurseries and hospitals. In schools, nursery nurses work in nursery, reception and infant classes alongside the teacher, providing and supervising educational and play activities. They may also be involved in providing out-of-school care at after-school clubs and on holiday schemes. Nursery nurses in hospitals can work in maternity and special care units, and on children's wards. Day nurseries, both private and local authority, employ nursery nurses to care for children under 5 whose parents are unable to care for them during the day. Nursery nurses can also be employed in clinics, residential homes, the community, family centres and private homes as nannies.

Entry, qualifications and training

You don't necessarily need academic qualifications, but many employers and course providers expect you to have three to five GCSEs grades A–C. You can study for a two-year full-time NVQ level 3 award or you can work as a nursery assistant and study for qualifications part-time. There are several different awards towards which you can work, including: CACHE Level 3 Diploma in Child Care and Education, the BTEC National Diploma in Children's Care, Learning and Development and NVQ level 3 in Children's Care, Learning and Development. The government now expects all professionals to work towards Early Years Professional Status (EYPS). There are several ways to achieve this and how you do it will depend on what qualifications you already have, how much experience you have and which particular pathway your employer supports and encourages. EYPS is an addition to, not an alternative to, the qualifications listed above.

Everyone working with young children has to undergo a Criminal Records Bureau (CRB) check to ensure that they have no criminal convictions that would make them unsuitable for this work.

Personal attributes

You must really enjoy working with children. You have to be patient, calm, imaginative and practical. You need to be well organised and good at working as part of a team. You should be observant, safety conscious, sensitive and very good at communicating with children. You will also have to be able to build up good relationships with parents and other professionals.

Earnings

Trainees earn £10,000 to £12,000. Qualified nursery nurses earn £14,000 to £18,000 and nursery managers can earn £25,000 to £38,000.

Info

National Day Nursery Association
www.ndna.org.uk

Office for Standards in Education Children's' Services and Skills (Ofsted)
0845 640 4045
www.ofsted.gov.uk

Childcare Careers
www.childcarecareers.gov.uk

Council for Awards in Care, Health and Education (CACHE)
0845 347 2123
www.cache.org.uk

CHIMNEY SWEEP

Chimney sweeps clean and remove soot and other debris from chimneys and flues of open fires, wood-burning stoves and other oil, gas, coal or wood-burning heating and cooking appliances. Cleaning chimneys reduces the risk of chimney fires and the levels of dangerous emissions. This work had gone into decline, but increasing numbers of people are installing wood-burning stoves because they are considered a more environmentally friendly and economical form of heating. The work involves inspecting the job to be done and then removing soot and debris with special vacuum equipment and old-fashioned brushes. As a chimney sweep you remove the soot and dirt you have collected and leave the premises clean and tidy. You also advise customers on how to maintain or operate chimneys, flues and appliances safely.

Entry, qualifications and training

Nearly all chimney sweeps are self-employed, so you have to fund your own training, purchase of equipment and insurance. No formal qualifications are necessary, but a background in practical, physical work is a useful start. The National Association of Chimney Sweeps (NACS) offers training and advice. Other than this, you may be able to find a local chimney sweep who is prepared to offer you some on-the-job training. A driving licence and vehicle are essential, as you will need to transport equipment and travel between customers.

Personal attributes

You have to be reasonably physically fit and be a good practical problem solver, with a systematic and tidy approach to your work. You also need to be good at talking to customers. Being self-employed, you need to know how to market, promote and manage your business.

Earnings

Since most sweeps are self-employed, earnings depend on the number of customers you have and what you charge per job. Prices vary from £30 to £90 per chimney. The work is also seasonal – most people have their chimneys swept from early spring to late autumn, not mid-winter when they are using their fires and stoves.

Info

National Association of Chimney Sweeps (NACS)
01785 811732
www.chimneyworks.co.uk

Guild of Master Sweeps
www.guild-of-master-sweeps.co.uk

ConstructionSkills
01485 577577
www.cskills.org

CHIROPODIST (OR PODIATRIST)

(see Podiatrist)

CIVIL AVIATION

The civil aviation sector relates to all the occupations in the world of civil aircraft flying, including passenger and goods transportation. The key roles associated with civil aviation are outlined below, but there are other jobs – working as a baggage handler, as an information assistant at an airport or in security positions are all part of the world of civil aviation.

Aeronautical engineer

(see also Engineering)

Air traffic engineers are responsible for the efficient operation of the wide range of sophisticated telecommunications, electronic systems and specialist equipment needed in air traffic control centres, airports and other specialist centres. This involves the installation, calibration and maintenance of radar, air-to-ground communication systems, navigational and landing aids, computer data and processing equipment, and visual display units. Opportunities may exist for engineers to look after day-to-day maintenance and, at graduate level, for field management, installation and development work.

Air cabin crew

Flight attendants (air cabin crew) look after the safety, comfort and welfare of passengers. Before a flight they check stocks of equipment, welcome passengers on board and go through safety routines. During the flight they serve food and drink and on budget airlines they also sell these items. They must be ready to respond in a crisis, such as a passenger being taken ill or, more rarely, something going wrong with the flight.

Aircraft maintenance engineer

(see also Engineering)

Aircraft maintenance engineers make sure that aircraft are airworthy. They maintain, service and overhaul the aircraft, their engines and equipment, working to very high standards set by the Civil Aviation Authority (CAA). Every part of every job is checked and certified. Engineers usually specialise in either mechanics or avionics, and work on major overhaul or on 'turnarounds' – the work carried out after each flight. Apart from working with airlines, other opportunities are found with firms that specialise in aircraft maintenance. There are also a few openings for professional engineers in works management, production, planning, and research and development.

Air traffic control

The safe and efficient movement of all aircraft through British air space and airports is the responsibility of National Air Traffic Service (NATS) air traffic control officers and assistants. With the aid of sophisticated radio, radar and computer systems and with visual checks on visibility and weather conditions made from the control tower, they ensure that aircraft are kept a safe distance apart and that pilots are well advised as to their position and prevailing conditions, given clearance to land and directions to loading bays. Air traffic controllers mainly work for NATS, although there may be limited opportunities with other employers, such as local authorities or aircraft manufacturers. All must hold a CAA licence stipulating the service they are qualified to give and where they can operate. Some of the more routine tasks, such as checking flight plans, updating weather information, logging aircraft movements and keeping runways clear, are carried out by air traffic control assistants. Prospects for promotion to officer level are good, air traffic control staff are employed to work at any location within the country.

Airline customer service agent

Airline customer service agents work for individual airlines, handling companies, and airports and terminals. They deal with passengers from the moment they check in to when they board their flights. They are responsible for checking in luggage as well as customers. Customer service agents have to ensure that unaccompanied children or other passengers with special needs are safely escorted to their flights and they are also expected to calm nervous passengers before they board their planes.

Airline pilot

Commercial pilots in the UK fly fixed-wing aircraft and helicopters. Before take-off the pilot must prepare a flight plan, study the weather, make sure that the craft is airworthy, check that the cargo and fuel are safely loaded and work out estimated arrival times. Little time is spent actually flying the aeroplane manually. The pilot spends most of the time carefully monitoring sophisticated computer-controlled automatic flying, navigational and communications systems. Pilots keep in touch with air traffic control and must be prepared to deal with sudden changes in weather and other conditions. Pilots work irregular hours but their actual flying time is strictly controlled.

Most UK pilots are employed by one of the major carriers of passengers and goods, and when flying large aircraft they are part of a team. Opportunities for pilots of small aircraft and helicopters are to be found in flying executive jets, in the field of air taxiing, conducting aerial surveys, or as test pilots or flying instructors.

Entry, qualifications and training

Aeronautical engineer/Aircraft maintenance engineer

Entry to aircraft maintenance engineering is via craft, technician or student apprenticeships; entry qualifications depend upon the type of apprenticeship. The apprenticeships take the form of on-the-job training and part-time study at local colleges to prepare for aeronautical engineering/aircraft maintenance engineering qualifications offered by City & Guilds and Edexcel (BTEC)/SQA or the CAA. Qualified aircraft engineers (including those from the armed forces) have to meet certain practical experience requirements before they can take examinations to become licensed aircraft maintenance engineers. There are some full-time courses in aeronautical engineering and aircraft maintenance, usually lasting two and a half years.

Air cabin crew

Airlines usually train their own cabin crews at special centres on courses lasting four to six weeks. Applicants should be over 18, have a good level of general education to GCSE standard, preferably including English and maths, and have conversational fluency in at least one European language. Experience in a customer care setting can be helpful.

Air traffic controller

You need five GCSEs grades A–C, including maths and English, but 70 per cent of applicants have degrees, HNDs or other higher education qualifications. You must have good eyesight and colour vision and be physically fit. Most air traffic controllers train via the National Air Traffic Services (NATS) training scheme at Bournemouth Airport. You spend 13 weeks at the NATS college and after this your training lasts either six months, if you train as an aerodrome controller, or nine months, if you train as an area controller. You have to pass exams at several stages and not all trainees make it. After this there is a further supervised training period of 18 months.

Air traffic engineer

NATS runs a training scheme for graduate electrical/electronic engineers lasting a minimum of 15 months. The training is approved by the Institution of Engineering and Technology and after approximately three years will lead to chartered engineering status.

Airline customer service agent

There are no standard entry requirements, but individual airlines and handling companies set their own requirements. They normally ask for a good standard of education and may require you to have GCSE grade A–C in English. A foreign language qualification can also be useful, as can previous experience in customer service work. You will need to live reasonably near an airport and you may well need your own transport because shift work could make reliance on public transport difficult. You will have to undergo security checks and many companies also ask you to have a medical examination.

Pilot

UK pilots are required to hold a licence issued by the Joint Aviation Authorities (JAA) which represent the civil aviation departments of a group of European states that have collaborated to set common safety standards called Joint Aviation Requirements. Licence holders can work as pilots in any of the JAA member states. Full details of licensing requirements and organisations providing approved courses can be obtained from the CAA (see the Info box). Training to be a commercial pilot costs £50,000–60,000 and may be integrated (*ab initio*) or modular. Helicopter courses tend to be more expensive. Most applicants wishing to undertake integrated courses are sponsored privately or by an airline. Such sponsorship is highly competitive and difficult to obtain. Trainees are generally expected to contribute to training costs either while training or by repaying some of the fees once in employment. An alternative entry route is via a short-service flying commission with either the RAF or the Royal Navy. All pilots are expected to attend retraining and refresher courses throughout their careers.

Entry requirements for sponsored pilot training vary between airlines, but most ask for a minimum of two/three A levels or equivalent, including maths and physics. Many airlines recruit graduates up to the age of 26. Eyesight must be of a very high standard. Normal colour vision and an excellent level of health and fitness are essential.

Personal attributes

Aeronautical engineer/Aircraft maintenance engineer

Maintenance engineering requires a combination of practical interest, mechanical aptitude, accuracy and manual dexterity. Engineers must be willing to adapt and to retrain. Very high standards and a responsible attitude are also most important.

Air cabin crew

Air cabin crew must be reassuring and approachable, smart, have lots of energy and stamina and have the confidence and the ability to act quickly and decisively in a firm but polite and tactful manner.

Air traffic control officer

The work is stressful; officers need to be able to assimilate and interpret a great deal of information and instantly act upon it. They must be able to react quickly if conditions suddenly change, and be healthy, reliable and emotionally well balanced; good eyesight and colour vision are also important.

Air traffic engineer

Normal colour vision, great care, accuracy and a basic understanding of the practical applications of electricity and magnetism are required.

Airline customer service agent

You need excellent customer service skills. Delays and changes to flights mean customers are often stressed, anxious or angry. You need to keep calm and follow procedures quickly, but without cutting corners. You must be smart, tidy and presentable and reasonably physically fit.

Pilot

Pilots must be very well balanced, physically fit, have stamina, be mentally and physically alert and ready to respond quickly to changing conditions. They must be unflappable, confident, self-assured leaders with considerable technical skill.

Earnings

Airlines operate in a competitive and difficult market. This has affected wages. Earnings vary according to your job – air cabin crew or airline pilot, for example. Each airline sets in own rates of pay. As a guide, air cabin crew and customer service staff start on £12,000 to £14,000. Air traffic controllers earn £10,000 during training and £15,000 to £18,000 on being appointed. Once validated, after two years, salaries rise to £45,000 to £50,000. Pilots earn around £75,000 to £80,000 flying jet aircraft, much less for turboprops. They often have to pay a bond of £15,000 to the company that employs them and often have to pay for much of their own training.

Info

Global ATS Ltd
www.global-ats.com

BAE Systems Cwmbran Training College
01633 835 123
www.cwmbrancollege.com

British Air Transport Association (BATA)
020 7222 9494
www.bata.uk.com

The British Air Line Pilots Association (BALPA)
020 8476 4000
www.balpa.org

British Women Pilots Association (BWPA)
www.bwpa.co.uk

Civil Aviation Authority (CAA)
020 7379 7311
www.caa.co.uk

GoSkills (The Sector Skills Council for Passenger Transport)
0121 635 5520
www.goskills.org

Guild of Air Traffic Control Officers (GATCO)
01949 876405
www.gatco.org

National Air Traffic Services (NATS)
01489 616001
www.nats.co.uk

People 1st for Hospitality, Leisure, Travel and Tourism
0870 060 2550
www.people1st.co.uk

CIVIL SERVICE

Even with government cuts and merging of departments the Civil Service is a very large employer. Civil servants work in a many occupations and professions, carrying out the work of government. Work ranges from advising ministers on policies to dealing with daily enquiries about planning issues, benefits payments or education. While departments do their own recruitment and set entry requirements for specific jobs, there is an overall structure across most departments. This structure means you can decide at which level you would like to enter and what sort of work appeals to you.

Work falls broadly into three groups: corporate services, which are concerned with finance, IT, human resources and communications; operation services, which is the day-to-day delivery of services through government offices, including all the face-to-face dealings with the public; and policy delivery, which is concerned with developing and implementing policies, working very closely with the government.

Administrative officers and administrative assistants

Administrative officers and administrative assistants carry out the daily clerical and customer contact functions in every department and agency. Their work may involve dealing directly with the public, such as answering telephone enquiries, gathering information, processing documents, keeping records and entering data into computer systems.

Junior managers/executive officers

Junior manager is the next step up the ladder after administrative officer. Junior managers are responsible for running small teams who carry out day-to-day functions for every department and agency. Tasks and responsibilities include motivating and training members of the team, carrying out annual appraisals and preparing and presenting reports on work progress to senior managers. They also have to deal with problems. If, for example, a client is unhappy with the service he or she has received, this will be referred to the junior manager in the first instance. After two years' successful work as a junior manager, it is possible to apply to join the Fast Stream management development programme.

Fast Stream development programme trainees

The Civil Service offers a fast track accelerated training programme for recruits who want to get into senior management. Fast Stream entrants can be placed within many central government departments, and there is a special training route for anyone who wants to join the Diplomatic Service and a further pathway called the European Fast Stream. This places trainees in departments where there is a strong focus on European issues.

There are also some specific professional areas that have their own Fast Stream programmes. These include Fast Stream Economists, Fast Stream Statisticians and Fast Stream Technology in Business pathways. Government Communications Headquarters at Cheltenham also has its own Fast Stream training scheme.

Entry, qualifications and training

As numbers of jobs in the Civil Service are cut back, competition for all posts at every level is likely to be fierce.

At whatever level you enter, a great deal of your training will be on the job. All civil servants have to be either UK nationals or from a Commonwealth or EU country. For some posts, only UK nationals are accepted. Each department or agency sets its own entry requirements, but there are some common guidelines. To become an administrative assistant or an administrative officer you do not need any formal qualifications. In practice, you often need five GCSEs grades A–C. Many applicants have A levels or are graduates. Many junior manager/executive officer posts ask that you have two A levels.

All Fast Stream applications must be made online. The schemes open for applicants in September each year and you have the option to express an interest in more than one scheme and department. Fast Stream graduate trainees need a good honours degree, a first or a 2.1, to be considered for the programme. Fast Stream Economists must have a 2.1 in economics. Fast Stream Statisticians must have at least a 2.2 in a numerate discipline. Fast Stream Technology in Business trainees must have a 2.1 in a business, engineering, technical, mathematical or scientific discipline.

Applicants to the Diplomatic Service must have either a degree or several years' work experience. They must pass a medical, undergo rigorous security checks and be prepared to work anywhere in the world. The Diplomatic Service also participates in the graduate Fast Stream programme.

For posts at all levels, departments often set aptitude tests of various kinds, which are designed to measure the kinds of skills that will be needed to do the job effectively. There is strong competition for Fast Stream posts in all areas.

For undergraduates considering a career in the Civil Service, there are a number of work experience and vacation work opportunities available; see the Civil Service Recruitment website.

Because the Civil Service has a structured route to development and promotion, it is possible to move into higher-level jobs through experience and performance if you do not meet the initial selection criteria for those posts.

Professional occupations

There are also many opportunities in the Civil Service and its agencies for people with a wide range of vocational and professional skills. There are posts for accountants, actuaries, architects, engineers, chemists, physicists, biologists, vets, lawyers, surveyors, IT specialists and many more. For many of these posts applicants need to have relevant professional and vocational qualifications in particular areas such as science, engineering, law or finance. See the Civil Service Recruitment website for more details.

Personal attributes

Of course, there is some variation in these according to the type of work you are involved in and the level of responsibility you have. All civil servants should have an interest in delivering high quality services and information to government, members of the general public and to other organisations. Civil servants need to be flexible, able to cope with change, be good at working under pressure and good at communicating in both written and spoken English. Beyond this, there are specific skills you will need to help you perform your own role effectively.

Earnings

Salaries for administrative assistants range from £12,700 to £15,500. For administrative officers the range is £14,000 to £22,000. Junior managers earn between £20,000 and £25,000. Fast Stream salaries start at around £26,500 and are around £37,500 at the end of a four- to five-year training period. There are small variations between different departments and agencies. Many posts attract performance-related pay bonuses and there are higher salaries for people working in London or Brussels.

Info

Civil Service Careers
www.civilservice.gov.uk/jobs

CLEANER

Cleaners may also be referred to as cleaning operatives or domestic service assistants. While most of us think of cleaning as cleaning and tidying domestic premises, the work goes far beyond this. As well as being employed by individuals to work in private houses, cleaners are employed by contract cleaning companies. They clean hospitals, restaurants, industrial premises, office blocks, shops, passenger vehicles and public buildings. Some cleaning companies specialise in house clearance or in cleaning up after fires, floods or other disasters. What your daily tasks involve will depend very much on the premises in which you work, but could include cleaning carpets, hard floors, walls, kitchen and bathroom surfaces and appliances, furniture and other fixtures and equipment.

Entry, qualifications and training

There are no formal entry requirements to get into this work, though in some areas you may be able to undertake an apprenticeship – employers set their own individual requirements. If you work for a cleaning contract company, training is provided on the job and there are good opportunities to progress to supervisory level in this sector.

Personal attributes

This is work where personal attributes are far more important than qualifications. You must be reliable and trustworthy. Depending on the size of operation you work for, you may have to have good team skills or be confident working on your own. If you work in private houses you will have to impress clients with your honesty and integrity. In all instances you need a thorough approach to your work and you must be physically fit.

Earnings

Cleaners working full-time hours earn £12,000 to £13,000. You can earn £14,000 to £16,000 as a supervisor or working in highly specialised cleaning. Cleaners working in private houses charge by the hour and this can range from the National Minimum Wage, just over £6, to £20.00 if you work in an expensive location where your services are in demand; £6.00 to £9.00 is more usual.

Info

British Institute of Cleaning Science
01604 678710
www.bics.org.uk

Asset Skills
08000 567160
www.assetskills.org

Jobcentre Plus and local
newspapers for job adverts

CLOTHING INDUSTRY

(see also Fashion)

The clothing industry is diverse and complex, with products ranging from off-the-peg garments that are turned out in thousands, to exclusive *haute couture* designs from top fashion houses. There are job opportunities in large factories, small workrooms, with large wholesaling firms, in small family businesses and on production lines. The largest sections of the industry are men's and boys' outerwear, women's and girls' outerwear, children's clothing, bespoke tailoring (made to measure) and dressmaking. More specialised areas such as millinery and glove making are relatively small. Skilled workers are generally in great demand in most areas.

Pattern cutter

Pattern cutters work with clothing designers and clothing technologists. They produce the pattern templates from working drawings produced by fashion designers. They either cut patterns by draping material over dummies and cutting the pattern or they have standard cardboard patterns which they develop and alter to create different styles. Increasingly, pattern cutters use computers to help create their patterns.

Entry, qualifications and training

Some fashion design companies and clothing manufacturers offer apprenticeships in pattern cutting. You must have four GCSEs grades A–C to apply for these. Your GCSEs should include English, maths and a design subject. Many trainee pattern cutters have a relevant Foundation degree, degree or diploma in clothing technology. Some fashion design degree and diploma courses include relevant technical pattern-cutting skills. The London College of Fashion offers part-time and short, intensive pattern-cutting courses. Training is mostly on the job, but there are several NVQ and diploma courses for which you can study while employed.

Pattern grader

Pattern graders produce scaled-up and scaled-down versions of an original pattern (made by a pattern cutter), so that manufacturers can make the same garment in different sizes. Technology plays a key role in pattern grading. Graders use scanning technology to produce extremely accurate patterns in different sizes.

Entry, qualifications and training

Most people start as pattern grading assistants and work their way up after a period of about two years. It is also common to do an apprenticeship in pattern grading with a clothing manufacturer or fashion design company. You can also get into pattern grading or a similar technical role after a degree or BTEC HND in clothing technology and production.

Sample machinist

Sample machinists work to produce sample garments for customers and designers. As a sample machinist, you may work on a number of different product lines or concentrate on a particular style, for example sportswear or evening wear. You also work with a variety of materials, including cotton, wool, synthetics and leather. Sample machinists have to follow carefully the instructions on colour and fabric given by the designer. They then stitch and press the garment to give the designer a clear idea of what the finished item will look and feel like and how it will hang. Experienced sample machinists often take on a quality control role for other machinists.

Entry, qualifications and training

Sample machinists usually start as sewing machinists making up garments once the samples and the design have all been completed. There is a wide range of City & Guilds craft and design courses available in textile machining, machine embroidery and pattern cutting. If you have four GCSEs you may also be able to take an apprenticeship with a clothing manufacturer or fashion design company. Training is on the job.

Sewing machinist

Sewing machinists stitch garments together once the design has been finalised, the material cut and the sample garments completed. They normally work for clothing manufacturers and may be responsible for just one part of production, eg turning up hems, making buttonholes, stitching seams or fitting sleeves.

Entry, qualifications and training

No formal qualifications are needed, but many companies will set a practical test to ensure you have appropriate manual dexterity skills. If you are interested in progressing to becoming a sample machinist or a pattern cutter, you may wish to take an apprenticeship. In this case you will need four GCSEs, usually including English, maths and a design subject.

Personal attributes

To work in any of these jobs you need an interest in clothing and textiles. For pattern cutting you should have good technical drawing and computer skills and the kind of numerate skills that mean you can take very precise measurements. You should have an eye for detail and design. Sample machinists need an understanding of fabrics, good hand and machine sewing skills and an understanding of the production process.

Earnings

Sewing machinists start on between £12,000 and £13,000. Pattern graders earn between £12,000 and £16,000. Trainee pattern cutters and sample machinists start on between £12,000 and £20,000. The range is wide because fashion design companies tend to pay higher starting rates. Experienced pattern cutters and sample machinists can earn more than £20,000.

Info

Skillset Careers
08080 300 900 (England and Northern Ireland)
0808 100 8094 (Scotland)
0800 121 815 (Wales)
www.skillset.org/careers

Textile Institute
0161 237 1188
www.textileinstitute.org

COASTGUARD

Whenever a swimmer is dragged out to sea by a dangerous current, a boat is capsized by strong winds, a ferry passenger falls overboard or a ship runs aground on a sandbank. HM Coastguard coordinates the search and rescue. At its centres around the coast of the British Isles it is responsible for approximately 10,500 miles of coastline and a million square miles of sea.

At these centres, a constant watch is kept on international distress frequencies, satellite, radio and telephone communications, all of which are responded to immediately. HM Coastguard works with and can call upon many resources for search and rescue, at sea including lifeboats, helicopters, tugs and local rescue organisations. For onshore rescues, such as people or animals being stranded on cliffs or trapped in mud, they call upon teams of auxiliary coastguards.

Entry, qualifications and training

Most entrants start as watch assistants. For this you need good basic literacy, numeracy and IT skills, and a strong interest in maritime affairs. Watch officers need GCSEs grades A–C in English and maths, or their equivalent. For applicants without formal qualifications, the Maritime and Coastguard Agency can set competency tests. Watch officers must also have extensive experience of the sea. Many watch officers have been in the Royal Navy or the Merchant Navy, or have had other first-hand experience of the sea. Auxiliary coastguards must be aged 16 or over. Posts are open to UK nationals and to EU and Commonwealth citizens. Applicants must be physically fit, with good hearing and eyesight.

All recruits attend a training course at the Maritime and Coastguard Agency's Training Centre in Dorset, after which training is a combination of classroom and practice-based assignments.

Personal attributes

As a coastguard you will have to take important decisions quickly and calmly. You need a clear speaking voice and the ability to work with modern communications equipment. You should have good leadership skills and work well as part of a team.

Earnings

Trainees earn £13,500 to £15,500 – watch assistants earn £17,000. Watch officers earn £21,000. Coastguards may also earn additional money for working shifts.

Info

Maritime and Coastguard Agency
www.mcga.gov.uk

COLOUR SCIENCE AND TECHNOLOGY

Colour technologists are concerned with producing dyes and pigments that have a wide range of applications, including the textile, paint, rubber, plastics, paper, leather and foodstuffs industries. They must ensure that exact colours can be produced at an economic price and in the right quantities whenever they are needed. They are often involved in research and development projects. Technologists are also employed in sales, management, buying, development and research, quality control, customer liaison and technical services departments (depending on the industry involved and the expertise needed).

Textile technologists may work in the design, manufacture and operation of textile machinery, and in the design, production, colouration, finishing and manufacture of fibres, yarns and fabrics of all types.

Entry, qualifications and training

You can start as a technical assistant, a technician or a graduate trainee. Many applicants are graduates, but if you have good A level grades, especially chemistry, you may well get in as a technician. Larger companies often run formal training schemes of a year to 18 months. Preferred degree or HND subjects include analytical chemistry, applied chemistry, chemistry, colour science, maths, business studies and textiles technology. Some entrants are recruited with art degrees or HNDs in art and design. Most training is on the job and usually includes frequent short courses to ensure that you remain up to date with all the latest technical developments.

Personal attributes

You need very good colour vision and technical ability, plus persistence in solving problems. You should be good at working as part of a team and also be able to develop a good sense of business awareness and the ability to work with and listen to customers or clients.

Earnings

New entrants earn £17,000 to £20,000 as technicians and £22,000 to £29,000 as graduate trainees. Salaries at senior level are £30,000 to £55,000.

Info

Oil and Colour Chemistry Association (OCCA)
020 7598 1584
www.occa.org.uk

The Society of Dyers and Colourists (SDC)
01274 725138
www.sdc.org.uk

The Textile Institute
0161 237 1188
www.textileinstitute.org

COMPLEMENTARY MEDICINE

The popularity and range of complementary medicine and therapies have grown in recent years. The occupations shown here are therefore not exhaustive, but give a cross-section of the more established ones. Some not covered here include colonic therapy, colour therapy and crystal healing. Here are some sources of further information common to most of these therapies and treatments.

Info

Institute for Complementary and
Natural Medicine
020 7922 7980
www.i-c-m.org.uk

Skills for Health
0117 922 1155
www.skillsforhealth.org.uk

General Regulatory Council for
Complementary Therapists
www.grcct.org

Federation of Holistic Therapists
0870 420 2022
www.fht.org.uk

Complementary and Natural
Healthcare Council (CNHC)
0203 178 2199
www.cnhc.org.uk

Acupuncturist

Acupuncture is a system of treatment that involves the insertion of fine needles into one or more points of the body to restore the overall health of the person and help alleviate symptoms from which they may be suffering. Acupuncture can also be used for relieving pain, and in China it is used to anaesthetise patients during operations. It has been practised in China and other Far Eastern countries for thousands of years and is a growing profession in the UK. Many health professionals, for example nurses and physiotherapists, train as acupuncturists.

Entry, qualifications and training

To practise as an acupuncturist you must take an in-depth course (usually around three years full-time or the part-time equivalent). Acupuncture is currently unregulated, but you can work towards membership of a professional body, such as the British Acupuncture Council (BAcC) or the Acupuncture Society. The British Acupuncture Accreditation Board (BAAB) has approved several courses that lead to membership of the BAcC. To get onto a BAAB approved course you normally need at least five GCSEs grades A–C, including a science. Some colleges may require two A levels, including a science subject. The BAcC website lists courses and their entry requirements. If you already have healthcare qualifications, these may gain you entry onto a course and you may be exempt from parts of the course. At present acupuncturists do not have to be registered with a professional body to practise, but the Health Professions Council may develop a compulsory registration scheme in the near future.

Personal attributes

You must enjoy working with people and be good at putting them at ease – acupuncture is a treatment that makes many clients initially nervous. You need a real interest in biology, health and preventive care and you must have good, confident manual dexterity. You need a good business sense if you are self-employed and the ability to organise your own time and keep accurate records.

Earnings

Most acupuncturists are self-employed and charge between £40 and £90 per session. An experienced practitioner, working full-time hours, would see about 30 clients a week. Annual earnings are between £19,000 and £35,000.

Info

British Medical Acupuncture Society
01606 786782
www.medical-acupuncture.co.uk

British Acupuncture Council (BAcC)
020 8735 0400
www.acupuncture.org.uk

Acupuncture Society
www.acupuncturesociety.org.uk

Alexander technique practitioner

Alexander technique practitioners teach a form of physical and mental well-being. Practitioners, usually working one-to-one with clients, teach them to develop better posture, poise, balance and coordination. They teach through demonstrating certain physical exercises and techniques, through manipulation, referred to as 're-coordinating', and through explaining and teaching relaxation techniques. Practitioners aim to teach a technique that can be applied to all aspects of daily life. Some clients may simply want to improve their sense of poise or well-being; others may wish to try the technique to help with emotional problems or physical aches and pains. Actors, musicians and other performers may employ Alexander technique practitioners to improve posture, presence and comportment.

Entry, qualifications and training

There are no formal entry requirements, but you do need a good general education, and academic subjects that cover biology, physiology or anatomy are useful. A background in social care, social work, counselling or healthcare might also be useful. Most people who become practitioners have started as clients, found the technique useful and developed the desire to teach it to others. There are three separate training bodies: the Society of Teachers of the Alexander Technique (STAT), the Professional Association of Alexander Teachers (PAAT) and the Interactive Teaching Method (ITM); they have details of training opportunities at introductory/foundation and practitioner level. You will have to fund your own training. The training covers anatomy, physiology, biology and the science of movement. It also includes supervised practical sessions with clients.

Personal attributes

Practitioners must be good communicators able to explain things but also good at listening and being understanding. Practitioners also have to feel physically comfortable with other people and to promote that same sense of ease in their clients. They must have a genuine interest in physical and mental health issues and be able to develop a good grasp of scientific and practical matters. Usually self-employed, they also need appropriate financial and marketing skills.

Earnings

Almost all Alexander technique teachers/practitioners are self-employed, charging anything from £20 to £50 per session – most sessions last about half an hour.

Info

Society of Teachers of the Alexander Technique 020 7482 5135 www.stat.org.uk	**Professional Association of Alexander Teachers (PAAT)** 01746 761 024 www.paat.org.uk

Aromatherapist

Aromatherapists use the organic essential oils from aromatic plants to treat a whole range of physical and emotional symptoms. Based on discussing a client's symptoms, lifestyle, diet, overall state of health, etc, the aromatherapist prescribes a combination of essential oils to treat the person. This is done either by massage, or by giving a client oils to use in their baths, on their pillows, or to scent their rooms. While aromatherapists may work in beauty salons, they are also employed by healthcare organisations and often work closely with GPs, nurses and other healthcare professionals.

Entry, qualifications and training

There are no specific academic qualifications but certificate and diploma courses are run at a number of state and private colleges. Some courses set particular entry requirements such as a GCSE in biology and they may also set admissions tests. The length of courses varies from a weekend to an evening a week over one or two years. The longer courses offer a much greater depth of study.

Personal attributes

Aromatherapists must be very good at putting people at ease. They must be caring, patient and good listeners. They must be comfortable with close physical contact with other people.

Earnings

Many aromatherapists are self-employed and charge between £20 and £55 an hour. Aromatherapists who are employed earn from £16,000 to £23,000 a year.

Info

Aromatherapy Council
www.aromatherapycouncil.co.uk

Chiropractor

Chiropractic is a healthcare profession concerned with, but not limited to, the diagnosis, treatment and prevention of structural and functional disorders affecting the musculo-skeletal system. Common complaints include low back and leg pain, headaches and neck and arm pain, as well as sports injuries. Working in a primary contact profession, a qualified chiropractor may be approached directly, without a medical referral, by patients seeking help.

Chiropractors are trained to utilise a wide variety of diagnostic techniques, including X-ray. Manual manipulation (adjustment) of spinal and extremity joints as well as soft-tissue structures is the most common treatment method employed. They will also offer advice on nutrition, rehabilitative exercises and modifications to activities of daily living. There is an increasing demand for chiropractic services and employment prospects are good both in the UK and in Europe.

Entry, qualifications and training

To practise as a chiropractor you must be registered with the General Chiropractic Council (GCC). To join the register you need to complete a GCC accredited degree or Master's qualification in chiropractic; see the GCC website for a list of approved courses. You need three A levels, including physics, biology or chemistry. If you do not have the qualifications mentioned above, you may be able to take a one-year preliminary course (offered by all GCC approved institutions). To have had work experience, paid or voluntary, in a caring profession will strengthen your application for all these courses.

Personal attributes

Manual dexterity and practical skills as well as a sound theoretical knowledge of the body are necessary. An ability to communicate with patients and inspire confidence is important.

Earnings

Earnings are determined by the number of patients and how well established the practice is. Clients are usually charged per session at £25 to £60 per hour. A new entrant earns up to £15,000 per year. With experience it is possible to earn £30,000; a large practice will pay an experienced person up to £40,000.

Info

British Chiropractic Association
www.chiropractic-uk.co.uk

United Chiropractic Association
www.united-chiropractic.org

General Chiropractic Council (GCC)
020 7713 5155
www.gcc-uk.org

McTimoney Chiropractic
Association
www.mctimoney-chiropractic.org

Scottish Chiropractic Association
www.sca-chiropractic.org

Homeopath

Homeopathy is a system of healing that assists the natural tendency of the body to heal itself. There are three main principles of homeopathy. First is treating like with like – what produces the symptoms of a disease may also cure it; the patient is treated by a small amount of the substance causing the symptoms and the natural defences are stimulated. Second, the lower the dose the better the result. Third, the remedy should be unique to the particular patient at a particular time. Homeopathic remedies may be used to treat almost any reversible illness in adults, children or animals.

Many newly qualified homeopaths set up in partnership in a clinic with other homeopaths and some now work with GPs in fund-holding practices. Homeopathic patients may come privately or be referred by GPs. Medical homeopaths (doctors who have trained in homeopathy) work as GPs, private practitioners or in one of the NHS homeopathic hospitals.

Entry, qualifications and training

Medical doctors who have been qualified for a minimum of two and a half years may take a postgraduate course at one of the five teaching centres accredited by the British Homeopathic Association.

Candidates who are not medically qualified have a choice of institutions and courses. Several organisations register homeopaths as professionally competent. The largest, the Society of Homeopaths, is involved in developing professional education and is currently establishing a formal procedure for accrediting courses in homeopathy. There is a database of recognised courses on its website.

Personal attributes

Homeopaths must have an interest in people, an ability to consider and interpret information and be good listeners and communicators.

Earnings

Earnings depend on earning fees from clients who normally pay by the hour for sessions – £25 to £100 per hour; £35 to £50 an hour is the most likely rate. Annual earnings range from £15,000 to £45,000.

Massage therapist

Massage therapists use several different techniques, but they all involve using their hands and fingers to manipulate soft tissue. Most massage therapists are self-employed, but they may work in beauty salons, sports centres and private health clinics, or occasionally for the NHS. Massage therapists work with people who are in pain or suffering stress. They work with sports men and women who have suffered injury and they may work with babies and their parents to help calm babies and improve the bond between parent and child. There are many different techniques and schools of massage; Indian head massage, sports massage and body massage are some of the key specialisms.

Entry, qualifications and training

At present, this is an unregulated profession, so there are no agreed training routes, but the General Council for Massage Therapy (GCMT) recommends intending massage therapists to take an in-depth course. They have developed training guidelines and suggestions of what topics every course should cover and they should be able to give you useful guidance. Most massage therapy training is private, so you will have to pay for the training yourself. Entry requirements for training courses vary, but most will expect you to have five GCSEs grades A–C, including English and a science subject.

Personal attributes

You must have excellent communication skills, able to reassure and put people at their ease. You will have to be a good listener too. You need to be physically fit with good stamina and an interest in science and health. If you are self-employed you will also have to have the right administrative and organisational skills to run your business. In many settings you will also have to work as part of a team.

Earnings

Self-employed massage therapists charge between £25 and £70 an hour. If you work in a beauty salon you will probably earn between £14,000 and £16,000 a year. Many experienced massage therapists, who are skilled in a variety of massage techniques, may earn more than £30,000.

Info

Massage Training Institute
020 7254 7227
www.massagetraining.co.uk

Sports Massage Association (SMA)
0870 005 2678
http://www.thosma.org

Guild of Infant and Child Massage
01889 564 555
www.gicm.org.uk

Naturopath

Naturopaths work in private practice; naturopathy is not offered by the NHS. They believe in treating the whole patient and in encouraging the body to cure itself, so do not generally give drugs which, they consider, often treat the symptoms without dealing with the actual cause of a problem. A naturopath uses treatments designed to correct total body chemistry; diet is seen as a major factor and patients are encouraged to eat more natural food. Hydrotherapy is often used to stimulate the blood to a specific area of the body or to draw it away from another (by applying cold packs to combat throbbing headaches, for example).

Naturopaths also need to be skilled in psychology since they recognise that physiological complaints may frequently be caused by psychological problems. Any remedies used tend to be nutritional, herbal or homeopathic, and naturopaths may also be trained in acupuncture or other systems of alternative or complementary medicine. In the UK, naturopathy is closely linked to osteopathy, and many naturopaths are qualified osteopaths, using these skills in treating their patients.

Entry, qualifications and training

Two graduate courses are offered by the British College of Osteopathic Medicine in London: a BSc (Honours) degree in Osteopathic Medicine combined with a Naturopathic Diploma and a BSc (Honours) degree in Naturopathic Medicine.

The usual minimum entry requirements are three good A levels or equivalent, one of which should be chemistry. Mature students may be considered on an individual basis, taking into account their academic and life experiences.

Personal attributes

Professional skills must be combined with a sympathetic and caring manner.

Earnings

Salaries vary depending on hours worked, number of patients and fee scales. Fees range from £25 to £100 an hour.

Info

The General Council and Register of Naturopaths 0870 745 6984 www.naturopathy.org.uk	British Naturopathic Association 08707 456984 www.naturopaths.org.uk

Osteopath

Osteopathy is a system of diagnosis and treatment where the main emphasis is on conditions affecting the musculo-skeletal system. Osteopaths use predominantly gentle manual and manipulative methods of treatment to restore and maintain proper body function. They work in private practice and are increasingly being asked to work as part of mainstream medicine. All osteopaths are required to register with the General Osteopathic Council (GOsC).

Entry, qualifications and training

To practise as an osteopath, you need to take a degree approved by the GOsC. You then have to register with the GOsC. If you have other medical qualifications you may be able to take a shorter postgraduate course. You can find a list of all approved courses on the GOsC website. You normally need five GCSEs grades A–C and two or three A levels, including at least one science. Osteopathy degree courses combine academic work and periods of practical placement. Before you can register with the Council you need to have a medical, character reference and a Criminal Records Bureau (CRB) check. You also need to take out your own liability insurance. Once you are working as an osteopath you have to complete 30 hours of continuing education each year as part of your professional development.

Personal attributes

You have to be genuinely interested in working with people, able to put them at ease and gain their trust. You must have a keen interest in science and be physically fit. If you are self-employed, you must be good at managing and marketing your services.

Earnings

Most osteopaths are self-employed and earnings are based on the rates they charge per treatment and consultation, usually between £25 and £75 per session. In your early career earnings will probably be around £20,000; later on, earnings can be up to £40,000.

Info

General Osteopathy Council (GOsC)
020 7357 6655
www.osteopathy.org.uk

Reflexologist

A reflexologist applies pressure to the foot, or to the hands, to stimulate the reflexes, which acts as a treatment to release tensions in the body, improving circulation and stimulating the body's own natural healing processes. A usual session conducted with a client involves applying pressure to the hands and feet, to clear blockages and improve circulation, easing tension and restoring the body's natural balance to all organs and parts of the body.

Entry, qualifications and training

Reflexology courses are available at colleges of further or higher education and private centres throughout the UK. The number of hours of study required by courses varies between 60 and 200. Most courses are private and there is a fee, but grants may be available.

Personal attributes

A reflexologist helps people and is sensitive and sympathetic to the client's needs and condition. It is essential to have good communication skills, including listening and understanding. The work involves solving problems. Reflexologists must be logical thinkers able to offer a solution to health problems and understand when to refer patients to suitable medical practitioners.

Earnings

Newly qualified reflexologists earn £14,000 to £20,000. Experienced reflexologists with plenty of clients can earn around £30,000. Most reflexologists are self-employed so income is dependent on the number of clients seen and the geographical location. Some reflexologists may get contracts to work in hospitals, care homes, health clubs, etc.

Info

Association of Reflexologists
0870 5673320
www.aor.org.uk

Reflexology Forum
www.reflexologyforum.org.uk

Reiki healer

Reiki healing is a form of energy-based healing founded in Japan. Reiki healers endeavour to guide energies through the bodies of their clients, attempting to activate natural healing processes within the body. There are many systems of Reiki, but they all aim to help physical, emotional, mental or spiritual problems. Reiki is used to treat pain, stress and tiredness and it aims to induce calm and increase clients' energy levels. It is sometimes used in conjunction with traditional and other complementary therapies.

During a Reiki session, the client lies fully clothed on a bed or sits in a chair while the healer places his or her hands in a sequence of positions over the client's body. The whole body is treated rather than specific symptoms or areas. Treatment can take between one and two hours. Reiki is non-diagnostic, non-interventionist and non-manipulative and no pressure is applied.

Entry, qualifications and training

There are no specific academic entry requirements, though many Reiki healers will have qualifications in other aspects of healthcare, counselling, or complementary therapies. You should have experience of working with people and you also need to undergo some Reiki healing yourself, to experience how it operates. Training is through one-to-one sessions with a Reiki master or teacher.

Training courses in Reiki are also offered at a number of colleges at introductory and advanced level. It is possible to gain a certificate or diploma awarded by an exam body such as the Vocational Training Charitable Trust (VTCT) or the Open College Network (OCN).

Personal attributes

You must have very good interpersonal skills. You need to be able to put people at ease, reassure them and listen to them. You need to have an open mind and a positive attitude about how Reiki healing works. You must be physically fit. If you are self-employed you need some business awareness, and financial and marketing skills.

Earnings

Most Reiki healers are self-employed, charging for each individual healing session. Fees range from £20 to £75 an hour. What you can charge varies according to your geographical location and your level of experience.

Info

Reiki Healers and Teachers Network
www.reikihealersandteachers.net

UK Reiki Federation
0870 850 2209
www.reikifed.co.uk

Reiki Association
www.reikiassociation.co.uk

Reiki Council
www.reikiregulation.org.uk

COMPUTING

(see Information and Communication Technology)

CONSERVATION

Conservation falls broadly into two categories: cultural heritage and the environment. They are each concerned with protecting and preserving – the former our cultural history and the latter the natural environment.

Conservator

Conservators and restorers look after historic buildings, paintings, pieces of sculpture, ancient books, historic tapestries, carvings, pieces of furniture and other objects. Conservators examine items for any signs of damage or deterioration. They do their best to ensure that objects are looked after properly, and protected and preserved in the most effective ways possible. Finally, they may take steps to restore them to something as close as possible to their original condition.

Conservators have to understand the effect of the environment on different materials, and to ensure that objects are not stored or displayed in harmful conditions. They have to be aware of and be able to control light, humidity, temperature and sources of pollution. They employ many different scientific techniques and they make photographic records of their work.

Entry, qualifications and training

Most conservators have a degree. You need either a degree in art followed by a specialist postgraduate qualification in conservation, or a degree in a specific area of art, eg ceramics and glass, or textiles. The Institute of Conservation lists relevant courses on its website. Highly skilled and experienced craftsmen and women who do not have a degree may also be able to get into conservation work if they can demonstrate their practical skills and knowledge of working with specific materials.

Personal attributes

Conservators must have a blend of interests in artistic, scientific and technical matters. They have to pay close attention to detail and be prepared to work patiently and extremely carefully. They also need to be good communicators, being able to explain their requirements and concerns convincingly.

Earnings

New entrants earn between £19,000 and £22,000. This rises to around £20,000 to £25,000 after two or three years' experience. Senior conservators can earn between £27,000 and £35,000. If you develop a really good reputation and are able to work on prestigious pieces, you may earn more than this. The cultural and arts sector has been hit by cuts, so salaries may remain somewhat static in this sector.

Environmental conservation

(see Environment)

CONSTRUCTION

(see also Building Surveyor and Civil Engineering)

Construction is a broad sector. Houses, flats, schools, hospitals, shops, factories, theatres, restaurants, garages, sports stadia, hotels, stables, care homes and warehouses or all examples of buildings. The construction industry encompasses a wide range of occupations involved in the construction and fitting out of new buildings and redeveloping and refurbishing existing building stock.

Construction trades

There are many different construction trades: carpenters, painters and decorators, electricians, plasterers, plumbers and roofers. While they each require specific knowledge and technical skills, they share similar patterns of training and professional qualifications. Check the Entry, qualifications and training section at the end of this entry to find out about the different ways to train and qualify.

Carpenter

There are several different jobs covered by the general term 'carpenter' – what they all have in common is that carpenters work with wood. They use wood to make doors, window frames, skirting boards, floorboards, cupboards and all the other woodwork you can think of in any domestic, public or commercial building. Some of the different roles include bench joiners, who prepare doors and window frames in a workshop ready for other workers to install them in properties;

carpenters and joiners who work on site or inside or outside buildings, fitting cupboards, doors, window frames, etc; and wood machinists who prepare floorboards and skirting boards in the workshop ready for the carpenter and joiner to fix in place and finish.

Demolition operative

Demolishing a building properly and safely is one of the most highly skilled areas in construction.

Demolition operatives use heavy machinery to bring down walls, buildings and other structures. They have to be acutely aware of safety, calculating exactly how a building will collapse. They are also involved in clearance of the site once the building has been razed to the ground.

Roofer

Roofs come in many different shapes and sizes and are made from many different materials. It is the job of roofers to fix roofs onto buildings and to ensure that these roofs are safe and weatherproof. Within roofing there are several different specialist trades: felt roofing, tiling and slating, lead roofing and many more. You may choose to work mainly with one of these materials and become a specialist, or you may decide to work with all the different types of roofing material.

Scaffolder

Scaffolders build scaffolding that might be used in demolition, but more significantly in construction. They build scaffolding from steel tubes and wooden platforms, and it is essential they build scaffolding that is safe for other construction workers to stand on and work from.

Steeplejack

Steeplejacks work not just on steeples, but on any high structures, chimneys, clock towers, etc. They have to work at a great height, using special safety equipment, but also have to have a good working knowledge of many different trades because they are likely to have to carry out repairs to and with many different materials: glass, wood, paint, plaster, mortar, etc.

Interior and finishing trades

Once a basic structure has been completed by bricklayers, carpenters, roofers, etc, there is still a great deal of work needed to make the building comfortable to live or work in and useful for the purpose for which it has been built. Ceiling fixers, floor layers, glaziers, painters and decorators, plasterers and plumbers are examples of some of the interior and finishing trades on offer.

Ceiling fixer

Ceiling fixers and dry liners install ceilings, especially in large modern buildings with large expanses of high ceiling. They build structures to fit large sheets of plasterboard to, and cover the whole thing with a very thin layer of plaster.

Electrician

This is a major construction industry career with many different options and pathways. You can see full details on page 151.

Glazier

Glaziers work with glass, installing glass windows, doors and glass partitions. They have to be skilled in cutting and fixing glass, from basic double-glazing to more ornate glass effects.

Painter and decorator

No building looks complete until the important finishing touches of painting, wood staining and papering have been applied. Painters and decorators work inside and outside all kinds of buildings, from private houses to large warehouses, shops and offices.

Plasterer

This is a highly skilled occupation, as plasterers have to line walls or ceilings with a layer of even, smooth and attractive plaster to act as a basis for painting, wallpaper or other finishes. They have to work quickly, achieving the desired finish before the plaster dries out. Some plasterers go on to develop skills in ornamental and decorative plasterwork.

Plumber

Plumbers install and maintain all the necessary pipes, valves, tanks, boilers, etc that keep water and heating systems flowing through any building. They install and maintain drainage systems and repair flashing on roofs.

Trowel trades

If you work with brick or stone you will learn one of these trades. Of the many construction occupations available, these offer you the chance to be creative as well as using practical skills.

Bricklayer

Bricklayers build the external and internal walls of all kinds of buildings, from private houses to large hospitals, hotels and offices. They build garden walls and lay patios. They work mainly with ready-prepared bricks, building them up in layers, working to produce smooth and weatherproof results.

Stonemason

Stonemasons have employed their skills for hundreds of years, using natural stone as their basic building material. Today stonemasons work both restoring historic buildings and building modern structures. This is highly skilled work and a flair for design as well as practical ability is very important.

Supervisory roles

With so many different workers involved in building projects, both large and small, it is very important that there are people to take overall responsibility for employing workers, purchasing materials, health and safety, and day-to-day management.

Site manager

Many site technicians become site managers, taking on more responsibility for larger projects and being in charge of everything that happens on the site.

Site technician

Site technicians get involved with the general running and safety of the site. Your role would include hiring and buying materials and machinery, and organising people and equipment. It would be your responsibility to ensure that budgets and plans are followed, and that everything meets technical requirements.

To become a site technician, you will need to have a strong knowledge of building methods and materials, and health and safety requirements, which you will have to teach workers on your site. You will need good communication and organisational skills, a high level of competence in computing, and work well as part of a team.

There are no specific academic entry requirements to train as a site technician, though it is helpful to have GCSE/Standard Grade passes in science, maths and technology for the measurements and planning.

Construction project manager

Construction project managers have overall responsibility for the planning, management, coordination and financial control of a construction project. It is their responsibility to see that the clients' wishes are adhered to and that the project is completed on time within the agreed budget.

Entry, qualifications and training

While understanding the many different ways to train and qualify appears daunting, there are really three ways into construction trades at craft and technical levels. These are through having relevant work experience, through an apprenticeship, or through a college course followed by training with an employer. If you already work on a building site as a labourer, your employer may be prepared to support you through training in one of the building trades.

If you would like to serve a traditional apprenticeship (TA) in a construction trade, you need to find an employer who will take you on and provide the work experience while sending you on day-release to college. During your apprenticeship you normally work towards NVQ levels 2 or 3. How many apprenticeships are on offer and in what trades varies throughout the country; ConstructionSkills has up-to-date information on availability. To do an apprenticeship you normally need three or four GCSEs grade A–C, including maths, English and a technical subject. These requirements do vary though, so check with local colleges and employers.

There are many full-time courses in construction available at local colleges. Entry requirements and exact qualifications vary widely. Many courses lead to an intermediate construction award (ICA) and if you achieve one of these, you may be able to progress to a shortened apprenticeship known as a programme-led apprenticeship (PLA).

If you are still at school and are thinking about careers in construction, a few schools have introduced a new diploma course for 14- to 19-year-olds. It only started in September 2008, so as yet there is no data on how employers view it, but it may be an option you wish to discuss.

Many building contractors now insist that you have a Construction Skills Certification Scheme (CSCS) card to work on their sites. The card is proof of your skills and competence. To get your card you must pass a health and safety assessment and have an NVQ or equivalent qualification. The CSCS helpline and website offers further information.

Personal attributes

While a variety of trades have been described and each has its special requirements, there are many skills and qualities that are important for all these occupations. You need to have a special interest in and feel for the particular material you are working with – wood, metal, plaster, stone, etc. You must be good at measuring and calculating, working out how much material you will need, and measuring exactly to ensure that something fits.

For all jobs you must be physically fit, though some work, such as bricklaying, is especially demanding. You may have to climb up and down scaffolding, work outside in unpleasant weather, or work in cramped spaces such as somebody's loft.

You need to get on with people. You often work as part of a team, and if you progress to supervisory or management roles you have to be organised and be good at motivating other people. If you are working in private houses, you must be polite, pleasant and trustworthy, and good at coming up with solutions to problems. If you become self-employed you must develop good business and financial skills.

Earnings

For construction trades, pay on completion of an apprenticeship is between £16,000 and £20,000. Labourers earn £15,000 to £17,000. Experienced construction trades workers can earn up to £30,000 if they have supervisory or training responsibilities.

Salaries for management posts range from £21,000 to £33,000. Construction has been hit particularly hard by the current economic climate and this has affected the amount of overtime, contract work and other benefits available.

Info

Construction Skills Certification Scheme (CSCS)
0844 576 8777
www.cscs.uk.com

ConstructionSkills
0344 994 4400
www.cskills.org

CRAFTS

Crafts include a diverse mix of occupations which are all concerned with the designing and making of useful and/or beautiful objects. Such objects can be made of glass, wood, porcelain, metal, leather or living flowers and plants. The medium In which you choose to work affects the skills you require and the training you need to follow. Work is at many different levels, from taking part in a fairly. routine production process in a factory to designing and making individual pieces. Here are some common sources of information for many craft occupations.

Info

The Crafts Council
0207 806 2500
www.craftscouncil.co.uk

Design Council
0207 420 5200
www.designcouncil.org.uk

Arts Council England
0845 300 6200
www.artscouncil.org.uk

Creative and Cultural Skills
(The Sector Skills Council for Craft,
Cultural Heritage, Design, Literature,
Music, Performing, and Visual Arts)
020 7015 1800
www.ccskills.org.uk

Cabinet maker

(see Carpentry)

Florist

The florist's job involves designing and creating flower arrangements and displays such as table decorations, bridal bouquets, sprays and wreaths, as well as selling cut flowers and plants. Florists work mostly with fresh flowers and plants, but may also use silk or other artificial and dried flowers, grasses and natural objects. Some florists buy from flower markets; others have stock delivered from wholesalers, local nurseries or overseas producers. The work can include providing office displays, making arrangements for banquets, functions and receptions, and decorating hotels and public buildings. Florists generally work a 40-hour week, including Saturdays.

Entry, qualifications and training

You don't need formal qualifications to train as a florist and most florists train on the job while studying part-time for relevant NVQs in floristry at levels 2 and 3. Helping out in a florist's shop or joining a flower arranging group can strengthen your application.

Personal attributes

You must love working with flowers and plants and have an artistic flair for colour and design. You also need good customer skills, helping people plan flowers for weddings and funerals. You need good business skills if you wish to work for yourself or manage a shop. You are often responsible for choosing and purchasing the flowers you use.

Earnings

Trainees in earn around £11,000. With experience you can earn £16,000 to £19,000. If you manage a shop you could earn £23,000 to £25,000. If you become self-employed earnings vary, but can be £30,000 plus if you are successful.

Info

British Florist Association
0844 800 7315
www.britishfloristassociation.org

National Association of Flower Arrangement Societies
www.nafas.org.uk

Lantra
0845 707 8007
www.lantra.co.uk

Jewellery trade

Design

Jewellery designers craft a wide variety of items either by hand or using methods of large-scale production. These may be very expensive, traditionally styled pieces using gold or platinum, cheaper costume jewellery using synthetic stones and base metals, or fashion accessories made from beads, plastic or wood.

Although there are a few openings for designers of expensive jewellery, the more costly costume jewellery and mass-produced jewellery, there is more scope for original designers on either a freelance or artist/craftsperson basis, making fashionable ranges with semi-precious stones.

Manufacture

The jewellery, silverware and allied industries encompass a vast range of specialist skills. Apart from mounting and silversmithing, other skills needed to support these occupations include gem setting, engraving (hand and machine), enamelling, chasing, engine turning, spinning, electroplating and polishing.

Entry, qualifications and training

To work in a jeweller's shop you do not need any formal qualifications, but some employers do expect you to have GCSEs in maths and English. Training is usually with a more experienced jeweller and you can take NVQs levels 2 and 3 in retail sales and retail operations.

You can study for a Professional Jewellers' Diploma with the National Association of Goldsmiths (NAG). This covers introductions to precious metals, gemstones and hallmarks (the marks that certify a precious metal's quality). This is a distance-learning course which lasts about 18 months. NAG also runs a Professional Jewellers' Management Diploma designed for shop managers or people who would like to become shop managers. There are several independent training courses available for jewellers; the Jewellery and Allied Industries Training Council (JAITC) holds details of these (see the Info panel for contact details).

In the jewellery manufacturing trades there are a number of apprenticeships available. Most jewellery designers have a degree in three-dimensional design and have specialised in jewellery design within that course.

Personal attributes

For retail jewellery work you have to have good communication and customer care skills and a real interest in the products you are selling. You should have an eye for detail and an awareness of colour and fashion. You need good numeracy skills and you should be highly dextrous, easily able to handle small and expensive items carefully. Anyone working in jewellery manufacture must be practical and careful, with an interest in scientific and technical processes as well as artistic effect.

Jewellery designers have to be artistic and imaginative, with a good understanding of the properties of different metals, gems and other materials. They also need to be good at promoting their products and have a sound understanding of business.

Earnings

Pay for people working in jewellers' shops is from £12,000 to £16,000. Store managers earn between £17,000 and £25,000. Some own their own businesses, including online jewellery stores. In manufacturing, salaries range from £14,000 to £18,000 depending on your level of skill and experience.

Jewellery designers earn between £15,000 and £25,000. Some designers with flair and good market instincts can earn far more than this, especially if they are designing jewellery for the rich and famous.

Info

Creative and Cultural Skills
(The Sector Skills Council for Craft,
Cultural Heritage, Design, Literature,
Music, Performing, and Visual Arts)
020 70158100
www.ccskills.org.uk

Design Council
020 7420 5200
www.design-council.org.uk

The Goldsmiths Company
020 7606 7010
www.thegoldsmiths.co.uk

Goldsmiths Company Directory
www.whoswhoingoldandsilver.com

National Association of Goldsmiths
(NAG)
020 7613 4445
www.jewellers-online.org

Skillsmart Retail
0800 093 5001
www.skillsmartretail.com

Jewellery and Allied Industries
Training Council (JAITC)
www.jaitc.org.uk

Leather craftworker

Leather craftworkers make and repair leather items. These include clothing, footwear, furnishings and accessories like handbags and wallets. Some leather craftworkers specialise in products such as saddles and bridles for horses, book covers or weapons and armour for historic societies or theatre companies. The work involves cutting various types of leather from patterns, hand or machine stitching pieces of leather together, fitting fastenings such as buckles, adding linings of other materials and applying finishes such as wax or stains.

Entry, qualifications and training

It is not straightforward to get into leather craftwork. You may be able to do an apprenticeship in textiles that includes leather work. Alternatively you may be able to do a college course in fashion and textiles that includes leather work, particularly all the practical skills you need to work with these materials.

If you are particularly interested in saddlery, the Worshipful Company of Saddlers and the Society of Master Saddlers run the Saddlery Apprenticeship Scheme which lasts for four years. You may need to relocate to take up training or employment, especially if you are thinking about rural leather crafts. The Leather Connection website includes useful information about relevant education and training. A lot of training is on the job, learning skills from more experienced craftworkers, but there are several NVQs you can work towards. These include Leather Production levels 2 and 3, Leather Goods level 2 and Footwear and Leather Products Manufacture level 3.

Personal attributes

You need good manual dexterity working with a range of highly specialised tools and equipment. You should have a real interest in the field in which you work, whether this is a rural craft like saddlery, or high fashion. You should be able to work accurately, taking measurements and adding fine detail. You may also need good customer skills.

Earnings

New entrants earn £11,000 to £14,500 – possibly less during an apprenticeship. Experienced craftworkers can earn up to £20,000.

Info

Leather Connection
www.theleatherconnection.com

Society of Master Saddlers
01449 711 642
www.mastersaddlers.co.uk

Skillset Careers
08080 300 900 (England and Northern Ireland)
0808 100 8094 (Scotland)
0800 121 815 (Wales)
www.skillset.org/careers

Picture framer

Picture framers frame pictures and other art works of all styles, working for galleries, artists or customers who want a picture, photograph or poster professionally framed. They also frame 3-D objects such as dried flowers, sea shells, models and 3-D art works. They work with many types of materials, including wood and metal. They often advise their customers on what type of frame would best suit a particular piece of art, on some occasions visiting the location where the art is to be displayed.

Entry, qualifications and training

There are no formal entry qualifications for this work, though there are several short and part-time courses run on how to become a picture framer. The Fine Art Trade Guild is the trade association for the sector. You can attain its Guild Commended Framer award by taking tests that are offered at centres throughout the UK. The award is internationally recognised as the qualification for the framing industry.

The Guild also awards advanced qualifications in textiles and mount design and cutting. Guild members are listed in the Guild directory. Membership of the Guild also helps you keep current with new ideas and fashions and to be kept informed of any further courses that might prove useful for you.

Personal attributes

You need a flair for design, and a good appreciation of how to use both colour and texture. You need very precise practical skills, able to measure, cut and work with great accuracy. You need to be able to work well with people when giving advice, but you also spend a great deal of time working on your own. Since picture framers are almost always self-employed, you also have to have good business and marketing skills.

Earnings

Earnings range from £12,000 to £18,000 if you are working the equivalent of full-time hours. Many picture framers do this work part-time and combine it with another job or other activities.

Info

Fine Art Trade Guild
020 7381 6616
www.fineart.co.uk

Potter/ceramic designer

Potters make and design objects from clay. They work with basic earthenware and fine porcelain, making everything from basic kitchen- and tableware to ornaments and individual pieces of art. They may design items for the mass market that will be made on a factory production line. At the other extreme they make expensive individual items to be sold through galleries and displayed at exhibitions. Designers working with mass-market producers will have to liaise with buyers, production managers and other staff and will often play a quality control role in the whole process. Designers who are successful enough to work for themselves will work in a studio with their own wheel, kiln, etc.

Entry, qualifications and training

Most pottery/ceramics designers are graduates with a degree in ceramics or 3-D design. If you are considering a course, it is worth checking what practical skills the course covers in addition to its artistic and creative content. To be taken on by a company or a design studio you will need to put together a portfolio of photographs of your work. If you are self-employed, there is a wide range of courses available through local adult education institutes and short-course details are also available from the Studio Pottery website. It is important if you are self-employed to keep up to date with new trends in design, new materials, glazes, techniques, etc.

If you wish to work in the more routine work on the manufacturing side, you will not need formal qualifications.

Personal attributes

You must love creating something with your hands and have a flair for design and good awareness of colour. You need to be imaginative, creative and practical. You need good people skills, being able to interpret design briefs given to you or for working with buyers from shops and galleries. If working for yourself, you need good business acumen.

Earnings

If you are employed by a company or studio, starting pay is around £17,000, rising to £25,000. If you are self-employed, income is much more difficult to predict and can be much lower than for employed designers. Like many art and craft careers, potters may have to boost their artistic earnings by taking on other, more routine work. Many potters increase their income by teaching on pottery courses.

Info

Studio Pottery
www.studiopottery.co.uk

Thatcher

Thatchers are self-employed craftspeople who roof, re-roof or repair thatched buildings with long straw, combed wheat straw, reed and other materials. The materials and methods they use have to preserve the building in its original form.

A thatched roof gives good insulation against heat and cold and lasts 20 to 50 years. A roof is thatched by taking off the old thatch and then pegging down layers of new straw or reed.

Entry, qualifications and training

Academic qualifications are not essential. Thatching can be learnt on the job as an apprentice to a Master Thatcher. Training takes four to five years. The Countryside Agency runs a training scheme for people of all ages, leading to NVQ level 2 in Thatching.

Personal attributes

Thatchers need to be robust, good with their hands and not mind bad weather or heights. They also need common sense, and the ability to make decisions and to deal with customers.

Earnings

Salaries start at between £13,000 and £16,000, rising to £24,000 with two or three years' experience. In some regions it is possible to earn more than this because there is a high demand for thatches.

Info

New Entrants Training Scheme
01432 365314
www.hct.ac.uk

Thatching Information Service
01920 438710

National Society of Master Thatchers
c/o The Secretary
15 High Street
Steventon
Abingdon
Oxfordshire OX13 5RZ

CUSTOMS AND EXCISE

Customs officers work for Her Majesty's Revenue & Customs (HMRC) and the UK Border Agency's Border Force. For officers based at ports and airports (detection officers), the work is sometimes high profile – seizures of drugs or the prevention of human trafficking. Much of the work is more routine but vital, checking people, luggage and documents to ensure that nothing illegal is being brought in or removed from the country. Officers are also responsible for the collection of a range of taxes and duties. They visit businesses, ensuring that the correct duty is being paid on petrol, alcohol or tobacco, for example.

Entry, qualifications and training

You can join either as an administrative assistant or assistant officer or as a direct entrant customs officer or detection officer. To join as an assistant you need five

GCSEs grades A—C, including maths and English. For direct officer entry you must also have two A levels. If you do not meet these selection criteria HMRC do set selection tests to assess your suitability. These test your communication and teamwork skills as well as English and maths. The majority of training is on the job.

Personal attributes

You must be able to get on with people, being polite, tactful and able to question and listen carefully. You should be honest and fair and be able to analyse complex information. For much of the work on the excise and VAT side you must have good numeracy skills.

Earnings

Assistant officers earn just under £16,000, officers earn £21,000 to £28,000 and higher grade officers earn £25,000 to nearly £39,000. At all levels you may earn more through extra payments for working unsocial hours.

Administrative grade salaries are between £12,759 and £19,500. Junior managers earn between £20,000 and £25,000. Senior managers can earn more than £40,000.

Info

HMRC
www.hmrc.gov.uk

Civil Service Careers
www.civilservice.gov.uk/jobs

DENTISTRY

There are many roles besides that of dentist – all of them must be registered with the General Dental Council in order to practise in the UK.

Dentist

Dentists work to keep teeth and gums healthy. They try to prevent, detect and treat tooth decay and gum disease. This involves examining, filling, crowning and extracting teeth, scaling, and cleaning teeth and gums. They design and fit dentures and plates and take corrective measures for teeth growing abnormally. Cosmetic dentistry, whitening or fixing veneers to teeth, is also a developing area of their work. They are also involved with the rectification of fractured jaws and surgery of the mouth. Much of the dentist's work today is highly technical and requires a lot of manual dexterity. There is growing emphasis on preventive work, and the dentist is expected to counsel and educate.

Opportunities exist both in the UK and abroad. In general, dental practice dentists work on contract to the NHS, but growing numbers work in private clinics. Some work in hospitals, community services, school services or the armed forces. There are also opportunities for dentists to work in university dental teaching and research.

Specialist areas of dentistry include paediatric dentistry orthodontics and oral and maxillofacial surgery.

Entry, qualifications and training

To practise as a dentist you must have completed a five-year degree in dentistry at one of the UK's 14 dental schools. To get a place on one of these courses you must have three A levels (grade requirements vary from AAA to ABB), which must include chemistry and either maths or physics. Graduates with science degrees can also get into dental school: some courses are specifically designed for graduates. Some dental schools offer a pre-dental foundation year in science for graduates without suitable science qualifications.

All entrants are assessed at the interview stage on a clearly defined list of skills. These are: strong academic ability, self-discipline, commitment to completing this long and demanding degree course, manual dexterity and technical dental skills, plus the ability to maintain intense concentration for prolonged periods and to build relationships with patients and colleagues, high-level communication and interpersonal skills for interaction with patients of all ages and backgrounds, an interest in the welfare of others and a sympathetic manner, good administrative and managerial abilities, information technology skills owing to the increasing use of computers for keeping records and accounts, and for digital imaging of radiographs and intra-oral photography. After completing your degree you have to do a period of vocational training with an approved dental practitioner.

When you have graduated from dental school you begin a period of work-based vocational training, working under supervision in an approved dental practice. Many graduate dentists undertake the recently introduced General Professional Training (GPT), which offers structured training in hospital and general practice settings.

As a qualified dentist you can specialise by doing further postgraduate training in a specific area of interest, for example orthodontics (straightening or moving teeth).

Personal attributes

As is clear from the skills required by dental schools, you have to be strong academically, with excellent manual dexterity and a real ability to work well with people. You have to be very resilient: most patients are stressed and/or uncomfortable when they visit a dentist, so your people skills contribute enormously to your potential success.

Earnings

Dentists' earnings are affected by the type of work they do and the balance of NHS and private work they undertake. Trainees during their period of vocational training earn around £30,000. Dentists who have completed their training earn between £60,000 and £80,000. Some work, such as private cosmetic dentistry, can be very lucrative and take earnings to more than £150,000. The most senior consultant dentists in the NHS earn £170,000.

Dental hygienist

Dental hygienists clean, polish and scale teeth and in some cases prepare patients for oral operations. Through lectures and practical experience they also endeavour to educate children and adults on the importance of proper dental care. Dental hygienists work to the written prescription of a dentist.

Entry, qualifications and training

Applicants for the Diploma in Dental Hygiene must be over 18 with five GCSE passes, including biology and English. They also need two years' experience as a dental nurse or two A levels or equivalent. Manchester University offers a three-year BSc in oral health science. Graduates work as oral health therapists, which combines the skills of a hygienist and therapist.

Personal attributes

Manual and visual dexterity is required. Candidates should have an ability to communicate in order to educate patients in good dental hygiene practice. The ability to work in a team is important.

Earnings

Newly qualified dental hygienists earn between £21,000 and £27,000; experienced hygienists earn between £32,000 and £39,000. In some fashionable private practices, earnings can be higher than this.

Dental nurse

Dental nurses prepare the surgery and get the appropriate instruments ready. During treatment they assist the dentist by passing instruments, mixing materials, taking notes from the dentist's dictation for records and making sure the patient is comfortable at all times. Once the patient has left, the dental nurse tidies the surgery and sterilises all the instruments. Sometimes, particularly in general practice, dental nurses also help with reception work – making appointments, taking payments, dealing with the paperwork, meeting and reassuring patients.

Entry, qualifications and training

Many dentists like to train their own assistants and expect applicants to have four GCSEs, including English, maths and a science. Dental nurses must obtain NVQ level 3 in Oral Healthcare or pass the National Certificate of the Examining Board for Dental Nurses. Preparation for this exam can be either at evening or day-release courses or via a full-time college course lasting one to two years. Dental nurses also have to complete two years' practical training in a dental practice.

Personal attributes

Candidates should be equable, sympathetic and have an agreeable nature and an ability to communicate. Good administrative and managerial skills and the ability to work in a team are important.

Earnings

In private practice, earnings vary depending on type of practice and its location. In the NHS, dental nurses earn close to £16,000, while team leader nurses in large practices or hospital dental departments can earn up to £25,000.

Dental technician

Dental technicians design and fabricate a wide variety of different materials and equipment to make crowns, dentures, metal plates, bridges, orthodontic braces and other appliances prescribed by a dentist.

Entry, qualifications and training

To work as a dental technician you must be registered with the General Dental Council and to obtain registration you must complete a dental technician course. These are offered at BTEC diploma, Foundation degree and degree level. You can either study full-time or apply for a traineeship with a private dental laboratory or a hospital and study on a part-time basis. This usually takes four to five years.

Personal attributes

Good technical skills and the ability to work in a team need to be combined with good people skills, being able to put people at ease, listen to questions and address patients' concerns.

Earnings

Qualified dental technicians earn £22,000 to £28,000, less during training. Senior technicians or laboratory managers may earn up to £35,000.

Dental therapist

Dental therapists work in local authority clinics and hospitals, assisting dentists by carrying out simpler forms of treatment such as fillings and the extraction of first teeth. They also give guidance on general dental care. Dental therapists must always work to the written prescription of a dentist.

Entry, qualifications and training

To become a dental therapist you must take either a diploma in dental therapy or a degree in oral health sciences, including modules on dental therapy and hygiene. The British Association of Dental Therapists (BADT) can provide details of relevant dental schools; diploma courses last two years, degree courses three years.

To get onto either course you need five GCSEs grades A–C, including human biology, plus two A levels. If you are already a qualified and experienced dental nurse you may be able to do a course without meeting the usual academic requirements.

Personal attributes

You must be very good at working with people, able to reassure, be calm, encourage and teach. You should have an interest in science and healthcare and you should also be practical, with good manual dexterity and good eyesight. You must be physically fit and resilient.

Earnings

Pay starts at around £21,000 to £26,000. With experience, and working in private practice, you can earn considerably more than this.

Info

NHS Careers
0345 60 60 655
www.nhscareers.nhs.uk

British Dental Association
020 7935 0875
www.bda-dentistry.org.uk

General Dental Council
020 7887 3800
www.gdc-uk.org

British Society of Dental Hygiene
and Therapy
0870 234 0752
www.bsdht.org.uk

National Examining Body for
Dental Nurses
01253 778417
www.nebdn.org

British Association of Dental Nurses
(BADN)
www.badn.org.uk

British Association of Dental
Therapists (BADT)
0845 257 3487 (11am to 3pm)
www.badt.org.uk

DIETICIAN

A dietician is an authority on diet and the application of the principles of nutrition. Dieticians working in hospitals collaborate with medical staff, other healthcare professionals and catering staff in planning the correct balance of foods for all the patients, depending on their general state of health and medical requirements. Dieticians are also employed by local health authorities to work with general practitioners, in health centres and clinics dealing with infant welfare and antenatal treatment. Some dieticians may now be employed directly by fund-holding GPs. They are also called upon to educate other healthcare professionals in nutrition. Other opportunities for dieticians exist in education, research, the food industry and the media. Increasingly, dieticians work in a freelance capacity.

Entry, qualifications and training

To work as a dietician in the NHS you need either a degree in dietetics or human nutrition or a postgraduate qualification in dietetics. If you choose to do a degree, then you must have three A levels grades A–C, including chemistry and one other science. If you opt for the postgraduate route, then you need a good honours degree in a life science, medicine or nutrition. You should check with the British Dietetic Association (BDA) to ensure that the course you are considering meets the approved professional standards.

If you do not want to go through higher education, you may be able to start work as a dietetic assistant in the NHS and train to NVQ level 3 in Allied Health Professions (Support) Dietetics. Applicants for assistants' posts need to have four GCSEs grades A–C, usually including maths, English and a science.

Personal attributes

You have to be extremely good at talking to people, listening to them and explaining complex information in a way that can be easily understood. You also have to be able to tell people things they would rather not hear. You have to have an aptitude for and an interest in scientific and medical concepts. You have to be able to work well as part of a health professionals team. You may also need presentation skills to explain ideas to groups of people rather than always working one-to-one.

Earnings

Dieticians start on between just under £23,000 and £27,500. Experienced dieticians can earn £31,000 to £33,500 and team leaders can earn close to £40,000. Some dieticians are self-employed and their earnings are based on the fees they charge clients. Others work in private clinics specialising in advice on weight loss or coping with allergies, for example, and here earnings may be higher than in the NHS.

Info

Health Professions Council (HPC)
020 7840 9812
www.hpc-uk.org

British Dietetic Association (BDA)
0121 200 8080
www.bda.uk.com

NHS Careers
0345 60 60 655
www.nhscareers.nhs.uk

DISC JOCKEY

Disc jockeys (DJs) select, play and mix music at clubs, private parties and on radio stations. They use a variety of high-tech equipment for mixing, pitch control and cross-fading, and may also be responsible for lighting and multimedia effects. A DJ's personality may be the key to success or otherwise of a radio show. At live events it is up to the DJ to create the right atmosphere and read the audience. What is required at a family party is going to be very different from what makes a successful club or dance venue.

Entry, qualifications and training

A strong interest in and enjoyment of different music styles is essential, and it is useful to have an interest in technology and electronics. Some DJs specialise in specific music genres such as soul, funk, hip-hop and pop. Most are self-taught and usually begin their career by volunteering their services at clubs, radio stations or to friends. It is useful to send a tape demonstrating DJ skills when asking for work.

Personal attributes

DJs must have a lively personality, a sense of fun and natural creativity. They need to have a good knowledge of and genuine interest in music and be able to interact well with an audience.

Earnings

Sometimes you have to start off doing unpaid work. Very often you are paid by the session, anything from £50 to £300, most sessions lasting a few hours. Really experienced club and radio DJs with an established reputation can earn up to £1,000 per session.

Info

Creative and Cultural Skills (The
Sector Skills Council for Craft,
Cultural Heritage, Design,
Literature, Music, Performing, and
Visual Arts)
020 701 5 1800
www.ccskills.org.uk

Skillset Careers
08080 300 900 (England and
Northern Ireland)
0808 100 8094 (Scotland)
0800 121 815 (Wales)
www.skillset.org/careers

RadioCentre
020 7306 2603
www.radiocentre.org

The Radio Academy
020 7927 9920
www.radioacademy.org

DIVING

Diver

Divers work for many different employers. Some work in the oil and gas industry, surveying, checking and building rigs and pipelines. They work for the police, searching and retrieving evidence or attempting rescues, for the media in underwater filming, and for fish farms, checking stock and equipment. They may also work for surveying companies or for archaeological research. Divers work in the sea, in rivers, in lakes, canals and reservoirs. Divers also work as instructors, either training others to become professional divers or working in outdoor education and leisure, teaching people who are interested in recreational diving. They normally specialise in a particular type of diving and this is determined by how deep they have to dive and by what kind of breathing apparatus they use.

Entry, qualifications and training

You must be extremely physically fit to train as a diver. You must pass a strict medical before you can start to train and you have to pass annual medicals throughout your diving career. Both the medical and the diving training course you complete have to be approved by the Health and Safety Executive (HSE) before you can work as a commercial diver.

While you don't need academic qualifications for the actual diving, you may well need qualifications relevant to the industry in which you are working. Scientific divers often have a degree in oceanography. Others may have a degree in surveying. For work in the offshore oil and gas industry, you may need welding or other construction qualifications.

The police and the Royal Navy train their own divers, so you will have to pass their selection procedures.

Personal attributes

As well as physical fitness, you must be able to work in hazardous and frightening conditions. You should have a great awareness of safety issues at all times, and you must be very thorough in checking equipment and following procedures.

Earnings

Divers are usually paid by the day. Rates vary enormously, from £130 a day for inshore work for a surveying or civil engineering company, to as much as £1,000 a day for some offshore work in the oil and gas industry. You need to bear in mind that most divers will probably only complete 200 dives a year.

Info

The Underwater Centre
01397 703786
www.theunderwatercentre.co.uk

Professional Association of Diving
Instructors (PADI)
0117 300 7234
www.padi.com

Cogent (The Sector Skills Council
for Science Based Industries)
01925 515200
www.cogent-ssc.com

International Marine Contractors
Association
020 7824 5520
www.imca-int.com

DOMESTIC APPLIANCE SERVICE

(see also Gas Service Engineer)

Domestic appliance service engineers service and repair all kinds of household goods, including washing machines, fridges, televisions, DVD players – in fact all kinds of electrical and gas appliances. Service engineers work for retailers, for manufacturers and for servicing companies and some are self-employed. As well as replacing worn or damaged parts in appliances, they may offer routine servicing, checking that everything is running smoothly and removing dust, limescale or other debris from appliances. They also advise customers on the best way to care for their appliances.

Entry, qualifications and training

While no formal qualifications are necessary, in practice most organisations will expect you to have qualifications and background experience in at least two of the following areas: electrics, electronics, gas fitting, mechanics, plumbing and refrigeration. There are several relevant Edexcel BTEC and City & Guilds courses at levels 2 and 3. Look for courses with units in consumer goods or specialist options on TV, DVD and PC repair and maintenance. People aged 16 to 24 who are interested in this work could consider an apprenticeship in electrics, gas fitting or plumbing. Training is usually provided by the employer and consists of new trainees assisting and learning from a more experienced engineer until they are able to take on more complex jobs or work on their own.

Personal attributes

As well as good practical skills and knowledge of a wide range of appliances, you must have good problem-solving ability and you must be good at dealing with people. You must be polite and friendly to customers, good at explaining problems, and able to listen to their concerns.

Earnings

Pay starts at between £13,000 and £16,000. With a few years' experience this rises to £16,000 to £22,000. Anyone with highly specialised skills, such as gas servicing, may earn £25,000 or more.

Info

Gas Safe Register
0800 408 5500
www.gassaferegister.co.uk

Domestic Appliance Service Association
www.dasa.org.uk

DRIVING

Although many jobs require you to drive a vehicle, the occupations in this section refer to those which require professional driving skills.

Chauffeur

Chauffeurs drive clients to their destinations, doing their best to ensure that their passenger(s) are comfortable on the journey and arrive safely and on time. Politicians, celebrities, senior executives and wealthy private individuals are among the possible clients of a chauffeur. Some chauffeurs work for one family or individual. Others might work for a large business driving various company members around. Some chauffeurs work for limousine hire companies driving wedding or funeral cars. As well as driving, your duties could include helping clients in and out of cars, assisting with luggage, providing information about the journey and being generally helpful.

Entry, qualifications and training

No formal academic qualifications are required, but you must have several years' driving experience and a full, clean UK driving licence. Some employers like you to have an Advanced Driving Certificate from the Institute of Advanced Motorists. For some posts you will need a foreign language and perhaps other skills such as car maintenance or gardening, if your time spent actually chauffeuring is likely to be fairly limited. Many chauffeurs have worked as taxi drivers or have been in the police force or armed services.

Personal attributes

You must have excellent driving skills, and be careful, confident and sensible. You need to be polite, smart and tactful and able to respect people's privacy and use your discretion. You must be flexible, calm and reasonably physically fit.

Earnings

Pay starts at £13,000 to £17,000. With experience earnings rise to around £25,000. Some posts bring other benefits such as accommodation or a lot of foreign travel.

Info

Institute of Advanced Motoring
020 8996 9600
www.iam.org.uk

GoSkills (The Sector Skills Council
for Passenger Transport)
0121 635 5520
www.goskills.org

British Chauffeurs Guild Ltd
020 8641 1740
www.britishchauffeursguild.co.uk

Courier

Couriers deliver and collect parcels, generally in larger towns and cities. Around 10,000 couriers work in Central London. Mostly the delivery or collection is in the same city, sometimes in a different one and very occasionally in another country. Most couriers use a motorbike, which they may be required to buy. Couriers carrying packages abroad travel by air.

In large and congested cities there is an increasing trend for couriers to travel by pushbike, and some couriers use small vans.

Entry, qualifications and training

Couriers don't need formal qualifications, but good literacy skills are important. You must be aged 17 or over and have a driving licence appropriate to the vehicle you are to drive, eg motorcycle, car or van. A basic knowledge of motor vehicle maintenance can be valuable and motorcycle couriers usually have to provide their own vehicle, plus its road tax and insurance. Once you are employed you can work towards NVQs levels 2 and 3 in Carry and Deliver Goods. Units include road safety and customer care.

Personal attributes

Good, safe driving skills and an ability to deal with people are both important. You are often under a great deal of pressure to be quick, so you must be able to cope with this and not compromise safety. Sometimes knowledge of foreign languages can be useful.

Earnings

Couriers start on between £12,000 and £16,000 and with experience they can earn £17,000 to £22,000. Motorcycle couriers in London can earn £24,000. Remember that out of these earnings you may have to pay for fuel, insurance and the maintenance of your vehicle. Many couriers are self-employed. Some employers pay bonuses for good attendance, reliability and punctuality.

Info

Skills for Logistics
01908 313360
www.skillsforlogistics.org

Driving instructor

Driving instructors teach clients how to drive in preparation for all categories of the Driving Standards Agency's theory and practical driving tests. Instructors can also provide post-test training for the Pass Plus scheme as well as prepare clients for advanced driving tests, such as the DIAmond Advanced Motorists test.

The industry is now very much structured to self-employment, with instructors either having their own business or existing as an independent operation within a franchise agreement.

Entry, qualifications and training

Driving instructors must be registered with the Driving Standards Agency (DSA). To register to train you must have held a full UK/EU driving licence for four years and you must not have been disqualified from driving at any time in the last four years. You will have to pass criminal record checks and a series of tests. You can get a starter pack containing all the information you need from the DSA; it also provides information on approved training courses. Driving schools and other specialist training schools run the training courses and the length and cost of training varies.

You take your theory test first and you can attempt this as many times as you like. Once you have passed this, you have to pass a special driving test and a test of your ability to teach. You must do all three tests within a two-year period. When you have passed you can join the Driving Instructors' Association (DIA) register of approved instructors. The DIA offers the chance for continuing professional development and advanced training and you can take an NVQ level 3 in Driving Instruction.

Personal attributes

As well as excellent, safe driving skills you need an ability to work really well with your students. People learning to drive may be nervous, anxious and lacking in confidence, or alternatively they may be careless and over-confident. You have to be able to work flexible hours and if you become self-employed you have to have good organisational and business skills.

Earnings

Earnings come from hourly charges to learner drivers – £15 to £28 per hour. On qualifying you are likely to earn around £16,000 in your first year, and with experience £23,000 to £25,000. Experienced instructors who have built up a reputation could earn £30,000 plus.

Info

GoSkills (The Sector Skills Council for Passenger Transport) 0121 635 5520 www.goskills.org	Driving Instructors' Association (DIA) 020 8665 5151 www.driving.org

Large goods vehicle driver

This work ranges from driving conventional flat-bodied lorries that can carry a variety of loads to driving lorries designed for one purpose, such as car and animal transporters and milk tankers. Drivers often take a load from A to B and then carry one back from B to A in the UK or across Europe. As well as driving, lorry drivers may have to help with the loading and unloading of goods. Drivers of potentially dangerous products must know how to handle them safely and certification is required.

Entry, qualifications and training

To drive a large goods vehicle you must be aged at least 18, have good eyesight, pass a medical and have good general standards in maths and English. You may not need formal qualifications, but some employers may prefer GSCE maths and English.

There are two ways to get your large goods vehicle (LGV) licence. If you are already working for a transport operator, it might train you. If you are not employed by an operator, you could fund yourself through a driver training school before looking for work.

The LGV licence is divided into two categories: Category C1 allows you to drive rigid vehicles up to 7.5 tonnes, while Category C allows you to drive rigid vehicles over 7.5 tonnes. You can then take a further test that allows you to drive vehicles with trailers (category C+E).

Courses take one to three weeks and cover driving skills, basic mechanics, and loading and securing loads. The test includes vehicle safety questions, specific manoeuvres such as reversing into a bay, 25 miles of road driving and a theory test based on the Highway Code and LGV regulations. See the Business Link website for a list of approved LGV training providers.

Personal attributes

You must be a good driver with a thorough understanding of road safety, and the patience to tolerate long drives and heavy traffic. You must be happy spending many hours on your own, but also be able to work with warehouse employees and customers and remain pleasant and friendly.

Earnings

When you qualify you are likely to earn between £13,000 and £15,000. Experienced drivers earn £18,000 to £21,000. Drivers of fuel and chemical tankers can earn up to £30,000. There are sometimes opportunities to earn more through overtime.

Info

Road Haulage Association
01733 261131
www.rhaonline.co.uk/courses

Skills for Logistics
01908 313360
www.skillsforlogistics.org

Freight Transport Association (FTA)
0871 711 2222
www.fta.co.uk

Light goods or delivery van driver

Delivery van drivers deliver all kinds of goods, from supermarket shopping orders to parcels or fresh flowers. You may also be driving valuables such as cash from banks or other premises. The work is not just about driving. Delivery van drivers normally load or help load up the van, plan the most efficient route for deliveries, take the goods from the van to the customers and get customers' signatures for receipt of goods. They may also be collecting parcels from customers to take to some central point. Compared to a large goods vehicle driver you are usually working in a smaller geographical area, say the delivery range of a supermarket or a flower shop. This is not always the case: some parcel delivery companies operate across large distances and across many regions.

Entry, qualifications and training

You don't need formal qualifications for this work, though if you join via an apprenticeship your employer may require you to have three or four GCSEs grades A–C. In all cases you need a reasonable standard of maths and English, good eyesight and a clean driving licence. Depending on the size and type of vehicle you are driving you may need an additional licence. In all cases you will need to obtain a Certificate of Professional Competence (CPC). You can find more information about this and licences on the directgov motoring website. Training usually starts with an introductory course about relevant paperwork, local routes, etc. Some employers may then put you through your CPC. If you wish to drive vehicles carrying valuables, you will have to undertake additional training such as defensive driving.

Personal attributes

You need to enjoy and be good at driving. You should be physically fit and not mind bad weather. You need good communication skills and to be friendly and pleasant to customers. You must be able to balance the need to work quickly and efficiently with the necessity of being a calm and safe driver.

Earnings

Drivers earn between £12,500 and £20,000 depending on geographical location and the kind of company you work for. Pay is higher if you are driving valuables. Some employers pay bonuses for doing a certain number of deliveries, per day, week, etc.

Info

Skills for Logistics
01908 313360
www.skillsforlogistics.org

Security Industry Authority
(for driving/delivering valuables)
0844 892 1025
www.sia.homeoffice.gov.uk

Directgov
www.direct.gov.uk/en/motoring

Passenger transport

(see also Engineering, Railway Work and Logistics)

As well as drivers, there are many other jobs involved in passenger transport, including customer services, engineering and maintenance, information technology, logistics and marketing.

Bus/coach driver

Bus and coach drivers transport passengers either on local or long journeys. Bus drivers work mainly on shorter routes in particular towns or cities, or between a small number of these. Their work involves taking fares, checking passes, giving information about timetables and assisting passengers who may have difficulties, such as a disability or bulky luggage. Coach drivers tend to take people on longer journeys, say between cities or even countries. They may also take people on tours to see sites of special interest or to view impressive scenery. While their work is similar to that of bus drivers, they may also have to load luggage, give information about the sites or countryside through which they are driving and check that all passengers who should be on board are on the coach. Some bus and coach drivers may also be involved in community transport, driving school buses for example.

Entry, qualifications and training

Your essential qualification for this work is a Passenger Carrying Vehicle (PCV) licence. To drive a bus or a coach you must be aged 21, or 18 to drive a minibus. Many bus and coach companies will take you on and train you to gain your PCV, so long as you already have a full, clean EU driving licence. You can train independently through a driving school; you need to check with local driving schools whether they offer this training option. A recent EU Directive requires PCV drivers to obtain a Certificate of Professional Competence (CPC). You can get this through periodic short training courses and your employer company should be able to help with this. The Transport Office website carries more details about this. Some employers will give you the opportunity to train to NVQ level 2 in Passenger Transport.

Companies set their own entry standards, but many will expect you to have three or four GCSEs and you will have to meet their medical requirements.

Personal attributes

Safety awareness is paramount. It is the responsibility of any driver to be ever conscious of the safety of his or her passengers. You need to be calm and patient in congested traffic, and with difficult passengers. Your people skills are very important: you need to be polite, helpful and good at giving information. You may also need to be firm and assertive in some situations.

Earnings

New drivers earn between £12,000 and £15,000 – with experience drivers earn up to £19,000. Some coach drivers may also earn additional money in tips.

Info

GoSkills (The Sector Skills Council
for Passenger Transport)
0121 635 5520
www.goskills.org

Transport Office
www.transportoffice.gov.uk

Taxi driver

A 'taxi' is a traditional hackney carriage (like the black London taxis). The hackney carriage driver is allowed to 'ply for hire' – drive around the streets looking for passengers – and can be flagged down by a 'fare' (passenger). They may also operate from taxi ranks (known as 'standing for hire') in the streets. A private hire vehicle, on the other hand, has to be booked over the telephone or in person at the office from which it operates. Drivers therefore spend a good proportion of their time waiting around for passengers. Hours for both types of driver are generally long and unsocial (since there is a good deal of evening or night work, as well as weekend and public holiday work). Drivers may be owner-drivers or work for a company.

Entry, qualifications and training

Taxi drivers must be at least 21 years of age to be granted a licence, although in practice, because of insurance requirements, most are over 25. A valid Group A driving licence and relevant driving experience are also necessary. Hackney carriage drivers are legally bound to take the shortest or quickest route to a passenger's destination. Trainee drivers usually have to pass special tests, known as 'knowledge tests', to prove that they know their way about sufficiently well. These tests are generally oral, the most demanding being the Knowledge of London Test, which is required before drivers may operate in the capital. This usually takes some 18 months to two years to complete. Specialised training schools exist and there are also special training schemes for the disabled and for people who have been in the forces. In London, too, an additional driving test must be passed before a licence is granted.

Personal attributes

Driving in traffic demands a calm, unflappable personality, with lots of patience. Drivers also need to have a good memory. In addition, a taxi driver must be 'of good character', as a licence will not be granted to anyone who has committed certain offences.

Earnings

Almost all taxi drivers are self-employed and have to pay tax and National Insurance out of their earnings. Owner-drivers generally earn more than drivers employed by a company (who are often on a fixed rate), although they must also finance the repairs and servicing costs incurred by their own vehicles. Average earnings are around £14,000.

Info

GoSkills(The Sector Skills Council
for Passenger Transport)
0121 635 5520
www.goskills.org

National Private Hire Association
0161 280 2800
www.phtm.co.uk

Transport Office
www.transportoffice.gov.uk

ECOLOGIST

Ecology draws on a combination of biological science, environmental science and geography. Ecologists work in and study ecosystems (whole environments and the living organisms within them). These organisms include people, animals, plants, birds and insects of every kind. An ecologist studies how these different organisms interact and what external influences might help to either maintain the balance or cause the destabilisation of the whole system. Many ecologists study one particular group or organism, eg amphibians – some work on particular types of project, eg restoring a former industrial landscape to a wildlife conservation area. Ecologists look at the impact of proposed developments such as housing, quarrying, fishing or agriculture on the area proposed for such a development. Day-to-day work could include carrying out field studies, testing samples in the laboratory, organising school or other educational visits to wildlife conservation areas, or presenting results of research to planning committees, businesses and local community groups. Ecologists work for all of those bodies concerned with the natural environment, both statutory and non-statutory organisations.

Entry, qualifications and training

Ecologists are normally graduates or postgraduates in subjects including ecology, biology, botany, zoology and environmental science. The British Ecological Society website lists undergraduate courses. The Institute of Ecology and Environmental Management offers training courses at student and professional level. Much of the training is on the job. Work associated with the environment is always popular, so doing some voluntary work either before or during your university studies could strengthen your application for paid work.

Personal attributes

A passion for what you do is essential. The mix of skills you need depends a lot on your particular role. You may have to be very patient and happy working on your own if you are out collecting samples. If you are presenting a paper on a planning issue you will need to be a confident communicator. You often need to be able to work as part of a team and you must have a thorough and methodical approach to much of your work.

Earnings

Ecologists earn £20,000 to £25,000. Senior project managers and ecological consultants can earn £35,000 to £45,000.

Info

Institute of Ecology and
Environmental Management
01962 868626
www.ieem.net

Society for the Environment
0845 337 2951
www.socenv.org.uk

Field Studies Society
0845 3454071
www.field-studies-council.org

British Ecological Society
0207 685 2500
www.britishecologicalsociety.org

ECONOMIST

Economists work for central and local government, regional development bodies, higher education institutions, banks, insurance companies, trade unions and international organisations. They apply economic theory and knowledge and give advice on a whole range of topics related to the economy and finance. They study statistical data and trends to try to interpret and predict how the economy will perform. Their work may cover interest rates, taxation, employment policies, trends in consumer behaviour, what we buy and what we spend. Economists devise methods for sampling data, determine how to analyse data and how to translate them into information that can be used to inform policy decisions, solve problems or plan strategies.

Entry, qualifications and training

Economics is a graduate profession. You need a degree either in economics or in economics in combination with business, finance or law. In these cases the majority of your modules should still be in economics, and must cover micro and macro economics. You need a 2.1 or better and many employers look for high A level grades too. If you have a degree in another subject you may get into economics, but only by completing a postgraduate course in economics. Competition for posts is fierce and you can improve your chances by joining your student industrial society or something similar to demonstrate your interest in business and economics. The Civil Service runs an annual recruitment scheme for graduate economists. Most training is on the job, where you might be sent on several short courses as well as being supervised and guided by senior staff.

Personal attributes

Economists need excellent written and spoken communication skills, and to be good at translating technical and mathematical concepts into everyday language. They need good research skills, and to be able to analyse and interpret a wide variety of data. They need good judgement and must be able to work with great accuracy. They have to be able to work under pressure and manage their own workloads effectively. IT skills are also important.

Earnings

New entrants to the profession earn between £28,000 and £35,000. After three to five years' experience salaries rise to between £40,000 and £50,000. Many salary packages include other benefits such as private health insurance.

Info

Government Economic Service (GES)
020 7270 4835
www.ges.gov.uk/

Royal Statistical Society (RSS)
020 7638 8998
www.rss.org.uk

Society of Business Economists
01264 737552
www.sbe.co.uk

ELECTRICIAN

The distribution of electricity to every home and business and the installation, maintenance and repair of every kind of electrical equipment are the daily work of electricians and electricity distribution workers. There are many types of work, including domestic wiring, work on roads and railways, on lifts, laboratory equipment or individual domestic appliances. There is also a growing area of work concerned with installing solar panels, photo voltaic cells and other sustainable technologies.

Auto electrician

(see Motor Industry)

Electricity distribution worker

We probably only think about electricity distribution work when we suffer a power cut. To be of any use to any of us, electricity must be transmitted from power stations to its many destinations. It is electricity distribution workers who look after these electrical networks that supply electricity to every home, commercial property or installation of any kind. It is their job to help maintain and sustain a safe and constant supply of electricity. Distribution workers usually specialise in one of three areas. These are overhead work, which involves building and maintaining the overhead power lines that we can all see. Secondly, you could be a cable joiner, fixing and joining underground cables and also connecting domestic and commercial customers to the electricity supply. Thirdly, you could work to fit, repair and maintain the equipment at electricity substations. Day-to-day tasks could include keeping equipment in good working order, installing and dismantling equipment such as transmission cables, assembling or removing components, finding and diagnosing faults and inspecting and testing equipment.

Entry, qualifications and training

You don't always need formal qualifications to get into this work, though many employers offering training do ask for a good general education and may require GCSEs grades A to C in English, maths and a technical subject. You might get into this via an apprenticeship and employers offering apprenticeships in this work set their own entry requirements. The apprenticeship is likely to lead to relevant NVQ-level qualifications and which of these you work towards will depend on which area of transmission work you are training to work in. If you have other relevant experience in construction trades you may be able to get into this work.

Personal attributes

You must have good manual dexterity, good eyesight and perfect colour vision. You need to be practical and happy to work in uncomfortable positions, up on a pylon or down a hole for example. You have to be able to work as part of a team and your observation of health and safety matters is truly essential.

Earnings

Apprentices earn £12,000 to £15,000 but experienced workers can earn £25,000 to £45,000.

Info

Energy & Utility Skills
0845 077 9922
www.euskills.co.uk

Electrician

An electrician might rewire your house, install the complex wiring for a hospital operating theatre, repair the cables that keep traffic lights working, or set up the lighting system in a theatre. He or she might also repair faulty electrical equipment, from a domestic storage heater to the systems that keep the air conditioning running in a large building. Work on domestic wiring could include fitting wiring to sockets or light switches, fitting fuse boxes and circuit breakers and testing all the wiring you have just installed to ensure that it is safe. If you are rewiring, rather than working on a new development, you would also need to discuss with customers where they would like sockets and light fittings to go. On commercial properties you may be laying cables that support computer networks and connecting computers and other equipment to power points. You could also be installing fire alarms and other security systems, testing systems and repairing reported faults.

Entry, qualifications and training

To qualify as an electrician you must achieve an electrotechnical NVQ level 3. There are various routes to achieving this, but the most common, provided you are between the ages of 16 and 24, is to do a three- to four-year apprenticeship. These are mainly employer-based, but include some college work and practical and written assessments. Though it is not always essential, many employers require you to have GCSEs grades A–C in English, maths, technology and a science subject. If you are not eligible for an apprenticeship you can do college-based City & Guilds courses at GNVQ levels 2 and 3.

Electrotechnical NVQ level 3 offers several different pathways, including electrical installation, electrical maintenance, electrical instrumentation and associated equipment, installing highway electrical systems, electrical panel building and electrical machine rewind and repair. A great deal of training takes place on the job.

Personal attributes

You must have good practical and technical skills and be able to follow technical drawings and diagrams. You should be reasonably fit, and for some jobs you need to be able to cope with heights or working in confined spaces. You should have good colour vision. You need to be able to work on your own, or as part of a team, and you must have good communication skills and be able to talk to people without using a lot of technical jargon.

Earnings

At the start of an apprenticeship you will earn around £12,500, rising to £18,000 at the end of your training. Newly qualified electricians earn around £19,000 to £24,000, but experienced electricians can earn much more than this. Many electricians are self-employed, which means earnings are related to how much work they can get and what they charge.

Info

Engineering Council UK (ECUK)
020 3206 0500
www.engc.org.uk

SEMTA (The Sector Skills Council
for Science, Engineering and
Manufacturing Technologies)
01923 238 441
www.semta.org.uk

Women into Science and
Engineering
www.wisecampaign.org.uk

ENGINEERING

The Engineering Council's definition of engineering is 'the application of science and maths to the solving of practical problems and the making of useful things'. Engineering covers many occupations and is integral to the success of every other industry. Employment opportunities exist in industry, academia, local authorities and the armed forces.

Acoustics engineering

Acoustics engineering involves the measurement, management regulation and control of the noises and vibrations that surround us in our homes, workplaces and environments such as restaurants, shopping centres, railway stations or dance venues. Work could involve carrying out noise assessments on buildings to make sure sound insulation methods meet Building Regulations, conducting environmental noise surveys, or examining how changes to building design can affect noise levels. The work often requires computer modelling as well as actual monitoring. Some acoustics engineers work in the recording industry, contributing to the design of studios. Other highly specialised areas include designing medical equipment such as ultrasound scanners which use sound to diagnose or treat medical conditions.

Aerospace engineering

Aerospace engineering is one of the most technically advanced areas of engineering. It is exciting and rewarding, involving leading-edge technology, variety, skill and innovation. This diversity means that career opportunities can be found across the entire global aerospace spectrum, from research, design, manufacture and maintenance, through to operation and support. However, the recent downturn in the aerospace industry significantly reduced opportunities, and it may be some time before the good employment prospects once offered by the industry return.

Agricultural engineering

The main areas in which agricultural engineers are involved are: design and production of agricultural machinery; planning, design and construction of farm buildings and associated equipment; field engineering – irrigation, drainage and land resource planning; and service engineering, involving the sale, servicing, repairing and installation of farm machinery. They are also involved in forestry engineering, amenity and ecological engineering, and precision farming using satellite positioning systems.

Automotive engineering

In the vehicle manufacturing industry engineers may be employed in design, development, production, operations management and maintenance activities. In motor vehicle servicing, the work tends to be at craft level, with some engineers using their technical base to develop into motor vehicle engineering management. Currently, NVQs in Vehicle Mechanical and Electronic Systems Maintenance and Repair are offered at levels 2 and 3.

Biochemical engineering

This involves the application of engineering principles to industrial processing. Biochemical engineers are involved in the research, design, construction and operation of plant used for the processing of biochemicals such as those used in effluent treatment, fermentation and the production of drugs.

Biomedical engineering

Biomedical engineers, also referred to as clinical engineers or bioengineers, work on the research, design, development and maintenance of technology and equipment used to meet patients' clinical needs both during and after medical treatment. They work in the fields of instrumentation, rehabilitation and biomaterials. They build and test prototypes, run clinical trials and evaluate the performance of equipment and materials. Examples of their work include new heart valves, replacement joints and new types of hearing device.

Building services engineering

(see also Construction)

Building services engineers are concerned with heating and ventilation, refrigeration, lighting, air conditioning, electrical services, internal water supply, waste disposal, fire protection, lifts, and acoustic and communication systems. The work involves the planning and design of engineering systems, and supervision of contracts, working in collaboration with architects, surveyors, structural engineers and builders.

Chemical engineering

Chemical engineers are concerned with large-scale processes, not always in the chemical industry. The term 'process engineering' is often used to describe their work, as they are more interested in the physical factors involved in a process than in the chemical reaction itself. Chemical engineers are employed in the oil, chemical, pharmaceutical, food, brewing and process industries.

Civil engineering

Civil engineering plays an important part in everyday life. Civil engineers devise, plan and manage development in vital areas – the design and construction of state-of-the-art roads, dams, harbours, railroad systems, bridges and airports. Civil engineers also play an important part in the provision of electricity and water supplies, and in managing traffic and transport. Every project is unique and involves the expertise of a team of people who plan, design, build and maintain these essential assets.

Communications engineering

Communications engineers work for large telecommunications organisations, government departments and small companies specialising in communications technology. They are responsible for overseeing the developing, installation and day-to-day management of communications projects of many kinds. Their work involves discussing project briefs, sourcing appropriate materials and products, conducting site surveys, managing staff and finding solutions to technical problems. Communications engineers are usually graduates with a telecommunications engineering, physics or computer science degree.

Control engineering

This is a multidisciplinary field involving electrical and electronic engineering, maths, computer science, instrument engineering and mechanical engineering. Specialisation in control engineering often follows the study of another branch of engineering.

Electrical and electronic engineering

The technology of electrical engineering deals with heavy current, while electronic engineering deals with light current. Applications of heavy current include electrical machinery of all kinds, generating stations and distribution systems. Light current is used for such products as transistors, microprocessors and telecommunications equipment. The two fields are often interdependent and training is closely related. Electronics is a rapidly developing field and offers excellent opportunities, as do the allied disciplines of computer and software engineering.

Energy engineering

This branch of engineering is concerned with the use, production, distribution, conversion and conservation of energy, with due regard to the environment. Energy engineers are employed across the whole spectrum of industry, as energy management and control are essential elements in containing costs, reducing pollution and addressing environmental concerns. The majority of openings are in major fuel industries (including renewables), consultancy and research.

Environmental engineering

Environmental engineering is a developing and increasingly important profession. Environmental engineers work for local authorities and private companies, large and small. Their work is concerned with assessing the impact of human activity on the environment. The three main areas in which they work are waste management, land reclamation and pollution control. Their work involves visiting many different kinds of site, liaising with surveyors, engineers, scientists and other organisations. They may use computer models to simulate the environmental impact of particular activities.

Fire engineering

This involves the application of engineering principles to the assessment, prevention and inhibition of fire risk within buildings, manufacturing plant and industrial processes. The various stages include the use of mathematical principles in the assessment of fire risk, the application of scientific principles to fire safety practices and the use of management techniques for the inhibition and prevention of the onset and spread of fire.

Fire engineers are employed in the fire services, architectural and building design, project management, insurance assessment, industrial processing, the aircraft industry, environmental health and any area of safety where the possibility of fire or combustion represents a hazard.

Gas engineering

Gas engineering involves specialisation in the use, transmission and distribution of gas (natural or manufactured), or in the production of gas, or in related fields such as exploration.

Geotechnical engineering

Geotechnical engineers often have a background in civil engineering or geological science. Applying the science of rock and earth mechanics, they work out how the ground will behave if tunnels are bored into it or buildings and other structures built into and onto it. They also work on civil engineering and construction projects to help ensure that the environment of the ground around the project is preserved. They can tell where flooding or erosion, for example, might cause problems.

Instrument engineering

(see also Control Engineering)

Instrument engineers are concerned with the measurement of pressure, temperature and so on, designing, installing and maintaining instrument systems.

Manufacturing systems engineering

This branch of engineering deals with the skills required to operate new manufacturing systems: computerised production, computer-controlled assembly, robotic systems and flexible manufacturing systems.

Marine engineering

This discipline is related to offshore engineering under the general title of 'maritime engineering', which involves engineering systems and equipment in a maritime environment. Both marine and offshore engineers are involved in design, research, consultancy, survey, manufacture, installation and maintenance activities, the former with vessels of all sizes and types, the latter with offshore platforms, sub-sea installations and under-sea vehicles. Employment opportunities exist within firms offering design and research activities, engine- and shipbuilding firms, classification societies, government bodies, the Merchant Navy and the Royal Navy.

Materials engineering

Materials engineers work in a diverse range of industries, working on the research and development of new materials to advance technologies; innovating and modifying materials to improve the performance and efficiency of existing products; and investigating the failure of products or structures. They work with all types of materials, including plastics, metals, alloys, glass, ceramics and composites. Some of the industries they work in include telecommunications, power generation, sport and medicine. Materials engineers have developed materials used in modern tennis rackets, replacement hip joints and internet broadband connections; these are just a few examples. Most materials engineers have a degree in materials engineering or materials science, or a degree in applied physics or chemistry.

Mechanical engineering

Mechanical engineering is the biggest branch of the engineering industry. It involves the skills of designing, developing, producing, installing and operating machinery and mechanical products of many types. The field is enormous in scope, and most engineers specialise in a particular area. Other branches of engineering, such as electrical and civil engineering, overlap with mechanical engineering to a certain extent.

Mechanical engineers are employed in almost every sector of industry. Some of the largest areas of employment are machine tools, railway engineering, aerospace and the automobile industry.

Mining engineering

In Britain, most mining engineers are employed by companies in mining areas, working for consultants who monitor mining activity and subsidence. They need some knowledge of related disciplines such as mechanical, electrical and civil engineering, and to understand geology and surveying in relation to mining. The majority of openings in metal mining are overseas.

Nuclear engineering

Nuclear engineering involves the applications of nuclear energy and associated research and development. The work of designing and constructing nuclear reactors and the management of nuclear power stations through waste management and storage and decommissioning of plant is carried out by nuclear engineers.

Offshore engineering

Offshore engineers are concerned with the construction and operation of drilling platforms and wellheads, and other engineering issues related to the exploitation of offshore oil and gas.

Operations engineering

Operations engineers are concerned with specifying, evaluation, acquisition, commissioning, inspection, maintenance, asset management and disposal of facilities, systems, vehicles and equipment. Career opportunities exist at craft and technician level in the servicing and maintenance of a wide variety of industries, of which transport is the largest. Chartered and incorporated engineers may be engaged in asset or fleet engineering management, requiring multidisciplinary engineering, commercial and legal knowledge and encompassing health and safety, reliability, environmental and economic factors, or in specialised inspection roles. Many technicians build on their practical skills by further career development to aspire to these more senior positions.

Petroleum engineering

Petroleum engineers are concerned with exploration and drilling for oil. They obtain and interpret information – for example, the quantities and quality of oil discovered.

Process engineering

Process engineers work in large and small companies manufacturing all kind of products. They develop efficient industrial processes to make the huge range of products on which modern society depends, including food and drink, fuel, artificial fibres, pharmaceuticals, chemicals, plastics, cosmetics, cleaning products, energy and clean water. Their role can be similar to that of chemical engineers.

Production engineering

Production engineers develop and improve manufacturing techniques. They are responsible for designing production systems to ensure that products can be manufactured to the specified design, in the right quantities, at the right price and by the required date. Their work overlaps with production management.

Recording engineering

(see Broadcasting)

Structural engineering

Structural engineers are concerned with the design and maintenance of the framework and fabric of large structures such as bridges, motorways and office blocks.

Transport engineering

Transport (or traffic) engineers are concerned with managing the best use of roads and related facilities, and work mainly with road traffic. Transport planners, who are not necessarily engineers, are concerned with the provision of all types of transport. The current priority is to provide an integrated transport system.

Water engineering

Water engineers mostly work for water companies and river authorities, ensuring the supply of fresh water, and dealing with the reclamation and disposal of water which has been used.

Entry, qualifications and training

Since engineering includes many careers, this outline of qualifications and training is a general guide. The various engineering bodies and the relevant sector skills councils provide more detailed information.

It is difficult to move from one engineering profession to another. You need to decide at an early stage which type of engineering you wish to pursue.

Graduate engineers

Most professional engineers are graduates who have completed a degree in just one type of engineering. There are degrees available in all the types of engineering described in the previous paragraphs. For most degrees in technical subjects you will need three A levels, although grade and subject requirements vary between institutions and subjects. Physics, maths, chemistry and other science subjects are often required. Many engineering degree courses offer the option to spend a year out in industry. Once you have completed your degree and are in employment, you are likely to work towards becoming a chartered engineer, working towards professional examinations through the relevant engineering organisation, eg the Institute of Mechanical engineers.

Professional engineers are likely to have responsibility for research and development, problem solving, managing work teams and projects and bringing creative ideas to the whole engineering process.

Technician engineers

For many types of engineering, if you do not wish to study for a degree you may be able to get in at technician level. This usually means you should have five GCSEs grades A—C, including English, maths and a science subject. Your employer may give you the opportunity to train to NVQ level 3 in a relevant subject. You can also consider college courses offering City & Guilds or BTEC qualifications. Cogent, SEMTA and Summit Skills websites offer plenty of information. You may also be able to train through an apprenticeship. Check your local Jobcentre Plus and Connexions careers office for details of what is on offer locally.

Every engineering production line, construction site, processing plant or scientific laboratory will employ a number of staff to handle the day-to-day processes, quality testing, looking after equipment, and doing all the routine work to keep systems running. For these jobs, entry requirements vary greatly, but many will not require formal academic qualifications.

Personal attributes

Professional engineers, in whatever discipline they choose to specialise, require excellent problem-solving, scientific and technical skills. They need to be imaginative in finding solutions to difficulties and they need to have a rigorous and thorough approach to research and testing. They also need good teamwork skills and good project management and human resource management skills. Working at technician or more junior levels, you may need good numeracy skills and good manual dexterity.

Earnings

Salaries for graduate entrants vary across the many fields of engineering. Starting salaries around £21,000 to £26,000 cover most branches and these rise to £27,000 to £50,000 with experience. Some engineers become senior project managers with higher salary potential. Technician engineers earn between £16,000 and £28,000.

Info

Institute of Engineering and Technology
020 7240 1871
www.theiet.org

Engineering Council
020 7240 7891
www.engc.org.uk

Engineering Training Council in Northern Ireland
028 9032 9878
www.etcni.org.uk

The Institute of the Motor Industry
01992 551 521
www.motor.org.uk

Cogent (The Sector Skills Council for Science Based Industries)
01224 787800
www.cogent-ssc.com

SEMTA (The Sector Skills Council for Science, Engineering and Manufacturing Technologies)
0808 100 3682
www.semta.org.uk

Summit Skills
01908 303969
www.summitskills.org.uk

Women into Science and Engineering
020 7227 8421
www.wisecampaign.org.uk

Women's Engineering Society (WES)
01438 765506
www.wes.org.uk

Institute of Agricultural Engineers
01525 861096
www.iagre.org

Institution of Chemical Engineers
(IChemE)
01788 578214
www.icheme.org

Chartered Institute of Building
Services Engineers
020 8675 5211
www.cibse.org

Institution of Civil Engineers (ICE)
020 7222 7722
www.ice.org.uk

British Computer Society (BCS)
(relevant for electronics engineers)
0845 300 4417
www.bcs.org

Energy Institute
www.energyinst.org

Institute of Materials, Minerals and
Mining (IOM3)
020 7451 7300
www.iom3.org

Institution of Mechanical Engineers
(IMechE)
020 7222 7899
www.imeche.org

Institute of Nanotechnology
01786 447520
www.nano.org.uk

Nuclear Institute
www.nuclearinst.com

Institute of Physics
020 7470 4800
www.iop.org

Institute of Physics and Engineering
in Medicine
01904 610821
www.ipem.ac.uk

NHS Careers (relevant for materials
engineers and biomedical
engineers)
0845 606 0655
www.nhscareers.nhs.uk

Royal Aeronautical Society
020 7670 4300
www.aerosociety.com

ENVIRONMENT

Occupations in the environment sector are concerned with the protection and preservation of the natural world in which we live.

ENVIRONMENTAL CONSERVATION

Environmental conservation covers several activities from recycling waste to habitat management. It does not just involve green issues but is about making the best use of scientific knowledge to produce solutions for a sustainable environment. Conservation includes the protection of rural and urban landscapes, plants and animals and countryside recreation. This includes protection and management of rivers, coastal zones and waterways, together with their fisheries and fish stocks.

There are opportunities in a range of organisations from government departments to the voluntary sector. Competition for jobs is high but there can be a lack of applicants with experience, which often needs to be gained through voluntary work. A large proportion of those working for conservation organisations do so on a voluntary, casual or part-time basis. It is estimated that 47,000 paid employees work in this sector alongside 200,000 volunteers. The majority of those in permanent jobs have higher education qualifications. Many of the permanent jobs are with government agencies and include the following.

Countryside conservation officer

Countryside conservation officers are involved in the protection and appropriate development of all types of countryside and rural environment. Their work is varied. They may be involved in implementing schemes to protect or improve the landscape, or they may advise on the environmental impact of proposed developments. They may put into practice schemes to protect particular plants, birds, insects and animals, or in creating new habitats for these plants and animals. The work may also involve educating the public about how to use the countryside appropriately and negotiating with other land users, or preparing reports for planning committees and other formal bodies. Conservation officers are employed by local government, government agencies, charities such as the National Trust and the Woodland Trust, and environmental consultancies.

Entry, qualifications and training

For most jobs you need a degree, preferably in a subject such as ecology, geography or environmental conservation. This is a very competitive field, so you also need some good practical skills. The majority of people who get full-time paid work of this sort have done some voluntary work first for one of the countryside organisations. Check the Info panel for the major countryside organisations in the UK. Once you are employed there are plenty of courses you can do to increase your knowledge and skills in specific areas, eg woodland, birdlife, or coastal erosion.

Personal attributes

These vary according to your particular responsibilities and tasks, but a love of the countryside is always essential. Interest in geography, botany and zoology may be important. You should be good at keeping records and measuring scientific data of various kinds. You should be prepared to work outside, but also be able to communicate effectively at meetings or in an educative role.

Earnings

New entrants earn £15,000 to £19,000. At management level salaries can be £20,000 to £30,000. Many of the employing organisations are charities operating on tight budgets. Salaries can be higher working for consultancies.

Countryside ranger/warden

Countryside rangers are responsible for the day-to-day management of areas of countryside such as common land, heaths, woodland or wetlands. They undertake practical work such as tree planting or carrying out field surveys to determine how prevalent particular species are in a specified area. Rangers patrol sites, making sure that footpaths, bridges and gates are in good order. They can also provide advice and help to members of the public, keeping an overall eye on safety. They may also have responsibility for managing budgets and for organising exhibitions, or conducting educational tours of sites.

Entry, qualifications and training

You do not need any formal qualifications to do this work, but you will almost certainly have to do some voluntary work. Some conservation organisations offer a range of short training courses to volunteers in subjects such as species identification, hedge layering, coppicing and risk management. You can also do City & Guilds courses in environmental conservation, for which you do not need any formal qualifications.

Personal attributes

As well as a passion for the countryside you should be very practical and confident in using tools and equipment. You need good communication skills and for many posts you also have to have reasonable office and IT skills.

Earnings

Starting salaries vary according to the type of organisation in which you are employed. Local authority salaries for rangers are around £17,000; other countryside management organisations may pay up to £20,000. Voluntary organisations may pay around £15,000.

Info

Lantra
0845 707 8007
www.lantra.co.uk

Natural England
0845 600 3078
www.naturalengland.org.uk

National Trust
www.nationaltrust.org.uk

Institute of Ecology and
Environmental Management (IEEM)
01962 868626
www.ieem.net

British Trust for Conservation
Volunteers (BTCV)
01302 388883
www.btcv.org.uk

Recycling officer

Recycling officers work mainly for local councils, planning and developing policies to help local people recycle as much waste material as they can. Recycling officers organise schemes to recycle glass, paper, cans and plastic. They may also organise and manage schemes to encourage residents to make compost, either on their own properties or at central points set up by the local authority. Reducing waste is an important and very topical area of local authority work, so the significance of this area of work has increased. Recycling officers are also involved in organising publicity about recycling. They often attend meetings of both formal bodies such as parish councils and informal societies such as gardening clubs.

Entry, qualifications and training

While there are no formal academic entry requirements, most successful applicants have either a degree or a Higher National Diploma. The most useful subjects include environmental science, earth studies, geography, or any science subject. If you don't have a degree, then plenty of useful paid or voluntary work on recycling projects strengthens your application. If you can offer relevant NVQs at levels 2 and 3, this also helps. NVQs at levels 2 and 3 are available in Recycling Operations, Waste Management and Environmental Conservation. Much of the training is on the job. You are likely to need to do frequent short updating courses, because technology and knowledge are changing rapidly in this field.

Personal attributes

You must be a good communicator, able to present written information and oral reports. You should be well organised, good at prioritising, and you need reasonable IT skills. Being able to manage teams of people is very important.

Earnings

New entrants earn between £20,000 and £25,000. Salaries may be lower if you work for a community organisation. With experience and considerable management responsibility salaries rise to £30,000 to £40,000.

Info

Energy & Utility Skills
0845 077 9922
www.euskills.co.uk

Chartered Institution of Wastes Management
01604 620426
www.ciwm.co.uk

Waste Management Industry Training & Advisory Board (WAMITAB)
01604 231950
www.wamitab.org.uk

Waste and Resources Action Programme (WRAP)
0808 100 2040
www.wrap.org.uk

Environmental health officer/practitioner

Environmental health officers (EHOs) are enforcers, educators and advisers, and are employed in both the public and private sectors. Their responsibilities include pollution control, including noise control, environmental protection, the inspection of food and food premises, health and safety in workplaces and in the leisure industry, and the control of housing standards, particularly in the private rented sector. Much of their time is spent out of the office, dealing with the public and visiting premises of all types.

Entry, qualifications and training

The usual route to becoming an environmental health officer/practitioner is through a degree in environmental health. You can either do a three-year degree, followed by a one-year work placement, or a four-year degree that includes a third-year work-based training placement. If you have a science degree, you can also enter the profession by doing a postgraduate course in environmental health. In all cases, your course should be accredited by the Chartered Institute of Environmental Health (CIEH) in England, Wales and Northern Ireland, or the Royal Environmental Health Institute of Scotland in Scotland. Alternatively, if you have an HNC, HND or Foundation degree in science, you may be able to enter directly into the second year of a degree. If you have A levels or an HND you may prefer to work as an environmental health technician for a local authority. From this point, with your employer's support, you can do the environmental health degree on a part-time basis while continuing to work in an environmental health department. As a trainee environmental health officer you have to keep a detailed portfolio of your work and also pass the professional qualifying exams of the CIEH.

Personal attributes

EHOs need a broad mix of skills. They have to be able to deal with complex legal and scientific information. They must be able to explain the law to members of the public or other non-lawyers. They should be diplomatic and calm, but at other times they will also have to be assertive and determined.

Earnings

Starting salaries are between £27,500 and £33,000. There is some weekend and late evening work involved and this may attract additional payments. At management level salaries are £35,000 to £60,000.

Info

Chartered Institute of Environmental Health (CIEH) 020 7928 6006 www.cieh.org	Food Standards Agency 020 7276 8000 www.food.gov.uk
Environment Agency (EA) 0870 8506 506 www.environment-agency.gov.uk	Royal Environmental Health Institute of Scotland 0131 225 5444 www.rehis.org

Pest control technician

Pest controllers control not only mice, rats, cockroaches and ants that may be damaging foodstuffs in a factory, hotel or private home, but also rabbits, moles, birds and foxes that attack farmers' crops. They work for local authorities and private firms. Service staff are employed to lay traps and set poison. There are also opportunities for graduates in research and management.

Entry, qualifications and training

Qualifications in pest control are usually preferred, although at assistant level full training is provided on the job, including day or block release to achieve a recognised qualification, such as British Pest Control Association courses. The British Pest Control Association and the Royal Society for the Promotion of Health have merged their basic pest control qualification – BPC Diploma Part 1 and RSPH Certificate in Pest Control. As part of this partnership, other BPCA examinations, including the advanced level certificate (BPC Diploma Part 2), the fumigation certification scheme and the Certificate for Surveyors – Pest Control (CSPC), are brought under the joint BPCA/RSPH umbrella.

Personal attributes

This is not a job for the squeamish and the work demands a mature outlook, an ability to get on with many kinds of people, to work in varying conditions and to work alone. The ability to drive is important.

Earnings

Pay is between £14,000 and £17,000. With experience and qualifications you can earn £25,000 to £28,000. Many pest control technicians set up their own small businesses.

Info

Asset Skills
08000 567160
www.assetskills.org

British Pest Control Association
(BPCA)
0870 609 2687
www.bpca.org.uk

National Pest Technicians
Association (NPTA)
01949 81133
www.npta.org.uk

Royal Society for Public Health
020 3177 1600
www.rsph.org.uk/

EVENTS ORGANISATION

Events organiser

'Events organiser' is a job title that covers many similar work roles. These jobs include conference or exhibition organiser and events, conference or exhibition manager or coordinator. What all these jobs have in common is that the events organiser/manager is involved at every stage of organisation, right through from the first planning meeting to being there at the event, to ensure that everything runs smoothly and successfully. Events include trade fairs, exhibitions, festivals, fundraising events, product launches, training events and social occasions. Events can be small and local, or large and international. They may last for one evening or as long as a week. What the different job titles denote is the specific types of event for which you are responsible. These might be exhibitions, conferences or social events such as parties or weddings.

The work involves meeting clients to discuss what they want from the event, agreeing budgets and researching and booking appropriate venues, catering and entertainment. The work also involves checking health and safety issues and logistical planning. The events organiser also attends the event itself to solve any problems that arise on the spot.

Entry, qualifications and training

People move into events organisations and management from a variety of backgrounds. You don't necessarily need any formal qualifications, as relevant experience and the right blend of skills are often more important. There are, however, a growing number of events management courses at degree, Foundation degree and HND level. The Association of Events Organisers website carries details of these courses. Other useful degree subjects include business, marketing, public relations and hospitality.

Having practical experience in organising events is really important. If you have worked in hospitality, organising conferences and banquets at hotels, for example, this gives you a real advantage. Organising social events on a voluntary basis can also be valuable.

Training is very much on the job, as you normally begin as an assistant to a more experienced organiser/manager. There is a range of relevant NVQs towards which your employer may want you to work. Professional organisations such as the Association of Exhibition Organisers (AEO) or the Association for Conferences and Events (ACE) offer training and networking opportunities.

Exhibition designer

Exhibition designers are responsible for designing the displays and stands that form part of all kinds of exhibition. They may be working on large public exhibitions, trade fairs, or small temporary exhibitions set up by a business or a charity. The work involves discussing briefs with clients and producing sketches of ideas. These might be drawn by hand or computer-generated. Designers also have to liaise with suppliers and technical staff to ensure that the finished display matches the agreed brief.

Entry, qualifications and training

Employers prefer you to have formal qualifications in display design. It is sometimes possible to acquire these while working as an assistant designer. The British Display Society (BDS) provides details of relevant certificate and diploma courses. It is also possible to get into this work with a degree in a design-related subject such as 3-D design or interior design. There are now a small number of degree courses in exhibition design being offered. Check with the BDS for details.

Personal attributes

You have to have really excellent organisational and communication skills to succeed in this work. You must be a good administrator, keeping clear records and tracking the progress of any event. You must be able to establish relationships with new people very quickly and be able to lead teams of people who may not have worked together before. You must be creative, imaginative and calm in the face of crises.

For exhibition design you need good practical, technical and creative skills, as well as all the people skills required for other aspects of events organising.

Earnings

New entrants to both events organisation and exhibition design earn between £19,000 and £26,000. Senior managers earn between £35,000 and £45,000; some employers pay staff bonuses if events are successful. Some organisers, especially those dealing with social events such as weddings and parties, are self-employed and charge a fee according to the scale of the work involved. Exhibition designers start on around £16,000. With a few years' experience this rises to £25,000 to £35,000.

Info

Chartered Institute of Marketing
(CIM)
01628 427500
www.cim.co.uk

People 1st
0870 060 2550
www.people1st.co.uk

Association of Exhibition
Organisers
01442 285810
www.aeo.org.uk

Association for Conferences
and Events (ACE)
01480 457595
www.aceinternational.org

Association of British Professional
Conference Organisers (ABPCO)
028 9038 7475
www.abpco.org.uk

FARMING

Farming is an essential and changing sector. Resulting from economies of scale, farms have become larger and tend to specialise in just one or two areas, arable (the growing of wheat and other food crops), beef, dairy, sheep, poultry, etc. Farming is also more in the public eye. People have opinions on genetically modified food, food hygiene, animal welfare and whether crops should be grown as alternatives to fossil fuel. Though farms have become larger, farmers and managers have had to think of ways to diversity, such as bringing in leisure activities or opening farm shops on their premises. These developments have meant that jobs and work opportunities in farming have changed. Those working in farming have had to develop high levels of skill in, for example, managing a large dairy herd to maximise production or driving extremely sophisticated combine harvesters. Farmers have had to become good business people, negotiating with large buyers such as supermarkets to try to obtain the best prices for their products.

Agricultural contractor

Agricultural contractors work in many farming operations, including harvesting, crop spraying, weeding, lambing and sheep shearing – in short, all those tasks where extra labour is needed for a particular task or a particular season.

Entry, qualifications and training

You don't normally need specific entry qualifications, but you do need experience of those aspects of agricultural operations in which you wish to take on contract work. There are several relevant courses available for anyone who wishes to gain qualifications. These include BTEC First Diplomas in Agriculture and BTEC National Diplomas in Agriculture, City & Guilds National Certificate in Agriculture, C&G Advanced National Certificate in Agriculture, NVQ levels 2 and 3 in Agricultural Crop Production, NVQ levels 2 and 3 in Mixed Farming, and NVQ levels 2 and 3 in Livestock Production.

For some tasks, such as operating chainsaws or using pesticides, you are legally required to be trained and competent. The National Proficiency Test Council (NPTC) awards certificates of competence for chainsaw use. The NPTC offers many short courses in ploughing, crop spraying and other agricultural skills.

Personal attributes

You must be a practical problem solver, confident in handling and maintaining machinery. You need to be quick at establishing good working relationships with farmers and other landowners. You also have to be able to supervise and motivate teams of employees.

Earnings

Pay is determined by your level of skill and the work you are doing. Some agricultural contractors are paid very little more than the minimum wage, but average earnings are between £14,000 and £22,000 a year. Overtime can often be earned, because there are very busy times of year – harvesting, crop spraying, etc – contrasted with some very quiet times.

Info

National Proficiency Tests Council
(NPTC)
024 7685 7300
www.nptc.org.uk

Lantra
0845 7078077
www.lantra.co.uk

Agricultural engineer

(see Engineering)

Agricultural surveyor

(see Surveying)

Farm manager

Farm managers are employed by the landowner and are responsible for all aspects of the day-to-day working of the farm. They must plan ahead, organise the staff and work schedules, decide which crops to plant or which animals to rear, and keep a check on buildings and machinery. In addition, they must deal with the office work and accounts.

Farm worker

Farm workers are employed by farmers, who may well be big businesses, and by landowners to carry out practical and manual tasks on farms. The work could involve working with livestock, with crops or with a combination of these two. Your work could involve milking cows, feeding and checking sheep, cattle, pigs and poultry. It could involve preparing the ground to plant crops, harvesting those crops, or maintaining farm machinery. You could also work repairing and maintaining farm buildings. Most farms in the UK are large, and each farm employs few workers; nevertheless, you are likely to become a specialist in particular work such as dairy cows, arable crops or crops for energy generation. Many farms have to diversify to generate income, so the farm on which you work may have a farm shop, horses kept at livery or a local pheasant or partridge shoot on the land. Your work may involve helping with any of these or similar enterprises.

Entry, qualifications and training

When recruiting farm managers, most employers look for candidates who have hands-on experience of farming, but most farm managers now will also have a degree in agriculture or a closely related subject. Farm workers don't necessarily need any formal qualifications, though it may be an advantage if you have GCSEs in maths, English and a technical subject. There are many full- and part-time college courses in all the specialist areas of farm work.

Personal attributes

At whatever level you are working you must have a commitment to farming and a willingness to work in all weathers at any time of the year and to put in some unsocial hours. Farm workers need good practical skills and must be able to work alone, unsupervised or as part of a team. If you look after livestock you need a highly responsible attitude. Farm managers must be well organised, with good numerate and communication skills. They also need to be imaginative and good at marketing. A great awareness of health and safety and potential risks is important at all levels in farming.

Earnings

New-entrant farm managers earn around £20,000 to £27,000. Managers with a lot of responsibility managing large farms can earn £30,000 to £50,000. Basic grade farm workers earn 2p above the hourly rate for the National Minimum Wage, but many are on higher grades. There may be opportunities to work overtime at certain times of year. Average salaries for farm workers are between £12,000 and £18,000 at the start of your career, £18,000 to £22,500 with experience.

Info

Lantra
0845 707 8007
www.lantra.co.uk

FASHION

(see also Clothing Industry)

While much clothing manufacture is now done overseas, fashion in all its aspects is still an important part of the UK economy. The fashion industry covers all aspects of clothing and accessories for men, women and children, and falls into three main sectors: *haute couture* houses, where original model garments are made for individual customers; wholesale *couture*, where trends set by the *haute couture* houses are closely followed, and limited numbers of model garments in stock sizes are made for retail; and wholesale manufacture, which occupies the largest sector of the fashion industry. Here, the latest trends are adapted to styles that are attractive to the main market, and mass-produced at acceptable prices.

Designer

Fashion designers design garments for all levels of the fashion market. The majority work for high street stores, or their suppliers, designing garments that will be manufactured in their thousands. Some fashion designers work for more upmarket labels, designing products that are still for a mass market but which are produced in much smaller quantities. A few designers work in *haute couture*, designing individual one-off items. Fashion designers may specialise in particular types of clothing such as baby wear, evening wear, hats or sportswear. Some choose to specialise in designing accessories or footwear. Most fashion designers start by designing garments to someone else's brief, but a small number will design original items – this is probably the ultimate goal of most people who go into fashion design. Fashion designers start by making a sketch, often using computer-aided design (CAD), and work from this to the finished product. The work also involves liaising closely with buyers, sales managers and marketing professionals.

Entry, qualifications and training

It is increasingly difficult to get into this work without a degree, and preferably a relevant one in fashion, clothing technology, knitwear, embroidery, graphic design or art and design. If you have a degree in another subject, or you have not gone on to higher education, you really need to have worked in the fashion industry and have an impressive portfolio of your design ideas to show to a prospective employer. Training is rarely formal and is very much a case of 'pick it up as you go along'. Sometimes there are opportunities to undertake short training courses in new techniques or associated with new technology.

Personal attributes

Of course, a passionate interest in clothing, colour, design and fabrics is essential. In addition you need to be good at analysing trends and almost being able to second guess what will happen next. You have to be able to work as part of a team, cope under pressure, solve problems and have good drawing skills, both freehand and with computer software. You need to have a lot of self-confidence, and be good at promoting your ideas to others.

Earnings

In London, new entrants earn between £17,000 and £23,500. Outside London, it will be much less, but there are only a few opportunities outside London. Good junior designers who have worked for three or four years in design can earn £30,000 to £42,000. Freelance designers charge per item or per collection and rates vary widely, but some can earn more than £60,000 to £100,000.

Info

Skillset Careers
08080 300 900 (England and
Northern Ireland)
0808 100 8094 (Scotland)
0800 121 815 (Wales)
www.skillset.org/careers

Textile Institute
0161 237 1188
www.textileinstitute.org

Dressmaker

Opportunities for dressmakers occur in *couture* houses that make specially designed costumes for a particular collection or customer, in wholesale fashion houses making mass-produced garments, and in theatres both making and adapting costumes. Dressmakers may also be employed by large stores to carry out alterations, or they may be self-employed, making clothes either from home or from a workshop. Teachers of dressmaking are employed in schools, colleges and by adult education centres.

Entry, qualifications and training

No formal qualifications are necessary, but City & Guilds qualifications and NVQs are available. Some degrees and HNDs in clothing design or fashion have a dressmaking option.

Personal attributes

Dressmakers need to combine artistic and practical skills with an ability to follow instructions and to recognise problems as they arise and make the necessary adaptations. They may have to deal with temperamental designers and their customers.

Earnings

Earnings vary, but trainees earn between £12,000 and £14,000, and with experience dressmakers can earn £17,000 to £20,000. Many dressmakers are self-employed and can earn more, especially if they make items like wedding dresses or other special-occasion wear. Some dressmakers work part-time or as a second job.

Info

Chartered Society of Designers
(CSD)
www.csd.org.uk

Skillset Careers
08080 300 900 (England and
Northern Ireland)
0808 100 8094 (Scotland)
0800 121 815 (Wales)
www.skillset.org/careers

Model

Models work as 'live' or photographic models, generally showing clothes or accessories. Photographic and advertising models rely on an agent to get them work and handle the fees. Competition is intense and very few models get to the top of the profession.

Fashion models are employed full-time by couturiers, wholesalers or fashion stores as 'live' models. They have the garments draped and pinned on them during the design stages, and show them to the public. Live models must be tall, at least 1.72~m (5~ft 8~in). Photographic modelling involves posing in garments chosen to be illustrated in magazines, newspapers, catalogues or on advertising posters. This work is often out of season for the type of garments being modelled and some of the work is done abroad. Expenses include the provision of accessories, a good basic wardrobe and hairdressing.

Entry, qualifications and training

Private model schools run training courses for live and photographic modelling. Reputable schools will only take entrants whom they think will succeed, and will introduce them to agencies at the end of the training period. The London College of Fashion, a non-commercial college, offers a one-year full-time course leading to a certificate in fashion modelling. Students should have three GCSEs grades A–C or equivalent.

Personal attributes

A model must be able to work hard, be punctual and reliable, get on well with people, and have a great deal of common sense. Competition is intense and only those who can interpret what the stylist and photographer want will get to the top. A female model should be at least 1.72~m (5~ft 8~in) tall and have body statistics of about 86–61–86 cm (34–24–34 in). A male model should be at least 1.83~m (6~ft) tall. Models should have clear skin, good hands, nails and teeth, healthy hair and attractive features.

Earnings

Models normally work freelance and are paid per day or per job. Rates vary enormously depending on how well established you are and what kind of modelling you do. Routine modelling for clothing catalogues may pay £50 to £60 per day. At the top end of the profession these rates are between £600 and £1,000 per day. Working for a fashion house, rates vary from £10,000 to £40,000 per year. Remember that your agent may charge up to 20 per cent of your fee.

Info

Association of Model Agents
www.associationofmodelagents.org

Alba Model Information
0871 717 7170
www.albamodel.info

Equity
020 7379 6000
www.equity.org.uk

FILM AND TELEVISION PRODUCTION

This popular and highly competitive sector offers opportunities in film production, television and advertising. The majority of those working in film and TV are self-employed freelancers. Film production involves both studio and location work. Anyone who is really serious about this work needs to develop personal marketing skills in addition to their creative craft skills.

Animator

Working as an animator you aim to bring drawings or models to life on screen. Your work could be used in animated short and full-length films, television cartoons, adverts, computer games, music videos, websites and movie visual effects. Producing an animation involves many stages and processes, from generating ideas to building models and editing the final piece. Each stage can involve several specific tasks and job roles, including production designers who create the look; storyboard artists who take the script or ideas and show the story in a visual way; layout artists also draw how each shot will look. In production – digital painters touch up colours; animators and modellers follow the storyboard and use computer or stop-frame animation to create movement and personality.

Announcer

Announcers work to detailed and carefully timed scripts, communicating information to the viewer from a soundproof 'behind the scenes' office. They sometimes write or adapt their own material and need to be able to work on their own.

Archivist/librarian

(see also Archivist)

Archivists and librarians collect, collate, preserve and make available collections of recorded visual, sound, written and other materials for use by various productions. Archives are valuable business resources, and some archivists are now involved in selling and marketing materials.

Art and design

(see also Art and Design)

The art and design function is to create a visual effect to meet the needs of the production, creating manual or computer-generated graphics.

Camerawork

Workers in this area operate and assist with still, film and video cameras to record images as directed, using different techniques.

Costume/wardrobe

The wardrobe department interprets the production requirements in terms of costumes and accessories to ensure historical accuracy and an accurate portrayal of the style and ethos of the period.

Direction

The director is responsible for achieving the creative, visual and auditory effect of a production and, equally importantly, motivating a team.

Film, video and audio tape editing

Raw tape or film is shaped to interpret the requirements of the director, either by physical cutting (film) or by selecting sequences and re-recording onto a master tape using sophisticated computer equipment.

IT specialist

IT specialists support many aspects of broadcasting, film and video, either within the companies or as consultants, providing and maintaining relevant systems and software.

Journalist

(see Journalism)

Lighting

Lighting specialists ensure that the stage or set is correctly lit to meet the needs of the production.

Make-up and hairdressing

(see Beauty and Hair for Make-up Artist)

Marketing and sales

Marketing and sales staff work in an international marketplace to raise revenue for broadcasters or film makers. Airtime is sold, sponsorship and co-production rights are negotiated and spin-off products, such as books, toys and DVDs are developed.

Model maker/prop maker

Model makers and prop makers work not only in film and TV but in the theatre too. They make all kinds of props from moving models to fake jewellery, replica weapons and even fake food. Model makers and prop makers use a wide range of skills, including carpentry, sculpting, casting, sewing, painting, welding and computer-aided design (CAD). It may well be that some prop makers develop experience and a reputation for being especially skilled in one or two of these areas.

Producer

Producers perform a variety of management and operational roles to bring together the many elements of a production, either in a studio or on location. Often responsible both for the initial concept and raising the essential finance, they are the team leaders.

Production assistant

Production assistants provide high-quality administrative and secretarial support to the producer and director at every stage of production, coordinating all activities and preparing schedules and scripts.

Production manager

Production managers organise all essential support facilities for the team, from accommodation and transport to on-set catering. They will also roster crews and arrange payments.

Production operative

Production operatives perform the operational duties of the production such as vision mixing and autocue operations.

Researcher

Researchers support the producer, helping to turn ideas into reality – providing and following up ideas, contacting and interviewing people, acquiring relevant factual material and writing briefings for presenters.

Runner/gofer

This job is the traditional entry-level job for the industry. Bright, highly motivated – often highly qualified – people act as general assistants, taking messages, making deliveries, being indispensable, and learning the basics of the commercial business.

Setcraft/props

People working in this area construct the scenery, sets and backdrops to meet the production brief, reflecting both historical accuracy and the required design and style. They also maintain sets during a production, and operate any mechanical features as directed. Props (hired or made) are used to dress the set.

Sound

Sound craftspeople interpret the requirements of a production in terms of sound collection. During post-production they may be involved in recording, editing and dubbing, using a range of sophisticated equipment.

Special effects

Special effects designers create and operate effects for a production, within technical limitations and budget, and operate the necessary machines.

Transmission

Technicians and engineers work to exhibit the production in a high-quality form, which can involve projecting images or operating transmission equipment linking electronic signals from the studios to a transmitter.

Writer

(see also Writer on page 419)

Writers work to produce or edit scripts for a variety of radio, television, DVD or film productions.

Entry, qualifications and training

The film and television industry has changed rapidly over the past decade and one of the results of this has been that at all levels and whatever your specific job, you need to be multi-skilled and flexible. While formal academic qualifications are not essential, this is an exceedingly competitive field, the result being that many entrants to all jobs within the film, TV and video industry are graduates. Degrees in communications, multimedia, photography, media studies, film and television are particularly useful. These courses are also extremely popular and thus entry is competitive. Look for courses where you get the chance to use state-of-the-art technology and where there may be opportunities for work placements or at least contacts with the industry.

If you wish to get into production/direction you may have to start in research or marketing, or as a production assistant – whichever, most careers in this sector require you to work your way up from the bottom, or be prepared to make sideways transfers.

Skillset, the Sector Skills Council for the Creative Industries, provides a range of free and subsidised training courses and works closely with the industry to try to ensure that employees are training in appropriate skills. Some television companies offer graduate training schemes, but unsurprisingly, these are massively over-subscribed.

Personal attributes

You need either to have creative flair and imagination, or to be able to see the value of these and support them. For many roles you need good technical skills and the ability to work carefully and patiently, maintaining good powers of concentration. You need excellent people skills, as you are often working in situations where the whole team is under pressure and you have to be able to keep calm. In many situations, you need to be good at promoting yourself and your ideas.

Earnings

With so many different jobs in this industry, here are some examples of pay to give a flavour of the range of possible earnings. Runners are paid between £13,000 and £14,500, but the experience is extremely useful. Trainee production assistants earn between £12,000 and £15,000. Experienced production staff earn between £19,000 and £25,000. Technicians earn between £16,000 and £26,000. Directors' salaries are not necessarily high, if they are working for small companies on low-budget productions.

Many staff work freelance and are paid on a daily basis or a fee per contract. BECTU sets rates in the industry. Your own fee-negotiating skills are often important in this field.

Info

BBC
020 8752 5942
www.bbc.co.uk

British Film Institute (BFI)
020 7255 1444
www.bfi.org.uk

Broadcasting Entertainment
Cinematographic and Theatre
Union (BECTU)
www.bectu.org.uk

Skillset Careers
0808 100 8094
www.skillset.org

FIREFIGHTER

Firefighters work to save life and rescue property in emergencies. Fighting fires is only one aspect of their work. They are called to emergencies such as road traffic accidents, plane or train crashes, explosions and chemical spillages. They also rescue people or animals stranded in high places or stuck in mud. The Fire Service also advises on fire safety through education programmes. They offer advice on fire protection and prevention for existing properties and new buildings. They also conduct inspections of premises such as hotels and hospitals to ensure that adequate fire alarms and proper escape routes and action plans to deal with emergencies are in place.

The Fire Service is administered by local authorities, and each authority is responsible for its own recruitment and selection procedures. The armed services and the British Airports Authority also have their own fire services.

Entry, qualifications and training

No formal qualifications are necessarily required, but since each brigade sets its own entry requirements some may require GCSEs in maths and English. You must be aged 18 or over to train as a firefighter. In order to pass the National Firefighter Selection Tests you have to fill in a detailed application form and pass a physical fitness test, a medical and a range of aptitude tests. The training is on the job, with frequent courses on new risks, better procedures, etc.

Personal attributes

As a firefighter you have to be calm and courageous, prepared to go into dangerous situations, but sensible enough to tackle things calmly. You must be good at reassuring frightened or injured people and at working as part of a team. You may also be involved in teaching about fire prevention and safety, so you must enjoy dealing with people.

Earnings

Trainee firefighters start at around £22,500. On achieving full competence, the rate for a firefighter is between £28,000 and £29,500. Firefighters working in London earn an additional £4,500. Crew managers earn £35,000 plus, and a station manager earns around £40,000.

Info

Skills for Justice	Fire Authority for Northern Ireland
www.skillsforjustice.com	028 9266 4221
	www.nifrs.org

FISH FARMER

Fish farming is a relatively small but growing industry. Declining fish stocks and concerns about sustainability have made farming fish increasingly viable. Most fish are farmed for the table, but some are also produced to stock lakes and reservoirs for the leisure industry. The most commonly farmed fish are salmon and trout, but tilapia, bream and other species are also being farmed. Shellfish such as mussels, oysters and scallops are also farmed commercially. Fish farm managers, technicians and other workers are employed on commercial fish farms, private estates and by environmental organisations. The work is varied. You might buy in young fish and rear them to adulthood or breed new stock by hatching eggs from adult fish. Typical tasks include feeding fish either by hand or through automated feeding systems, checking the health of fish and the quality of the water they live in, moving fish from one tank or pond to another according to their weight and size, and finally, harvesting fish for the table or to sell to other fish producers.

Entry, qualifications and training

If you wish to join this industry as a manager or assistant manager, you normally need a relevant degree. There are a small number of fisheries degrees available in the UK. You may also be able to get into management with a degree in another subject such as agriculture or environmental management. If you wish to start at technician level, you may not necessarily need formal qualifications, though you could consider a part-time BTEC first diploma in Fisheries Husbandry or a two-year full-time BTEC National Diploma in Fisheries Management.

Once you are working in fish farming, you may want to consider taking Institute of Fisheries Management part-time certificate and diploma courses in fisheries management. You need to consider geographical location when you are thinking about this career. The majority of farms are in Scotland, though there are a few in the south of England and a scattering in other places.

Personal attributes

You need to have a real interest in the scientific aspects of what you are doing. You have to enjoy working with living organisms. You have to be prepared to work in all weathers and conditions. You may have to work as part of a team, but you also have to be happy and confident in working on your own.

Earnings

Fish farm technicians earn between £14,000 and £18,000. Assistant managers earn around £25,000 and managers of large fish farms can earn up to £38,000. For some posts accommodation may be provided, though occasionally this may only be a caravan.

Info

Institute of Fisheries Management
0115 982 2317
www.ifm.org.uk

Lantra
0845 707 8007
www.lantra.co.uk

British Trout Association
0131 472 4080
www.britishtrout.co.uk

FISHING

Fishing covers work on many kinds of commercial boats, from single-handed vessels to large factory ships employing crews of 15 to 20. The usual progression for fishermen and women is to start as deckhands, work up to mate and finally to fishing vessel skipper. Fishermen and women work on inshore vessels that stay close to the shore and on vessels that go limited distances out to sea. They also work on vessels that go far out into the ocean.

Fishing vessel deckhand

Deckhands help with everything from gutting and cleaning the fish caught to preparing food for other crew members and keeping the boat clean and orderly. They repair nets and also help set up trawling and hauling equipment.

Fishing vessel skipper

Skippers are responsible for the management of every voyage. They have to plan where to fish and take responsibility for navigation and for health and safety aboard the vessel. They oversee the use of the vessel's fishing gear and other technical equipment. They manage the workload of the crew and deal with any problems that arise.

Entry, qualifications and training

To become a deckhand you don't need any formal qualifications, though previous experience of the sea and boating or sailing of some kind is useful. Most people train through training schemes organised around the UK; contact the Sea Fish Industry Authority for details. If you have had some useful experience, it may be worth approaching a skipper directly to see if he or she will take you on. Training is on the job, but if you progress to become a mate or a skipper you can take NVQ level 3 in Marine Vessel Operations (Mate) or Marine Vessel Operations (Skipper).

Personal attributes

As either a deckhand or a skipper you must have good eyesight and hearing and be physically fit and have a lot of physical courage. The work is often dangerous as you have to deal with wind, storms and cold seas. You must be able to tolerate working with a small group of people, often in cramped, uncomfortable conditions. You need to be able to tolerate long periods away from home, family and friends.

Earnings

There are wide variations in earnings for deckhands and skippers. Earnings are based on the size of the catch and the value of the fish caught. Salaries for deckhands and skippers are between £11,500 and £26,000. Skippers on large commercial vessels can earn considerably more than this. Income is also affected by legal restrictions on size of catch and the number of days on which a vessel is permitted to leave port to fish.

Info

The Seafish Industry Authority
01472 252300
www.seafish.org

Maritime and Coastguard Agency
(MCA)
www.mcga.gov.uk

FLORISTRY

(see Crafts)

FOOD SCIENCE AND TECHNOLOGY

The food industry is a significant employer. With the vast array of food products now available and concerns about healthy eating and the impact of the food we consume on the environment, food production is much discussed. Food scientists and technologists use food science and other scientific approaches to turn raw materials into finished products for the consumer in an industry that is becoming increasingly sophisticated.

The majority of those qualifying in food science are employed in a variety of positions in the food industry, which covers not only the manufacture of food but its ingredients, food packaging and the manufacture of food-processing machinery. Positions exist in production, quality assurance or in product or process development. The growth of 'own label' products has led to additional opportunities in the food retailing sector, where technologists are responsible for developing new products, identifying suppliers, and ensuring the quality of the product from manufacture, through distribution to the store and, ultimately, to the consumer's table. Those keen to secure a career in research will find opportunities in government service, in research associations, as well as in commercial organisations and the universities. There are additional opportunities in environmental health, education, consultancy, public health laboratories and in technical publishing and journalism.

Entry, qualifications and training

There are several routes into this work. You can start as a lab technician with a food or drinks manufacturer. For this you normally need four GCSEs, including maths and a science. If you are successful, you can then study part-time for higher qualifications and progress to technologist-level jobs. You could study a degree in food technology; you normally need two or three A levels, including biology or chemistry, to do this. If you have one A level there is a range of BTEC HNC and HND full- and part-time courses for which you could apply. Exact course requirements vary, so check with colleges. If you have a degree in an unrelated subject, there are some postgraduate courses in food safety and food quality management that could gain you entry. The Institute of Food Science and Technology careers website provides information on all these options.

Personal attributes

You need a real interest in food and food preparation, combined with an aptitude for an interest in science. You should be a good communicator, able to share ideas or enforce legislation if necessary. You must be careful and methodical and acutely aware of food safety and hygiene issues. You should be able to work well in a team, but able to work on your own too. If you are involved in recipe development you should be creative. If you are involved in research, you need an enquiring mind.

Earnings

At technician level, salaries start at around £20,000. Graduate food technologists earn between £23,000 and £27,000. If you have 5 to 10 years' experience and management responsibility, salaries range from £30,000 to £45,000.

Info

Improve Limited
0845 644 0448
www.improveltd.co.uk

Institute of Food Science and
Technology (IFST)
020 7603 6316
www.ifst.org.uk

IFST Careers
www.foodtechcareers.org

Chartered Institute of Environmental
Health (CIEH)
020 7928 6006
Careers website: www.cieh.org

Chartered Institute of Environmental
Health (CIEH) Course finder
020 7827 5800
www.cieh-coursefinder.com

FORENSIC SCIENTIST

Films and television have probably been responsible for bringing a not always accurate portrayal of forensic science to public attention. Most forensic scientists work for independent organisations which provide forensic science services to the police, public health laboratories, universities and companies that deal with specialised areas such as fire investigation or examining questioned documents. Forensic scientists examine and try to identify, by means of analytical chemistry, molecular biology and microscopic analysis, samples of materials such as clothing, hair, blood, glass, paint and handwriting, in order to provide evidence to expose criminals, the location of a crime, the weapons used, and other relevant details.

Entry, qualifications and training

This is a fiercely competitive graduate-entry profession. The most relevant degrees are biology, chemistry, biochemistry, crop and soil science, materials science, pharmacology and physiology. While there are many undergraduate degrees in forensic science, not all of these qualify you as a forensic scientist. You should check individual course details very carefully. Most forensic scientists also have relevant postgraduate qualifications and some laboratory work experience. Most training is on the job, but you are also likely to have to attend several short courses to improve your knowledge and skills.

Personal attributes

You must have an enquiring and logical mind. You should be patient and able to pay attention to really small details. You should have good scientific skills and knowledge and you must be persistent. Excellent written and oral communication skills are also vital.

Earnings

Trainee forensic scientists earn from £20,000 to £23,000. You may start higher up the scale if you have a postgraduate qualification. After around two years salaries are £25,000 to £35,000. Senior forensic scientists can earn £50,000.

Info

The Forensic Science Society	Forensic Science Northern Ireland
www.forensic-science-society.org.uk	www.fsni.gov.uk
Skills for Justice	Forensic Science Service (FSS)
www.skillsforjustice.com	www.forensic.gov.uk

FORESTRY

Trees, woodlands and forests cover some 13 per cent of the land area of Britain. Forests and woodlands have to be managed so that they can provide many resources. They are used to harvest timber for the construction industry, for furniture making and for paper production. Recreational activities like walking, cycling and horse riding are permitted in many woods and forests and so suitable routes have to be maintained. They are wildlife havens for plants, birds, mammals, reptiles and insects. Some grazing of stock, particularly traditional breeds of cattle and ponies, is being developed in some of our forests. Forestry officers and forestry workers are employed either by private companies or environmental organisations that manage forests and woodland or by contractors.

Forestry officer

Your role as a forestry officer would depend very much on the type of forest or woodland you are managing and what its primary functions are, eg timber production, recreation or wildlife proliferation. Your responsibilities would almost always involve the supervision of other forestry workers and contractors. Your work may involve planning planting programmes and supervising such planting. You might have to organise both the harvesting and sale of timber. Some woods and forests have visitor centres and part of your role could be to manage this. You would be responsible for the monitoring and care of wildlife in the forest and you may have to provide information to the public on nature trails or on what tracks and paths they are allowed to use for which activities.

Forestry worker

Forestry workers take on a wide range of tasks that support all the forest's commercial and environmental activities. Forestry workers plant, prune and cut down trees. They tidy up the forest floor, perhaps removing weeds or debris from tracks and paths. They often build or maintain fences, gates and stiles.

Entry, qualifications and training

What qualifications you need depends on whether you are hoping to start as a forest worker or to get into forestry management. In either case some voluntary work with a woodland or forestry-based organisation is a very good starting point. The Woodland Trust is one such organisation, but there are others. Check the Volunteering England website to find out about local opportunities.

To become a forest worker you do not need any formal qualifications. You could choose to study full- or part-time at an agricultural college where you could complete a BTEC National Diploma in Forestry and Arboriculture. If you are already employed in forestry, your employer may be happy for you to do a course part-time. Whether the course is full- or part-time, you should check with the college as it may have formal entry requirements, eg GCSEs including maths and science. Passing one of these courses will enable you to progress to skilled worker level and then on to management. If your work involves using a chainsaw or applying pesticides you will have to pass proficiency tests before you are allowed to do this. The National Proficiency Test Council provides information about these tests, but your employer can also help you arrange to take these.

If you prefer to go straight into forestry management, then you will need to do a degree or HND course in forestry or a related subject such as countryside management.

Personal attributes

You have to be extremely practical and very safety conscious. You must have a real love of woodlands, forests and trees and an interest in nature. You should be very happy to work outdoors in all sorts of weather conditions. You will often be working on your own and unsupervised, so you have to be comfortable with this, but also good at working as part of a team.

Earnings

Basic grade forest workers start on around £12,000, while skilled workers earn between £15,000 and £19,000. Supervisors earn around £20,000 and forestry managers may earn up to £27,000. Occasionally accommodation is provided, but this is by no means standard practice.

Info

Forestry Commission
www.forestry.gov.uk

National Proficiency Tests Council
024 7685 7300
www.nptc.org.uk

Royal Forestry Society (RFS)
www.rfs.org.uk

Volunteering England
www.volunteering.org.uk

Lantra
0845 707 8007
www.lantra.co.uk

Institute of Chartered Foresters
0131 240 1425
www.charteredforesters.org

FOUNDRY WORK

Foundry work supports many other industries. It makes metal-cast components such as propellers, turbines, crankshafts, all types of machinery, and domestic items such as fireplaces.

Foundry workers are employed in several specialised tasks. Patternmakers produce template models, which are used to create moulds for casting metal. They make the models with a range of materials, such as wood, metal, plastic and wax. Moulders make moulds into which molten metal is poured to make castings. Foundry process operators are employed in one of several roles, including mill operator, cupola attendant, looking after the furnaces, wax assembler – putting together the wax patterns, ladle person (or caster) – transferring molten metal from the furnace to the moulds, die caster – operating die casting machines, fettler – grinding surplus metal off castings with abrasive wheels.

There are also limited openings for foundry technologists, metallurgists, chemists and engineers in research and development. Graduate trainees are recruited to production and administrative management posts.

Entry, qualifications and training

While you don't need formal qualifications it may help if you have already worked in another area of engineering, manufacturing or production and/or if you have a forklift licence. There may be opportunities to do an apprenticeship in foundry work; what is available varies from region to region. If you want to do an apprenticeship you may need three GCSEs, including one technical subject. Much of your training will be on the job, but your employer may give you opportunities to study for engineering qualifications. If you cannot get in through an apprenticeship and do not have previous experience, a college BTEC or City & Guilds course in engineering could improve your prospects. Vocational diplomas for 14–19-year-olds have recently been introduced in the manufacturing sector. These combine school or college study with work experience and may provide a further route into foundry work. You need to be physically fit to do foundry work and some employers may require you to pass a medical as part of the selection process.

Personal attributes

You must be physically fit with good stamina. You have to be extremely safety conscious at all times. You must be able to follow instructions and work as part of a team. You may have to work on several different projects and you need a high level of concentration.

Earnings

Trainee foundry operatives earn between £13,000 and £18,000. With experience, this rises to £20,000 to £24,500. You may earn more if you have additional supervisory or other responsibilities.

Info

SEMTA (The Sector Skills Council for Science, Engineering and Manufacturing Technologies)
0845 643 9001
www.semta.org.uk

Institute of Cast Metal Engineers
www.icme.org.uk

FUNDRAISING

Fundraising managers work mainly for charities, but also for pressure groups, community projects and other organisations. They are responsible for overseeing all those activities that help their organisations to generate income. Their varied activities include working with advertisers and marketing specialists to decide how to target a particular audience; working with businesses to obtain corporate funding such as the sponsoring of a project; and organising special fundraising events. They are also responsible for managing trading through charity shops or mail order catalogues; keeping in touch with donors; and organising and supervising the work of volunteers. The particular mix of tasks varies greatly. Large charities may employ fundraising managers who specialise in just one of the above areas. Working for a small charity, you may have to turn your hand to anything and everything.

Entry, qualifications and training

While there may be no specific entry qualifications, many fundraisers are graduates with a degree in business studies or marketing. This work is now highly competitive and organisations have to consider who will really be able to help them generate income. A background in advertising, public relations, finance or marketing is ideal. Having done some voluntary work for your chosen charity, or for something similar, can also strengthen your application.

The Institute of Fundraising offers a part-time foundation course in the basics of fundraising, for people who have just embarked on this career. It also offers a certificate in fundraising management, which is equivalent to NVQ level 4. A great deal of training is informal and on the job.

Personal attributes

A full range of excellent interpersonal skills is essential. You must be persuasive, good at negotiating and able to speak confidently to groups of people. You need good business sense, IT skills and numeracy, and the knack of spotting an imaginative solution or coming up with an appealing idea.

Earnings

Fundraising managers earn between £19,000 and £25,000. With experience and working for a large organisation it is possible to earn more. Some vacancies with small organisations or community groups will be less well paid and many may be part-time with pro rata pay for hours worked.

Info

Institute of Fundraising
020 7840 1000
www.institute-of-fundraising.org.uk

Working for a Charity
020 7520 2512
www.wfac.org.uk

Volunteering England
www.volunteering.org.uk

Volunteer Development Agency
www.volunteering-ni.org

Volunteering Wales
www.volunteering-wales.net

Volunteer Scotland
www.volunteerscotland.org.uk

FUNERAL WORK

The main occupation in this sector is that of funeral director, and the role of embalmer is also an important one. Many others are employed linked to this work: crematorium attendants, drivers, grave diggers and general administrators, for example.

Funeral director

Funeral directors collect the deceased from hospital or their residence and prepare them for burial or cremation, which may include embalming. Most funeral premises include private viewing rooms for family visits. The funeral director often makes all the funeral arrangements on behalf of the family, such as the date, time and place of any ceremony and interment or cremation. The funeral director places the relevant notice of death and acknowledgement of thanks for sympathy in newspapers, pays all the fees, arranges flowers, transports the coffin and mourners to and from church/crematorium, and will act as a collection point for flowers, or donations in lieu, if desired.

Funeral directors may be employed by large firms such as cooperative societies, or by small family-run concerns. In remote rural areas, a local carpenter or other craftsperson may also work as a funeral director.

Entry, qualifications and training

Those wishing to obtain the Diploma in Funeral Directing must register with the National Association of Funeral Directors (NAFD) and will also have student membership of the British Institute of Funeral Directors (BIFD). Full details of the diploma course are forwarded to each student. Every student must follow the foundation module – there are no exceptions.

A satisfactory standard must be reached in the foundation module before proceeding to the diploma. A student will be required to have 24 months' experience and have arranged 25 funerals before the diploma is awarded. NVQs levels 2 and 3 in Funeral Services are available for those employed within the profession.

Personal attributes

Tact, sympathy and a reassuring, helpful nature are essential to funeral directors when they are advising the bereaved. They also need to combine administrative ability with technical expertise in the varied preparations of funeral arrangements. On-call and out-of-hours work is an integral part of the job and an ability to adapt to irregular hours is essential.

Earnings

Salaries vary depending on size of firm, many of which are family concerns. Average earnings are between £15,000 and £30,000.

Info

National Association of Funeral Directors (NAFD)	British Institute of Funeral Directors (BIFD)
0845 230 1343	www.bifd.org.uk
www.nafd.org.uk	

Embalmer

Embalmers work with the bodies of the deceased, working to preserve and present the body from the time of death until the time of burial or cremation. It is special work, because how a body looks to loved ones and friends of the deceased is very important. Embalmers wash, disinfect and dress bodies. They wash hair and apply cosmetics. They may use plaster of Paris or wax to preserve or restore the appearance of a body after injury or illness. They work closely with funeral directors and arrangers, so that they are aware of any special requests concerning clothing, jewellery or culture-specific practices connected with the bodies of the deceased.

Entry, qualifications and training

While you do not need formal qualifications, GCSEs in maths, English and science, especially chemistry and/or biology, are useful. You have to train with a tutor who is registered with the British Institute of Embalmers. Your training is usually through part-time or distance learning and you do this while working for a funeral director. If you successfully complete your course you can then register with the British Institute of Embalmers. At this stage you can either work for a chain of funeral directors or work freelance, offering your services to smaller, family-run firms.

Personal attributes

You have to be sensitive and aware of how those who have lost a loved one are feeling, yet you must be practical and not at all squeamish yourself. You have to have good manual dexterity for delicate work, be able to work on your own and above all have a dignified and responsible attitude to your work.

Earnings

Embalmers earn between £12,000 and £19,000. A few with a lot of experience can earn up to £30,000.

Info

British Institute of Embalmers
01564 778991
www.bioe.co.uk

FURNITURE AND FURNISHING

Furniture manufacture

Modern furniture production for the mass market employs a wide range of people. In factories, staff work on production lines, cutting, joining, finishing and assembling complete items or flat-packed products. Staff employed in purchasing departments source suitable materials, while sales and marketing staff with wholesalers and retailers promote and sell furniture products. In addition to these roles, whose equivalents may be found in other industries and businesses, there are a number of specific jobs associated with furniture production.

Furniture designer

As a furniture designer you could be designing furniture for the mass market, furniture to be made in very small quantities, or one-off items. You could be designing furniture made from a range of materials, wood, MDF, even metal or plastics – think of garden and conservatory furniture, for example. You might be designing office furniture or an expensive individual item commissioned by a customer.

If you work for the mass market, and the majority of designers do, your role will mainly involve drawing and designing the specifications for an item and perhaps being involved in making a prototype. If you are designing individual items, you may make the whole item yourself from start to finish.

Entry, qualifications and training

Most designers have a relevant degree, or HND; most appropriate subjects include furniture design, 3-D design, and furniture technology and product design. Some skilled craftspeople who get into the bespoke market, making individually commissioned items, may not have formal academic qualifications but may simply have built up a reputation through work they have already completed.

Personal attributes

Wherever you aim to place yourself in the furniture design market, you will have to have creative flair, imagination and a range of practical skills. For the mass market you will need good drawing and computer-aided design skills. You will need to understand the properties of various materials and be aware of costing and budgets for these materials. You will also have to be able to work as part of a design and production team. If you are working in more of a niche market, you may be self-employed and have to have all the appropriate self-marketing and business skills.

Furniture restorer

Furniture restorers repair, restore and preserve antique furniture. They have to use techniques from woodwork, metalwork, cabinet making, conservation and French polishing. Restorers often need to use modern materials such as resins to repair old pieces of furniture. The work can involve anything from a minor repair, putting a handle back in place, to completely rebuilding an impressive dining room suite. One important aspect of the work is to be able to agree with a client what is realistically achievable with a particular piece of work.

Entry, qualifications and training

The British Antique Furniture Restorers Association (BAFRA) can give advice on how to train to do this work. While there are not necessarily any formal entry qualifications, many furniture restorers do have degrees in furniture design, or other art or conservation-related subjects. BAFRA has lists of recommended courses. If you do not wish to go through a degree course, there are City & Guilds courses in furniture construction offered at a small number of colleges.

Personal attributes

Patience and the ability to pay meticulous attention to fine detail are very important. You have to have good practical and technical skills and a good eye for understanding what a particular piece of furniture would have looked like in its original state. A genuine interest in antiques and history will also make the work more enjoyable. On large projects, say in a stately home, you may be working as part of a large conservation and restoration team.

Upholsterer

Upholsterers make the padding and soft coverings for furniture such as chairs, sofas, stools and mattresses and headboards for beds. They work with a range of materials, from natural fibres such as woollen cloth, cotton, leather or suede, to modern, synthetic materials. Upholsterers work in two distinct areas – mass manufacturing or individually crafted pieces of work. The work involves planning the work, advising on fabrics and estimating costs, preparing patterns and templates, cutting out fabric, fixing webbing and springs, covering frames with padding and fabric using stitching, staples, tacks or glue, making cushions and adding finishing decorations and trimmings.

Entry, qualifications and training

You don't necessarily need formal qualifications, but if you choose to work in mass production, your employer may encourage you to work towards an NVQ level 1 in Supporting the Production of Furniture. If you wish to work for yourself or in a small craft centre or workshop then a City & Guilds qualification in furniture production could be very useful for you. Building up experience via short courses run by local colleges can be a very useful starting point.

Personal attributes

You need a good eye for design, especially an awareness of colour, texture and the impact created by different fabrics. You have to have good practical skills and good drawing skills, either freehand or computer-aided. If you work for yourself, you need appropriate business and self-marketing skills.

Earnings

New designers working for the mass market start on £17,000 to £20,000. With experience this rises to £25,000 to £50,000 – although not many reach the top end. In niche markets salaries range widely and are based on experience and reputation. Restorers earn between £20,000 and £40,000. Upholsterers working for the mass market earn £12,500 to £16,500. Working as an individual craftsperson you could earn around £17,000, but earnings can be much higher than this if you make it into expensive niche markets such as individually designed and produced one-offs in expensive and luxurious fabrics.

Info

Arts Council England
0845 300 6200
www.artscouncil.org.uk

British Design Innovation (BDI)
01273 621378
www.britishdesigninnovation.org

The Chartered Society of Designers (CSD)
020 7357 8088
www.csd.org.uk

British Antique Furniture Restorers
Association (BAFRA)
01305 854822
www.bafra.org.uk

Crafts Council
020 7806 2500
www.craftscouncil.org.uk

Creative and Cultural Skills
(The Sector Skills Council for
Craft, Cultural Heritage, Design,
Literature, Music, Performing,
and Visual Arts)
020 7015 1800
www.ccskills.org.uk

The Design Council
020 7420 5200
www.designcouncil.org.uk

GARDENING

Gardening, also known as amenity horticulture, involves not only planting and caring for flowers, trees and shrubs, but also the routine jobs of cleaning out flower beds, sweeping leaves and, in the winter, shovelling snow.

Gardener

(see also Landscape Architect)

Gardeners may be employed by local authorities to care for parks or school and hospital grounds, work for a garden centre or landscape contractor, or be self-employed. Some local authority employment may be replaced by private companies in the near future. Heritage gardening is a growth area and involves working for organisations such as the National Trust, English Heritage, and other private gardens.

Entry, qualifications and training

You don't always need formal qualifications to become a gardener. Training is given on the job, often as part of an apprenticeship; NVQ levels 1–3 are available. Some employers will require you to have three or four GCSEs grades A–C. Full-time training courses in horticulture are available at colleges throughout the country, from first diploma level. The Royal Horticultural Society offers a limited number of opportunities for practical training and plantsmanship at its gardens at Wisley, Rosemoor and Hyde Hall. Voluntary internships for four or more weeks are available for those studying horticulture at college, and at a number of schools work experience placements are available for secondary pupils.

Personal attributes

You must have a real interest in the plants you work with, whether they are commercial fruit and vegetables or ornamental flowers and shrubs. You should be very practical and happy to work in all weathers, and you must be patient – some of your work takes a long time to come to fruition. For some gardening jobs you need an eye for design and colour. You should be comfortable working on your own, but able to talk to people about their gardens, their crops and their ideas.

Earnings

Most people employed in commercial horticulture are paid on a nationally agreed scale which is revised annually for agricultural workers. The scale is graded and you are paid according to your levels of experience and the work you do. At the start of your career this rate is around the minimum wage and annual income is about £11,000. With experience and training this rises to £18,000. Many gardeners are self-employed, charging an hourly rate of anything from £7.00 to £20.00 an hour.

Info

Lantra
02476 696996
www.lantra.co.uk

Royal Botanic Gardens Kew
www.rbgkew.org.uk

Horticultural Correspondence
College
01249 730326
www.hccollege.co.uk

National Proficiency Tests
Council (NPTC)
024 7685 7300
www.nptc.org.uk

Royal Horticultural Society (RHS)
www.rhs.org.uk

LGcareers (careers in local
government)
www.lgcareers.com

GAS SERVICE ENGINEER

Gas service engineers, also known as gas service technicians or gas service fitters, work in people's homes and on business premises, installing, servicing and repairing appliances and systems such as cookers, boilers and central heating systems. They test controls and safety devices to ensure that they are working and they locate and repair gas leaks. Often they specialise in installation, servicing or repair, but some gas service engineers will work in all three areas.

Entry, qualifications and training

The usual route to qualification is through a technician-level apprenticeship lasting between three and four years. You need four GCSEs grades A–C, including English, maths and science, and you must have perfect colour vision. Most apprentices start at age 16, but you can start up to the age of 24. Successful completion of the apprenticeship also leads to an NVQ level 3 award.

To work as a gas fitter, installer or service engineer, you must register with the Gas Safe Register, which will check your qualifications and ascertain that you have had suitable training and work experience before allowing you to register.

Personal attributes

You must be practical, able to handle tools and instruments, and you must be able to apply technical knowledge to practical problems. You have to be able to work on your own or as part of a team, and it is important that you are polite and friendly and enjoy meeting and dealing with people. Having an acute awareness of safety issues is essential.

Earnings

Trainees earn between £12,500 and £15,000, and newly qualified technicians earn between £17,000 and £20,000. With several years' experience you can earn up to £26,000.

Gas network engineer

Gas network engineers lay and service the gas pipelines that supply domestic and commercial premises. The work involves digging holes using mechanical digging equipment, using maps and plans to trace where you need to dig, laying and repairing pipes, connecting homes and businesses to the gas network and dealing with emergency leaks.

Entry, qualifications and training

You do not need formal qualifications to work as a gas network engineer, but if you train through an apprenticeship you will normally need four GCSEs grades A–C, including maths, English and a technical subject. If you are not joining through an apprenticeship, you will have an advantage if you have experience and/or qualifications in engineering or building services. You will also need a driving licence.

Personal attributes

You need to be physically fit and you must be able to follow plans and instructions accurately. You need to have a keen awareness of safety issues and you should be good at working as part of a team. As you progress, you may need to develop supervisory responsibilities too.

Earnings

Apprentices and new entrants earn £12,000 to £14,000. Once you have completed your apprenticeship or built up some experience, salaries rise to £18,000 to £25,000. With supervisory responsibilities earnings can be £32,000 plus.

Info

Gas Safe Register
0800 408 5500
www.gassaferegister.co.uk

British Gas Recruitment Centre
www.britishgasjobs.co.uk

Energy & Utility Skills
0845 077 9922
www.euskills.co.uk

GEOLOGY

Geology, often referred to as geoscience, really encompasses a range of careers. Geoscience is concerned with the understanding of the earth, its rocks, minerals and fossils, the dynamics of how the continents move, why earthquakes occur and what its 460-million-year history can tell us. There are highly academic fields of geology, the discovery, collection, classification and analysis of fossil remains of flora and fauna from millions of years ago. Geoscience is also concerned with very practical and current questions, advising on whether a particular site is suitable for the building of a bridge, a dam or a tunnel, working out where natural resources such as oil, gas and metals can be found and how safely they can be extracted.

Some geologists work as lecturers in higher education; others who are interested in some of the scientific rather than the scientific/commercial applications work in some of the following.

Palaeontologist

Palaeontologists study fossils and all the layers of rock that make up the earth's crust to try to find out more about the physical history of the planet, the pattern of past climate changes, or the movements of whole land masses, for example.

Seismologist

These are the scientists we hear from when earthquakes and tsunamis are being reported on – why they have occurred, how powerful they were and what we might do to predict where these dangerous phenomena are next likely to occur.

Volcanologist

Volcanologists make a close study of active volcanoes and the area that surrounds them. They also look at extinct and dormant volcanoes to try to better predict when and where the next eruptions are likely to occur. They spend time working in and around craters as well as being based in laboratories. What comes out of volcanoes gives them a chance to study the structure of the core of the planet.

Geologists who work mainly in the extraction industries locating and extracting oil, gas, metals, minerals and soil fulfil some of the following roles.

Engineering geologist

Engineering geologists analyse the underlying structure of major construction sites before tunnels, pipelines, bridges, harbours, docks and buildings are begun. They identify potential problems and advise on the best materials and construction methods to use. They analyse and assess soil, rocks, water courses and other ground conditions. They take into account environmental conditions and they work to ensure that construction projects will be safe in the short and long term.

Mining geologist

Whether companies are extracting rock and stone, minerals, metals, coal or precious metals and gemstones, mine geologists provide advice and expertise on the geological aspects of development and production in mine, pit and quarry sites. In overseeing drilling and surface exploration programmes, they help to determine likely directions for future development.

Seismic interpreter

Seismic interpreters use data generated by movements in the rocks below the earth's surface to work out exactly what quantities of oil and gas are stored beneath the surface. They use complex computer software and data from satellite stations to help them in their work.

Geotechnician

Geotechnicians support the work of geoscientists. They are based mainly in laboratories and their work involves preparing and analysing rock samples to discover their chemical make-up. Some geotechnicians work at drilling sites, logging data and monitoring activity.

Entry, qualifications and training

Geoscience, except for technicians, is a graduate profession. Degrees in geology, geophysics, geo-engineering, geochemistry, earth sciences or similar subjects may all be acceptable. Many geologists also have a postgraduate qualification. To get onto one of these degree courses you normally need A levels, including maths and one science. While this is a competitive area of work in some ways, geologists with good qualifications are likely to be in considerable demand because resources are getting harder to locate and more difficult to extract. You may be able to get a job as a junior geotechnician if you have five GCSEs grades A–C, including English, science and maths, but some employers prefer you to have A levels, an HND or a degree. There are only a few science-based HNDs which specialise in geology and geoscience.

Personal attributes

You need a strong interest in the area of geoscience in which you want to work. You have to have a rigorous scientific approach to your work, be able to construct surveys, analyse and interpret data. You have to be good at working as part of a team, but also able to work independently. You need good powers of observation – to be quick to spot any changes in data. For some jobs you have to be able to work in physically hard conditions, on oil rigs, up a volcano, etc.

Earnings

Geoscientists earn between £30,000 and £45,000. Project leaders and other senior geologists can earn £50,000 to £60,000. Salaries are highest in the oil and gas industry; this is also the work where you may have to spend long periods away from home. Geotechnicians earn between £18,000 and £29,000. The higher salaries are, once again, paid in the oil and gas industries.

Info

Natural Environment Research
Council
01793 411500
www.nerc.ac.uk

British Geological Survey
0115 936 3143
www.bgs.ac.uk

Geological Society
020 7434 9944
www.geolsoc.org.uk

GLASSMAKER

Glassmaking covers many types of products and hence many different production methods. Some glassmakers work on industrial processes, manufacturing double-glazed windows for buildings, glass for the automotive industry or glass containers such as milk bottles, wine bottles or jam jars. Some manufacturers produce glass fibre and tough but delicate glass for scientific equipment. A different aspect of glassmaking is based in small studios or workshops making individually blown pieces of glass such as ornaments or bases, or making stained glass objects.

If you work in mass-production glass you are likely to work on one or more of the following processes. You could be mixing the basic ingredients of glass, silica, soda and lime. These are mixed with various additives and with scrap glass and then the whole mixture is heated to very high temperatures. The next process is to shape the glass, either by kiln forming or blowing the glass. Once the glass is cool it may have to be cut, ground or laminated to make the finished product. Finally, some objects will need to be decorated by sand blasting, acid etching or engraving.

Working in a craft studio or workshop, you are likely to be involved in the whole process of designing, mixing, heating, blowing and decorating objects made from glass.

Entry, qualifications and training

To work in mass-market manufacture you do not need formal qualifications, though GCSEs in science and/or art could be useful. To be a glassmaker in a craft workshop or studio you normally need a degree in a relevant subject such as glass and ceramics, applied art and design or decorative arts. To get a place on one of these courses, you need to have a portfolio of work, though it does not have to be in glass or ceramics but rather must show your artistic flair.

Personal attributes

In both manufacture and craft glass making you need good manual dexterity, hand–eye coordination and colour vision. In both you also need to be very health and safety conscious. In manufacture, you must be able to work as part of a team, to follow procedures and processes with great accuracy and patience. In craft work you need artistic flair as well.

Earnings

In glass manufacture, salaries start at around £14,000 rising to £18,000 to £23,000 with experience. Senior and supervisory roles can earn up to £27,000. In craft work there is great variation as many glassmakers are self-employed, but £15,000 to £24,000 is a rough guide.

Info

International Glass Centre
Dudley College
www.dudleycol.ac.uk

Proskills UK (The Sector Skills
Council for the Process and
Manufacturing Sector)
www.proskills.co.uk

British Glass
www.britglass.org.uk

British Society of Scientific
Glassblowers
www.bssg.co.uk

Creative and Cultural Skills
(The Sector Skills Council for Craft,
Cultural Heritage, Design, Literature,
Music, Performing, and Visual Arts)
020 7015 1800
www.ccskills.org.uk

HAIRDRESSING

Hairdresser

Hairdressing is a significant business in the UK. Hairdressers work on all aspects of hair styling, including cutting, styling, perming, straightening, colouring, applying highlights and incorporating hair extensions or other hair pieces. Salons or individual stylists may specialise in male or female hairdressing, or a niche market such as specialist colouring, Afro-Caribbean or ethnic hairstyles. As a junior stylist in training, you may have to help out with other work in the salon, washing hair, booking appointments, cleaning and tidying. Hairdressers work in salons, hotels, airports, cruise liners, hospitals and prisons; some work as freelances. There are over 170,000 hairdressers in the UK.

Entry, qualifications and training

You don't always need formal qualifications to become a hairdresser. You can either train at a salon, where you may go on day-release to a college or to the salon's own training centre. Alternatively you can do a full- or part-time college course in hairdressing or barbering. NVQ levels 1, 2 and 3 are available in Hairdressing. Salon and college entry requirements vary, but you may need four GCSEs grades A–C, including English, maths and an arts subject. There may be apprenticeship schemes in hairdressing available, but this varies across local areas. Where there are apprenticeships available you are again likely to need four GCSEs. Vocational diplomas for 14–19-year-olds have recently been introduced in hairdressing; these combine school or college study with work placement, but are not available in every area.

Personal attributes

Hairdressers should have a genuine interest in people, a natural friendliness, the ability to stay calm under pressure, creative ability and an eye for detail. A presentable personal appearance is also essential. Hairdressers must not have skin conditions that can be affected by chemicals.

Earnings

Trainees earn around £11,300 to £13,000. Stylists earn £16,000 to £21,000. There is a lot of regional variation and salaries also depend on how fashionable the salon is deemed to be. Top stylists can earn more than £30,000. This is work where you can sometimes make additional money from tips. It is also possible to become self-employed, visiting people in their homes to cut, colour, perm and style their hair. In this case, what you earn depends on what you charge.

Info

| Hairdressing and Beauty Industry Authority (HABIA) | Freelance Hair and Beauty Federation (FHBF) |
| www.habia.org | www.fhbf.org.uk |

HEALTH AND SAFETY

Health and safety adviser

Health and safety advisers work for every kind of organisation, from multinationals and government agencies to small businesses. Advisers work in partnership with employers, employees, directors and trade unions, and are responsible for ensuring that all safety legislation is adhered to and that suitable policies and practices are put in place. They help organisations minimise safety risks and they are often involved in staff training.

Health and safety inspector

Health and safety inspectors work to assess and improve every kind of work practice and the health and safety applications attached to it. In the UK one person is killed every day at work, and inspectors working for the Health and Safety Executive (HSE), which is a government agency, are constantly working to try to reduce this statistic. Inspectors check work premises, from building sites to farms and factories, and they have legal powers to demand changes. They are also called in to investigate when accidents do occur.

Entry, qualifications and training

It is possible to become an adviser without a degree, if you have plenty of work experience in management, engineering, science or health, but there is a move towards making this a graduate-entry profession. Degrees in occupational health, engineering, health science and management are the most favoured; each subject has specific A level entry requirements. Graduates or HND holders of any subject can become health and safety inspectors, but again there is a preference for subjects such as engineering, environmental health and physics.

If you are accepted by the HSE you undergo a two-year structured training programme. This involves a combination of short courses and on-the-job training.

Personal attributes

To become a health and safety inspector you have to be extremely observant and thorough in your approach to what you see and what you are told. You have to be an excellent communicator, able to explain to someone why a work station or a production line may be unsafe. You need to persuade people to do the right thing, but be firm enough to take action if they do not. You need to be a well-organised administrator.

Earnings

Health and safety advisers earn between £18,000 and £25,000. Trainee health and safety inspectors earn around £26,000 with a rise of around 10 per cent on successful completion of the two-year training period. Senior health and safety inspectors can earn around £40,000.

Info

Health and Safety Executive (HSE)
www.hse.gov.uk

Examination Board in Occupational
Safety and Health (NEBOSH)
0116 263 4700
www.nebosh.org.uk

Institution of Occupational
Health and Safety (IOSH)
0116 257 3100
www.iosh.co.uk

British Safety Council
020 8741 1231
www.britsafe.org

HEALTH SERVICE (NON-MEDICAL)

Healthcare is supported by a whole range of non-medical jobs which form an essential part of healthcare services. Some of these services are provided by the National Health Service (NHS), others such as catering, cleaning or laundry are often provided by companies that are contracted to do this work on behalf of the NHS.

Catering staff

Cooks, housekeepers and kitchen assistants working either for the NHS or for catering companies provide a range of hospital meals. They have to cater for special diets and try to provide a range of tempting food. Working within a tight budget is a key skill in this work.

Clerical and administrative staff

The NHS employs large numbers of clerks, secretaries, telephonists, receptionists and other administrative workers. Some of this work involves patient contact, eg receptionists at clinics, or ward clerks. Other work is more behind the scenes, ordering supplies, booking appointments and updating records.

Domestic services staff

Domestic services staff are either employed by the NHS or by private companies that have contracts to clean health service premises and also launder all the sheets, pillow cases, towels, etc.

Estates staff

Hospitals, clinics and other NHS premises need building services engineers to ensure that lighting, heating, air conditioning and other environmental management systems work at all times. Architects and surveyors are needed to design new premises or plan refurbishment of existing older properties.

Information science and technology

Computer systems of many kinds are important for keeping records, monitoring care and sharing information. All kinds of IT staff are employed, from data input clerks to systems development.

Management

This is a very broad term. The NHS employs managers in finance, human resources, strategic planning, performance monitoring and the day-to-day running of every kind of health service establishment.

Porters and messengers

Porters move patients and equipment from one part of a hospital or other healthcare centre to another. Messengers take important messages from one department to another. Even in these days of electronic communications, urgent messages are delivered by messengers.

Scientists

(see Medical and Healthcare Science)

Sterile services staff

Sterile services staff clean and sterilise all medical equipment. Some of this equipment is highly technical, so disinfecting it and preparing it for use is a painstaking and complex task. Applicants for this work usually need GCSEs in English, maths and a science.

Entry, qualifications and training

These vary considerably for different jobs. It is worth consulting specific career areas such as Accountancy, Biomedical Engineering, Hospitality, Human Resource Management, Information Technology and Secretarial work. For some work, such as being a porter or a kitchen assistant, you may not need any formal academic qualifications. For most management posts you need either a degree or professional qualifications in a relevant area such as accountancy or management studies. Posts in science, engineering or information technology will require relevant qualifications from GCSE to postgraduate level.

Personal attributes

The common thread for all these jobs is a genuine commitment to working within and for healthcare and wanting to deliver a good service to patients. For any work involving patient contact, being sensitive and caring is important. All jobs require you to be a good communicator and to be able to work very well as part of a team. Particular jobs require specific practical skills such as cooking, IT skills or being good with technical equipment.

Earnings

Apart from doctors and the most senior managers, all NHS staff are paid on a clearly defined scale. New entrants to junior posts such as kitchen assistant, porter or junior administrative assistant are paid between £13,900 and £17,000. Once you have supervisory functions and/or additional responsibilities, salaries rise to £18,800 to £21,300. Jobs in IT, human resources and management start at £22,000 rising to £37,800; senior managers in all functions can earn far more than this. This salary information is a guide only, because there are so many different points on the scale. The NHS Careers website sets out detailed information.

Info

NHS Careers
0345 60 60 655
www.nhscareers.nhs.uk

Health Learning and Skills
Advice Line
08000 150850
nextstep.direct.gov.uk

HEALTH VISITOR

(see Nursing Professions)

HEALTHCARE ASSISTANT

(see Nursing Professions)

HORTICULTURE

Horticulture refers to the commercial cultivation of flowering plants, shrubs, ornamental trees, soft fruit such as raspberries and strawberries, fruit trees, vegetables and herbs. Horticultural work occurs in a range of settings, including garden centres, plant nurseries, parks and formal gardens, market gardens, community horticulture projects and large farms. The main horticultural jobs are described below, but in addition horticultural specialists may work in teaching at agricultural colleges, in advisory work on new projects, or in areas such as marketing. Currently research on more sustainable methods of horticulture that use less water or fewer pesticides is a significant area of research and development.

Arboriculturist

Arboriculturists are tree specialists who develop expertise in the planting, care, management and production of trees of every kind, from orchard fruits and native English woodland trees to exotic varieties. They study sites to assess their suitability for particular trees and carry out surveys of tree populations and attempt to analyse and solve any problems that stop the trees thriving. They often work for formal gardens, parks, local authorities or conservation bodies. Their role may cover supervising other manual workers carrying out activities like pruning or planting. They may also help to resolve disputes over trees on boundaries, or decisions on whether a particular tree should be preserved.

Entry, qualifications and training

You can either enter this work with a degree in arboriculture or forestry management, or work towards appropriate professional qualifications once you have had some work experience with a forestry or woodland management organisation. If you take this second route, you may not need any formal qualifications. Professional qualifications include the Arboricultural Association Technician's Certificate in Arboriculture, the Royal Forestry Society's Professional Diploma in Arboriculture (DipArb (RFS)) or the Institute of Chartered Foresters' Professional Examination (with arboriculture options).

Personal attributes

You need a genuine interest in trees and conservation. You must also have a scientific and logical approach to your work. You must be a good communicator, able to supervise others and put across your ideas to groups or individuals. You should be physically fit and happy working in all weathers.

Earnings

New entrants earn around £17,000, but with either a degree and/or considerable experience, earnings are £20,000 to £28,000.

Horticultural manager

As a horticultural manager you will be responsible for the day-to-day care of plants and the supervision of staff. Your exact tasks will vary enormously, depending where you are working, for example, in a garden centre, a market garden or a commercial nursery. You may be involved in a lot of hands-on work, watering, feeding, pruning and planting. You may also be involved in working out costs, developing new products and markets, managing and training staff and negotiating with suppliers or dealing with queries from customers.

Entry, qualifications and training

You may not need formal qualifications to get into this work; many managers have worked their way up from more basic jobs. Individual employers set their own entry requirements and some will expect you to have three to four GCSEs, including maths, English and a science. Some managers have a degree in horticulture or a related subject.

Personal attributes

You need a blend of good practical and interpersonal skills. You should have a real interest in plants and be prepared to develop highly specialised knowledge. You must be able to motivate other people and ensure that work is carried out carefully. You should also be able to deal well with customers, being helpful and informative, or with suppliers, using good negotiating skills.

Earnings

Comprising many types of employer, earnings range from £16,000 to £40,000. Most people doing this work earn between £20,000 and £25,000.

Horticultural worker

Horticultural workers carry out all the daily tasks associated with planting, growing, caring for, propagating and harvesting flowers, shrubs, vegetables, fruit and trees grown for commercial or amenity purposes. Your day-to-day tasks could include sowing seeds, taking cuttings, checking plants for signs of pests and diseases, and pruning, tidying and moving plants. Your job could include some landscaping work and you may also deal with customer queries if you are working in a garden centre or nursery.

Entry, qualifications and training

You don't need formal qualifications to get into this work, though some employers will expect you to have GCSEs in maths, English and science. There are several part-time qualifications at NVQ levels 1 and 2 towards which you can work once you are in employment.

Personal attributes

You have to have a real interest in plants of all kinds and enjoy growing them and making them thrive. You need good practical skills and you must be physically fit with good manual dexterity. You should be able to follow instructions and then work on your own. You should also be able to work as part of a team. You may also have to work directly advising members of the public.

Earnings

Pay starts at £12,000 to £13,000 rising to £15,000 to £17,500. You may earn more as you take on supervisory or other responsibilities.

Info

Lantra (The Sector Skills Council for the Environmental and Land-based Sector)
02476 696996
www.lantra.co.uk

Institute of Horticulture (IoH)
020 7245 6943
www.horticulture.org.uk

Royal Botanic Garden, Edinburgh
0131 552 7171
www.rbge.org.uk

Royal Botanic Gardens, Kew
020 8332 5000
www.kew.org

Royal Horticultural Society (RHS)
0845 260 5000
www.rhs.org.uk

LGcareers (careers in local government)
www.lgcareers.com

Institute of Chartered Foresters
0131 240 1425
www.charteredforesters.org

Arboricultural Association
01242 522152
www.trees.org.uk

Grow careers
Advice Line: 0845 707 8007
www.growcareers.info

HOSPITALITY AND CATERING

Hotels, restaurants, fast food outlets and cafes and catering companies are an important employment sector, offering many different opportunities at all levels, from managers and supervisors to craft workers. As well as jobs specific to the sector, there are opportunities for cleaning staff, administrators, receptionists and IT staff.

Chef/cook

In addition to creating and supervising the preparation of all kinds of different dishes, a head chef/cook has to be trained in the management of a kitchen, being responsible for the staff and the organisation of their workload, planning the menus, budgeting, ordering and approving the necessary ingredients, and maintaining high standards of efficiency and hygiene. Chefs are employed in hotels, restaurants, industrial organisations (such as offices or factories), institutions (such as hospitals, schools and universities or colleges) and in the armed forces. In large establishments the chef de cuisine is in overall charge, while there may be a number of chefs de partie (in charge of their part of the kitchen) and a number of commis chefs (still learning the trade).

Entry, qualifications and training

No formal qualifications are necessary, but depending on which training route your employer wishes to put you through, you may need four GCSEs, including English and maths. If you want to study full- or part-time at college before you start training with an employer, you can study for BTEC National Certificates and Diplomas in Hospitality and Catering; you need four GCSEs grades A–C to get a place on one of these courses. You can study for NVQ courses to levels 1, 2 and 3, either full-time before you start work or part-time while you are training in a kitchen. There are also apprenticeships (leading to NVQ level 2) and Advanced Apprenticeships (leading to NVQ level 3) available in food preparation and cookery. These last 12 and 24 months, respectively. There are also some NVQ level 4 courses available in kitchen and larder, confectionery and patisserie.

If you have five GCSEs and two A levels, there are several Foundation degree courses available in food preparation, including professional cookery, professional patisserie, culinary arts, culinary creativity and hospitality. Vocational diplomas for 14–19-year-olds have recently been introduced in the hospitality sector, combining school or college study with work experience. At present there are only a few of these available.

Personal attributes

Chefs need a real passion for food and a creative attitude to making the best use of ingredients, whether they work in a top restaurant, a country pub or a hospital canteen. Despite the impression sometimes given on TV, being able to keep calm under pressure is a great asset. Chefs must be good team leaders and motivators, able to get people to work well together.

Earnings

Trainee chefs earn between £12,500 and £15,000. Chefs in charge of a section of the kitchen earn between £16,000 and £20,000. Second or sous chefs earn around £22,000 and head chefs earn up to £30,000. A head chef in a large, high-quality hotel running a large kitchen can earn £40,000 to £50,000. The hospitality industry has been hit by the recession, which has held back some salaries.

Fast food/restaurant manager

The responsibilities of fast food and restaurant managers vary very much according to the kinds of outlet in which they work. Fast food managers work mainly for chains that operate burger, pizza and fried chicken eateries, for example. As a fast food outlet manager your responsibilities are mainly for organising the work of the staff team, making sure that everyone works quickly and efficiently and solving problems if they arise. You are likely to be responsible for the food preparation area, as well as the customer service and eating areas. You have a major role in training new staff. As a restaurant manager you might be working in a large hotel, a small independent restaurant, a national chain of eateries or a fast food outlet. Restaurant managers tend to work front of house, welcoming guests, and ensuring that service is good and customers are satisfied. You will certainly be liaising with kitchen staff, but management of that area is likely to be the chef's domain.

Entry, qualifications and training

You don't necessarily need formal qualifications to become a fast food manager. Many managers begin as counter service staff, then become shift supervisors and from there progress to management. A few companies do offer graduate training schemes and accept graduates from any discipline. If you are interested in food and catering there are degrees in hospitality management, culinary arts management and hotel and catering management available at several universities. In all cases a great deal of training is on the job, but your employer may send you on short courses at college or run in-house, and there is a wide variety of catering and management qualifications you could consider.

Personal attributes

You have to have excellent interpersonal skills. The balance of how much time you spend with customers or managing your staff team depends very much on the kind of establishment for which you are working. In all instances you need to be polite, friendly and calm if problems arise or under pressure. In fast food management you need to be very aware of health and safety and food hygiene issues.

Earnings

Assistant managers earn between £18,000 and £22,500 and managers earn £20,000 to £26,000. At the luxury end of the restaurant business, a manager may earn up to £40,000. Working for fast food chains it may be possible to move into area or head office management roles with salaries of around £30,000.

Kitchen porter

The term 'porter' is a little misleading because kitchen porters are involved in far more than the unloading of deliveries. Kitchen assistant might be a more accurate term. These staff work with food preparation staff to keep the kitchen clean, hygienic and safe. They load and unload dishwashers, put away crockery and cutlery, wash items than cannot be put in a dishwasher and generally sweep and tidy the kitchen and keep work surfaces clean.

Entry, qualifications and training

You do not need formal qualifications to become a kitchen porter or kitchen assistant, but individual employers may ask for GCSEs in English and a science subject. If you want to use kitchen porter as a step on the ladder to other work in catering, it is certainly useful to have three or four GCSEs grades A–C. Training is on the job, though you may attend short courses such as food hygiene or health and safety awareness.

Personal attributes

You need to be very practical, quick to react to situations and see what needs to be done. You have to be able to work as part of a team and be able to cope with a fairly frantic work environment, where tempers may become frayed. You need to pay attention to detail.

Earnings

Kitchen porters/assistants earn around £12,500 to £14,000, maybe up to £16,000 in a large kitchen where they also have supervisory responsibilities for junior kitchen porters.

Hotel manager

As a hotel manager, you oversee all aspects of running a hotel, from housekeeping and general maintenance to budget management and marketing. Large hotels may have several departmental managers, eg restaurant and catering, conferences and functions, leisure facilities and domestic services, each reporting to one overall manager. Hotel chains may also have regional management teams, providing some central services such as purchasing of goods and supplies. Managers are responsible for everything from setting and managing budgets to staff recruitment and dealing with customer complaints. The work may involve marketing and developing business plans and new initiatives.

Entry, qualifications and training

There are two main routes to qualification: attending a college or university as a full-time student, or joining a training programme operated by an employer or an organisation that works with employers to provide training, such as the Hotel and Catering Training Company (HCTC). In the latter case, entrants learn on the job and attend college or a training centre on a short-course or day-release basis. Recruits on the work-based training programme will generally acquire NVQ awards. An increasing number of employers are offering Modern Apprenticeships, which provide a route to higher-level technical or supervisory posts, and NVQs at level 3. Full-time courses are available in hospitality-related subjects, including HNDs, Foundation degrees and degree courses.

Personal attributes

Managers need to be well motivated with good interpersonal and team skills. You have to be very well organised and a good problem solver. You need excellent communication skills, be able to get the best out of your team and to work well with customers.

Earnings

In small hotels managers earn £16,000 to £20,000 – £20,000 to £30,000 in medium-sized hotels. A manager of a large, successful hotel, or working for a chain of hotels in a head office management job, can earn up to £60,000.

Hotel receptionist

(see Receptionist under 'Business')

Waiting staff

Waiting staff wait at tables in restaurants, cafes, wine bars, hotels and some fast food outlets. They may also work for catering companies at functions such as weddings, parties, sporting or cultural events.

Waiting staff take customers' orders and pass these to the kitchen. They bring food to the table and in some instances may have to cook food such as flambéed desserts at the table. Some customers will also ask advice about what to eat or how a particular dish is prepared before placing an order. Waiting staff also set and clear tables before and after meals. They may also be responsible for adding up bills and taking payments from customers. They are the main link point between the kitchen and the customer.

Entry, qualifications and training

You do not need formal academic qualifications to do this work; having the right personal approach is far more important. Many waiting staff do have formal qualifications, including GCSEs in English and maths. Qualifications are more important, though not essential, if you hope to use your waiting work as a stepping stone to more senior roles.

Personal attributes

You have to look clean, tidy and presentable and have a friendly welcoming manner. You have to be practical, accurate in taking orders and adding up bills, good at working as part of a team and able to cope with pressure. You have to be patient; not all customers are entirely reasonable.

Earnings

Waiting staff earn between £12,000 and £14,500. Head waiters or section heads may earn £16,000 to £18,000. Many waiting staff are paid by the hour and earn close to the minimum wage. Many also make extra money from tips.

Info

People 1st, Skills Council for Hospitality
0870 060 2550
www.people1st.co.uk

Publican/licensee

Publicans manage licensed premises, mainly pubs and bars. They work for breweries, pub chains or for themselves running a free house. The publican/ manager runs the premises, which may include a restaurant, fruit machines and overnight accommodation, and is responsible for stock control, staff management and the overall standards of drink, food and customer service. Pubs and bars vary enormously, from lively late-night city centre bars providing music and other entertainment to quiet rural pubs serving a local village clientele. The demands that these different settings make on their managers will vary considerably.

Entry, qualifications and training

Many publicans/licensees work their way up to this position by starting work as a barperson and gradually taking on more responsibility. Alternatively, pub chains and breweries may take people onto management training schemes and give them appropriate training and experience to take on a pub or bar of their own. Each employer sets its own selection criteria, but some will expect applicants to have HNDs, a Foundation degree or a degree in a relevant subject such as business studies, marketing or hospitality. A good track record in work that involves customer service and taking on considerable responsibility is also a big advantage. Licensees must be aged 18 or over, have no criminal convictions and be able to satisfy the local authority that they are a suitable person to hold such a licence.

Personal attributes

You have to have excellent organisational and budgeting skills. You must be good at leading and motivating other people. You should enjoy working with members of the public, being able to provide a listening ear or a firm instruction as the need arises. You must be calm but able to react quickly in any potentially difficult situations, such as when dealing with customers who have drunk too much.

Earnings

Trainee and assistant managers earn between £15,000 and £21,000. Experienced managers generally earn between £25,000 and £30,000. Income may be related to turnover or to brewery and pub chain bonus schemes. If you are running your own establishment, your income will depend on how well that business does. In all cases, you are likely to have to work long hours to earn your living.

Barperson

Bar staff work in pubs, bars, restaurants and hotels, selling and serving alcoholic and non-alcoholic drinks to customers. In some cases they may also be responsible for taking food orders, selling snacks, etc. In some bars they will also have to know how to mix an extensive range of cocktails.

Entry, qualifications and training

You don't need formal qualifications to do this work. You must be aged 18 or over and you must have very good people skills. Some experience in retail or other customer care work is valuable.

Personal attributes

You should be friendly and helpful. You must be able to keep calm in what is often a very hectic, crowded and noisy environment. You should be able to use your initiative and work well as part of a team.

Earnings

Much of the work is part-time and many bar staff are paid the minimum wage, though this can be increased through tips. Annual income works out at between £12,000 and £15,000.

Info

British Institute of Innkeeping (BII)
01276 684449
www.bii.org

Wine and Spirit Educational Trust
(WSET)
020 7089 3800
www.wsetglobal.com

People 1st
0870 060 2550
www.people1st.co.uk

HOUSING OFFICER/MANAGER

Housing officers manage housing for housing associations, local authorities, charities and some groups of private landlords. The work can be very varied. Housing officers allocate properties to people waiting for tenancies and organise exchanges of properties between tenants. They carry out inspections of properties to ensure both that the tenant is looking after them as they should and that the landlord (housing association, local authority, etc) carries out appropriate repairs, maintenance or improvements. The housing officer has to deal with problems such as antisocial behaviour or rent arrears. He or she may be the one who has to instigate legal actions if problems persist. Some housing associations or charities provide accommodation for specific groups of people, such as those who are recovering from problems with substance abuse, or frail, elderly people. In these instances and in many other cases, part of the housing officer's role is to liaise with other authorities such as social services, schools and healthcare professionals. Collecting statistics and presenting reports can also form part of the role. Many people wanting to become housing officers start in customer services dealing with tenants' enquiries via e-mail or telephone.

Entry, qualifications and training

You don't necessarily need formal qualifications to work in this sector, though most housing officers do have A levels or equivalent. Individual employers may require you to have a degree or Foundation degree in a relevant subject such as social policy or administration. Many housing officers start in other, more junior roles in a housing organisation and work their way up. You can work towards levels 2, 3 and 4 qualifications in housing through the Chartered Institute of Housing (CIH). You can work towards these whatever your job in housing or indeed, if you are a tenant.

Personal attributes

An interest in improving people's living conditions, good interpersonal skills, effective organisation skills, sensitivity to an individual's needs and flexibility are all important.

Earnings

As a trainee, or working mainly in customer service dealing with telephone, e-mail and personal enquiries, salaries range from £15,000 to £17,000. As a more experienced housing officer having a caseload and dealing with more challenging problems, salaries range from £20,000 to £30,000. Senior housing managers earn £30,000 to £45,000. There is regional variation and salaries are also affected by whether you work for a local authority or a housing association.

Info

Asset Skills 01392 423399 www.assetskills.org	**National Housing Federation (NHF)** 020 7067 1010 www.housing.org.uk
Chartered Institute of Housing (CIH) 024 7685 1700 www.cih.org	**Royal Institution of Chartered Surveyors (RICS)** 0870 333 1600 www.rics.org

HUMAN RESOURCES

The field of human resources (HR) deals with all the functions in a business or organisation that relate to staff issues, such as recruitment, training and development, and employment. In some businesses the term 'personnel' is used, although 'human resources' is more commonly used now.

Human resources officer/manager

The role of an HR professional can vary and is largely dependent on the individual organisation's needs and the value that the organisation's senior managers place on the HR function. It can include working at a strategic level on a range of HR policies, processes and practices in relation to the business needs of the organisation. More commonly, however, HR advisers work on day-to-day issues such as recruitment, contracts of employment, payroll, training, induction, disciplinary and grievance procedures, redundancy programmes, equal opportunities policies and setting up staff support systems. In large organisations, individuals may specialise in one of these areas, but in smaller companies they will deal with all aspects of the job.

Entry, qualifications and training

This is a mostly graduate profession, unless you have a great deal of relevant experience. Any degree subject is usually acceptable, but business, psychology and human resource management could give you an advantage. You can also take postgraduate qualifications in human resource management. To do this, you normally need a degree, but other applicants with HNDs and/or relevant work experience might also be successful. Some people get into HR having worked in other areas of management, or having done administrative jobs in HR departments. The Chartered Institute of Personnel and Development (CIPD) offers a range of professional qualifications for which you can study while working. Check its website for further details.

Personal attributes

You have to have a broad range of management skills for this work. You should be highly organised, with good administrative and basic IT skills. You need to be good at building relationships with people; you must have integrity and sensitivity, but also be assertive. You need to be able to interpret and explain legal and statistical information.

Earnings

Typical starting salaries for graduates range from £22,000 to £26,000. At senior levels salaries range from £35,000 to £80,000. This wide variation is accounted for by the range of size and type of companies and organisations that employ human resources managers. Location, type of industry and number of staff employed are all important factors in determining pay.

Training officer/manager

Training officers work in medium-sized and large firms and organisations, national and local government, emergency services and voluntary organisations. They are responsible for identifying training requirements, designing training programmes, delivering training to individuals or groups and evaluating the success of training.

Entry, qualifications and training

This is an area of work that people move into after gaining experience in other posts or following general HR experience. A professional qualification is advisable. The CIPD offers a certificate in training practice for those new to the profession or with limited experience. NVQs in training and development at levels 3–5 are available.

Personal attributes

You need to be happy and confident presenting to or facilitating groups of people. You need to be a good problem solver and able to get people to change their attitudes. You must also be well organised, positive and enthusiastic. Sometimes you will have to be creative and imaginative, developing your own training materials.

Earnings

Salaries start at between £19,000 and £22,000, sometimes a little more in London.

Info

Chartered Institute of Personnel and Development (CIPD)
020 8612 6200
www.cipd.co.uk

HYPNOTHERAPIST

Hypnotherapists help people deal with a whole range of problems, from stress and anxiety to giving up smoking, losing weight or increasing self-confidence. They work by putting their clients in a deeply relaxed state where they can then absorb positive ideas that will help them deal with difficulties or to change their behaviour in some way.

Entry, qualifications and training

While there are no specific academic entry qualifications to become a hypnotherapist, the three main hypnotherapy organisations are working towards regulating the profession. The three main certificate-awarding and training bodies are the National Council for Hypnotherapy (NCH), the Hypnotherapy Society and the General Hypnotherapy Register (GHR). You need to contact these organisations to obtain course details. There are some postgraduate courses in hypnotherapy. To do one of these, you must already have a degree; psychology or healthcare subjects would again be particularly useful, though not essential. A background in healthcare, counselling or psychology would also be very useful. The courses provide training in the theory and practice of hypnotherapy. If the profession becomes regulated, then more clearly supervised training is likely to result.

Personal attributes

You must have very good communication skills, be able to talk to people, listen to them and put them at ease. You have to have an extremely responsible and mature attitude to your work. A pleasant, calm voice is also an asset. Since you are likely to be self-employed, you need good organisational and financial skills too.

Earnings

The majority of hypnotherapists are self-employed and charge per session. Charges for one session vary from £40 to £150, depending on whether you are seeing someone just once for a specific issue, or whether you are offering a series of weekly sessions. Newly qualified hypnotherapists earn between £15,000 and £21,000 if they work hours that equate to a full-time job.

Info

The General Hypnotherapy Register
(GHR)
01590 683770
www.general-hypnotherapy-register.com

Hypnotherapy Society
0845 602 4585
www.hypnotherapysociety.com

National Council for Hypnotherapy
(NCH)
0800 952 0545
www.hypnotherapists.org.uk

Skills for Health
0117 922 1155
www.skillsforhealth.org.uk

ILLUSTRATION

(see Art and Design and Medical Illustrator)

IMAGE CONSULTANT

Politicians, pop stars, sports personalities, business people, fashion specialists – even whole businesses – all of these and others might choose to employ an image consultant. An image consultant looks at the kinds of visual impression made by someone in the public eye and helps them work out how to create maximum impact and appear in a style that supports the message they want to put across. This might be flamboyant or serious, dynamic or thoughtful. Image consultants advise on appropriate clothing to wear, what colours suit a person, what hairstyle(s) they might use, what style of make-up to apply, where to shop, how to stand, sit, etc. They may recommend to a client that he or she get some voice coaching, or be seen taking part in a particular activity. Image consultants normally work from their own homes, so they need to have a suitable office area. They will also visit clients and accompany them on shopping trips, to hair salons, manicurists, etc. They help clients prepare for photography sessions or press conferences. They might also work with a client who is about to give a presentation of some kind.

Entry, qualifications and training

There are no specific entry requirements and not that many job opportunities. It is likely to be a second career after a background in one or more of the following areas: fashion, hairdressing and beauty, public relations or marketing.

Personal attributes

You need to be a confident communicator with a real sense of style – of what works and what does not. You need a good eye for colour and an interest in fashion. You have to be good at establishing your clients' trust and confidence, since you are advising them on very personal aspects of their appearance and how they come across. You also have to listen to them and work with them so that they are comfortable and effective when they use your suggestions.

Earnings

There is little data available; nearly all image consultants are self-employed. People who can afford to employ image consultants generally have quite a lot of money, though, and successful image consultants earn between £30,000 and £40,000 a year.

Info

The Institute of Image Consulting
0800 781 1715
www.inst.org/image-consulting-courses

IMMIGRATION OFFICER

Immigration officers and assistant immigration officers work for the UK Border Agency, which is part of the Home Office. They work at the nearly 50 air and seaports checking passports, visas and work permits and interviewing any travellers who are non-EU or non-British citizens entering the United Kingdom. Immigration officers have to try to establish why people are visiting the UK and check that the reasons given are really the case. They may be involved in surveillance work and in arranging to remove people from the United Kingdom who do not have the right to remain.

Entry, qualifications and training

You may not need formal entry qualifications, though a good general education is an advantage. The Border Agency sets its own selection tests, which are designed to assess your powers of written and spoken communication and your ability to take responsibility. You must be aged between 18 and 64. Having a foreign language can also be an advantage. For many roles you need a driving licence and for most posts you must be a British citizen. Training is on the job and there is a clear career development and promotion structure in the Border Agency.

Personal attributes

You need good powers of observation, a calm but firm manner and the ability to work closely as part of a team. You may need to take quick decisions and you must be able to take responsibility.

Earnings

New entrants earn close to £21,000, rising to £33,000 for senior officers. There may also be additional payments for working unsocial hours.

Info

UK Border Agency	Civil Service Jobs Online
www.homeoffice.gov.uk	www.civilservice.gov.uk/jobs

INFORMATION SCIENCE

Information science is the collection, classification, storage and retrieval of information and knowledge, and the main occupations relating to this are outlined below.

Archivist

Working as an archivist, you manage and preserve collections of historical records and documents. The collections you work with are of all types, from books, photographs and maps to audio, film and electronic files. Collections may belong to government, hospitals, universities, businesses, museums, libraries, families or individuals. Your day-to-day work is likely to include making sure materials are stored correctly and kept in good condition, identifying, dating, cataloguing and indexing archive materials, helping people to use the archives and carrying out research. You may also be expected to give talks about the collections you manage and to seek out and negotiate the purchase of new material to help extend or complete your collections.

Entry, qualifications and training

The main qualification is the postgraduate diploma in archive management, which is run at six UK universities. To be accepted on to one of these programmes you need a good honours degree, usually a 2.1. Any discipline is acceptable, but history, or a subject where you have had to research original source material, will be particularly useful. Many entrants start as records clerks or assistant archivists. In fact, such work experience is very important if you want to complete a postgraduate diploma. Many applicants also do quite a lot of voluntary work to strengthen their applications. Your paid or voluntary experience must be in an archive or records management department, not a library. The Society of Archivists keeps a list of suitable paid and voluntary training places. Tracking down employers who can provide experience can be quite hard – universities and local government offices have some of the largest archive and records departments.

Personal attributes

A passionate interest in history and in original source material is essential. You should be logical, well organised and good at paying attention to detail. You meet all sorts of people in this work, so good communication skills and a real commitment to customer service are very important. At senior level you also need to be good at managing members of a team.

Earnings

The Society of Archivists suggests a minimum of £22,000 for newly qualified archivists. Higher salaries tend to be paid in academia. Senior archivists earn between £35,000 and £60,000.

Info

The National Archives
www.nationalarchives.gov.uk

Society of Archivists
01823 327030
www.archives.org.uk

Museums Libraries and Archives Council
www.mla.gov.uk

Information scientist

Rather like librarians, information scientists organise, manage and develop information systems. Working with IT and paper-based systems, they store, analyse and retrieve information and distribute it to interested clients. They work for many types of organisation and with all kinds of information, including scientific, technical, legal, commercial, financial and economic. As well as cataloguing and indexing information and dealing with enquiries, information scientists often have to analyse statistics or write reports summarising highly technical or specialised information.

Entry, qualifications and training

This is a graduate profession and unless your degree is in librarianship or information science/management, you also have to do a one-year postgraduate qualification. Competition for places on these courses is fierce, and you need a year's experience in a library or information centre of some kind before you start your course.

Personal attributes

You must be able to get on well with people and enjoy dealing with enquiries. It is important for you to have good IT skills: experience of handling databases is particularly useful. You should have a good memory and either a breadth of knowledge or highly specialist knowledge in a particular field such as law or science.

Earnings

Trainees earn between £18,000 and £20,000. Newly qualified professionals earn £22,000 to £28,000. With further professional experience information scientists earn between £30,000 and £40,000 – a few more than this.

Info

Institute for the Management of
Information Systems
www.imis.org.uk

Chartered Institute of Library and
Information Professionals (CILIP)
020 7255 0500
www.cilip.org.uk

Association for Information
Management (ASLIB)
020 7253 3349
www.aslib.com

Librarian/information manager

Librarians and information managers anticipate the information needs of their clients, acquire that information by the most efficient means possible on behalf of their clients, and may well analyse it and repackage it for the client. Information may come in the form of a book or journal, or may be extracted from databases in-house, on CD ROM or online. Librarians and information managers need to be able to use the internet and show others how to do so.

Information needs to be organised to make it accessible to users by indexing, cataloguing and classifying. Librarians and information managers promote and exploit the library's collection to users of the library or information source and assist them with any enquiries. They work in public libraries and schools, universities and colleges, in government, in the law, in hospitals, business and industry, and also in accountancy, engineering, professional and learned societies and in virtually all areas of economic activity.

Entry, qualifications and training

Library assistants are usually required to have four to five GCSEs or equivalent, to include English language; training is on the job. Part-time or distance-learning vocational courses leading to City & Guilds and SQA qualifications are available to library assistants in post. NVQs levels 2–4 in Information and Library Services are also available. To qualify as a professional librarian or information officer and gain Chartered Membership of the Library Association, a degree or postgraduate qualification accredited by the association is necessary.

First degree courses, postgraduate diplomas and Master's are jointly accredited by the Library Association and the Institute of Information Scientists. A full list of the courses offered by 17 universities is available through the Library Association website. The Library Association and Institute of Information Scientists have joined together to create a new organisation, the Chartered Institute of Library and Information Professionals.

Personal attributes

Librarians and information managers need to be well educated, with an outgoing personality, and able to communicate with people at all levels with clarity, accuracy and tact. They need intellectual curiosity, breadth of knowledge and a logical and methodical approach to seeking out, organising and presenting information. A good memory is also useful. Management skills and an interest in working with computers are important assets.

Earnings

Library assistants earn from £15,000 to £18,000. Newly qualified librarians earn £19,000 to £24,000. Chartered librarians earn between £23,000 and £28,000. The Chartered Institute of Library and Information Professionals (CILIP) produces annual salary guidelines.

Info

Institute for the Management of
Information Systems
www.imis.org.uk

Chartered Institute of Library and
Information Professionals (CILIP)
020 7255 0500
www.cilip.org.uk

Association for Information
Management (ASLIB)
020 7253 3349
www.aslib.com

INFORMATION AND COMMUNICATION TECHNOLOGY

Information technology is a part of most businesses and organisations of every kind. In many different jobs you are likely to have some involvement with information technology, whether you are processing payments, providing information to customers, communicating with colleagues, ordering stock or managing production systems – these are just a few examples of how you might use IT, even though your job title may not relate directly to IT functions. The careers described in this section, however, are those where working with information technology, its users and its customers, is central to your job. IT is always in a state of development and it is impossible to cover every job title relevant to this sector, but many of the most representative career options are described here. Roles in marketing and training are also relevant to this sector.

Applications developer

Applications developers (sometimes referred to as applications programmers) translate software requirements into concise and precise programming code. Most applications developers specialise in a specific development environment, such as e-commerce, e-learning or computer games. They develop detailed knowledge of particular computer languages. Their main activities involve writing specifications and designing, building, testing, implementing and sometimes supporting applications using computer languages and development tools.

Computer games developer

Computer games developers design interactive games for PCs and for games consoles. They create and test new games and refine and update existing ones. Development of games is very much a team effort, where professionals with different areas of expertise, eg animation, design, graphics and sound engineering, all have to work together. The starting point is the original idea or concept, with all these aspects of the technology contributing to a successful finished title. There are now some degree courses available in computer games development.

Computer service and repair technician

Technicians are employed by retailers, manufacturers and organisations that make extensive use of computers in their business. Regular upgrading of office systems means that a substantial amount of time is spent on installing and checking new systems, the rest being spent on diagnosing and correcting faults.

Database administration

Organisations obtain and store information about their customers, accounts, orders or stock levels on computers. The database manager takes responsibility for maintaining these and for security, access and the legal use of information held.

Forensic computer analyst

This is a relatively small but growing area of IT specialist work. Forensic computer analysts work for the police and various government agencies helping to tackle IT crime. The work may involve investigating computer hacking, internet fraud, the downloading of pornography, terrorist networks and industrial, commercial and political espionage. You are likely to need a relevant IT degree or industry qualification to get into this work.

Hardware engineer

Engineers design, develop and undertake research into computers and the computerised components of cars and appliances. They are involved in manufacture, installation and testing. As well as dealing with engineering issues they need to be aware of safety, efficiency and environmental factors.

Help desk adviser

Help desk advisers give advice to customers by telephone, by e-mail and by online diagnosis. They are the first line of support for customers who are experiencing difficulties with hardware and software. They work with their customers to identify faults and suggest solutions. If they cannot help the customer to solve the problem, they may refer them to a second line of support. Help desk advisers work for retailers, manufacturers, internet service providers and in-house for many large organisations such as businesses, universities or government departments.

Multimedia programmer

The key to being a successful multimedia programmer is that you have to have both creative and imaginative skills and good technical IT skills. Multimedia programmers add all those functions that make a product multimedia. They write computer programs or create websites that draw together multimedia features such as text, sound, graphics, digital photography, 2/3-D modelling, animation and video, working to a designer's specification. Multimedia products work on particular 'platforms', predominantly the internet, as well as interactive television, information kiosks, DVDs, CD ROMs, computer games consoles and mobile phones.

Network engineer

A network is a system of computers and other communication equipment linked to exchange information. This could be used to enable staff to share information through a company intranet or for global communication via the internet. Network engineers advise clients on options and benefits, as well as installing and testing equipment. They also diagnose faults and maintain the hardware, software and cabling systems.

Software engineer

They have a similar role to that of programmers but use this in technical and engineering settings. They may, for example, work on systems for contact centres or air traffic control. Most have a degree in software engineering or a related computer science. Many universities ask for maths A level or equivalent for entry to such courses. As most commercial and manufacturing functions now have established IT systems, the work undertaken by software engineers has shifted emphasis from creating new systems to using existing software and devising appropriate interfaces to integrate it with new products.

Systems analyst

Systems analysts work on delivering the best IT solutions for an organisation's needs. They examine how and where computerised systems would be of benefit, assess the hardware needed and look at the most cost-effective solutions. Systems analysts then work with programmers and supervise software production.

Systems support staff

Systems support staff work for suppliers of software and hardware, internet service providers or the computer departments of large companies. They provide technical support to users, often via the phone or e-mail. The work involves establishing what the problem is, helping the client put things right or deciding to refer the problem to other specialists. It requires detailed product knowledge as well as extreme patience and excellent communication skills. Training is often on the job, with entrants coming from a variety of backgrounds in which they have been able to demonstrate high levels of computer literacy.

Web designer

(see also Art and Design)

Web designers design and plan websites either for their own company or for clients. The complexity of the task varies according to the nature of the site, and can include extensive use of multimedia or implementing secure systems for financial transactions. A considerable amount of time is spent testing sites and checking they are user-friendly. Once the site is working properly, designers upload it to a server and may be responsible for registering it with search engines in terms of both content and design.

Designers need an in-depth knowledge of the internet and must be up to date with technological developments. Many designers work on a freelance basis. The availability of jobs in this area is decreasing as increasingly sophisticated software packages are making web design less of a specialist area.

Entry, qualifications and training

Many employers set their own entry requirements, but are increasingly asking for academic or vocational qualifications, from NVQs to degrees. Applicants for posts may be asked to take aptitude tests to assess their numeracy, logic, accuracy, thinking speed and verbal reasoning. Systems analysts and programmers are generally expected to be graduates. Entry to computer science degrees is normally with two or three A levels or equivalent, including maths. Web designers need knowledge of HTML and Java as well as familiarity with web design software such as Dreamweaver and Flash. Technicians and network engineers usually have a related National Diploma or vendor qualifications.

There are a large number of computer-related courses, and entry requirements vary according to the nature of the course. A growing number of Foundation degrees with flexible entry requirements are becoming available. Product-specific and professional qualifications are offered by companies such as Microsoft, Cisco and Novell and by professional bodies such as the British Computer Society (BCS), the Help Desk Institute and the Institute for the Management of Information Systems.

Employment-based training opportunities include Modern Apprenticeships for school leavers and Graduate Apprenticeships for those from non-IT disciplines. Many companies run their own programmes as well as sending trainees on relevant external courses.

Personal attributes

The balance of skills that are most important varies between some of the above roles, but excellent problem solving, analytical and technical expertise and the willingness to develop with technological advances are all essential, though to different degrees. Being able to work under pressure, being part of a team and communicating well, especially to less technically trained colleagues, are equally important.

Earnings

Encompassing many careers, a range of entry levels and work for different types of employer, the range of salaries is wide. Here are a few typical examples. Help desk advisers start on £15,500 to £17,000 and network engineers £19,000 to £24,500. Web developers start between £17,000 and £24,000. Jobs that involve management or sensitive areas such as computer security will pay much higher salaries – £30,000 to £50,000.

Info

British Computer Society (BCS)
0845 300 4417
www.bcs.org

British Interactive Media
Association (BIMA)
01277 658107
www.bima.co.uk

e-skills UK (The Sector Skills
Council for Business and
Information Technology)
020 7963 8920
www.e-skills.com

Institution of Analysts and
Programmers (IAP)
020 8567 2118
www.iap.org.uk

Institute for the Management of
Information Systems
0700 002 3456
www.imis.org.uk

Intellect UK
020 7331 2000
www.intellectuk.org

National Computing Centre (NCC)
0161 228 6333
www.ncc.co.uk

Skillset (Sector Skills Council for
the Creative Industries)
020 7713 9800
www.skillset.org

INSURANCE

The insurance industry is a significant employer in the UK. Many large insurance companies, providing insurance cover for every kind of item, situation and mishap, are based in the UK or have large operations here. There are many different career pathways open to people who have an interest in working with people and with financial information.

Account manager

As an insurance account manager your key role would be to ensure that your company's insurance policies are recommended by brokers and financial advisers to their clients. You would arrange meetings with brokers and advisers to ensure that they are aware of new products that you are developing. You might work with other members of the insurance team to develop new products as a result of requests from brokers on behalf of their clients. You could be involved in producing marketing literature or in training customer service staff to provide appropriate information on your insurance products. You could be responsible for monitoring brokers and advisers to see that they sell your products according to industry codes of practice.

Broker

Insurance brokers are the link between customers and insurance providers. They have a detailed knowledge of insurance products, whether this is life assurance, motor insurance, buildings insurance or any other specific field. They do not work for one insurance company – they work for customers trying to find the most appropriate insurance cover at the best possible price.

Claims administrator

Claims administrators, sometimes known as claims settlers or claims technicians, deal with policy holders who are making claims. Administrators issue forms, explain procedures to customers, gather further information and issue payments where claims are simple. If there is some dispute or the claim is very complex, they may have to refer it to their managers. Claims administrators work for brokers or for insurance companies. They normally specialise in a particular type of insurance, eg motor or household.

Claims inspector

When anyone makes a claim on their insurance, the claims inspector assesses the claim to ensure that it is truthful and also to check that the insurance company is liable for payment. Inspectors carry out detailed inspections of damaged goods or property and their work often involves interviewing claimants either in person or by telephone.

Loss adjuster

Loss adjusters carry out very similar work to that of the claims inspector – the key difference is that they are independent. They investigate claims on behalf of insurance companies. They assess the causes of loss or damage, and make sure that the insurance claim is valid and covered by the policy. They can deal with all kinds of insurance claim, including damage by fire, flooding, theft or accident.

Risk surveyor/analyst

Insurance risk surveyors, also known as insurance risk analysts, work for general insurance companies, brokers, or firms of specialist surveyors. Their main role is to advise about risk, based on technical knowledge, experience and good practice. They visit sites such as commercial premises or engineering works and produce detailed reports on any particular risks associated with the site. They can also advise people on how to reduce the impact of these risks.

Insurance technician

Insurance technicians provide all the day-to-day administrative and clerical back-up that keeps the insurance industry going. They are often referred to as insurance clerks or insurance administrators. The work includes sending out routine correspondence such as policy renewal reminders, entering data onto computer systems or sending out marketing information. Exact tasks and responsibilities vary according to what kind of insurance organisation and for what department they are working.

Underwriter

Underwriters assess the financial risk involved in insuring particular items, premises or projects. They calculate the prices for insurance premiums, aiming to fix on a price that will be profitable for the insurer but also competitive for potential customers.

Entry, qualifications and training

Insurance claims administrators and technicians usually need four or five GCSEs grades A–C, including English and maths. Exact requirements vary from firm to firm. Accounts managers often start as technicians and work their way up. For brokers and underwriters, different firms set their own entry requirements. These vary from five GCSEs grades A–C to two A levels or a degree in a mathematical subject. Many firms like you to have had some experience in insurance or other financial work. Study for examinations from the Chartered Insurance Institute while working is usual and takes two to five years depending on the level you are working towards.

Brokers are regulated by the Financial Services Authority (FSA) and need to meet the FSA's training and competency standards. Brokers who deal in long-term investments such as pensions and life assurance need an approved qualification from the FSA.

Loss adjusters normally have several years' experience in the insurance industry or in other professional fields such as accountancy, law or surveying.

Personal attributes

People working in insurance must have excellent written and spoken English, be able to talk to people and write concise accurate reports. Some roles require good negotiating skills and the ability to deal with sensitive situations. Some degree of numeracy skill is important for all jobs. To be an underwriter, you need to be able to analyse complex statistical information.

Earnings

New-entrant brokers earn £17,000 to £23,000 – £20,000 to £40,000 with experience. For jobs that involve the sale of insurance products, part of your salary is earned through commission or bonuses. Claims managers earn around £19,000 to begin with – up to £60,000 if managing a large department. Loss adjusters start on £18,000 to £25,000, possibly rising to £45,000. The picture is very similar for underwriters. Technicians start on £12,999 to £19,000. In all cases achieving professional qualifications is likely to boost salaries.

Info

Financial Skills Partnership
0845 257 3772
www.directions.org.uk

Chartered Insurance Institute
020 8989 8464
www.cii.co.uk

ifs School of Finance
01227 818609
www.ifslearning.ac.uk

DiscoverRisk
www.discoverrisk.co.uk

INTERIOR DECORATOR

(see Construction Trades)

INTERIOR DESIGNER/INSCAPE DESIGNER

Interior designers work for commercial organisations as well as undertaking private commissions. They are responsible for the interiors of buildings (whereas an architect is responsible for its shell). Interior design can cover materials for floors and ceilings, fitments and fittings, and colour schemes, along with electrical and spatial planning. The commercial organisations may be offices, hotels, pubs, stores or banks. Interior designers may work with architects, have their own consultancies, or work in design units within large organisations.

Entry, qualifications and training

Most interior designers have a degree in one of the following subjects: fine art, fashion and textile design, product design, interior design or graphic design. It is possible to get into this work without a degree if you have really demonstrable creative flair or a lot of relevant experience. Most training is on the job, working closely with more experienced and established designers. It can be valuable to do short courses on photography, desktop publishing and new product knowledge, in order to remain current.

Personal attributes

As well as an eye for colour and a feel for fabric, you need considerable technical and product knowledge and technical drawing skills, either on paper or with computer-aided design (CAD). You need to be able to work closely with other people and, if you work freelance, you should be confident enough to promote your own work.

Earnings

Salaries start at between £16,000 and £22,000, but if you have established your reputation you may earn far more. If you work freelance you can charge £30 or more an hour. What you can charge depends upon geographical location and upon personal recommendations of your work.

Info

Design Council
www.designcouncil.org.uk

British Institute of Interior Design
www.biid.org.uk

Chartered Society of Designers
(CSD)
www.csd.org.uk

Creative and Cultural Skills
(The Sector Skills Council for Craft,
Cultural Heritage, Design, Literature,
Music, Performing, and Visual Arts)
020 7015 1800
www.ccskills.org.uk

JEWELLERY

(see Crafts)

JOURNALISM

Journalists write and produce material for print, broadcast and digital media. Twenty-four-hour news and new ways of receiving that news have had a great impact on this sector. Newspapers, magazines, radio, television and internet news channels offer myriad opportunities for journalists, though every one of these opportunities is hotly pursued by many applicants. New technologies have blurred some of the demarcation lines between jobs in journalism. In national media there may still be clear distinctions between editors, reporters, sub-editors, production editors, features editors etc, but in smaller business-to-business (trade) magazines one person can be concerned with editing, commissioning, sub-editing and production-editing tasks.

Editor

The editor of a publication is responsible for its policy, content and the appointment and organisation of staff. An editor will prepare schedules for content and build up key relationships with external bodies. An editor of a publication will become the spokesperson for the title and will be expected to speak at conferences and to comment publicly on issues of importance. The editor works closely with the different groups within the team, including writers, production staff, advertising sales team, marketing and the publisher (*see also* Publishing). The editor will hold regular editorial meetings to discuss current work and to plan forthcoming features. The editor will also oversee the editorial budget. Section editors (newspapers and magazines) specialise in specific areas, run their own teams of journalists and commission articles for their sections. Typical newspaper sections include home affairs, foreign affairs, health, media, education and travel.

Entry, qualifications and training

Most editors have come from a background in journalism and have worked their way up to the job, and so may have journalism qualifications.

Personal attributes

The mix of skills you need depends partly on how large a publication you are working for, but certainly team leadership. Good planning skills and the ability to meet deadlines are essential. Being able to create and maintain a 'house style' in both appearance and content is very important.

Earnings

Earnings vary according to whether you edit a trade magazine, a local free newspaper, a paid-for regional paper, a popular weekly or monthly magazine, or a national daily newspaper. At the lower end, editors of trade magazines or free local newspapers earn between £25,000 and £35,000. At the top end, editors of national daily papers may earn £80,000 to £90,000. Editors of regional newspapers and well-known magazines earn between £40,000 and £60,000 – more for some magazine titles.

Journalist

Journalists/reporters find, research and write news articles and features for newspapers, magazines, special-interest periodicals, news agencies, radio, television and the internet (see Broadcast Journalist). Most reporters start out on local papers where they cover a mix of stories, from weddings to council meetings. Local reporters are generally expected to multi-skill and might be expected to write the local news or features, sub-edit or take photographs. They work irregular hours and must be able to produce accurate, interesting and readable copy quickly, often in noisy offices or even public places. Editors look for trainees with an interest in current affairs and events, an accessible writing style and a good use of grammar, and an understanding of the role of the local newspaper within its community. Good time management and being able to work under pressure are also important qualities as journalists have to work to strict deadlines.

Inexperienced journalists are expected to work their way up, starting with more routine jobs. Regional and local newspapers recruit trainee reporters and photographers under a training contract and some newspaper groups run trainee schemes. These schemes are open to school or college leavers who have not taken a specialist university or college course. Applications for traineeships should be made direct to the editor. Direct entrants to these schemes will be expected to attend block-release or day-release courses and to sit the National Council for the Training of Journalists (NCTJ) National Certificate or a National (Scottish) Vocational Qualification.

National papers generally employ reporters with some experience, and will look to journalists who have had experience on local newspapers. Trade magazine experience, where knowledge of a specialist area has been developed, is also a route to entry into the national press. Occasionally national newspapers advertise for trainee recruits, but these opportunities are rare.

Trade magazines are also a route into the industry. Many magazines are produced on a monthly or fortnightly basis and specialise in particular subjects.

Reporters on trade magazines are able to develop a specialist subject that can then be used to transfer to writing for national newspapers or to develop into a freelance career.

Experienced journalists have the opportunity to become feature writers or columnists for national newspapers. Feature writers suggest subjects for research, and produce longer than average articles dealing with topics not necessarily of current news value but of general interest. Feature writers will have developed an expertise or specialism within the subject they write about, and may have come originally not from a journalistic background but from the specialist area on which they write. Columnists often write about subjects from a personal point of view. Feature writers and columnists tend to be freelance writers working for a number of different newspapers, magazines and publishers, and will also work in broadcast media.

Entry, qualifications and training

There is always lively competition for this work. You can either train with a newspaper (known as direct entry), or take a course at college or university (known as pre-entry). If you opt for a course you need to check that it is accredited by the NCTJ. To get onto most courses you will need five GCSEs grades A–C, including English, and two A levels. If you already have a degree you may be able to take an 18-week fast-track course in journalism. Whether you train via work or through a course, competition for entry is extremely fierce. You need to do as much as you can to strengthen your application. Write articles for local newspapers or student magazines and try to get some voluntary work experience on a local newspaper. Journalism courses allow you to take the NCTJ preliminary certificate as part of your studies. Whether you enter journalism through a course or as a direct entrant, much of your training will be on the job, learning from more experienced colleagues.

Personal attributes

To be a good journalist you must have excellent writing skills and be able to adapt these to suit your particular audience. You should be good at researching information, talking to people, listening and encouraging them to talk to you. You need very good IT skills and you must be able to meet a deadline without fail.

Earnings

Trainees earn £15,000 to £21,000. Once you have completed your training, earnings are between £20,000 and £40,000, depending on whether you work for a magazine, a local or regional newspaper or a national daily. The most successful journalists can earn £100,000, but few reach this level.

Sub-editor

Sub-editors are journalists who work for national daily or weekly newspapers, local and regional newspapers, and magazines of every kind. They process all the copy that will appear in their publication to ensure that it is accurate, free of typographical errors and spelling mistakes, makes sense and reads well. Sub-editors take the stories written by journalists and reporters and rewrite the copy to make it fit the 'house style', adhere to word counts and remain within the law. The sub-editor is responsible for putting the story on the page and is often responsible for designing and laying out pages. Sub-editors write headlines, picture captions and summaries.

Entry, qualifications and training

Many sub-editors will have been trained as reporters and then specialised. The NCTJ runs short courses and distance-learning qualifications for sub-editors. The Periodical Publishers Association also runs courses for sub-editors.

Personal attributes

Sub-editors must be meticulous in their work. They are required to make quick decisions and to have the confidence to rewrite or cut the work of others. They must be able to work under pressure and to meet deadlines.

Earnings

Sub-editors start on between £18,000 and £24,000, depending on the title they work for. Senior sub-editors earn from £25,000 to £55,000. Top salaries are paid only to chief sub-editors on national newspapers.

Info

National Union of Journalists (NUJ)
www.nujtraining.org.uk

Skillset Careers
08080 300 900 (England and Northern Ireland)
0808 100 8094 (Scotland)
0800 121 815 (Wales)
www.skillset.org/careers

National Council for the Training of Journalists (NCTJ)
01799 544014
www.nctj.com

Newspaper Society
www.newspapersoc.org.uk

Broadcast journalist

Broadcast journalists work in radio, television and online. Unlike print journalists, almost all broadcast journalists take a postgraduate pre-entry course. Some journalists still make the transition to broadcasting from newspapers, but it is increasingly regarded as a specialist branch of the profession in its own right. As in print, broadcast journalists will need to have good communication skills, an enquiring mind, knowledge of current events and a sense of what makes a news story. The ability to speak clear, standard English is important. Both the BBC and ITN run traineeships for entrants into broadcast journalism.

Experience in radio journalism can be found in hospital, community and college radio. This can be used as evidence of interest and experience when applying to courses – many postgraduate courses will require a recorded news story as part of their application procedure.

Entry, qualifications and training

You can move into broadcast journalism from newspaper or magazine journalism and join a new-entrant training scheme with a TV or radio broadcaster – this is referred to as direct entry. You can complete a degree or postgraduate qualification in broadcast journalism – this is known as the pre-entry route. You can also get details of courses from the Broadcast Journalism Training Council. If you have a degree in journalism, media studies or politics this may strengthen your application for a training position. This is a fiercely competitive field and any voluntary work for community radio could be helpful.

Personal attributes

You have to be an excellent communicator, able to speak clearly and with confidence. You need to be able to listen and to question and to be sensitive or persistent as required. You also need good writing and research skills. You have to be able to work under pressure and to meet deadlines.

Earnings

Salaries on training schemes are between £16,000 and £19,000. Once you are qualified, these rise to £25,000 to £40,000. Top broadcast journalists who are household names can earn far more than this – some in the region of £100,000 plus.

Info

Broadcast Journalists' Training Council
01778 440025
www.bjtc.org.uk

Radio Academy
020 7927 9920
www.radioacademy.org

The RadioCentre
020 7306 2603
www.radiocentre.org

National Council for the Training of Journalists (NCTJ)
01799 544014
www.nctj.com

Skillset Careers
08080 300 900 (England and Northern Ireland)
0808 100 8094 (Scotland)
0800 121 815 (Wales)
www.skillset.org/careers

Press photographer

(see Photography)

Web content editor

Web content editors research, write, edit, proof and update material on websites. This material includes images as well as text. Just like any magazine or newspaper journalist or editor, web content editors try to ensure that what they produce is appropriate to their target readership. Web content might include local and national news, opinion, information about products and services, factual information or entertainment. Editors work closely with technical staff who develop and design websites. Web content editors also liaise closely with the clients for whom they are writing, editing and updating material.

Entry, qualifications and training

There is no one route for entry into this work. Many web content editors have worked as journalists. Some have worked in IT or marketing, and many have considerable experience in the profession or subject with which they are going to work. Knowledge of desktop publishing and photo imaging packages can greatly increase your employability.

Personal attributes

You need excellent writing skills, with a good grasp of English grammar. You should be creative, but not lose sight of the importance of detail and accuracy. You should be able to write to very specific word counts or house styles and you should be able to communicate really well with other members of your team.

Earnings

New entrants earn between £19,000 and £23,000. With three or four years' experience, and depending on the size of the organisation you work for and where you live, this can rise to well over £30,000.

Info

Society for Editors and Proofreaders
020 8785 5617
www.sfep.org.uk

Skillset Careers
08080 300 900 (England and Northern Ireland)
0808 100 8094 (Scotland)
08000 121 815 (Wales)
www.skillset.org/careers

World Wide Web Consortium (W3C)
www.w3.org

e-skills UK (The Sector Skills Council for Business and Information Technology)
www.e-skills.com

National Union of Journalists (NUJ)
www.nuj.org.uk

LABORATORY TECHNICIAN

(see also Medical and Healthcare Science)

Assisting with research, helping to diagnose diseases, measuring pollution levels and developing new products – these are some of the tasks laboratory technicians help to undertake. Laboratory assistants ensure that equipment is clean and in working order. They set up experiments and investigations and record data. They may also be involved in stock control, monitoring and ordering chemicals, equipment and other supplies. Laboratory technicians work in education, in medicine, in the pharmaceutical industry, in food science and in research laboratories of every kind. Those working in education help school and college students to use equipment safely and record results correctly, and they may be involved in demonstrating how to conduct experiments.

Entry, qualifications and training

You can get into laboratory technician work with four GCSEs grades A–C, so long as you have maths and one science. However, many employers now expect applicants to have GTEC, HNC or HND qualifications, a Foundation degree, or a degree in a science subject, eg biotechnology or chemistry. It is also possible to start as a laboratory assistant and work towards qualifications on a part-time basis. There are several qualifications to choose from: NVQ levels 2, 3 and 4 in Laboratory and Associated Activities or NVQ levels in Clinical Laboratory Support. You could also study part-time for a BTEC HND/HNC or Foundation degree while working, rather than before joining this profession. If you work in a school science laboratory, CLEAPSS, the School Science Service, offers several professional development courses. Because technology is changing fast, your employer, whether you work in healthcare, education or research and development, is likely to send you on short courses to keep you up to date with changes and developments.

Personal attributes

You need a genuine interest in science and in the kinds of projects on which you are working. You need to have a very thorough and careful approach to all your work, be able to follow procedures and record results accurately. You will need a range of technical and IT skills, though the precise nature of these varies from job to job. You have to be good at working as part of a team. If you are working in schools or colleges, you may have to explain and demonstrate experiments and procedures to students and assist them in their work, so good training and information-giving skills are important.

Earnings

Laboratory assistants earn £13,500 to £16,000. Starting salaries for technicians are between £15,500 and £21,000. Senior technicians earn £20,000 to £27,000. Private sector laboratories tend to pay the highest salaries, especially in 'cutting edge' fields of biotechnology.

Info

NHS Careers 0345 60 60 655 www.nhscareers.nhs.uk	Association for Science Education (ASE) www.ase.org.uk
SEMTA (The Sector Skills Council for Science, Engineering and Manufacturing Technologies) 0800 282167 www.semta.org.uk	CLEAPSS Schools Science Service 01895 251496 www.cleapss.org.uk

Animal technician

A very specific role in a laboratory is that of the animal technician. Animal technicians are the staff responsible for the care and welfare of animals used in biomedical, pharmaceutical and other fields of research. Governments around the world require that new medicines have been extensively tested on animals before allowing human clinical trials. Testing is also undertaken on veterinary medicines and other products which may have an effect on human health. Animal technicians are responsible for caring for the animals, undertaking observations, sampling for the scientific studies, and ensuring that the strict laws controlling their use are followed at all times. Applicants should have a genuine desire to work with animals and must demonstrate concern and respect for their well-being.

Entry, qualifications and training

The minimum entry qualifications are five GCSEs at grade C or above, but some entrants have A levels or a degree. The Institute of Animal Technology (AIT) offers five levels of qualification, from a basic one-year certificate to a postgraduate MSc.

You can get exemption from certain modules of these courses if you can offer sciences at A or degree level. These qualifications can be taken as distance-learning modules or at local colleges through day-release courses.

Personal attributes

You have to be comfortable handling animals and you must be kind, caring and calm when doing so. You also have to accept that you will have to do things that are stressful for animals, so you need to be prepared for this. You must be practical, thorough and meticulous, since you have to record scientific information accurately.

Earnings

Trainees earn £12,000 to £15,000 and from £15,000 to £20,000 for qualified technicians, but there is no national agreed rate for this work. A senior laboratory manager can earn up to £35,000.

Info

Lantra	Institute of Animal Technology
02476 696996	(AIT)
www.lantra.co.uk	www.iat.org.uk

LAND AND PROPERTY

The land and property sector covers many occupations connected with the management, sale and purchase of land and property.

Estate agent

Estate agents are responsible for the sale, letting and management of any kind of property – factories, shops, offices and farms as well as residential property. In many cases they also deal with valuation and survey work, and offer other services such as auctioneering and financial services advice. Large firms provide a wide range of these services through specialist departments employing qualified professionals, particularly in the area of surveying and valuation. Dedicated sales staff fulfil the role of property negotiators, and in the majority of smaller firms with just one or two branches a combination of these functions will be found.

Entry, qualifications and training

You don't necessarily need formal qualifications to become an estate agent. Relevant experience and the right skills are extremely important. At the moment there are not many graduates in this profession, but some large estate agent chains do run graduate training schemes. Where this is the case, a degree in a relevant subject such as surveying or business may put you at an advantage.

Many people start work in an administrative role with an estate agent and work their way up. In this case, each agent sets its own entry requirements, but many expect you to have GCSEs in English and maths.

You normally start as a trainee sales negotiator and receive on-the-job training from more experienced agents. The National Association of Estate Agents (NAEA) offers a range of distance-learning professional qualifications for estate agents. Qualifications cover residential property agency, commercial property agency, property letting and management, and property auctions.

Personal attributes

You must be outgoing, with very good people skills. You should be a good negotiator. You should be well organised, able to keep track of several things at the same time. You should have good written as well as spoken English and you should have a genuine interest in property.

Earnings

Trainees earn between £13,000 and £20,000, and once you handle sales you earn commission on properties sold. This can take earnings to £20,000 to £50,000. Estate agency is in the front line when there are fluctuations in the property market, so you can easily lose commission-based earnings.

Info

National Association of Estate
Agents (NAEA)
www.naea.co.uk

Royal Institution of Chartered
Surveyors (RICS)
0870 333 1600
www.rics.org

Asset Skills
01392 423399
www.assetskills.org

Gamekeeper

Gamekeepers work on large country estates for private landlords, management firms and private syndicates that wish to organise a shoot. They rear the game birds and fish, and protect them from poachers and predators. They must ensure that the proper environment for the game is maintained, and on shooting days they organise the beaters.

Entry, qualifications and training

There are no formal entry qualifications, but gamekeepers must have a driving licence, be good at handling a dog, and be suitable to apply for a shotgun licence. There are part- and full-time City & Guilds and BTEC courses in gamekeeping, and gamekeeping and countryside management. Some of these courses may set specific entry requirements. The training is on the job and most gamekeepers start as an assistant or under keeper.

Personal attributes

You have to love being outside in all weathers and have a real interest in nature. You need to be very practical, good with your hands and physically fit. It is important that you are very observant, both of animal and plant life and of safety issues. You are on your own for a great deal of the time, but you must be able to communicate well with other people when shoots or other events are taking place.

Earnings

Gamekeepers earn between £11,500 and £18,500. Many posts include free or subsidised accommodation, and a suitable motor vehicle.

Info

National Gamekeepers Organisation www.nationalgamekeepers.org.uk	**Lantra** 02476 696996 www.lantra.co.uk
Scottish Gamekeepers Association www.scottishgamekeepers.co.uk	

LANDSCAPE MANAGEMENT AND DESIGN

(see Gardening)

LANDSCAPE ARCHITECTURE

Landscape architecture as a profession covers the three divisions of design, management and science.

Landscape designer

Designers are trained in the planning and design of all types of outdoor spaces. They use design techniques based on their knowledge of the functional and aesthetic characteristics of landscape materials, and of the organisation of landscape elements, external spaces and activities. Their work ranges from large-scale landscape planning to the preparation of schemes for the short- and long-term development of individual sites. It also includes preparing detailed designs, specifications, contract drawings and letting and supervising contracts. Some practitioners are also qualified in other disciplines such as planning and architecture, and the landscape designer draws on many fields in order to promote new landscapes and sustain existing ones.

Landscape manager

Landscape managers employ management techniques in the long term care and development of new and existing landscapes, and also in determining policy and planning for future landscape management and use. They have particular expertise in the management and maintenance of landscape materials, both hard and soft, based on established principles of construction, horticulture and ecology. In addition, the landscape manager will have a thorough knowledge of budgetary control procedures, property and resource management, especially related to labour requirements and machinery, and the letting and administration of contracts.

Landscape scientist

Landscape scientists explore and investigate the flora, fauna and geology of an area to be landscaped or which has already been landscaped. They survey areas to find out what impact landscape projects will have on wildlife. They suggest strategies to encourage new wildlife into an area. They are involved at all stages of a project, from initial planning through to monitoring wildlife and other natural phenomena in an area once a project has been completed.

Entry, qualifications and training

The recognised professional qualification for those working in all aspects of landscape architecture is Member of the Landscape Institute (MLI), which entitles the use of the title Chartered Landscape Architect. There are three divisions: Design, Management and Science. Associate Membership, the first step towards achieving this, is gained after completing an accredited degree. Two years' relevant work is required as an Associate Member before taking the Institute's Professional Practice Examination and progressing to full Professional Membership. A list of accredited courses is available from the Landscape Institute.

Personal attributes

Those working in design need creativity, imagination, a practical outlook, interest in the landscape and an enthusiasm for working outdoors. Those in management require good organisational and interpersonal skills, consistent application and a practical outlook. Scientists need enthusiasm for the subject, technical commitment and good communication skills.

Earnings

New graduate landscape architects and scientists earn around £24,000. For fully qualified and chartered landscape architects, salaries range from £25,000 to £45,000. Some landscape specialists earn £50,000 plus. There is much variation according to whether you are working for a corporate development company landscaping gardens of expensive commercial premises, or working on a project funded by a voluntary body, for example.

Info

Lantra
02476 696996
www.lantra.co.uk

Landscape Institute
020 7299 4500
www.landscapeinstitute.org

Institute of Ecology and
Environmental Management (IEEM)
01962 868626
www.ieem.org.uk

LAW

The legal profession includes many occupations, all working on legal matters of one kind or another. The word 'lawyer' is a generic term that people use to describe both solicitors and barristers.

Advocate/barrister

Barristers have expertise in advocacy, and represent their clients in court. They are independent sources of legal advice and can advise clients on their case. Usually, they are hired by solicitors to represent a case in court and only become involved once advocacy before a court is required. They plead the case on behalf of the client and the client's solicitor. Barristers usually specialise in particular areas of law, such as criminal, chancery (estates and trusts), commercial, and common law, which includes family, housing and personal injury law. Most barristers are self-employed; working from offices referred to as chambers. Some work for government departments or agencies such as the Crown Prosecution Service. An increasing number of employed barristers work in private and public organisations such as charities or trade unions. In Scotland the role and responsibilities of an advocate are similar to those of a barrister in England and Wales. The work of a barrister or advocate is likely to include taking instructions from solicitors, studying and working out how to proceed with each particular case, answering complex legal questions raised by solicitors or by cases through researching complicated points of law and writing opinions on legal matters. If a case is to go to court the barrister will have to prepare for this and then appear in court speaking and questioning on behalf of either the defence or the prosecution.

Entry, qualifications and training

This is a highly competitive, almost exclusively graduate profession. In England and Wales you will need either a good law degree (2.1) or a good degree in another traditional academic subject. Some universities offering law degrees also require you to pass the National Law Admissions Test (LNAT). If your degree is not in law, you must take a one-year full-time or two-year part-time course – the

Common Professional Exam (CPE) or Graduate Diploma in Law (GDL). After this, the route is the same for everyone. You must get a place on the Bar Professional Training Course (BPTC). This is also offered as one year full-time or two years part-time and there is a central clearing system for applications. Applicants for the BPTC also have to join one of the four Inns of Court before starting the course. On completing the BPTC, hopeful barristers apply for a pupillage in a set of barristers' chambers (their word for offices). After completing a pupillage, the next stage is to get a tenancy to practise in a set of chambers. All stages are exceedingly competitive.

In Scotland, advocates need to pass a postgraduate diploma in law and spend two years practising as a solicitor before being called to the bar.

Personal attributes

As it will be necessary to understand and interpret complex legal wording into clear basic English, barristers must have an excellent command of the English language and a meticulous understanding of the use of words. Barristers must understand and talk knowledgeably about technical matters in order to be able to cross-examine the most expert witness, for example on complex aspects of technology. It is also useful if barristers present a highly confident and self-assured manner and can put on a 'good performance' in court. Since the work is confidential, a barrister needs to be trustworthy and discreet.

Earnings

Most barristers' earnings are based on the fees they charge. Trainees during pupillage earn around £10,000. After this the range is from £25,000 to £300,000. Salaries in the Crown Prosecution Service are between £30,000 and £80,000.

Info

The Bar Council
020 7242 0082
www.barstandardsboard.org.uk
www.barcouncil.org.uk

Law Careers
www.lawcareers.net

All About Law – The Law Careers
Website
www.allaboutlaw.co.uk

National Admissions Test for Law
(LNAT)
www.lnat.ac.uk

Barrister's clerk/advocate's clerk

The barrister's clerk is the administrator or manager of the business chambers, deciding which briefs to accept, which of the barristers in the chamber to give them to, and negotiating the fees with the solicitor. The accounts, the barristers' appointment books and the efficient day-to-day running of the office are all part of the job of an experienced clerk.

Entry, qualifications and training

The minimum qualification is four GCSE pass grades at A–C in academic subjects. Training is on the job and juniors can apply through the Institute of Barristers' Clerks to attend a two-year part-time Edexcel (BTEC) national certificate course studying organisation, finance, management, law, marketing and chambers administration. On obtaining the certificate, juniors may apply, after five years' service, for qualified Membership of the Institute of Barristers' Clerks.

Personal attributes

In order to manage efficient chambers and the barristers who work from them, a barrister's clerk needs good organisational skills, the ability to lead a team as well as be part of a team, and to get on with the general public. A good command of written and spoken English and an appreciation of the necessity for absolute confidentiality at all times are vital to success in this career.

Earnings

Clerks start on £15,000 to £18,000. Junior clerks with two or three years' experience earn £20,000 to £25,000; senior clerks may earn £60,000 to £80,000 plus a performance-related bonus.

Info

Institute of Barrister's Clerks
020 7831 7144
www.ibc.org.uk

Court staff

Court administrative officer

Court administrative officers and court administrative assistants ensure the smooth day-to-day running of the courts. They book cases, allocate cases to courtrooms, prepare lists of the day's cases and send out correspondence. They may also be involved in the collection of fines and providing information to members of the public. More senior administrative officers lead teams of assistants, ensuring that all the tasks listed above are carried out efficiently.

Entry, qualifications and training

To work as an administrative assistant you require two GCSEs grades A–C and to be an administrative officer you need five GCSEs grades A–C. If you have other useful administrative experience, you may be considered without these formal qualifications.

Personal attributes

You must be able to deal calmly and politely with people. You should have good organisational skills and be able to stay calm in a busy environment. You should be able to pay attention to detail and work well as part of a team.

Court legal adviser

Court legal advisers, sometimes referred to as court clerks, are legal advisers who give advice to unpaid (non-stipendiary) magistrates who are trying cases in the magistrates courts. They are qualified lawyers, but they do not take part in the decision making about judgments and sentencing. As magistrates do not have to be legally qualified, it is the court clerks who ensure that magistrates interpret and apply the law correctly.

Entry, qualifications and training

Court legal advisers have to be either qualified solicitors or barristers, who themselves must have either a law degree or an approved postgraduate legal qualification. Court legal advisers follow a set training programme and also learn by working with more experienced clerks, finding out about the many different areas of work – road traffic, licensing, fines enforcement, sentencing, etc.

Personal attributes

As well as a real interest in and broad knowledge of the law, court legal advisers must be logical thinkers, capable of undertaking fairly detailed research. They must be discreet, sensitive and calm, but also able to remain detached when dealing with stressful and upsetting situations.

Court usher

Whether you are a defendant, a witness, a jury member or a lawyer, it is the responsibility of the court usher to ensure that you know where you should be, what you should do and how you should do it. Ushers ensure that the courtroom is prepared and that everyone is present. They call witnesses and defendants, label evidence and administer the taking of oaths. At Crown Court, where a jury trial is taking place, court ushers escort members of the jury to and from the courtroom. They remain on duty outside the jury room while the jury is in discussion and they take messages between the jury and the judge.

Entry, qualifications and training

You do not necessarily need any formal qualifications to become a court usher, though you would be expected to have a good general level of education. Previous work experience of dealing with the public and handling difficult situations are more important than professional qualifications. Your training will be on the job and you start by shadowing another usher. You will probably be sent on several short in-house courses. Skills for Justice has recently introduced NVQ levels 2 and 3 qualifications in Court Operations, so you may have the opportunity to work towards one of these.

Personal attributes

These are really important. You have to be trustworthy and truthful and you must have excellent people skills, be able to remain calm, reassure and explain, but be confident if people are hostile or difficult. You have to be well organised and pay attention to detail.

Earnings

Court administrative assistants and ushers are paid between £14,000 and £15,000, while court administrative officers earn between £16,000 and £21,000. Trainee court legal advisers start on £21,000 to £21,500, rising to £29,000 on completion of training.

Info

Skills for Justice
www.skillsforjustice.com

Northern Ireland Court Service
www.courtsni.gov.uk

Her Majesty's Courts Service
020 7189 2000
www.hmcourts-service.gov.uk

Court reporter

Court reporters attend court sittings and take down a complete report of all the evidence, the summing-up or judgment and, on occasions, the speeches of counsel in the various cases. Formerly, the proceedings were taken down in shorthand; now a palantype or stenograph is used. This is a typewriter-like machine that enables the reporter to achieve 200 words per minute. In addition, computers may be used to prepare transcripts, with all the advantages of on-screen editing and speed of preparation. The work sometimes involves travelling to a number of different courts. The majority of verbatim reporters begin their careers in the courts but can also work for Hansard, producing reports of proceedings in the House of Commons and the House of Lords. Television subtitlers also use the skills of verbatim reporting.

Entry, qualifications and training

While there are no formal academic entry requirements, the reality is that most court reporters have A levels or equivalent. Applicants need to have proven ability in written or machine shorthand (usually over 180 words per minute), good typing speeds and excellent spelling, grammar and punctuation. Legal experience can also be an asset. Details of full-time, part-time and distance-learning courses are available from the British Institute of Verbatim Reporters. In Scotland, there are no college courses but training is provided on the job by working alongside an experienced reporter.

Personal attributes

Like anyone concerned with the courts, reporters must be discreet, honest and trustworthy, as most of the work is confidential. Reporters must show a high degree of accuracy.

Earnings

Pay is from £16,000 to £20,000. Many court reporters work freelance and can earn anything from £60 to £325 a day. What you earn depends on how complex and demanding your work is.

Info

British Institute of Verbatim Reporters www.bivr.org.uk	Ministry of Justice 020 7210 8500 www.justice.gov.uk
Signature 0191 303 1155 www.signature.org.uk	

Legal executive

A legal executive is a professional lawyer employed in a solicitor's office or in the legal departments of commerce and central and local government. The training and academic requirements in a specified area of law are at the same level as those required of a solicitor. Consequently, with few exceptions, a legal executive is able to carry out tasks that are similar to those undertaken by solicitors. The main areas of specialisation are conveyancing, civil litigation, criminal law, family law and probate. In addition to providing a worthwhile career in its own right, the legal executive qualification provides access to those wishing to qualify as solicitors via the Institute of Legal Executives (ILEX) route. In Scotland, the term 'legal executive' is not used, but solicitors engage assistants to do similar work.

Entry, qualifications and training

The minimum entry requirement is four GCSEs, including English, but A-level students and graduates are welcome. As an alternative, the Institute accepts a qualification in vocational legal studies, and has special arrangements for students who are over 21. In the main, training is on a part-time basis so that there is potential for trainees to 'learn while they earn'. For those already working in a legal environment, but with no formal legal qualifications, an NVQ (level 4) in Legal Practice is available, and the Institute is the awarding body.

Personal attributes

An ability to communicate, both verbally and in writing, with people at all levels, absolute discretion and trustworthiness, together with meticulous attention to detail, are essential.

Earnings

Trainees earn between £16,000 and £22,000. Qualified legal executives earn between £25,000 and £50,000. Large city firms pay the highest salaries, which may include bonuses.

Info

Institute of Legal Executives (ILEX)
01234 841000
www.ilex.org.uk

All About Law – The Law Careers
Website
www.allaboutlaw.co.uk

Paralegal

Paralegals work for firms of solicitors, commercial companies and public sector bodies. They are not qualified solicitors or legal executives, but they develop considerable specialist knowledge. They normally specialise in a specific area of the law, such as conveyancing, probate or family law. Their work involves researching information, drafting and managing documents, attending client meetings, and some general clerical work. Paralegals also have to keep up to date with legal developments in their specialist field.

Entry, qualifications and training

While there are no specific entry qualifications for paralegals, many hope to become solicitors, barristers or legal executives. This means that many applicants for these posts have a law degree. In any case, some firms ask for four or five GCSEs grades A–C or two A levels. Training is on the job and there are City & Guilds courses leading to a certificate level 2 and diploma level 3 available in paralegal studies. The Institute of Legal Executives (ILEX) also offers part-time and distance-learning courses for paralegals.

Personal attributes

You must be very well organised, able to manage your time and prioritise your work well. You need excellent written English skills and should be interested in legal matters.

Earnings

Salaries for paralegals are between £18,000 and £25,000. In large city law firms earnings can be much higher – up to £70,000 plus large bonuses.

Info

Institute of Legal Executives (ILEX)
01234 841000
www.ilex.org.uk

Institute of Paralegals
020 7099 9122
www.theiop.org

National Association of Licensed
Paralegals
020 3176 0900
www.nationalparalegals.com

All About Law – The Law Careers
Website
www.allaboutlaw.co.uk

Solicitor

The role of the solicitor is to provide clients with skilled legal representation and advice. The clients can be individual people or companies, or any type of organisation or group. A solicitor may work on all kinds of legal matters, from house purchases to defence of people accused of crimes; from selling a corporation to drafting a complicated will or trust. Solicitors may also represent clients in all courts, but will often brief a barrister (see Barrister) to represent the client, and then act as a liaison between them.

Scottish solicitors can appear in all courts and tribunals in Scotland up to and including the Sheriff Court. They can also gain rights of audience, enabling them to appear in the higher courts by becoming a solicitor-advocate, or may brief an advocate to represent their clients.

While some solicitors may deal with a variety of legal problems, others specialise in a particular area, such as shipping, planning and construction, financial services or social security. Specialisation within the profession is increasing. The majority of solicitors work in private practice, with firms made up of several partners. Many others work as employed solicitors in commerce, industry, local and central government and other organisations.

Solicitors are instructed directly by clients and have a lot of contact with them. They have rights of audience in the magistrates' court and the county court. Unlike barristers, solicitors do not wear wigs but do wear gowns if they appear in the county court. Solicitors are governed by a professional body called the Law Society.

Entry, qualifications and training

The Law Society governs the training of solicitors in England and Wales, which takes place in two stages – the academic and the professional. Most, but not all, entrants to the profession are graduates. Some universities offering law degrees require applicants to take the National Law Admissions Test (LNAT). Fellows of the Institute of Legal Executives (ILEX) over the age of 25 with five years' qualifying experience do not need to complete the academic stage. Non-law graduates take the Common Professional Examination (CPE) or a postgraduate diploma in law; those with qualifying law degrees are exempt from this. The next stage, the vocational stage, is taken via the legal practice course, available at a number of colleges and universities. It is a one-year full-time or two-year part-time course. The trainee solicitor then has to undertake a two-year training contract with an authorised firm or organisation. There is always strong competition for these since there are more applicants than available places.

The Law Society of Scotland governs the training of solicitors in Scotland. It is possible to study for a Bachelor of Law degree at five Scottish universities: Aberdeen, Dundee, Edinburgh, Glasgow and Strathclyde. Alternatively, it is possible to take the Law Society's own examinations by finding employment as a pre-diploma trainee. After completion of the LLB degree or professional examinations, all graduates who would like to become solicitors must take the diploma in legal practice – a 26-week postgraduate course, which also offers training in office and business skills. After successful completion of the degree and the diploma, those who wish to become solicitors then serve a two-year training contract with a Scottish solicitor. Trainees must undertake a further two-week course of study, keep training records that will be examined and monitored by the Society, and take a test of professional competence. The trainees can then apply to the Law Society of Scotland for a practising certificate. All Scottish solicitors must hold a Law Society of Scotland practising certificate.

Personal attributes

A high level of academic achievement, integrity, good communication skills, patience, discretion, a good command of language and problem-solving skills are all required.

Earnings

The minimum salary on a training contract is £18,600. London firms may pay more – £30,000 to £32,000. After completing training, salaries are higher if you specialise in commercial law – £60,000 to £150,000. In non-commercial law, salaries are between £40,000 and £80,000.

Info

The Law Society
0870 606 2555
www.lawsociety.org.uk

Law Society of Northern Ireland
028 9023 1614
www.lawsoc-ni.org

National Admissions Test for Law
(LNAT)
www.lnat.ac.uk

Law Careers
www.lawcareers.net

All About Law – The Law Careers
Website
www.allaboutlaw.co.uk

LEISURE AND AMENITY MANAGEMENT

Leisure and amenity management can cross over into arts administration, to sport and physical recreation, to tourism and to appreciation of the natural environment. Leisure activities could include anything from taking a stroll in a park, visiting a country house or historic monument to learning to kite surf at an outward bound centre. Many of these activities are covered in other parts of this guide, but there is work specifically related to the leisure industry.

Leisure centre manager

Leisure centre managers are responsible for the day-to-day running of their centres. These health clubs and leisure facilities may be run by local authorities, private companies or form part of hotel leisure and spa facilities. Your work will depend on what range of activities your particular centre has to offer. It is always likely to include drawing up timetables of activities, coordinating special events, recruiting and training staff, developing marketing material and marketing strategies, and managing budgets.

Entry, qualifications and training

There are two ways to qualify in leisure management: by starting as either an assistant manager or a management trainee. Each employer sets its own entry requirements, but a good standard of education including GCSEs in English, maths and a science are usually necessary. A strong interest in sport and leisure and a track record of working with people are also important. While working as an assistant or trainee, the Institute of Sport and Recreation Management offers a number of qualifications for which you can work on a part-time basis.

Alternatively, you can take a degree in sports and leisure management, sports science, sports studies or similar and start work as a graduate manager or management trainee. Degrees in business, psychology or tourism may also be useful entry qualifications.

Personal attributes

You should have a genuine interest in sport and fitness. You need excellent interpersonal skills and to be good at motivating other people. You should be very well organised and have a flair for marketing and publicity. You should have some grasp of financial management and reasonable IT skills.

Earnings

Earnings range from £18,000 to £25,000 for assistant or trainee managers. Managers earn between £21,000 and £26,000, and senior managers running large facilities can earn £35,000 to £38,000.

Info

The Institute for the Management of Sport and Physical Activity
01509 226 474
www.imspa.co.uk

SkillsActive
020 7632 2000
www.skillsactive.com

LINGUISTICS, LANGUAGES AND TRANSLATION

Interpreter

Interpreters communicate between people who do not share a common language. They use two main techniques: simultaneous and consecutive interpreting. Conference interpreters usually work using the simultaneous method in a booth with headphones and communicative technology, allowing them to hear the speaker and interpret to their audience.

Very few openings are available for interpreters, even worldwide. Conference interpreters work at international conferences such as the United Nations or the European Commission and at the International Court of Justice, using simultaneous or consecutive interpreting. Some work for international agencies, others are freelance. Demand for conference interpreters in particular languages may fluctuate depending on the political and economic requirements of the day. Interpreters with specialist knowledge, such as engineering or economics, may have the chance to work at conferences on their subject. Interpreters may also work as guides in tourist centres, and to do this they must usually be accredited and trained as guides.

Demand for interpreting in the public services (police, courts, public health and local government) has led to the creation of the National Register of Public Service Interpreters, which covers a wide range of African, Asian, European and Far Eastern languages. This register is supported by the Home Office and the UK legal agencies. The Institute of Translation and Interpreting (ITI) can also help source qualified public service interpreters from its membership, as can numerous other commercial agencies.

Entry, qualifications and training

To take a degree course, two A levels or equivalent, including a foreign language, are normally required. At the newer universities and colleges, training in interpreting and translating is offered, combined with regional studies or technological or business studies, aimed at industry, commerce and international organisations. A list of these courses is offered by the Institute of Linguists and by ITI. Such degree courses usually involve work or study abroad. The Institute of Linguists Educational Trust also offers the only qualification in public service interpreting – the Diploma in Public Service Interpreting, which is mapped at between NVQ levels 4 and 5.

Personal attributes

Fluency in two or more languages should be allied with a natural feeling for words and phrases and a good ear. It is necessary to be able to think quickly, to remain alert for long periods and to be socially confident. Subject knowledge is essential, especially for simultaneous interpreting, which requires a degree of understanding and anticipation of subject matter and context.

Earnings

Interpreters new to the profession earn between £18,500 and £22,000, though there are not many salaried jobs for interpreters. The majority of interpreters work freelance and earnings vary from £150 to £700 a day. The languages you interpret, the complexity of information and the situations in which you work affect daily pay rates.

Info

National Centre for Languages
(CILT)
08456 12 5885
www.cilt.org.uk

Chartered Institute of Linguists
(IoL)
020 7940 3100
www.iol.org.uk

Institute of Translation and
Interpreting (ITI)
01908 325250
www.iti.org.uk

Sign language interpreter

British Sign Language (BSL) interpreters help deaf and hearing people to communicate effectively through the use of signing. They work for social service departments or organisations working for or with deaf people, while some work freelance or for agencies. As a sign language interpreter you might use your skills in many different kinds of setting and on different types of assignment. You could be aiding communication at business meetings, at police stations, in court, in a hospital, at a parents' evening, at a conference or at a theatre. Your work would involve preparing for your assignment by ensuring that you are aware of any specialised vocabulary you may need to sign. During an assignment you would have to listen or watch carefully as appropriate, to ensure that you communicate meanings as accurately as possible.

Entry, qualifications and training

To become a British Sign Language Interpreter you must achieve interpreter and BSL qualifications recognised by the Registration Department of Signature (formerly CACDP). You can qualify in either of the following ways: you can either do a degree or postgraduate diploma, or alternatively work towards NBQ level 4 qualifications in Interpreting (BSL/English). You can work towards this while you are already working in some other role with deaf people.

Personal attributes

You must have excellent communication skills and be able to listen carefully, work with speed and accuracy, and maintain intense concentration. You must be able to establish a good rapport with people very quickly. You will sometimes be working with clients who are in stressful situations such as courts or hospitals.

Earnings

As an employed BSL interpreter you can earn £20,000 to £35.000 a year. Freelance interpreters charge £25.00 to £30.00 an hour and can also claim travel expenses.

Info

Signature	National Centre for Languages
0191 383 1155	(CILT)
Textphone: 0191 383 7915	08456 12 5885
www.signature.org.uk	www.cilt.org.uk
Association of Sign Language	
Interpreters (ASLI)	
0871 474 0522	
www.asli.org.uk	

Translator

Translators work freelance from home, as staff translators within a commercial organisation whose main business is not translation, or within a translation agency. Normally, they only translate from another language into their mother tongue. The work translated varies from whole books to business letters and documents. Translators, especially those who specialise in work for publication, must be able to express themselves very well. In areas where the subject matter of the text is specialised, for example computing, maths or mountaineering, expert knowledge is required of the translator. A broad-based general knowledge is always an advantage. Translators may be responsible for finding their own work but may also be registered with a translation company or agency.

Entry, qualifications and training

Proficiency in a foreign language is obviously necessary, as is the ability to write well in the target language. An understanding of the culture of the relevant countries is important. Increasingly, there is a need to be computer literate. Most translators have a postgraduate qualification or a diploma in translation. First degree courses in translation are available at a number of universities and diplomas are available via the Institute of Linguists.

Personal attributes

Translators must be meticulous, conscientious, creative and persistent. The ability to carry out research, as and when necessary, and good interpersonal skills are also required.

Earnings

Starting salaries are between £18,000 and £23,000 – £25,000 to £30,000 for experienced translators. Many translators work freelance, in which case they are usually paid a fee per thousand words translated. This fee ranges from £80 to £220. The rate depends on the language(s) being translated. Translating Chinese characters commands the highest fees.

Info

Association of Translation
Companies (ATC)
020 7930 2200
www.atc.org.uk

Chartered Institute of Linguists (IoL)
020 7940 3100
www.iol.org.uk

Institute of Translation and
Interpreting (ITI)
01908 325 250
www.iti.org.uk

International Federation of
Translators
1 514 845 0413
www.fit-ift.org

National Centre for Languages
(CILT)
020 7379 5101
www.cilt.org.uk

LOCAL GOVERNMENT

Local government is responsible for developing local policies and delivering local services. In addition to the specific local government roles described below, local government provides education, social care, environmental health, leisure facilities and public protection. These departments employ appropriately qualified professionals, including teachers, social workers, lawyers, architects, trading standards officers, housing officers, engineers, environmental health officers and many more. Local authorities also employ specialists in finance, human resources and business management, and some specialised administrators such as registrars of births, deaths and marriages, and clerks to council committees. The LGcareers website gives details of the range of jobs on offer.

There is currently a decline in numbers of local government jobs and many of its functions may be undertaken by private contractors, looking for staff with similar skills to those required by local government departments.

Local government administrative assistant

Local government administrative assistants provide support in all council departments, eg housing, social services or planning. Your work will vary depending on where you work and what your specific role is, but many tasks are common to most administrative assistant posts. As an administrative assistant your work could include processing forms, answering queries on the telephone or at a helpdesk, sorting mail, filing, photocopying, inputting and updating information on computers, finding information and taking notes at meetings.

Local government officer

Local government officers are responsible for putting council policy into practice. Your day-to-day tasks will vary according to your particular role and responsibilities, but are likely to include supervising and training administrative staff, keeping records, dealing with enquiries, presenting and preparing information for committees or other meetings, monitoring performance, overseeing projects and managing budgets.

Entry, qualifications and training

Entry requirements vary between councils. For some administrative assistant posts you may need GCSEs, including maths and English; formal qualifications are often not required. Administrative officers usually need four or five GCSEs, including maths and English. Entry requirements for local government officers vary widely, depending on the job, and can be anything from four GCSEs, including maths and English, to a degree or equivalent qualification. Local authorities provide training on the job and support for part-time study for relevant professional qualifications.

Personal attributes

While every role demands particular knowledge and skills, there are some common threads that are essential for all employees. You must have a genuine interest in and commitment to serving your local community. Most jobs require a good level of communication skills, as they involve direct contact with members of the public. You should be flexible and able to work well as part of a team. You should also be prepared to take on responsibilities. Some jobs require good IT or numeracy skills.

Earnings

Administrative assistants are paid between £14,000 and £19,500, and local government officers are paid from £18,000 to £39,000 – more if you move into senior management. Salaries are higher in London than elsewhere and many councils pay performance-related bonuses.

Info

Local Government Careers
www.lgcareers.com

LOGISTICS

(see also Road Transport)

Logistics is the management of the moving of goods or materials from one place to another.

Freight forwarder

A freight forwarding firm will arrange for the most efficient means of the international transport of goods, and will ensure that all documentation, legal and insurance requirements are met, and customs duties paid. Freight forwarders may be individuals or firms; they may specialise in a particular method of transport, certain goods or countries. They may arrange for a number of different shipments to be grouped together for more economical transport. Some very large organisations have their own freight forwarding department or a subsidiary company.

Freight forwarders are usually located near ports or airports and in provincial centres. They employ people to deal with a wide range of clerical and administrative tasks, such as sales, personnel, timetabling, accounting and computer work.

Entry, qualifications and training

School leavers can enter the industry through the Modern Apprenticeship route. NVQs are available in International Trade and Services, Distribution and Warehousing Operations, and Organising Road Transport. There are several degree courses in international trade, logistics, supply chain management, transport, export studies and overseas business. Large companies may offer graduate training schemes for those with relevant degrees.

The Institute of Freight Forwarders offers an Advanced Certificate in International Trade that can be studied full- or part-time or by correspondence. The Institute of Logistics and Transport offers a range of professional qualifications from introductory to MSc level, which can be studied by distance learning.

Personal attributes

People working in freight forwarding need excellent problem-solving and communication skills. Accuracy and clarity are essential, as misunderstandings can cause major problems. IT skills are essential with the growth in internet trading and greater use of technology such as global positioning satellite (GPS) systems to plan and manage journeys. Geographical, cultural and religious awareness are also important.

Earnings

School leaver trainees are paid between £14,000 and £17,000. Graduate trainees working for larger companies start on £19,000 to £23,000. Senior managers in freight forwarding departments can earn £30,000 to £40,000.

Info

Skills for Logistics
01908 313360
www.skillsforlogistics.org

British International Freight
Association (BIFA)
020 8844 2266
www.bifa.org

Chartered Institute of Logistics and
Transport (CILT UK)
01536 740104
www.ciltuk.org.uk

Institute of Export
01733 404400
www.export.org.uk

Supply chain manager

Supply chain managers (also known as logistics or distribution managers) are the ones who ensure that food, drink, clothing, electrical equipment, in fact anything that you can buy from a retail outlet, arrives where it should when it should. The manager has to ensure that supplies neither run out nor build up in over-large quantities in warehouses, shops or anywhere along the supply chain. You can work either for a large retailer that has its own logistics department or for a logistics contractor that organises all the transport and distribution on behalf of retailers and wholesalers. Your responsibilities are likely to include planning delivery timetables, monitoring stock levels using computer databases, tracking the movement of goods through depots, and overseeing the ordering and packaging process ready for dispatch. You also have to monitor performance and try to come up with ways of making the whole process more efficient and cost-effective, and you are also responsible for recruiting and managing staff in the distribution department. Your work would involve close liaison with purchasing officers, warehouse managers and transport staff.

Entry, qualifications and training

There are two ways to get into supply chain management. Some people take a Foundation degree, HNC, HND or degree in a relevant subject such as transport management, supply chain management or international transport. Other subjects such as geography and business subjects may also include relevant modules. Some large companies prefer to recruit graduates for their management training programmes. However, it is possible to join a company in its distribution or logistics department and work your way up into a management role. You may also choose to take some relevant qualifications on a part-time basis if you choose this second route.

Personal attributes

You need good planning skills and you must also be able to pay attention to detail. You need to be numerate with good IT skills too. You have to be able to work under pressure and solve problems quickly and calmly. You must have a good range of people skills, be excellent at leading and motivating, good at soothing ruffled and agitated managers somewhere else along the supply chain and able to liaise effectively with others.

Earnings

Graduate trainees earn between £18,000 and £22,000. If you start by working your way up, your salary will depend very much on what job you are doing, but once you get into supply chain management your earnings are similar to those of a graduate trainee. In either case, once you have completed some training and built up a year or two of experience, salaries rise to £25,000 to £30,000. For very large operations, the most senior managers can earn £40,000 to £50,000.

Info

Chartered Institute of Logistics and .
Transport (CILT UK)
01536 740100
www.ciltuk.org.uk

Skills for Logistics
0870 242 7314
www.skillsforlogistics.org

MANAGEMENT CONSULTANT

Management consultants advise businesses and organisations of many sizes and types on all aspects of problem solving or improving the way that the business or organisation operates. They may, for example, offer financial advice, suggestions about recruitment and ideas on improving levels of staff motivation or methods of conflict resolution. They may advise on ways of reshaping the actual structure of a business.

The work could involve interviewing members of staff, observing activities, looking at written information about the company, accounts, future projections, etc. After having drawn various conclusions, the consultant will then suggest actions that the business could take to change things. This advice could involve working with key members of staff as well as providing written reports.

Entry, qualifications and training

Management consultants often move into this work after time spent in finance, marketing, project management, human resources or the armed services. The other route in is through a graduate training scheme offered by a management consulting firm. Preferred degree subjects include business, management, IT, economics and psychology. If you specialise in a particular area of consultancy, such as marketing or human resources, a relevant degree is helpful. You should have a 2.1 and an A level tariff of 320 points. Training is on the job, but many consulting firms provide extensive in-house courses. After about two years in the profession you are likely to have the option to take either a Master's in Business Administration (MBA) or a professional qualification linked to your area of expertise, for example finance, marketing or human resources.

Personal attributes

You need to be an excellent communicator, one-to-one, with groups and on paper. You should have good IT and numerical skills and the ability to analyse problems and suggest solutions. You should have a broad knowledge of business issues.

Earnings

New entrants earn £27,000 and £35,000, depending on location and the type of consulting. Experienced consultants earn between £35,000 and £60,000. This occupation can offer high salaries for very successful consultants – £60,000 to £125,000.

Info

Management Consultancies
Association
020 7321 3990
www.mca.org.uk

MANUFACTURING

Manufacturing encompasses many occupations, all of which are concerned with the large-scale production of goods and packaging.

Factory worker

Factory work is all about the manufacture of products of every kind: food, furniture, cars, clothing, electronic equipment – in fact, all goods that we use. A whole range of jobs support any manufacturing process: administration, research, engineering and marketing, but they are covered elsewhere.

The term 'factory worker' refers to workers who are involved in the production process – and specific tasks and duties vary depending on what is being produced. Workers may operate special machinery for building cars, work on a conveyor belt filling cans of drink, wash and grade raw fruit and vegetables to be processed, assemble complete items by putting components together, or monitor the quality and consistency of any product. The range is really very wide.

Entry, qualifications and training

For most jobs there are no specific academic requirements, although some employers may like you to have GCSEs in maths, English and technology. Many employers set their own entry tests to measure how well you are likely to perform the tasks you will be expected to do. There are now some GNVQs level 2 available in Performing Manufacturing Operations, and if you are under 24 years old there may be opportunities to do an apprenticeship in electrical, electronic or mechanical engineering.

Personal attributes

You need to be good at practical work and quick with your hands. It is important that you don't mind carrying out repetitive tasks and that you can keep your concentration while doing this. You must be able to follow instructions, pay close attention to safety and work well as part of a team.

Earnings

Starting pay is between £12,000 and £16,000, and if you take on some supervisory responsibility it can rise to £20,000. Many jobs include shift-work allowances.

Info

Vacancies are advertised in local papers and through Jobcentre Plus offices.

Packaging technologist

There are opportunities for packaging technologists with manufacturers of raw packaging materials, with companies that produce packaging and with companies that have a product to be packed. Many small firms do not have their own packaging adviser/technologist, and hire a consultant when the need arises.

The purpose of packaging is to protect, preserve, contain and present its contents. It also has a vital function in branding and brand awareness. Developing packaging that has a minimal impact on the environment and does not add too much to the carbon footprint of a product is also increasingly important.

There are career opportunities developing materials for packaging purposes, for designing equipment to manufacture or fill packaging, for structural design of parts, for graphic design on packs, for physical and chemical testing, and for quality assurance.

Entry, qualifications and training

Packaging modules are available in some first degree courses, and two universities offer an MSc in Packaging Technology. The Diploma in Packaging Technology from the Institute of Packaging is recognised as a qualification of excellence. It can be studied in three ways: residential, part-time and by distance learning.

Personal attributes

Technologists and scientists must be able to look at problems in a practical way and have the ability to communicate their ideas to others both verbally and on paper.

Earnings

New entrants earn between £15,000 and £20,000; senior technologists can earn £25,000 to £30,000, with research and development work attracting the higher salaries.

Info

Packaging Futures
www.packagingfutures.com

Institute of Materials, Minerals
and Mining
020 7451 7300
www.iom3.org/packaging

Sheet-metal worker/plater

Sheet-metal workers/platers are engaged in shaping, cutting and joining together pieces of metal. Sheet-metal workers work with thin metal sheet up to 3~mm thick, using a wide range of hand and power tools. They make such items as aircraft sections and car prototypes. Platers work with metal plates from 3~mm thick upwards. As well as hand and power tools, heavy presses are needed to bend the plate. Products include ship and submarine parts and industrial boilers.

Entry, qualifications and training

If you are between 16 and 24 years old and want to join a National Apprenticeship Scheme for Engineering Construction (NASEC), you need GCSEs (A–C)/S grades (1–3) in maths, English and a science. If you have engineering drawing, metal work or other practical subjects as well you may have an advantage. Applicants without the required entry grades may also be considered. These apprenticeships take up to three years and you train on the job, working alongside experienced sheet-metal workers. This apprenticeship leads to an NVQ level 3 award in Engineering Production. Older applicants can get into this work without GCSEs, but won't get the opportunity to do a full apprenticeship.

Personal attributes

You must have good manual dexterity and be able to concentrate for long periods of time. You should be good at following instructions, but able to work without direct supervision. Normal eyesight is essential and good colour vision is important.

Earnings

Starting salaries range from £14,500 to £17,000. With experience you can earn between £17,000 and £25,000.

Toolmaker

Toolmakers work in engineering, making a wide range of jigs used to guide cutting tools and to hold the work in position; fixtures, to hold metal for bending or welding or to hold parts together; press tools in different shapes and sizes for cutting parts; mould tools to make items such as fridge interiors or mobile phone cases and measuring gauges. Toolmakers are often involved in making small quantities of a new product when it is at the design and development stage. Toolmaker machinists make the tools, often specialising in just one kind:

Toolmaker fitters work on large structures that are constructed from many parts. They check all the parts, number them and then fit them together.

Entry, qualifications and training

If you are between 16 and 24 years old and want to do a NASEC apprenticeship, you need GCSEs (A–C)/S grades in maths, English and a science. If you have engineering drawing, metal work or other practical subjects as well you may have an advantage. Applicants without the required entry grades may also be considered. These apprenticeships take up to three years and you train on the job, working alongside experienced toolmakers. This apprenticeship leads to an NVQ level 3 award in Engineering Production. Older applicants can do BTEC Certificates in Manufacturing Engineering.

Personal attributes

You must have good manual dexterity and be able to understand engineering drawings. You should be good at following instructions, but able to work without direct supervision. Normal eyesight is essential and good colour vision is important.

Earnings

Starting pay ranges from £15,000 to £18,000. With experience you can earn between £19,000 and £25,000.

Welder

Welders join pieces of metal together by applying intense heat and melting the edges so that two pieces become one. The sorts of items welded are metal sections of aeroplanes, ships, oil rigs, cars and power turbines. Welders work in light and heavy engineering firms, in foundry work and in shipbuilding. Some plastics are also welded.

Welders work on all types of fabrication, from the manufacture of metal-frame chairs to high-quality, complex applications such as building a submarine.

Entry, qualifications and training

If you are aged between 16 and 24 you can do an Engineering Apprenticeship. There are no set entry qualifications for this, but many employers prefer you to have GCSEs in English, maths, technology and a science subject. If you have these GCSEs, this also offers a wider range of further qualifications you can take part- or full-time at college. These qualifications are also open to people of any age. There are several different NVQ awards related to welding, including fabrication and welding, performing engineering operations and welding with pipework.

Personal attributes

You must have good practical and technical skills and be able to concentrate for long periods of time. You should be good at following instructions, but able to work without direct supervision. Normal eyesight is essential and good near vision is important.

Earnings

Pay starts at between £14,500 and £17,000, and with experience you can earn £20,000 to £26,000, Highly skilled specialist welders may earn up to £30,000.

Info

Proskills UK (The Sector Skills Council for the Process and Manufacturing Sector)
01235 833844
www.proskills.co.uk/

Tecskills (Engineering Construction Industry Training Board)
www.tecskills.org.uk

Welding Institute (TWI)
01223 899000
www.twi.co.uk

MARINE SCIENTIST

Marine scientists study the life of the planet's oceans – their plants, their fish, their plankton, their mammals and their seabirds. They also study the geology of the seafloor and of coastal regions. Marine science encompasses many disciplines, including biology, botany, environmental science, geology and zoology. Marine scientists' work involves research and analysis of what is happening in the oceans and forecasting of what could happen. They may study the impact of climate change, underwater volcanic activity, fishing and water sports. Marine scientists work for a range of organisations, including those dealing with energy exploration for oil and gas, fisheries, renewable energy sources, marine conservation and wildlife protection.

Your work as a marine scientist could involve analysing samples, designing experiments, building computer models to simulate certain situations and writing detailed reports. In many cases you would conduct some of your work based on sea-going vessels and might even incorporate diving into your work routine. You would also be responsible for managing research budgets and junior members of the research team.

Entry, qualifications and training

There are a few degrees and postgraduate courses in marine science or oceanography. This is a degree-level career, but it draws on many other subjects, including biology, biochemistry, geography, geology and environmental sciences.

Personal attributes

Biologists need the same characteristics as all scientists: patience and the willingness to repeat experimental work and measurements to check results, a methodical way of working, good observation and accuracy.

Earnings

Research assistants earn £17,000 to £27,000, depending on your job title, role and what type of organisation you work for – public, private or voluntary body. If you have a PhD, your starting salary will be between £25,000 and £35,000.

Info

The Centre for Environment, Fisheries and Aquaculture Science (CEFAS)
01502 562244
www.cefas.defra.gov.uk

Institute of Marine Engineering, Science
020 7382 2600
www.imarest.org

Lantra: The Sector Skills Council for the Environmental and Land-based Sector
0845 707 8007
www.lantra.co.uk

The Marine Biological Association (MBA)
01752 633 207
www.mba.ac.uk

Marine Conservation Society
01989 566 017
www.mcsuk.org

Natural Environment Research Council (NERC)
01793 411500
www.nerc.ac.uk

Scottish Association for Marine Science (SAMS)
01631 559 000
www.sams.ac.uk

MARKET RESEARCHER

Market research is the collection and analysis of information about markets, organisations and people to support better business decisions. It is used to discover gaps in the market, to ensure customer satisfaction and to plan effective marketing campaigns. In a competitive environment, the more knowledge a business has about its customers, the more likely it is to succeed.

Over the past few decades, market research techniques have developed significantly, making it a more precise science. The methods used depend on the requirements of the business and the budget available, and include interviews with individuals, surveys by telephone, post and via the internet, and increasingly using mobile phone text messaging. These are used to gather quantitative (numerical) data. Qualitative research by face-to-face interviews with individuals or groups is geared to providing insight into why people hold the views they do, and provides greater understanding of customers. Interviewers are known as field workers, and their work, and that of the analysis personnel, is organised by the research executive, who is in overall charge of the project for a marketing executive or client, and is responsible for interpreting the results.

Every year, the Market Research Society (MRS) publishes the *Research Buyer's Guide*, which lists the majority of market research agencies in the UK and outlines the size of each agency, together with their areas of specialisation. The guide also details other organisations that can offer advice on getting started in market research; the online version of the guide is free at www.rbg.org.uk.

Entry, qualifications and training

Field workers do not need qualifications but must be articulate, persuasive and presentable. Applicants for research and executive positions will be expected to hold a degree. The majority of market research graduates are drawn from disciplines that require strong communication or analytical skills, such as languages, English literature, maths, psychology, geography, history, politics, science and IT. However, graduates with degrees as contrasting as zoology and theatre studies are also welcomed by the industry.

The Market Research Society offers a range of qualifications that are linked to the UK's National Qualifications Framework and are designed to suit a wide range of candidates, from those with no experience to practitioners seeking continuous professional development.

Personal attributes

Excellent communication skills and the ability to get on with people of all types are necessary. Analytical skills, numeracy and data interpretation are important.

Earnings

Market research analysts who interpret the data and results, or managers who plan and develop research, start on £22,000 to £26,000. Experienced research executives earn between £30,000 and £45,000. Market research interviewers working on a casual basis earn £50 to £80 per day. Interviewers who are permanent employees earn between £12,000 and £16,000.

Info

Association for Qualitative Research (AQR)
01480 407227
www.aqr.org.uk

Chartered Institute of Marketing (CIM)
01628 427500
www.cim.co.uk

Direct Marketing Association
020 7291 3300
www.dma.org.uk

The Institute of Direct Marketing (IDM)
020 8977 5705
www.theidm.co.uk

Ipsos MORI (polling organisation)
020 7347 3018
www.ipsos-mori.com/careers.aspx

Market Research Society (MRS)
020 7490 4911
www.mrs.org.uk

Social Research Association (SRA)
020 7388 2391
www.the-sra.org.uk

MARKETING EXECUTIVE

Marketing is the process of persuading us to buy or of raising the profile of products, services or causes. The role of marketing executive can be varied and demanding, since marketing covers many activities, including advertising, promotion, sponsorship, public relations, media relations and research. As an executive you could be involved in planning, developing and managing any of these activities. Marketing executives work either for specialist marketing consultancies or for in-house marketing departments working to sell, promote or increase market share of that business's products or services. Day-to-day tasks can include writing press releases, planning campaigns, liaising with customers, training sales staff, writing brochures or website entries, attending meetings, building up and maintaining good contacts in the media and, more elusively but very importantly, coming up with new ideas.

Entry, qualifications and training

There are two main routes into marketing. You either need a degree in a relevant subject such as marketing or a business-related subject, or you can get into marketing if you already have relevant experience in sales or customer services. The Chartered Institute of Marketing (CIM) offers several professional qualifications towards which you can work while employed. These courses cover all aspects of marketing and are pitched at several levels, from introductory to postgraduate diplomas.

Personal attributes

You must be an enthusiastic and energetic communicator, able to motivate staff and persuade customers and clients. You also need to be a good team member, able to listen to the ideas of others. You have to be a good organiser and great planner. You have to be a creative thinker, imaginative and able to come up with something new.

Earnings

New entrants earn between £22,000 and £28,000 – geographical location and the sector you work in affect pay. Senior marketing managers earn between £25,000 and £55,000. Some senior marketing executives can earn £100,000.

Info

Chartered Institute of Marketing (CIM)
01628 427500
www.cim.co.uk

Institute of Direct Marketing (IDM)
020 8614 0277
www.theidm.com

Communication Advertising and Marketing Education Foundation (CAM)
01628 427120
www.camfoundation.com

Arts Marketing Association
01223 578078
www.a-m-a.co.uk

MEAT INDUSTRY

The meat industry extends from work in a small retail shop through to supermarkets; from meat buying for large organisations such as hotels and caterers to the manufacture of meat and poultry products. There is also work connected with health and meat hygiene.

Butcher

Butchers prepare and sell meat, poultry, game and meat products. They work in small shops, supermarkets, markets, farm shops and farmers' markets. Some butchers also make their own products, such as pies or sausages. As well as cutting and preparing meat for sale, they deal with customers, offering advice on how best to prepare and cook meat and poultry. They are responsible for ordering and buying products and have to have a good knowledge of food safety and food hygiene.

Entry, qualifications and training

A good general education is necessary but there are no formal educational requirements. Training is on the job and courses are available at further education establishments and technical colleges, leading to examinations of the Meat Training Council. NVQs are available at levels 1–4, and Higher National Diploma/ Certificate qualifications. Modern Apprenticeships are available. Apprenticeships may be an option if you wish to train as a butcher – employers set their own entry requirements, but three to four GCSEs grades A–C may be required.

Personal attributes

Butchers need to be very practical, with good manual dexterity, and not squeamish. They must ensure that they and their work environments are really clean and hygienic and they must enjoy talking to people and giving advice. A good business sense is also useful.

Earnings

Trainee butchers earn £12,000 to £13,000. Skilled butchers earn between £14,000 and £19,000. Skilled butchers who are also section managers and who have responsibilities for sourcing and buying produce can earn £25,000 or more. In some geographical areas there is a shortage of skilled butchers.

Info

Worshipful Company of Butchers Guild
020 7600 4106
www.butchershall.com

Meat Training Council
01908 231062
www.meattraining.org.uk

Improve Ltd
0845 644 0448
www.improve-skills.co.uk

MEDICAL AND HEALTHCARE SCIENCE

Many scientific disciplines play a key part in medicine – in the development and testing of drugs and the monitoring of the performance of these drugs. Scientists contribute to the understanding of the processes of disease and damage to tissue, organs and systems, as well as to the development of equipment and techniques to improve diagnosis and treatment. There are very many jobs in medical and healthcare science, and those described here are examples from some of the different areas of science in medicine.

Life scientists and pathologists

Life scientists work in hospital laboratories, in community health and for other national agencies concerned with blood, health protection and organ transplant. Life scientists work in three broad areas: pathology, investigating causes and development of diseases; genetics, looking at genetic components of illness; and embryology, investigating the development of life and treatments for infertility. Some examples of these scientific roles are shown below.

Clinical embryologist

This is a rapidly developing field. Clinical embryologists are involved in research and investigation of various aspects of *in vitro* fertilisation (IVF) treatment and other programmes of assisted reproduction. This work involves the collection of eggs from patients for examination, checking fertility levels of individuals and the application of 'cutting edge' and sometimes controversial technologies.

Clinical immunologist

Clinical immunologists use sophisticated laboratory techniques to examine the effects on the immune system of syndromes such as AIDS and allergic conditions such as hay fever or asthma. They apply the knowledge they acquire to developing better treatments of these conditions. This is a fast-moving and developing area of medical science.

Clinical microbiologist

Clinical microbiologists work to diagnose all kinds of infections – bacterial, viral, fungal or parasitic. What they discover about the infections a patient has plays an important role in how that patient is treated: what antibiotics are given, for example. They also work for the Health Protection Agency helping prevent the spread of diseases.

Phlebotomist

Phlebotomists take blood samples from patients so that these samples can be analysed to diagnose diseases and other disorders. They have to take great care when collecting blood to disturb the patient as little as possible, to label the blood taken correctly and to ensure that it is taken to the correct laboratory. Phlebotomists also work for the blood donor agency, collecting healthy blood from volunteers.

Physiological scientists

Physiological scientists monitor the body's systems: breathing, hearing, sight, heart, liver, kidneys, brain, etc. They help investigate problems and produce information that will assist doctors in making diagnoses. In some roles they work to maintain many of the body's systems and functions during surgery. Many physiological scientists work directly with patients in outpatient clinics and on hospital wards.

Cardiographer

Cardiographers work in hospitals, operating the electrocardiograph (ECG) machines that monitor the functioning of the heart. They reassure patients and explain the procedure to them before fitting electrodes to the patient's body, ensuring they are correctly connected to the machine, and take readings that a doctor uses to make decisions about diagnosis and treatment.

Neurophysiology technologist

Neurophysiology technologists, also referred to as clinical physiologists (neurophysiology), work in hospital outpatient departments, in intensive care units and in operating theatres. Their work is concerned with monitoring and measuring activities in the central and peripheral nervous systems. They use highly sophisticated equipment to obtain their readings. They work closely with patients of all ages – a child who has suffered a brain injury, or an older person who has had a stroke, for example. They also work closely with other members of the healthcare team.

Perfusionist

Perfusionists (or perfusion scientists) work in operating theatres where patients are undergoing open heart surgery. The term 'perfusion' refers to the movement of liquid through tissue. The perfusionist ensures that oxygen is circulated through the patient's blood even when the action of the heart and lungs is temporarily stopped in order to carry out the surgery. Perfusionists use a range of complex machinery and monitoring equipment to carry out their work. They must alert fellow members of the operating team if they have any causes for concern.

Physical scientists and biomedical engineers

Physical scientists working in medicine develop ways to measure what is happening in the body, new ways of diagnosing and treating diseases and new equipment to aid in treatment. They also have to ensure that such equipment works safely.

Medical physicist

Medical physicists are involved in developing highly sophisticated equipment for measuring the effects of illnesses and disabilities. Medical physicists have developed X-ray and ultrasound scanning equipment and they use their research skills to refine and improve these techniques and technologies. They often work closely with radiographers in the field of nuclear medicine, treating cancer cells with the correct dose of radiation.

Clinical engineer

Clinical or bioengineers design equipment for monitoring, diagnosis, treatment and rehabilitation or research. They may design laser equipment or electronic aids for patients with disabilities. They examine the mechanics of the human body to see how to replicate the functions of particular organs or systems. They develop a detailed knowledge of materials and of engineering processes, and apply this technical knowledge in a medical environment.

Medical laboratory technician

All the scientific research and development work that goes on throughout the health service and in medical schools needs the support of medical laboratory technicians and assistants. Laboratory technicians work in all aspects of medical and clinical sciences, whether it is testing blood, screening cells for disease, or developing a new material to treat burns or wounds. Medical laboratory technicians assist scientists in setting up experiments, monitoring these experiments and recording the results.

Entry, qualifications and training

There are three levels of entry. For most of the healthcare science professions there is also a range of assistant roles that form an important part of the clinical science team. There are no set academic requirements, though many applicants have GCSEs grades A–C in maths, English and a science. These roles can be a stepping stone to further career development and eventual professional qualification. You can start work as a trainee or assistant, combining on-the-job training with study so that you learn as you earn.

If you have A levels or equivalent qualifications you can join as a trainee, combining work and practical training with part-time study for a degree or professional qualification in a specific area of healthcare science. Opportunities for graduates who wish to work in healthcare science are open to graduates from many science disciplines. There are some vocational degree courses that are specific to particular healthcare science roles and accredited by the relevant regulatory body. With most other science degrees you will need to undergo a period of further study, typically 18 months to two years, to extend your knowledge in your chosen specialism. This will lead to a postgraduate diploma or MSc and professional registration.

Personal attributes

If you are engaged in research and development you must have a rigorous and questioning scientific approach to your work – be good at problem solving and coming up with imaginative solutions. If your work involves contact with patients, you must have an understanding and reassuring manner, but you must also be able to avoid becoming too emotionally involved in your work. Many roles require you to have good practical skills, manual dexterity and the ability to be meticulous and highly observant. Many roles will also require you to use complex instruments and take careful recordings of results.

Earnings

Most NHS jobs are on a graded, structured pay scale, Medical laboratory technicians earn from £15,000 to £19,000. Most scientists start on the scale between £21,200 and £27,600, though senior scientists earn between £37,000 and £55,000.

Info

NHS Careers
0845 606 0655
www.nhscareers.nhs.uk

Health Professions Council (HPC)
0845 3004 472
www.hpc-uk.org

Institute of Biomedical Science
020 7713 0214
www.ibms.org

Association of Clinical Scientists
020 7940 8960
www.assclinsci.org

Health Learning and Skills Advice Line
08000 150850
www.learndirect-advice.co.uk

Institute of Physics and Engineering in Medicine (IPEM)
01904 610821
www.ipem.ac.uk

Society for General Microbiology
www.socgenmicrobiol.org.uk

Recruitment Centre for Clinical Scientists
020 7582 0866
www.nhsclinicalscientists.info

Association for Science Education (ASE)
01707 283000
www.ooo.org.uk

SEMTA (The Sector Skills Council for Science, Engineering and Manufacturing Technologies)
0800 282167
www.semta.org.uk

Medical illustrator

Medical illustrators employ a range of artistic and technical skills to produce photographs, drawings, videos and other digital images in healthcare settings. They produce material to help assess the effectiveness of treatment regimes by photographing patients at different stages of their treatment. They may produce material for medical textbooks, websites, lectures and other training and teaching activities. Some specialise in forensic work, taking pictures of non-accidental injuries or copying evidence from X-rays and slides.

Because medical illustrators use a combination of photography, video and drawing skills, there may be some opportunities to take work that allows you to develop special expertise in one or other of these areas. You are likely to spend your time working in hospital wards, operating theatres and clinics, as well as studios and technical laboratories.

Entry, qualifications and training

While it is not always necessary to have formal qualifications, it is now very difficult to get into this work without a Foundation degree, HND or degree in a relevant subject. The most useful subjects are graphic design and photography. It is likely that in the near future medical illustrators will only be able to practise if they are state registered. The exact date for this has not been finalised. However, when this does happen, all new entrants to this profession will have to have a relevant degree that meets the standards for registration. It is very useful if you can gain some relevant work experience with an NHS Trust medical photography department. You should also be able to produce a portfolio of your work at interview.

Personal attributes

This work demands a wide range of qualities and skills. You should have artistic and photographic ability and be competent working with technical equipment. You must have an interest in and some knowledge of biology, physiology, diseases and medical conditions. You have to have excellent interpersonal skills, and be sensitive and empathic when dealing with people who are anxious or vulnerable. You should be good at working as part of a team, but be able to get on with your own work unsupervised.

Earnings

Pay for new entrants is between £21,200 and £27,600. Senior medical illustrators earn between £28,000 and £37,000. Large teaching hospitals have much bigger medical illustration departments so these offer more scope for management jobs, which pay up to £39,000.

Info

Medical Artists Association
www.maa.org.uk

Medical Artists' Education Trust (MAET)
www.maet.org.uk

NHS Careers
0345 60 60 655
www.nhscareers.nhs.uk

Institute of Medical Illustrators
www.imi.org.uk

British Institute of Professional Photography (BIPP)
01296 718530
www.bipp.com

MEDICINE

Doctors work in many healthcare settings in both the National Health Service (NHS) and the private healthcare sector. In the NHS they work in GP practices, health centres, polyclinics and hospitals of every size and type. They can choose, through training, to work in one of very many different fields of medicine. In private practice doctors work in hospitals, clinics and medical centres.

General practitioner

Family doctors, or GPs, may offer healthcare to everyone in a particular geographical location. They will see children, adults and older people. They must be able to diagnose and deal with a broad spectrum of illnesses and disorders, mainly those common within the community, but also to recognise those that are rare. Increasingly, doctors also help their patients to cope with personal and emotional problems. They have to be aware of and take into account physical, psychological and social factors when looking after their patients. About 90 per cent of GPs now work together in group practices, allowing some specialisation.

GP practices are offering a greater range of treatments on their premises, including minor procedures, testing and screening. It seems likely that they will soon have greater administrative and financial responsibility if they become the health professionals responsible for commissioning the majority of healthcare for their patients.

Hospital doctor

Hospital doctors treat hospital inpatients and patients who come to the hospital through outpatient clinics. Hospital doctors work in one of 50 different specialist areas within medicine, treating illness, disease and infection. The specialisms fall into three main groups: medicine, surgery and psychiatry. During training they will learn about every aspect of health and with more experience choose a specialist area that interests them. Doctors choosing to work in medical areas can specialise in such fields as cardiology or paediatrics. They prescribe treatments or organise further investigations, and they monitor patients' progress. Surgeons perform operations of many kinds. They can choose to specialise in such areas as orthopaedics, repairing damaged and broken bones. Psychiatrists treat patients with mental illnesses such as anxiety or depression, prescribing drugs or behavioural or talking therapies.

Research and teaching

Research work is carried out in universities, hospitals, public health laboratories and other research establishments and pharmaceutical manufacturing companies. There are opportunities too for teaching in universities. Teaching may involve very little or no contact with patients, or it may be similar in content to hospital doctors' work. An academic career in medicine either through teaching or research is possible in practically all hospital specialities, general practice and public health medicine.

Entry, qualifications and training

To become a doctor in the UK you must take a five-year degree course in medicine recognised by the General Medical Council (GMC). To be accepted onto one of these courses you must have three A levels, normally two As and a B, including maths and two sciences. In Scotland you need five H grades and two Advanced Science Highers, one of which must be chemistry.

The GMC also approves some six-year degree courses in medicine designed for applicants who do not have the appropriate science grades. The additional year is a pre-medical course in science. In some cases, an Access to Higher Education course may be accepted. It is important to check carefully with the GMC, to ensure that you embark on an approved course.

As part of the selection process for a degree you may be asked to take a UK Clinical Aptitude Test (UKCAT). This test assesses behavioural and mental attributes relevant to people working in medicine. Check the UKCAT website to find out about participating universities and how to apply to take the test. All medical degrees combine practical training and clinical experience with academic learning. Having completed your medical degree you then undertake a two-year foundation programme gaining further experience and consolidating your learning.

Personal attributes

All doctors must have excellent interpersonal skills – these qualities have become increasingly important in selecting appropriate students for medical school.

Earnings

Junior doctors in postgraduate foundation training earn £33,000 to £41,000. Doctors in specialist training earn between £44,000 and £69,000. Hospital doctors earn from £45,000 and specialists earn £70,000. Senior consultants earn more than £150,000. GPs earn from £44,000 on qualifying to £80,000 plus.

Info

NHS Careers
0845 6060 655
www.nhscareers.nhs.uk

Royal College of Surgeons of England
020 7405 3474
www.rcseng.ac.uk

General Medical Council (GMC)
0845 357 3456
www.gmc-uk.org

UK Clinical Aptitude Test (UKCAT)
www.ukcat.ac.uk

Royal College of General Practitioners
020 7344 3051
www.rcgp.org.uk

Health Learning and Skills Advice Line
08000 150850
nextstep.direct.gov.uk

MERCHANT NAVY

The Merchant Navy refers to all non-military shipping and comprises cargo ships, tankers, ferries and cruise ships. The Royal Fleet Auxiliary also employs civilian crew. While different ships will carry different ranges of personnel – for example more engineers on a tanker, more cooks and hospitality staff on a passenger cruise liner – there is still a clear staffing structure on every ship and below are the main job titles and the work associated with them. In addition to the jobs outlined, ships employ catering staff and administrative staff. Cruise liners employ a whole range of additional personnel, including medical staff, hairdressers, activities coordinators and entertainers of many kinds.

Deck officer

Deck officers are responsible for every aspect of the ship, from its navigation to the management of the crew and the safety of passengers and crew. There are four grades of deck officer: captain or master, chief officer, second officer and third officer. The captain is in overall charge of the ship. The other three levels of officer share a range of responsibilities for navigation, cargo handling, safety of crew and passengers, supervision of crew, and management of overall maintenance. The levels of responsibility become greater for each deck officer grade.

Entry, qualifications and training

You can join as an officer cadet or marine apprentice if you have four GCSEs grades A—C, including English, maths and physics or combined science. You must also be sponsored by a shipping company or another training provider. There are also some opportunities to be sponsored through a Foundation degree or degree programme in science. These industry-sponsored courses include practical training on board ships as well as your academic studies.

Personal attributes

You must have good leadership skills and be able to motivate people and work as part of a team. You should have good technical ability and enjoy learning about equipment and systems. You have to be able to tolerate long periods away from home and sometimes work in rough and uncomfortable conditions.

Earnings

Officer cadet earnings are very low but once you are qualified as a junior officer you are paid between £20,000 and £23,500. Senior officers, that is, chief officers and captains on large ships, earn between £25,000 and £45,000.

Merchant Navy rating

Merchant Navy ratings are the crew members who work on the decks, in the engine room, handling the cargo and providing catering services on board ships. Exact duties vary according to the size and type of vessel and depending on what special skills or training you have. Work might include loading and unloading cargo, cleaning every part of the vessel and routine maintenance jobs.

Entry, qualifications and training

To train as a Merchant Navy rating you have to be taken on and sponsored for training by a shipping company or by the Royal Fleet Auxiliary. You need to apply directly to these. Each company sets its own entry requirements, but three or four GCSEs are a good guide. These should include English, maths and a science subject. If you have previous experience in engineering or in catering, this can give you a real advantage. Training is through a combination of college-based training and experience on board. You can work towards NVQs in marine support. You then have to make a choice between deck work, catering or engineering. If you continue with your studies you can go on to train as an officer.

Personal attributes

All ratings have to have a real interest in shipping vessels and in being at sea. You need to be physically fit and comfortable working in harsh conditions. The atmosphere is very different on a large tanker compared to an upmarket cruise liner – so you need to consider this when you decide what jobs to apply for. Teamwork is very important indeed. You need to be practical for all Merchant Navy work, but you will also need particular skills depending on whether you specialise in catering, engineering or deck management.

Earnings

Merchant Navy rating pay is low during training, though college fees and all living expenses on board ship are paid by the employer. Experienced ratings earn between £17,000 and £30,000.

Info

Merchant Navy Training Board
0800 085 0973
www.mntb.org.uk

Royal Fleet Auxiliary Service (RFA)
0845 60 40 520
www.royalnavy.mod.uk/The-Fleet/
Royal-Fleet-Auxiliary

A Career at Sea
www.careersatsea.org

Marine Society & Sea Cadets
020 7654 7000
www.ms-sc.org

METALLURGIST

Metallurgists are interested in the physical and chemical properties of metals and alloys, such as iron and steel, aluminium, copper and nickel. There are three different types of work for metallurgists. Chemical metallurgists are concerned with the extraction of metals from ore. They also study metal corrosion and fatigue. Physical metallurgists study the performance of metals under stress. Process metallurgists shape and join metals and select the best metal to use for particular jobs. Metallurgists work in research and development, design and manufacture, production management and quality assurance. Metallurgists may be at the forefront of new technologies, developing metals for new applications, or involved in the traditional manufacture of anything from razor blades to washing machines.

Entry, qualifications and training

This is almost always a degree-level career with preferred subjects being metallurgy, chemistry, physics, manufacturing engineering or similar. Occasionally you can join this profession if you have an HND in a relevant subject. For research and development posts, employers sometimes expect you to have a postgraduate qualification such as an MSc in metallurgy.

Personal attributes

Metallurgy demands an interest in scientific and technological subjects, an ability to solve practical problems and to work with other people on specific projects.

Earnings

Graduate entrants earn between £18,000 and £27,000. With a few years' experience earnings rise to between £30,000 and £37,000.

Info

Institute of Cast Metal Engineers
(ICME)
0121 601 6979
www.icme.org.uk/

Institute of Materials, Minerals and
Mining (IOM3)
020 7451 7300
www.iom3.org

Metals Industry Skills and
Performance
0114 244 6833
www.metskill.co.uk

Proskills UK (The Sector Skills
Council for the Process and
Manufacturing Sector)
01235 833844
www.proskills.co.uk/

METEOROLOGIST

Meteorologists are the people who tell us what the weather is going to do. While we are all aware of weather forecasting on television and radio, meteorologists provide information for many other clients too. People who want accurate weather forecasts include organisations involved in air transport, shipping, public service, the media, the armed forces and retail businesses. Individuals involved in air travel or water sports or outdoor pursuits such as climbing, farmers or sporting organisations – all of these can plan more effectively if they know what the weather is likely to do. Meteorologists collect data from satellites all over the world. They use computerised and mathematical models designed to make short- and long-range forecasts concerning weather and climate patterns. They also study the impact of weather on the environment, taking measurements, recording results and looking at patterns over time. The study of meteorology is one of the sciences most frequently used in the study of climate change.

The largest employer of meteorologists in the UK is the Met Office, but meteorologists are also employed by agriculture and fisheries organisations, the oil and gas industry, research organisations and the Environment Agency. Some work for small consultancies contracted to provide information for the kinds of organisations just listed.

Entry, qualifications and training

Meteorology is a graduate profession – many meteorologists also have postgraduate qualifications. The most useful degree subjects include maths, physics, meteorology, environmental science and oceanography. The Met Office usually takes entrants with a First or 2.1 degree. It is very unusual to get in with an HND or a Foundation degree. The Met Office has a Mobile Met unit (MMU) and it is possible to apply to be a forecaster for this unit if you have good A levels in maths and physics. Technical support staff and administrative staff employed by the Met Office do not need degrees, but from these roles it is not possible to become a meteorologist. The Met Office provides a structured training scheme for new entrants.

The Met Office offers a small number of highly sought-after summer placements which can provide really useful experience. Experience of computer modelling, even if it is not weather related, is also extremely useful.

Personal attributes

Of course, you must be interested in the weather – who isn't? In addition you have to have very good observational skills and the ability to generate and interpret highly complex data. You must be able to work as part of a team, and be able to communicate scientific information in such a way that it can be easily understood by the non-scientist.

Earnings

Graduate trainees in the Met Office earn around £20,000 and just under £25,000 once they have completed training. Experienced forecasters earn £25,000 to £35,000. Shift-work allowances may also be paid. Private weather consultancies may pay higher salaries, but they do not usually provide the training.

Info

The Met Office	Royal Meteorological Society
www.metoffice.com	www.rmets.org

MILK ROUNDSPERSON

(see Roundsperson)

MODELMAKER

Models can be made to represent almost anything: towns, office blocks, oil terminals, shopping centres, motorways, houses, cars and planes. They are often scaled-down versions of the real thing, but sometimes they can be enlargements. They are used to show what the real thing will look like, and if they are working models, they may be used as testers. Models are often used in television and films. Modelmakers work for firms specialising in such work, or sometimes branch out on their own.

Entry, qualifications and training

Formal academic qualifications are not necessary. Modelmakers may teach themselves or learn at evening class; some large firms offer apprenticeships. Edexcel (BTEC) courses in modelmaking are available at some FE colleges and some art colleges.

Personal attributes

Patience, manual dexterity, and a good sense of design, shape and colour are necessary. Modelmakers must be prepared to do one job for a considerable length of time; a project such as a model town could take up to a year to complete.

Earnings

Pay is between £18,000 and £22,000, though experienced modelmakers can earn up to £30,000.

Info

Institute of Engineering Design
www.ied.org.uk

Skillset Careers
08080 300 900 (England and
Northern Ireland)
0808 100 8094 (Scotland)
0800 121 815 (Wales)
www.skillset.org/careers

Design Council
www.designcouncil.org.uk

Creative and Cultural Skills
(The Sector Skills Council for Craft,
Cultural Heritage, Design, Literature,
Music, Performing, and Visual Arts)
020 7015 1800
www.ccskills.org.uk

MOTOR INDUSTRY

The motor industry provides job opportunities, from technical to sales and management roles. Whatever your particular role, you need a genuine interest in motor vehicles. The following section gives details of the most commonly found job titles and training routes in this industry.

Auto electrician

Auto electricians are motor vehicle technicians who have highly specialised knowledge of and skill in the complex electrical and electronic systems that are part of modern motor vehicles.

Entry, qualifications and training

To be an auto electrician, you need to do an apprenticeship. To start an apprenticeship you must have five GCSEs grades A–C, including maths and English. The apprenticeship combines on-the-job training with your employer and college-based learning. Through your apprenticeship you can gain an NVQ certificate.

Personal attributes

You must be good at working with your hands and able to solve problems. You must be good at working as part of a team.

Automotive engineer

(see Engineering)

Body repairer and refinisher

Body repairers and refinishers restore cars, vans, trucks and motorcycles to their original condition after accidents, damage or other wear and tear. This includes replacing windscreens and other glass, removing dents and rubbing away patches of rust. Repair and refinishing covers several different roles, including body repair, electrical, mechanical and trim repair, and vehicle valeting.

Entry, qualifications and training

For any job in body repair and refinishing, apart from car valeting, you need to do an apprenticeship. To be accepted for an apprenticeship you must have five GCSEs grades A–C, including maths and English. The apprenticeship combines on-the-job training with your employer and college-based learning. Through your apprenticeship you can gain relevant NVQ certificates.

Personal attributes

These vary according to exactly which aspect of body repair and refinishing you have chosen, but they all demand that you pay great attention to fine detail, that you can find ways to solve problems and that you are able to work as part of a team.

Roadside assistance and recovery technician

Roadside assistance and recovery workers are called to the scene of vehicle breakdowns. They have to make quick, accurate assessments as to whether they can repair the vehicle on the spot or whether it will have to be towed away. They also have to reassure vehicle drivers and passengers and explain to them clearly what the best course of action is.

Entry, qualifications and training

For this work you must be 21 years old and hold a full clean driving licence. Most successful applicants will already have worked for three years or more with motor vehicles, usually as a vehicle technician. Most technicians qualify through an apprenticeship.

Personal attributes

You need to be extremely responsible, with good technical skills and knowledge. You must be able to take decisions on your own and to solve problems. You must have good people skills, be polite, friendly and reassuring, and good at explaining technical problems.

Vehicle parts operative

Vehicle parts operatives deal with the ordering and management of the hundreds of separate parts that need to be replaced in every type of vehicle. Vehicle parts operatives have to be able to recognise any vehicle part and know that part's place in a vehicle. They have to liaise with customers, with technicians, with manufacturers and with distributors. The work involves ordering and finding stock, controlling stock levels and advising customers.

Entry, qualifications and training

To work as a parts operative, you need to do an apprenticeship. To be accepted on an apprenticeship you must have five GCSEs grades A C, including maths and English. The apprenticeship combines on-the-job training with your employer and college-based learning. Through your apprenticeship you can gain relevant NVQ certificates.

Personal attributes

You must be really interested in vehicles, be very well organised, able to work under pressure and good at dealing with people. You must be good at handling a lot of detailed information.

Vehicle salesperson

People working in vehicle sales, often called sales executives, sell cars and other vehicles to private and business customers. They have to know a great deal about cars, not just those they are trying to sell, but those they may be purchasing or taking in part exchange.

Entry, qualifications and training

There are no formal entry qualifications for this job. Many vehicle salespeople have worked as vehicle technicians or in other roles in the automotive industry. Some have come from a selling background in other sectors.

Personal attributes

Sales executives have to combine good technical knowledge with excellent people skills. You must be polite, friendly, prepared to answer detailed questions and able to offer clear explanations.

Vehicle technician

Vehicle technicians work to repair and maintain cars, vans, trucks and motorcycles. It is usual for technicians to specialise in just one of these groups of vehicles. Vehicle technicians also work at the many fast-fit centres that fit tyres, exhausts or other parts and systems. Some technicians specialise in MOT testing or in converting petrol cars to run on liquid petroleum gas (LPG).

Entry, qualifications and training

To become a motor vehicle technician (with the exception of fast tyre fitting) you need to do an apprenticeship. To start an apprenticeship you must have five GCSEs grades A–C, including maths and English. The apprenticeship combines on-the-job training with college-based learning. Through your apprenticeship you can gain relevant NVQ certificates.

Personal attributes

All motor vehicle technicians have to have a real interest in working with vehicles and be good at working with their hands. You often need to be a good problem solver and patient too – sometimes why something won't work is not obvious.

Vehicle valeter

Vehicle valeters clean and polish vehicles for individual customers and for car showrooms, and vehicle leasing and rental companies. Valeters clean the inside and the outside of vehicles. They may have to vacuum, clean windows and other glass, steam clean, wash, use high-pressure hoses and wax and polish vehicles. Some vehicle valeters combine vehicle pickup and delivery with their valeting work.

Entry, qualifications and training

There are no formal entry qualifications for this work, but if your job involves driving, you must have a full, clean driving licence. A mature attitude is important, and some experience in customer care work can be an advantage.

Personal attributes

You must be very thorough, good at paying attention to detail and you should be reasonably physically fit. You should be polite, friendly and trustworthy.

Earnings

Apprentices earn £11,500 to £14,000, rising to £16,000 to £20,000 on completing training. Experienced technicians can earn £25,000 plus. Car valeters earn between £12,000 and £15,000. Sales people normally earn a basic salary plus commission on each vehicle they sell; the basic salaries start at around £15,000 with a possible £5,000 in commission and bonuses. Many people with technical qualifications and experience go self-employed.

MUSIC

Music, whether popular, classical or jazz, is a career that appeals to many people. Becoming a performer in any genre is highly competitive. In addition to the specific roles described here, the music industry also employs people in marketing, finance and events management. It also crosses over with other industries such as arts administration and theatre.

Composer

Composers and song writers either write original pieces or devise new arrangements for pieces that have already been written, orchestral arrangements of piano pieces, instrumental versions of songs, jazz arrangements of classics, etc. It is very hard to make a living purely from composition, unless you have a really well-established reputation or can get a position as composer in residence – and there certainly aren't many of these. Once established, you may be commissioned to write pieces, film scores for example. The nature of composition has changed with the impact of powerful software, which enables you to cut out some of the basics of writing out music or structuring chords. No software, however, can replace flair, talent and imagination.

Entry, qualifications and training

For most people who wish to compose music, it is not a full-time job. There are no specific entry requirements, but many composers will have studied music, been through music college and are likely to play at least one instrument.

Personal attributes

A passion for music, creative energy and determination are the key qualities you need. If you want to have work commissioned, marketing what you do and getting yourself known are also very important.

Earnings

It is hard to say. Many composers make only part of their income from writing compositions. If they gain commissions they will charge a set fee for each particular piece of work. They can also earn money from royalties if recordings or sheet music of their work is sold.

Info

Incorporated Society of Musicians
(ISM)
020 7629 4413
www.ism.org

Associated Board of the Royal
Schools of Music (ABRSM)
020 7636 5400
www.abrsm.org

Musical instrument maker/repairer

Musical instrument makers and/or repairers build, repair, restore and maintain musical instruments of all kinds, from modern electric guitars to ancient pianos. Most repairers specialise in a particular instrument or family of instruments, such as woodwind, string, brass or pianos. Some develop special skills in restoring very old instruments, others make and build instruments using modern materials such as plastics and carbon fibres. One specialised field in musical instrument repair is piano tuning.

Entry, qualifications and training

You do not need specific qualifications to get into this work, but you do need careful training. You should certainly have excellent manual dexterity and a good ear. There are a few courses in musical instrument making and repair. These include the ASET Certificate in Classical Musical Instrument Technology at levels 2 and 3 and BTEC HNC/HND in Instrument Technology. London Metropolitan University offers Foundation degree and degree courses in musical instrument technology. You can find out about short courses in instrument repair from the National Association of Musical Instrument Repairers website. If you are interested in piano tuning, the Association of Piano Tuners provides details of training courses.

Personal attributes

As well as manual dexterity and a love of the instrument or instruments on which you wish to work, you need a range of people and business skills. Many instrument makers and repairers are self-employed, so you must be able to market your services and deal with potential customers.

Earnings

Salaries start at £14,000 to £18,000. Instrument repairers and makers with experience and a good reputation can earn more than £30,000. If you are self-employed, you will set an appropriate fee for the level of work involved and the length of time the job is likely to take.

Info

Institute of Musical Instrument
Technology
www.imit.org.uk

National Association of Musical
Instrument Repairers
www.namir.org.uk

Piano Tuners Association
www.pianotuner.orq.uk

Incorporated Society of Musicians
(ISM)
020 7629 4413
www.lsm.org

Musician (classical)

Whether you play an instrument or sing, musical training leading to a degree or equivalent qualification opens the door to a wide range of careers in music, including performing, teaching, administration, management, broadcasting, recording, journalism, publishing, promotion, librarianship and the retail trade.

Many professional musicians work on a freelance basis as soloists, orchestral players, commercial session musicians and in a variety of chamber music ensembles, including classical, rock, dance and jazz groups. A performer's working life often includes some teaching, master classes or community education work alongside regular and vital practice.

Some musicians arrange their own engagements, others have an agent or use a diary service to find work. For all performers, membership of a professional association or union is desirable.

There are opportunities, particularly for those who already play an instrument, to join the Army, the RAF or Royal Marines as a bands person.

Entry, qualifications and training

Entry to undergraduate courses of study usually requires a minimum of five GCSEs and one or more A levels, preferably including music. Full-time courses of study over three or four years, usually leading to a degree, are available at conservatoires (performance-based), universities (more academic) and colleges of higher education (broader spectrum). Singers require a longer training, often over six years. Conservatoires and universities also offer a range of postgraduate courses. Details of courses in performance, composition, musicology and teaching are available from the ISM website. The government introduced a training scheme for the music industry under the 'New Deal' initiative; details are available from Jobcentre Plus.

Personal attributes

A love of music, a positive and persuasive personality, robust physical and mental health, stamina, patience and excellent communication skills are essential for any career in music. Competition is fierce for performers, and only a very few talented musicians can establish a successful solo career. The ability to get on well with others helps to ensure good relationships with colleagues, managers and promoters to support career development.

Earnings

There is wide variation in earnings. Most musicians are self-employed and either have short contracts or are simply paid for individual jobs. There are some permanent salaried posts in orchestras, but many members of orchestras and bands of all types, as well as session musicians working in recording studios, are self-employed. What you earn depends on how much work you get, how good you are and how much your particular instrument or style is in demand. The Musicians Union (MU) can offer detailed guidance on what you might expect to be paid for work at your level and your instrument.

Musician (pop)

This career is desired by so many but achieved by only a few. Pop covers many styles – rock, heavy metal, folk, jazz, indie, etc – with trends for what is most popular shifting all the time. Pop musicians may be singers or play any instrument. The day-to-day work consists of practising your instrument or your singing, composing material, recording material and preparing for or going on tour. Not every pop musician is going to front a band or become a household name. Many singers and instrumentalists work as session musicians for bands either in the recording studio or on tour.

Entry, qualifications and training

There are no specific entry requirements – though a passion for your music is a good starting point. Being able to read music is useful, especially if you are going to work as a session musician. Many people learn the instrument they wish to play from a young age and hours of practice are a vital part of getting into this profession.

Personal attributes

You have to be enormously resilient and determined as well as talented. Many people will not achieve their dreams, or will work for a long time to achieve success. Success, if it comes, also brings demands on your time, your energy and your emotional resilience. You have to be able to cope with being very much in the public eye. How you look and how you present yourself are often very important too.

Earnings

Many pop musicians have to do other work to make ends meet, while the most successful earn enormous salaries. Equity, the performers' union, provides guidance on what session musicians can expect to be paid.

Music teacher

With music now placed as one of the foundation subjects in the National Curriculum, there is an increasing demand for music teachers. Opportunities range from private instrumental teaching to class teaching at primary, secondary and tertiary levels. Class teachers and some visiting instrumental teachers working in state schools require Qualified Teacher Status.

Private teachers set up and develop their own independent, studio-based business. The Incorporated Society of Musicians (ISM) sets professional standards for members who are listed in their Register of Professional Private Music Teachers. They set minimum hourly tuition fees, so that a reasonable income can be assured, and advise on business matters such as tuition contracts.

Entry, qualifications and training

Teachers require an appropriate teaching qualification, such as a PGCE (Postgraduate Certificate in Education). Details of courses in performance, composition, musicology and teaching are available from the ISM website.

Personal attributes

A love of music, a positive and persuasive personality, robust physical and mental health, stamina, patience and excellent communication skills are essential for any career in music.

Earnings

Earnings vary enormously. Guidance on rates of pay is available from the ISM. Hourly rates of £16–£20 are usual.

Info

Creative and Cultural Skills
(The Sector Skills Council for Craft,
Cultural Heritage, Design, Literature,
Music, Performing, and Visual Arts)
020 7015 1800
www.ccskills.org.uk

Incorporated Society of Musicians (ISM)
020 7629 4413
www.ism.org

Associated Board of the Royal Schools
of Music (ABRSM)
020 7636 5400
www.abrsm.org

Musicians Union
020 7582 5566
www.musiciansunion.org.uk

Equity
020 7379 6000
www.equity.org.uk

Rockschool
0845 460 4747
www.rockschool.co.uk

Music therapist

(see Therapy)

Piano tuner

(see Musical Instrument Maker/Repairer)

NAVAL ARCHITECT

A naval architect is an engineer who specialises in the design, construction and repair of sea-going craft, including cruise liners, Merchant Navy vessels, warships, submarines, ferries, pleasure craft and high-speed boats. Ship building has declined as an industry in the UK, but there opportunities to build and design small craft, especially in coastal towns. Some naval architects also work for the Maritime and Coastguard Agency inspecting ships in port to ensure that they are seaworthy. They also work on the design and construction of offshore installations such as oil and gas drilling rigs. As a naval architect you would work with construction and project teams checking specification and coordinating work. Your work could involve consulting with lawyers, scientists and accountants.

Entry, qualifications and training

The usual way to become a naval architect is with a degree or diploma accredited by the Royal Institute of Naval Architects (RINA). Approved subjects include naval architecture, marine engineering and ocean engineering. You need A levels in maths, physics and one other subject to study any of these accredited courses. Anyone with a qualification in another engineering discipline should check with the RINA to see whether it is acceptable, or what further qualifications and training they need to undertake. Without a degree or diploma it may be possible to take equivalent Engineering Council qualifications. Several companies are accredited to provide training. This training covers three areas: design, engineering practice and management services. After a minimum of two years' work experience you can apply to become a chartered or incorporated engineer with the RINA.

Personal attributes

A genuine interest in ships, boats and other vessels is a good starting point. You must have good technical engineering knowledge and a creative attitude to problem solving. Naval architects need good report-writing skills and the confidence and clarity to explain technical problems to non-technical people.

Earnings

Trainees start on between £23,000 and £25,000. Qualified and experienced naval architects earn around £40,000 to £50,000. Experienced and senior naval architects can earn £75,000.

Info

SEMTA (The Sector Skills Council for Science, Engineering and Manufacturing Technologies)
0845 643 9001
www.semta.org.uk

Royal Institution of Naval Architects (RINA)
020 7235 4622
www.rina.org.uk

Institute of Marine Engineering, Science and Technology (IMarEST)
www.imarest.org.uk

NURSING PROFESSIONS

Nurses, healthcare assistants, midwives and health visitors work in many different settings, including hospitals, health clinics, GP practices and the wider community. They work in the NHS, the independent healthcare sector, charities and voluntary organisations.

Healthcare assistant

Also known as health support workers, healthcare assistants work alongside nurses and provide basic care for patients. They help with treatments, keep wards tidy and complete basic paperwork. They work on general hospital wards, in clinics and outpatient departments, psychiatric hospitals, hospices and care homes. There are also opportunities for community-based work, providing physical care to individuals who might otherwise have needed to go into hospital or a residential care home.

Entry, qualifications and training

No prior qualifications are needed to start work as a healthcare assistant, but hospitals, care homes and other organisations do provide training and there is currently a drive to ensure that everyone doing this work will achieve at least NVQ level 2.

Personal attributes

Like qualified nurses, healthcare assistants must have patience, tact, tolerance and an ability to communicate with the patients in their charge. Physical fitness is essential as the job sometimes involves heavy work (such as lifting and turning patients).

Earnings

Newly qualified healthcare assistants earn from £13,700 to £17,000, more in London. Experienced healthcare assistants who have taken additional qualifications earn up to £18,500.

Info

NHS Careers	Health Learning and Skills Advice
0345 60 60 655	Line
www.nhscareers.nhs.uk	08000 150850
	nextstep.direct.gov.uk

Health visitor

Health visitors promote health and contribute to the prevention of mental, physical and social ill-health in the community. This involves educating people in ways of healthy living and making positive changes in the environment. Education may be achieved by teaching individuals or families in their own homes, in health centres, clinics, in informal groups, or through campaigns for the promotion of good health practices through local or national mass media.

The health visitor may work with people who are registered with a GP or who live within a defined geographical area. The work includes collaboration with a wide range of voluntary and statutory organisations.

Entry, qualifications and training

Applicants must hold a first-level nurse or midwifery qualification with post-registration experience. One-year health visitor courses are provided at institutions of higher education.

All approved programmes now lead to the award of Specialist Practitioner (Public Health Visiting/Health Visiting). These programmes are at a minimum of first degree level.

Personal attributes

Health visitors must be excellent communicators, able to convey information to all types of people without being patronising. They must have self-confidence, tact and a lot of common sense. They must be able to work alone, yet know when to seek advice. They should be confident, articulate public speakers.

Earnings

Newly qualified health visitors are paid £25,600 to £34,000. Team leaders and manager health visitors are paid £33,000 to £41,000.

Info

Community Practitioners and Health Visitors Association
020 7505 3000
www.amicustheunion.org/cphva

See also the Info panel at the end of the Nurse section.

Midwife

Midwives (who may be female or male) provide care and advice to mothers and fathers before, during and after birth; they are employed by the NHS in hospital and/or community settings, including home births, by private hospitals, or work independently. The midwife provides care during normal pregnancy and birth, and up to 28 days following the birth. The midwife will also care for women who have complications. The midwife is an integral part of the multidisciplinary team responsible for delivering care, working closely with obstetricians and other health professionals in ensuring the well-being of mothers and babies.

Entry, qualifications and training

To qualify as a midwife you need to complete a degree or diploma course in midwifery that is approved by the Nursing and Midwifery Council (NMC). Institutions running courses can set their own academic entry requirements, but there are broad general guidelines. For nursing diploma courses you need five GCSEs grades A–C, including English, maths and a biological science. For degree courses the same GCSE requirements apply, but you also need two A levels. Applicants must be aged 17.5 in England and Wales, 17 in Scotland and 18 in Northern Ireland. In England you must apply through the Nursing and Midwifery Admissions Service (NMAS) – the contacts for Scotland, Wales and Ireland are listed in the Info panel. Applicants who do not meet these entry requirements may be successful if they can demonstrate literacy and numeracy skills and provide some evidence that they have recently undertaken successful study of some kind. If you have a nursing degree or diploma (adult branch) you can do a 12- to 18-month midwifery diploma.

Personal attributes

Midwives must have extremely good interpersonal skills, and be caring, practical, friendly and encouraging. They must be able to work as part of a team, but also to take responsible decisions on their own.

Earnings

Newly qualified midwives earn between £21,200 and £27,600. Community midwives earn £25,000 to £34,000. Senior midwives and those involved in research and management earn £30,000 to £41,000.

Nurse

Nurses care for people of all ages who are ill, injured or suffering from mental, emotional or physical disabilities. They are based in hospitals, in clinics, in local GP practices, in schools, in the community and in industry. While there are many settings in which nurses work, there are four main branches that determine your career path: adult nurse, children's nurse, mental health nurse and learning disabilities nurse.

Adult nurses care for patients aged 18 and over in hospitals, clinics and other settings. They work with people who have long-term illnesses, who are recovering from surgery or who have suffered injury and trauma. Your daily tasks could include checking temperatures, blood pressure and respiratory rate, giving drugs and injections, cleaning and dressing wounds, administering blood transfusions and drips, and using hi-tech equipment. Once qualified, adult nurses may choose to specialise in fields such as operating theatre work, accident and emergency, coronary care and many more.

Children's nurses undertake the same variety of work as adult nurses, but their patients are all aged under 18 years. The work might involve caring for premature or newborn babies, or nursing older children who have long-term or terminal illnesses. Babies and young children may not be able to explain what is wrong, so children's nurses must develop good powers of observation.

Learning disabilities nurses work with people of all ages who need help with aspects of everyday living. These nurses may work in hospitals, in day care or residential settings, special schools and the community. The work normally involves assessing clients to see what they can do and where they need help, and then teaching, advising and developing programmes that help those people to reach their potential.

Mental health nurses work in hospitals, psychiatric units and the community. They work to support people who experience difficulties caused by conditions such as depression or anxiety. They work with people who have phobias, or who have suffered traumas through accidents or illnesses. Mental health nurses also work with people who have become dependent on alcohol or other substances. The work involves helping people to live and cope more effectively, whether this is through medication, talking problems through, or developing programmes of beneficial activities.

Entry, qualifications and training

You have to choose which of the branches of nursing interests you most, since the courses are each tailored to one of these branches. Having made this choice, the entry route for each branch is very similar. From 2013 all nurse training will be through a degree course, but there are currently a few remaining diploma courses. To get onto a diploma course you need five GCSEs grades A–C, including maths, English and one science. For a degree course you need the same GCSEs plus two A levels. Some institutions run advanced diplomas, which are pitched between the diploma and the degree-level course. There are other routes in. If you have graduated in another subject you may be able to do a two-year fast track course. All courses combine academic learning with practical experience. If you are a healthcare assistant and have NVQ level 3 qualifications you may be able to get full nursing qualifications on a part-time basis. All applicants for courses must have a Criminal Records Bureau (CRB) check. Once qualified, there are many opportunities for further training and developing specialist skills and knowledge in particular fields of nursing.

Personal attributes

While the balance of required skills and qualities may vary between the different branches of nursing, there are many requirements common to all. Nurses must be caring and compassionate and enjoy working with people. They have to be emotionally resilient, often dealing with distressing situations. Nurses must be practical and have good manual dexterity and confidence in handling specialised equipment. They need an interest in the science, anatomy and physiology that underpins health and illness. They must be very observant and also good at working as part of a healthcare team. In senior roles they must also be able to motivate, train, supervise and monitor the work of others.

Earnings

Newly qualified nurses earn between £21,250 and £27,600. With experience, specialist knowledge and management responsibilities, salaries are between £27,000 and £41,000.

There are opportunities to work overtime, which is paid at time and a half. These figures are based on working for the NHS. Some private sector salaries are higher, and some charity sector salaries are lower.

Info

Nursing and Midwifery Council
(NMC)
020 7462 5800
www.nmc-uk.org

National Leadership and Innovation
Agency for Healthcare (Wales)
01443 233333
www.wales.nhs.uk

Northern Ireland Practice &
Education Council for Nursing &
Midwifery
028 9023 8152
www.nipec.hscni.net

Nursing Careers Centre (NCC)
01 639 8500
www.nursingcareers.ie

OCCUPATIONAL THERAPY

Occupational therapists work with people who have physical, mental or social problems, either from birth or as the result of accident, illness or ageing. Their aim is to enable people to achieve as much as they can for themselves. They start with a thorough assessment of each client and his or her lifestyle to establish what the person wants to achieve. Treatment can involve adapting living and working environments, teaching coping strategies and discovering the most beneficial therapeutic activities.

Although occupational therapists often work as part of a team, they have more autonomy than other healthcare workers in the way they apply their knowledge and expertise. They work in hospitals, social service departments, individuals' homes, residential and nursing homes, schools, universities, charities and prisons. They may also work in private practice.

Employment and promotional opportunities are excellent and all UK-educated occupational therapists receive a qualification that is recognised by the World Federation of Occupational Therapists, giving them opportunities to work abroad.

Entry, qualifications and training

Entry to the profession is normally on completion of a full- or part-time degree in occupational therapy. Most courses require three A levels or equivalent; mature students will be considered without these academic requirements. Accelerated two-year full-time courses are also available to graduates of other disciplines. Part-time in-service programmes are also available for those employed as occupational therapy support workers or technical instructors. Some part-time courses can be studied irrespective of employment status. Although courses vary, all include the principles and practice of occupational therapy, behavioural, biological and medical sciences, and periods of clinical practice in a variety of hospital and community settings.

Personal attributes

You must be a good problem solver and be flexible, patient and sensitive. You have to be a very good communicator, encouraging and supporting clients, but also liaising effectively with other members of the health and social care team.

Earnings

Newly qualified therapists are paid on band 5 of the NHS pay scales, which range from just under £21,200 to a £27,600. Senior therapists are paid on band 6, from £25,000 to £34,000. Therapists with more management or other special responsibilities are paid on band 7, from just under £30,000 to £38,000.

Info

Health Professions Council (HPC)
020 7840 9812
www.hpc-uk.org

NHS Careers
0345 60 60 655
www.nhscareers.nhs.uk

British Association of Occupational Therapists/College of Occupational Therapists
020 7357 6180
www.cot.co.uk

OIL/GAS RIG WORK

There are various openings for personnel working on oil or gas drilling rigs, both onshore on land, and offshore out at sea anywhere in the world where there is oil and gas. Opportunities in all fields are generally limited to experienced and/or highly qualified applicants. An offshore rig has to be self-sufficient and is a combination of a factory, hotel and heliport. Catering and accommodation are similar to the provision onshore. Many of the routine factory tasks (such as cleaning and maintenance) are carried out by outside contractors and service companies.

Diver

(see also Diving)

Divers are employed in exploration and production work, as well as underwater repair work such as welding.

Drilling crew

The drilling crew is responsible for the drilling of wells, and the operation and maintenance of a variety of heavy machinery. The crew consists of a toolpusher who manages the team and is responsible for the safety and integrity of the operation, and a team of people including a driller, assistant driller and derrickman, who work on the tapering steel superstructure above the drill, roughnecks and roustabouts. A typical drill crew will number around 10 people. Progression to the role of driller is hierarchical, with people working through general labouring jobs (roustabouts), working on the drill floor (roughnecks) or at the top of the derrick (derrickman). The work is physical, from the operation of the drilling equipment to the cleaning and maintenance of pumps and equipment. A graduate drilling engineer and a range of other specialists, such as logging engineers, directional drilling specialists and mudloggers, will also work with the drill crew.

Engineer

(see also Engineering)

A production engineer supervises activities ranging from production and storage, gas compression and injection (to assist in the recovery of the oil), to tanker loading. The reservoir engineer is concerned with the behaviour of the oil accumulation or reservoir, and has to attempt to discover how much oil remains below ground and what the most effective methods of recovery are. Economics plays an important role. The maintenance engineer must ensure that all equipment is functioning properly, selecting and monitoring the companies under contract.

Geologist

(see also Geology)

The oil companies employ technical experts such as geologists, geophysicists, drilling and petroleum engineers, and seismic interpreters. Geologists collect and analyse data from a variety of sources to determine whether drilling might prove successful at a particular site, and to optimise production from existing oilfields. There are opportunities around the world.

Entry, qualifications and training

Engineers and geologists need relevant degrees. To join a drilling crew you do not necessarily need formal qualifications, but you must be aged 18 or over and are likely to have to pass a medical. Many people join through an apprenticeship scheme, and employers are likely to require four GCSEs grades A–C for this.

Personal attributes

You need to by physically fit, geographically mobile and emotionally resilient. It can be hard working for long periods, especially on offshore rigs. You need to be able to work really well as part of a team and have acute health and safety awareness.

Earnings

The harsh nature of this work leads to relatively high rates of pay. Roughnecks and derrickmen earn around £27,000. Drillers and assistant drillers earn from £32,000 to £50,000. Drilling engineers start on between £28,000 and £35,000, increasing to £35,000 to £45,000. Geologists and geophysicists are paid similar salaries to those earned by engineers. Annual leave is usually very generous if your job involves a lot of time working offshore.

Info

Cogent (The Sector Skills Council for Science Based Industries)
01925 515200
www.cogent-ssc.com

Institute of Materials, Minerals and Mining (IOM3)
020 7451 7300
www.iom3.org

Oil and Gas UK
020 7802 2400
www.oilandgasuk.co.uk

SEMTA (The Sector Skills Council for Science, Engineering and Manufacturing Technologies)
01923 238 441
www.semta.org.uk

Society of Petroleum Engineers
020 7299 3300
www.spe.org

Oilcareers
www.oilcareers.com

OPTOMETRY

Dispensing optician

Dispensing opticians supply and fit spectacles and contact lenses prescribed by optometrists (also known as ophthalmic opticians) and eye specialists. They can advise clients on different types of lens, such as varifocals or prescription sunglasses. They take precise measurements to ensure that the lenses work properly for individual clients and they also fit, adjust and repair spectacle frames. Most dispensing opticians work for high street chains or independent opticians in the retail sector and part of your role would be to sell and market your company's products and services. There are also some opportunities to work in hospitals and other healthcare settings.

Entry, qualifications and training

To practise as a dispensing optician you must complete a training course approved by the General Optical Council (GOC) and pass a professional examination administered by the Association of British Dispensing Opticians (ABDO). There are three routes to qualifying: a two-year full-time diploma; a three-year day-release course; or a three-year distance-learning course. Whichever route you choose you will need GCSEs grades A–C in English, maths and a science. Many course providers like you to have two A levels, including maths, biology or physics. The GOC provides a list of course providers, so check individual requirements.

Personal attributes

You must be pleasant, friendly, approachable and patient. You must also be good at handling delicate equipment and have reasonable mathematical skills for taking measurements and making calculations. It is also useful to have a grasp of fashion and style, since this is very important to many of your clients when they choose spectacles or lenses.

Earnings

Trainees and assistants without full qualifications earn £17,000 to £22,000. Qualified opticians earn £23,000 to £30,000. Many opticians run their own businesses, where earnings may be higher, but it is a competitive market.

Info

General Optical Council (GOC)
020 7580 3898
www.optical.org

Association of British Dispensing
Opticians (ABDO)
01227 738 829
www.abdo.org.uk

Optometrist

Optometrists (also referred to as ophthalmic opticians) are trained to examine eyes and test sight, detect and measure defects in healthy eyes and prescribe spectacles, contact lenses or other appliances to correct or improve vision. They must carry out whatever tests are clinically necessary to detect signs of injury or disease to the eye or elsewhere, and must refer these patients to a medical practitioner. Most optometrists work in general practice in a variety of arrangements, including independent businesses, partnership, as an employee of corporate bodies, as a franchisee or in the hospital eye service. There are also job opportunities in research organisations, academic departments, ophthalmic hospitals and clinics.

Entry, qualifications and training

Optometrists must be registered with the General Optical Council (GOC) before being permitted to practise in the UK. To obtain registration they must pass the professional qualifying exam run by the College of Optometrists. The exam is in two parts. For Part I you must gain a BSc honours degree in optometry. You can take Part II after completing a pre-registration year of supervised practice. The professional qualifying exam combines practical and oral assessment of the candidate's ability to manage patients and practise safely as an independent optometrist.

For a place on the degree course you normally need three A levels, two of which must be maths and science.

Personal attributes

Opticians need mathematical and scientific skills to make accurate observations and calculations. They also need an ability to get on with, and communicate effectively with, patients of all ages and backgrounds and to be able to put them at their ease.

Earnings

In the pre-registration year most optometrists earn around £18,000 to £22,000. If you do your pre-registration year in an NHS hospital the salary is close to £19,000. Hospital optometrists tend to be paid slightly more than their private practice colleagues once qualified – £27,000 to £33,000 in the NHS and £22,500 to £28,000 in private practice.

Info	
College of Optometrists	General Optical Council (GOC)
020 7839 6000	020 7580 3898
www.college-optometrists.org	www.optical.org

Orthoptist

Orthoptists diagnose and treat various abnormalities and weaknesses in the eye, such as a squint or double vision. Many patients are children, and special equipment and exercises are used to help correct any defects while they are still young. Orthoptists work closely with medical eye specialists and, where operations are necessary, with ophthalmic surgeons. Most orthoptists work within the NHS, in hospitals and clinics (including school clinics). There are also opportunities in private practice and teaching.

Entry, qualifications and training

To practise as an orthoptist you must pass a degree approved by the Health Professions Council (HPC). Details of approved degree courses are available from the HPC and also from the British and Irish Orthoptic Society. For these degree programmes you normally require five GCSEs grades A–C, including English, maths and two sciences. You also need two or three A levels, one of which must be biology.

Personal attributes

You need to enjoy working with people, be good at putting them at ease, and be patient and reassuring, especially when working with children. You need good powers of observation, good manual dexterity and good numeracy skills.

Earnings

Newly qualified orthoptists earn between £22,000 and £27,500. With experience you can earn more than £38,000. These figures are based on working for the NHS. In private practice, initial salaries may be lower than the NHS, but this gap is likely to close with experience.

Info

NHS Careers
0345 60 60 655
www.nhscareers.nhs.uk

British and Irish Orthoptic Society
020 7387 7992
www.orthoptics.org.uk

Health Professions Council (HPC)
(0)20 7840 9812
www.hpc-uk.org

PAINTER AND DECORATOR

(see Construction Trades)

PATENT ATTORNEY

A patent is a legal document that gives an inventor the right to claim an invention as his or her own work and to produce, sell or make the invention. It also protects the inventor from having his or her work and/or ideas copied by others. Patent attorneys have expertise in the field of intellectual property. They advise individual clients and companies on matters relating to patent law, and act on their behalf if they wish to patent an invention, or to register a trademark or a design in the UK or abroad. First, records are searched to gauge the likelihood of a patent being granted. The patent agent then draws up the particulars of the client's invention clearly and concisely, ensuring that it neither infringes another patent nor is liable to be copied without infringing its own patent. In cases where a client's patent has been infringed, the agent advises as to the best course of action. Patent attorneys are employed by private practice firms of patent consultants, industrial companies with a patent department, and the government.

Entry, qualifications and training

The minimum educational requirement for an attorney is a degree in a science or a technology-related subject. It is usually necessary to register as a patent attorney in the European Patent Office. This involves taking the European qualifying exams, for which a degree is necessary. Training is provided by your employer, and some patent agents choose to become patent examiners or work in-house for companies involved in research and development.

Personal attributes

You need a broad mix of skills: curiosity, the ability to assimilate new ideas, good analytical and critical skills, clear and concise thinking, and the capacity for logical and clear expression both in speech and in writing are all essential.

Earnings

Trainee patent attorneys earn between £27,000 and £33,000. Once qualified, salaries are between £50,000 and £70,000. Experienced patent attorneys can earn up to £100,000.

Info

Chartered Institute of Patent
Attorneys
020 7405 9450
www.cipa.org.uk

European Patent Office
www.epo.org

UK Intellectual Property Office
(UK-IPO)
0845 9 500 505
www.ipo.gov.uk

PERFORMING ARTS

Performing arts covers the many occupations that make up the world of cultural entertainment. Competition is keen and, because it is such a precarious profession, those entering it must be prepared for long periods of unemployment.

Circus performer

Circus performers entertain in many ways designed to be spectacular, amusing or both, from skilled high-wire acrobatics, trapeze work and tightrope walking, to juggling, fire eating and performing as clowns. They work in circuses that travel from place to place and in fixed venues such as theatres. Circus acts often form part of major events designed to impress, such as opening ceremonies for sporting or cultural events. Some circus performers may also get work as stunt performers in aspects of theatre other than circus. As a circus artist you may work on solo performances or on team displays.

Entry, qualifications and training

Having a real talent for what you do is far more important than academic qualifications. There are many courses in circus arts available, from short weekend courses, part-time courses at local adult education institutes, through to full-time two-year Foundation degree courses in London and Bristol. Some circuses and circus companies also run training courses. A full list of courses is available on the Circus Development Agency website.

Personal attributes

Of course, these very much depend on the particular circus craft you wish to pursue. For many you will need to be physically fit, agile and flexible and have a fair degree of physical courage. You will have to be prepared to learn and work hard at very specific sets of skills. You need to be confident and at ease in front of a crowd, and you must be able to work well with other people.

Earnings

Earnings vary widely. Many people working as circus performers earn less than £6,000 per year from their circus work, and are likely to do other work as well. Some circus craft people may earn far more than this – up to £23,000. Equity negotiates minimum pay rates per performance or per week.

Info

Creative and Cultural Skills
(The Sector Skills Council for Craft,
Cultural Heritage, Design,
Literature, Music, Performing, and
Visual Arts)
020 7015 1800
www.ccskills.org.uk

Circus Development Agency
www.circusarts.org.uk

Get Into Theatre
www.getintotheatre.org

Equity
020 7379 6000
www.equity.org.uk

Dance

Dance can be divided into the two main categories of theatre dance (ballet, modern and contemporary dance, jazz and tap) and social dance (ballroom, folk dance and disco). However, there are no hard-and-fast divisions between the different forms. The profession of dancing consists of two main areas: performing and teaching. Choreography, notation, dance animation and dance therapy are related areas of work.

Choreographer

Choreographers create and plan dance routines and oversee the execution of their plans by the dancers. Choreographers are often former dancers.

Dance notator

Notators are employed by dance companies to record their repertoire, and assist choreographers and rehearsal staff in the revival of choreographic works. Most notators are graduates of vocational dance schools or ex-professional dancers, as the work involves close and informed observation of the choreography, the ability to demonstrate the movement accurately and the ability to work effectively with professional dancers.

Dance performer

Many of those who wish to perform have had early training in ballet and/or other forms of theatre dance. Opportunities in ballet and contemporary companies are limited, and many dancers find their first employment in companies abroad. Dancers also work in pantomimes, shows and musicals, and on cruise ships. Professional performers find it useful to be members of Equity, the British actors' union.

Dance teacher

Teachers of dance can specialise in one area of dance teaching or teach in a variety of areas. The demand for teachers is high, especially as dance is now seen as a form of recreation. Teachers may work in commercial dance studios and professional dance schools both in the UK and abroad.

Entry, qualifications and training

Ideally, ballet students should attend a recognised residential establishment, such as the Royal Ballet School, from the age of 11 to 18. Means-tested financial assistance may be available to UK students. Dancers who want to become teachers must obtain the relevant qualifications, for which full-time and part-time courses are available. These generally have an entry requirement of four or five GCSEs at grade C and above. The Royal Academy of Dancing offers certificates, diplomas and degrees in classical ballet teaching. The courses are available on a part- and full-time basis.

Personal attributes

Dancers need to be hard working, self-disciplined both physically and mentally, dedicated and determined. They must be imaginative, able to express themselves artistically, and have a good sense of timing and an ear for music.

Earnings

Equity, the trade union for actors and performers, negotiates minimum rates for its members per performance or per week. Non-Equity members are often paid less than this, but dancers often accept these lower rates while they are trying to establish their careers. Experienced dancers can earn £500 a week and in London's West End rates are often closer to £700 to £800 a week.

Music

(see Music)

Theatre

(see Film and Television, Production for Lighting, Make-up Artist)

Many jobs, such as director, producer, lighting technician, prop maker, make-up artist and wardrobe manager, are common to television, film and in some instances (for example, sound technician) radio as well as theatre. There are also jobs in administration, front of house, taking bookings and selling programmes. There are jobs in marketing, advertising a theatre's activities or looking for sponsorship. There are practical opportunities such as carpentry. There are, however, some jobs that are specific to live theatre.

Actor

Acting mainly involves the interpretation of someone else's work and the communication of it to an audience, although there are opportunities for actors to write their own material. Actors are employed in various types of theatre (commercial, subsidised, community, fringe and theatre-in-education), and also in television, film, radio, and television and radio commercials.

Competition is keen and, because it is such a precarious profession, those entering it must be prepared for long periods of unemployment.

Entry, qualifications and training

Most potential actors attend drama school. The National Council for Drama Training is a useful source of information on accredited courses. A good general education is important, and some schools require GCSEs and A levels or equivalent. Training courses at established schools usually last two or three years. Entrance is by audition and is competitive. Further experience may be gained from working in a repertory company or in fringe theatre. This may be an alternative way of entering the profession, but it is becoming increasingly difficult to enter solely by this method.

Personal attributes

Acting requires a combination of intelligence, sensitivity and imagination, together with a good memory, determination and physical stamina.

Earnings

Many actors struggle to make a living through acting, especially in their early careers. Only 6 per cent of actors earn more than £30,000 a year. Equity, the actors union, sets minimum rates for its members – contact them for information. Actors are paid either per performance or per run of a play.

Stage hand

Stage hands, also referred to as stage technicians or crew, play an essential role behind the scenes, helping to ensure that props, scenery and special effects are exactly where they should be at just the right moment. Daily tasks vary, but can include helping carpenters to build, erect and paint scenery; moving scenery and furniture during a performance, either manually or with automated equipment; opening and closing stage curtains; and clearing and tidying the stage, studio or back-stage area after a performance. Stage hands also have to attend rehearsals to become familiar with a performance so that they know exactly what they have to do and can time it perfectly.

Entry, qualifications and training

You do not need formal qualifications – practical experience is more important. Many stage hands start as casual workers helping with large productions before they are able to get full-time work. Having experience of back-stage work through school, college, university or other amateur dramatics is extremely helpful. Having practical woodwork skills can also give you a good start. It is often worth approaching local theatre stage managers direct to see if they can offer you casual work. After this, training is very much on the job.

Personal attributes

You must be physically fit and happy to work at evenings and weekends. You must be able to maintain a good level of concentration, and work quickly, quietly and calmly during a performance. You should have a real interest in theatre and you must be able to work as part of a team.

Earnings

Full-time stage hands earn between £11,000 and £15,000, but there is not always full-time work available. Experienced theatre technicians with large companies can earn up to £20,000.

Stage manager

Stage managers are responsible for ensuring that all the technical and practical sides of rehearsals and live performances run smoothly. The stage manager is in charge of all stage hands and technicians and he or she has to ensure that everyone, including the performers, is in the right place at the right time. Typical activities for a stage manager include organising rehearsals, managing the props budget and the props themselves; liaising with other departments, eg lighting, set designers and wardrobe; cueing performers to go on stage, cueing sound and lighting staff; working closely with front-of-house staff; and keeping the 'prompt copy' of the script (which details the performers' positions on stage, script changes, and the props, lighting and sound needed for each scene).

Entry, qualifications and training

Most new entrants to stage management have degrees or professional diplomas in stage management and technical theatre. You can take a degree or diploma in this subject at drama school. Alternatively, you could take a degree in drama, stage management or practical theatre at a college or university. Some people who have worked as actors move into the stage management side of the profession. It is also possible to work your way up from a behind-the-scenes job such as a stage hand, but this route is becoming increasingly difficult. Practical experience is as important as formal qualifications. You must have had some experience of stage management through amateur dramatics, school, college, or university drama groups.

Personal attributes

You must be an excellent communicator with outstanding organisational skills. You should be able to liaise with people at every level in theatre. You need to be calm, quick at solving problems, able to take responsibility, good at motivating or pacifying others and easily able to think about several different things at once – a true multitasker.

Earnings

Salaries for assistant stage managers are from £16,000 to £24,000. Stage managers earn £21,000 to £40,000 or more. High salaries are few and far between because theatres often work on very tight budgets.

Info

Get Into Theatre
www.getintotheatre.org

Conservatoire for Dance and Drama
020 7387 5101
www.cdd.ac.uk

Creative and Cultural Skills
(The Sector Skills Council for Craft,
Cultural Heritage, Design,
Literature, Music, Performing, and
Visual Arts)
020 7015 1800
www.ccskills.org.uk

Equity (The Actors' Union)
020 7379 6000
www.equity.org.uk

The Independent Theatre Council
020 7403 1727
www.itc-arts.org

London Academy of Music and
Dramatic Art (LAMDA)
020 8834 0500
www.lamda.org.uk

National Association of Youth
Theatres
01325 363330
www.nayt.org.uk

National Council for Drama Training
020 7387 3650
www.ncdt.co.uk

PHARMACY

Pharmacists dispense and give advice on drugs prescribed by doctors or bought over the counter. They work either in the retail sector (community pharmacy) or in hospitals and other healthcare settings such as GP surgeries. A few pharmacists work in research for the pharmaceuticals industry.

Community pharmacist

Community pharmacists work for high street retail pharmacies and local health centres. They dispense prescriptions and ensure that medicines ordered on prescription or bought over the counter are supplied correctly, safely and in compliance with the law. They give advice to customers on what over-the-counter medicines might be suitable for their complaint, or they may recommend that the customer consult a doctor. They act as a link between doctors, patients and the pharmaceutical industry.

Hospital pharmacist

They dispense drugs for hospital in- and outpatients and work side by side with nurses, doctors and other health professionals to ensure that NHS patients receive the most appropriate medicines in the most effective way. In addition, in some hospitals, pharmacists manufacture their own products, take part in research work and come into direct contact with inpatients by accompanying medical staff on their ward rounds.

Entry, qualifications and training

Pharmacists must complete a four-year Master of Pharmacy degree, followed by one year's paid competency-based training and a registration examination. Entry to degree courses is with A level chemistry plus two other A levels or equivalent; maths and biology are preferred.

Personal attributes

As well as excellent relevant medical knowledge and the need to be very careful and accurate, it is also important that you get on well with people and can be patient and understanding. Pharmacists already have responsibility for handling dangerous drugs, and it seems likely that they will be given greater prescribing rights in the near future, when responsibility and decision making will be extremely important aspects of their skills mix.

Earnings

In the NHS, newly qualified pharmacists earn from around £22,000 to £27,600. Senior pharmacists and pharmacists with special responsibilities are paid from £34,000 to £45,000. Salaries for retail pharmacists are between £23,500 and £30,000.

Info

Royal Pharmaceutical Society
020 7735 9141
www.rpsgb.org.uk

NHS Careers
0345 60 60 655
www.nhscareers.nhs.uk

Association of the British
Pharmaceutical Industry (ABPI)
020 7930 3477
www.abpi.org.uk;
www.abpi.org.uk/our-work/careers

Health Learning and Skills
Advice Line
08000 150850
nextstep.direct.gov.uk

·Pharmacy technician

Pharmacy technicians work as part of the pharmacy team and are supervised by a pharmacist. Their duties can include the dispensing of medicines from prescriptions, preparing sterile medicines, assessing stocks of drugs, patient counselling, advising on health promotion issues and collecting and collating information on drugs from a variety of sources. Pharmacy technicians can work in chemists, hospitals, the armed forces, the prison service, or within the pharmaceutical industry.

Entry, qualifications and training

A nationally recognised qualification is the NVQ Pharmacy Services at level 3, which is available from approved centres. Entry requirements for this are generally four GCSEs at grade C or above, including English, mathematics and chemistry plus one other science. Mature applicants are welcome, and previous education and work experience are considered.

Personal attributes

As a pharmacy technician you should have a real interest in science and the ability to be accurate and careful. You should be able to deal sensitively and tactfully with people, be good at working as part of a team, and in some posts you may have to use sales skills as well.

Earnings

In the NHS, pharmacy technicians earn £22,000 to £27,600. The NHS also employs pharmacy support workers, who earn £15,200 to £17,000. In the private sector pharmacy technicians can earn up to £30,000.

Info

Royal Pharmaceutical Society
020 7735 9141
www.rpsgb.org.uk

NHS Careers
0345 60 60 655
www.nhscareers.nhs.uk

Association of the British
Pharmaceutical Industry (ABPI)
020 7930 3477
www.abpi.org.uk; www.abpi.org.uk/
our-work/careers

Health Learning and Skills
Advice Line
08000 150850
nextstep.direct.gov.uk

SEMTA (The Sector Skills Council
for Science, Engineering and
Manufacturing Technologies)
0800 282167
www.semta.org.uk

PHOTOGRAPHY

Photographers produce visual images of many kinds, either working to a brief given them by a client, or exploring subject matter they have chosen themselves. Photographers use a range of photographic equipment, including digital cameras (a few still use conventional cameras), lighting systems and computer programs developed to manipulate photographs. Some photographers also develop their own work, using either traditional darkroom methods or digital processing. The subject matter you work with is determined by the field of photography in which you work. Typical aspects of the job include choosing locations and subjects, selecting appropriate cameras and accessories, and setting up lighting and background. Photographers also have to compose the picture, whether this is discussing a pose with a model or arranging still-life objects.

Advertising/editorial photographer

Advertising photographers take pictures for magazines and brochures. These pictures either advertise a product or illustrate a story. Many advertising photographers specialise in particular subjects such as food, cars, portraiture or landscapes.

Corporate photographer

Corporate photographers work for large businesses and other organisations taking pictures for annual reports, promotional brochures or in-house journals. Some people working in this field become specialist industrial photographers, taking pictures of the manufacturing process as well as finished products.

Fashion photographer

Fashion photographers take pictures of models promoting clothes, shoes, jewellery, cosmetics and hairstyles. At the top end of the market they work for well-known magazines, taking pictures of models that people have heard of. At the other end of this market, photographers take hundreds of pictures for mail order catalogues.

General practice photographer

General photographers take pictures for a range of clients in their local community. A great deal of the work involves wedding photography, but these photographers often cover community events and family occasions. Many do some work for local newspapers that don't employ in-house press photographers. Those photographers who do specialise mainly in weddings or other special occasions are sometimes described as social photographers rather than general practice photographers.

Medical photographer

(see Medical and Healthcare Science)

Press photographer

While some reporters and journalists take their own photographers, there is still a specific role for a press photographer. Press photographers either work for a particular newspaper or magazine, or they work freelance, selling their images to whomever wishes to buy them. They take photographs that reflect everything from serious news and current affairs to sport and lifestyle pictures. A press photographer works to take images which best document an event or capture a moment. Some press photographer specialise in particular types of picture, eg sport, entertainment, celebrity or news events.

Scientific/technical photographer

Some photographers specialise in taking pictures for scientific journals and research papers. They may have to work with microscope slides as well as living subjects. The work of the wildlife photographer is a highly specialised aspect of this type of photography.

Entry, qualifications and training

While there are no formal entry requirements, this is a very competitive field. There are several courses you can do, and being able to combine a course with a good portfolio of your work and some relevant work experience is the best way to improve your chances of success. Courses are available at many levels, including City & Guilds, BTEC Certificates and Diplomas, A levels and degree courses. Many people start work as a photographer's assistant to gain basic skills and knowledge. The British Institute of Professional Photography (BIPP) awards the Professional Qualifying Examination (PQE) to photographers – the award is based on assessing a photographer's portfolio to ensure that it is of a good professional standard.

Personal attributes

These vary according to your chosen specialism, but all photographers must have the ability to perceive and re-create visual impact in a creative way. They must all be competent with technical equipment and normally need great patience. For most jobs, photographers must be able to work well with people, whether it is as subjects or as fellow members of a work team. They also need good business management skills.

Earnings

Initial earnings are between £12,500 and £21,000. Many photographers have to start as photographer's assistants and may earn less than this to begin with. Successful photographers earn between £20,000 and £30,000; a few may earn up to £60,000. Many photographers work freelance or are self-employed, where annual earnings range from £14,000 to £45,000.

Info

Association of Photographers
020 7739 6669
www.the-aop.org

British Association of Professional
Photographers
01296 336367
www.bipp.com

Creative and Cultural Skills
(The Sector Skills Council for Craft,
Cultural Heritage, Design, Literature,
Music, Performing, and Visual Arts)
020 7015 1800
www.ccskills.org.uk

Master Photographers Association
(MPA)
01325 356555
www.thempa.com

Photo Imaging Council
01883 334497
www.pic.uk.net

Skillset (The Sector Skills Council
for the Creative Industries)
020 7713 9800
www.skillset.org

Photographic technician

Photographic technicians work either in large photographic laboratories or in mini labs in high street stores. If you work in a professional laboratory, you may use traditional darkroom techniques developing films. Much of the work now on the high street and in traditional laboratories involves using computerised equipment producing prints or CDs from images taken on digital cameras. In both cases the work involves producing pictures of the best possible quality. Technicians check for quality, analyse problems and may give feedback to customers on what could have gone wrong. Based in high street stores, the work also involves dealing directly with customers, packaging pictures, and taking orders and payments.

Digital imaging technician

Digital imaging technicians work for professional photo finishing laboratories and picture libraries. The work usually involves discussing the format and finish of an image with a client, scanning images into a computer, using specialised software to manipulate the images, change colour, resize or crop a picture where appropriate, printing the finished image onto paper, saving it on CD or uploading it to a website. Digital imaging technicians are often responsible for building up banks of images that can then be purchased by clients.

Entry, qualifications and training

You may not need formal qualifications to work in a high street mini lab, though some employers may ask for GCSEs, including maths and a science. To work in a professional laboratory you are far more likely to need qualifications in photography, such as an HND, a Foundation degree, or a degree. If you want to work in digital imaging, it may also be helpful to build up a portfolio of images on which you have worked; you also need to be competent with relevant computer software packages such as Photoshop.

Personal attributes

In all cases you need a genuine interest in photography. For all positions you need good basic IT skills. To work for a professional digital imaging lab you need a high level of desktop publishing skill. You need good communication skills, to be able to explain problems to customers, or to clarify a brief from a client. You have to be good at working as part of a team.

Earnings

For photographic technicians, starting salaries are between £12,000 and £16,000 on the high street, possibly more in professional laboratories. Digital imaging technicians earn from £20,000 to £35,000.

PHYSICIST

Physicists study the world around us; they try to understand and explain why and how objects, including the universe itself, exist and behave in the way they do. As well as tackling these profound questions, physicists apply their knowledge in many practical ways – anything from the development of the next generation of mobile phones to the forecasting of climate change. Using mathematical techniques and computer modelling, they can have useful input into many industries. Physicists could be involved in the development of new medical instruments, the exploration of new methods of power generation or the investigation of artificial intelligence and robotics. Physicists work closely with many other scientists and engineers, including materials engineers, biomedical engineers, astronomers and information technologists. Physicists also work in teaching, academic research and scientific publishing.

Entry, qualifications and training

This is a complex and intellectually challenging profession. Employers normally require at least a good honours degree in physics, applied physics or engineering, but many applicants will also have a Master's degree or a PhD. To gain a place on a physics degree course you need five GCSEs and A levels in maths and physics. If you do not have these A levels you may be able to do a bridging course or a Foundation degree in science to meet these requirements.

Personal attributes

Above all, you need an enquiring mind and the ability to think in new directions and find imaginative ways of tackling problems. You also have to be logical and methodical in your thinking and you must be a good communicator. You have to be patient – you may be working on something for a long time before you get any answers, or the answers you would like. You have to be able to work successfully on your own, or as part of a team.

Earnings

New entrants earn £23,000 to £30,000. Research physicists who have just completed PhDs earn around £30,000. In industry, physicists earn from £30,000 to £55,000 plus. Senior researchers and project leaders in academia earn £35,000 to £45,000.

Info

SEMTA (The Sector Skills Council
for Science, Engineering and
Manufacturing Technologies)
0800 282167
www.semta.org.uk

Institute of Physics
www.iop.org

PHYSIOTHERAPIST

Physiotherapists treat patients suffering from a wide variety of diseases, conditions or injuries by physical means. They help people who have had a stroke to regain the use of lost functions, treat sports injuries and people with arthritis, and help children with cerebral palsy to learn to walk. The techniques used include massage and manipulation, exercise, electrotherapy and hydrotherapy. Most physiotherapists work in the NHS but there are many opportunities now for employment in industry, sports clinics, schools and private practice.

Sports physiotherapist

The increasing number of opportunities to work with sportsmen and women, both professional and amateur, has become a rather specialised and growing area within physiotherapy. Sports physiotherapists must hold a first-aid certificate and be a chartered physiotherapist. There is a special-interest group within the Chartered Society of Physiotherapy (CSP) for therapists who specialise in treating sporting injuries. There are also several postgraduate diplomas and Master's courses available in sports physiotherapy.

Entry, qualifications and training

To be registered with the Health Professions Council and the Chartered Society of Physiotherapy you must complete an approved degree in physiotherapy.

Entry requirements for these degrees in England, Wales and Northern Ireland usually include four AS levels at grade B, followed by three A levels at grade C or above, including a biological science. You also need five GCSEs grades A–C, including maths, English and a range of science subjects. In Scotland, you need five H grades (AABBB) with at least two science subjects. Appropriate Access to Higher Education courses may also be accepted.

Personal attributes

You must enjoy working with people, putting them at ease, explaining treatments and teaching exercises. You must have a good grasp of physiology and have good manual dexterity. You should be good at observing people and you also need to be able to work well as part of a team.

Earnings

Newly qualified physiotherapists in the NHS earn between £22,000 and £27,600. Senior physiotherapists earn £25,500 to £34,000. Physiotherapists with management responsibility earn up to £40,100. Some physiotherapists work in private practice, where earnings may be a little higher, but where there are fewer management posts.

Info

Health Professions Council (HPC)
020 7840 9812
www.hpc-uk.org

NHS Careers
0345 60 60 655
www.nhscareers.nhs.uk

Chartered Society of Physiotherapy
020 7306 6666
www.csp.org.uk

PLUMBER

(see Construction Trades)

PODIATRIST

Podiatrists used to be known as chiropodists. There are still some chiropodists in practice, but new entrants to this profession will train as podiatrists. Podiatrists are concerned with the health of feet. Those working in the NHS deal with problems caused by diabetes or arthritis and may work with those suffering from sports injuries. Ailments such as corns, bunions and malformed nails are more likely to be dealt with by those in private practice.

Podiatrists perform minor operations under local anaesthetic. They may work in the NHS in hospitals, clinics or health centres, or in private practice or large organisations. Many undertake postgraduate training to specialise in areas such as sports medicine, biomechanics or podiatric surgery.

Entry, qualifications and training

To practise as a state registered podiatrist you must take a degree in podiatry approved by the Health Professions Council (HPC). You then register with the HPC and The Society of Chiropodists and Podiatrists. To do a degree in podiatry you usually need five GCSEs grade A–C, including maths, English and a biological science. You also need three A levels, including one biological science. If you already have a degree in a biological science you can gain exemption from part of the degree course. Once you are in practice you must undertake annual continuing professional development activities monitored by the HPC.

If you do not wish to study for a degree, you can work in the private sector as a foot health practitioner and you can take a diploma in foot health care. Foot care practitioners can register with Foot Health Care Practitioners but you are not obliged to do so to practise. A similar role in the NHS is that of chiropody or podiatry assistant. Qualifications for these roles vary, but many employers and NHS Trusts require you to have three or four GCSEs grades A–C, including a science subject. Some NHS areas offer cadet or apprenticeship schemes in this work.

Personal attributes

You have to be good with people, able to reassure them and provide them with information. You need good practical skills with good manual dexterity. You should be able to work on your own, but also as part of a healthcare team. You need to be well organised and good at managing your own time. If you are in private practice you will also need good business skills.

Earnings

Newly qualified podiatrists working for the NHS earn between £22,000 and £27,600. With specialist responsibilities chiropodists earn between £24,500 and £33,500. Consultant chiropodists earn up to £39,000. The NHS Careers website contains detailed information on salaries. Private practitioners set their own charges, but generally earn between £20,000 and £30,000. Assistants or foot health practitioners earn between £15,000 and £21,200.

Info

Institute of Chiropodists and Podiatrists
www.iocp.org.uk

NHS Careers
0345 6060 655
www.nhscareers.nhs.uk

The Institute for Chiropodists and Podiatrists
01704 500477
www.iocp.org.uk

Health Professions Council (HPC)
0207 840 9812
www.hpc-uk.org

British Chiropody and Podiatry Association
01628 632449
www.bcha-uk.org

POLICE SERVICE

Police community support officer

Police community support officers (PCSOs) are a recent introduction to the police service. This work is done by civilians, rather than serving police officers, but they support and report to local police. They patrol public areas, providing a visible presence to reassure the public. In some areas they have powers to direct traffic or issue arrest warrants, and they often work at events such as football matches or public demonstrations.

Entry, qualifications and training

There are no formal academic requirements or age restrictions for applying to become a PCSO. Applicants must be UK, EU or Commonwealth citizens. Foreign nationals who have indefinite leave to remain in the UK and the right to work here are also eligible. While each police force sets its own entry requirements for PCSOs, they all tend to use similar selection criteria. You apply via an application form and after an initial screening of these forms you will be invited to an interview. You will also have to sit a written test and take part in role-play exercises to assess how you would cope with the range of situations the job throws up. Many forces set fitness tests, because you may have to undertake long foot patrols. Thorough background and security checks are made on all successful applicants. Having a criminal record does not necessarily exclude you from applying, but any convictions for violent or public order offences will certainly disqualify an applicant. Training takes between three weeks and three months, and is mainly classroom based; it covers many aspects of the work, including using computer systems, first aid, radio communications and patrolling.

Personal attributes

You need very good people skills, and to be confident dealing with difficult or sensitive situations. You need to be able to work on your own or as part of a team, to take decisions or seek support as appropriate. You must be able to keep calm in pressured situations and you should be able to remain alert and observant.

Earnings

Pay starts at £16,000 to £17,000, rising to £19,000 to £22,000 with experience. In some geographical locations salaries are higher – up to £26,000.

Police officer

Police officers are recruited as trainee police constables (PCs). PCs work in all aspects of policing, including preventing and investigating crime, maintaining public order and protecting people and property. PCs work from police stations or out on the beat, either on foot or in patrol cars. There are many opportunities to specialise in particular areas of police work once you have completed your probationary period.

There is a separate British Transport Police Force, which operates on passenger transport services to prevent crime, protect public safety and maintain public order.

Entry, qualifications and training

With police forces facing funding cuts, recruitment is likely to be limited and highly competitive. Each police force does its own recruiting, but they all work to a nationally agreed competency framework. While there are no formal educational requirements for joining the police service, there is a demanding selection procedure. Joining the police service is open to British or Commonwealth nationals and also to other foreign nationals who have no restrictions on their right to work in the UK. Applicants must be aged 18 or over. The first stage is to complete an application form and a medical questionnaire. If you are successful at this stage, you are invited to a selection centre to sit a variety of physical and psychometric tests. The physical fitness tests relate to tasks you would have to perform as a serving police officer. Sessions to help you prepare for these tests and to know what to expect are run throughout the UK several times a year.

The psychometric tests include written numeracy, literacy, information handling and reasoning tests, plus personality tests to assess your suitability for the demands of the job. The selection procedure also includes an interview and a full medical, with eyesight and hearing tests. You must have good vision and colour vision and be physically fit. If you pass the selection procedure, references are followed up and security checks, including your financial status, are made. Minor convictions or cautions do not necessarily preclude you from joining the police, but you must declare these.

New recruits work a probationary period of two years. During this time, training is a mixture of on the job with the local police service and college-based learning. Everyone goes through the Initial Police Learning and Development Programme. During this period, trainees work towards the NVQ level 3 in Policing and either during or shortly after this two-year period they are also expected to complete the NVQ level 4 in Policing.

As a probationer or serving officer you may be able to join the High Potential Development Scheme (HPDS), which offers accelerated training and development and helps your promotion prospects.

All policemen and women will undergo a wide variety of training throughout their career, enabling them to cope with changes in the law, social policy, information management and technology.

Personal attributes

You need a mature attitude and the ability to assess and weigh up situations quickly and then take appropriate action. You must be able to follow orders and have the confidence to instruct others. You must be able to stay calm in difficult situations and you must be emotionally resilient. You need excellent and varied people skills, to be able to be confident, assertive, diplomatic, reassuring, patient or firm as the occasion demands. You must be effective as part of a team, but also capable of working on your own.

Earnings

Salaries are set by individual police forces – the average starting salary is between £22,000 and £26,000, with incremental rises for each year of service. Sergeants earn around £40,000 and inspectors earn up to £50,000.

Info

Skills for Justice
www.skillsforjustice.com

Police Service of Northern Ireland
(PSNI)
www.joinpsni.co.uk

Police Service Recruitment
www.policecouldyou.co.uk

Scottish Police Entrance Test
www.police-recruitment.co.uk/
scottish-police-entrance-test.html

POLITICAL WORK

Though politics offers relatively few career opportunities, there are a number of jobs in politics associated with supporting the work of politicians, political parties, undertaking political research and lobbying political bodies on behalf of interest groups. There are also positions in administrative, human resource, information technology and financial roles with political organisations of every kind.

Elected politician

Politicians for the House of Commons, the Scottish Parliament, the Welsh Assembly and the European Parliament are all elected, so they don't 'apply' for their jobs in the traditional sense. Their work involves representing the concerns of their constituents and contributing to the process of decision making by joining in debates, asking questions and voting.

Political researcher

Many different kinds of organisations employ political researchers; MPs, political parties, trade unions, public relations consultancies and non-government organisations are the most likely employers. The work involves detailed research, by monitoring the media, the daily work of both Houses of Parliament and the institutions of the European Union. Researchers also provide detailed answers to questions on almost every topic imaginable.

Entry, qualifications and training

Politicians do not need specific qualifications and come from many different career backgrounds; law is one of the more common. There is a trend towards more people being 'career politicians' who work their way up through such jobs as political researchers or political party administrative staff. Most political researchers have at least a degree and may start by doing voluntary work.

Personal attributes

Politicians have to be good communicators who are well organised and able to balance the needs of their constituency work with demands in Westminster, or wherever they are based. Good organisational and interpersonal skills as well as a rigorous attitude to information research are essential for other political jobs.

Earnings

Junior research staff earn between £14,500 and £18,000; up to £20,000 in London. If you work for a politician, there are no general guidelines on what you should be paid. Senior researchers earn from £20,000 to £35,000. MPs earn £65,000, plus a range of additional allowances.

Info

Houses of Parliament
Information Office: 020 7219 3000
www.parliament.uk

National Assembly for Wales
029 2082 5111
www.wales.gov.uk

Northern Ireland Assembly
Communications Office: 028 9052 1333
www.niassembly.gov.uk

Scottish Parliament
0845 278 1999
www.scottish.parliament.uk

POSTAL DELIVERY WORKER

Postmen and women deliver mail to private and business addresses. They each have a round including several hundred addresses they visit on foot, by bicycle or by van. Postmen and women also sort the mail for their own rounds; some mail is still sorted by hand. Postmen and women may also be responsible for collecting mail from post boxes, local post offices and from business addresses.

Some postmen and women work at district or central offices, sorting mail to be sent to other areas of the UK or overseas.

There are many other delivery and administrative opportunities within the Post Office, including work for Parcelforce and work behind post office counters.

Entry, qualifications and training

There are no formal entry qualifications, but applicants have to pass an aptitude test that assesses their suitability for postal work. Once employed, it is possible to work towards NVQ level 2 in Mail Delivery Services. This covers mail sorting, mail handling and working with automated systems. Apprenticeships are available for applicants aged 16–18, but many postmen and women are taken on at age 18 or over. If your job involves driving, you must have a full, clean driving licence.

Personal attributes

You need good basic literacy and numeracy skills and you must not mind doing repetitive tasks. It is essential to be physically fit, reliable and honest. You need to be polite and friendly, but not mind working on your own.

Earnings

New postmen and women earn £15,000; this rises to around £17,500 after one year of service. It is also possible to earn more through working unsocial hours, taking on driving duties, or other responsibilities. With junior management responsibilities salaries rise to £18,000 to £21,000.

Info

Royal Mail Group plc
www.royalmailgroup.com

Skills for Logistics
01908 313360
www.skillsforlogistics.org

PRINTING

The purpose of printing is communication, whether the printed matter is books, magazines, newspapers, security documents or bank cards. Printers are also involved in other products, from wallpaper and floor coverings to advertising slogans on milk cartons. The printing industry covers a wide range of jobs in both factories and offices. It employs 200,000 people in 12,000 companies.

Camera/scanner operator

The reproduction of colour photographs is largely done by electronic scanners, requiring technical ability rather than the craft skills of the past.

Finishing department

Printed products are usually produced in large flat sheets or reels. To convert and finish sheets or reels into books, brochures or magazines, the material must be folded, stitched, sewn and trimmed. A range of specialised machinery is used to produce the finished product at high speed. Great care is needed at this stage to avoid faults, which could result in scrapping the product and financial loss to the company.

Graphic design

(see also Art and Design)

This is the most artistic job in the printing industry. Designers liaise with clients, understand their needs and transform ideas into high-quality printed products. A mastery of computers and a complete understanding of processes, techniques, typography and colour are required. Applicants normally enter the industry after a National Certificate diploma or higher-level course in graphic design.

Pre-press department

Most setting is via electronic transfer or CD. The pre-press operator uses a computer keyboard and mouse to set type and arrange the page, which is output to film or direct to the printing plate. An error in the pre-press department could result in the scrapping of thousands of books or products.

Printing department

This is where ink is applied to paper or other materials, by a variety of large and small printing machines. Such machines are complex and often computer controlled. They are managed by one or more craftspeople who control the physics and chemistry of the press to ensure that each copy produced is perfect.

Entry, qualifications and training

While you don't always need academic qualifications to get into printing, most companies do ask for GCSEs grades A–C in English, maths, science and IT. The range of qualifications acceptable for office and management jobs is wide. Some jobs require GCSEs; others are open to applicants with A levels or a degree. Training is mostly on the job, and the British Printing Industry Federation runs a number of short courses and also provides information on companies offering training. You can work towards a range of different NVQs, depending on what work you do and what is of special interest. Possibilities include Machine Printing levels 2 and 3, offering several options, such as lithography, web offset and screen printing; Digital Print Production levels 2 and 3, with units on machine operation, digital artwork and pre-press work; and Mechanised Print Finishing and Binding, covering finishing methods in general print and newspapers.

Personal attributes

For many roles in print you need good colour vision and excellent manual dexterity. You need to have a real interest in the finished product and how it looks. You should be keen to learn new skills and be able to adapt quickly as technology changes fast in this field. You should be able to work well as part of a team, but also to take responsibility for your own work.

Earnings

The variety of jobs results in a wide range of salaries. On the machine operating and finishing side, salaries start at £16,000 to £21,000. Where jobs are more technically demanding, earnings can reach £40,000. Managers earn £18,000 to £40,000. Many posts include shift-work allowances and opportunities to earn overtime.

Info

Proskills UK (The Sector Skills Council for the Process and Manufacturing Sector)
01235 833 844
www.proskills.co.uk

PrintIT!
www.printit.org.uk

British Printing Industries Federation (BPIF)
www.britishprint.com

PRISON OFFICER

The prison service

The prison service includes many types of institutions, from high security prisons to open prisons and young offenders' institutions. As well as prison governors and prison officers the prison service employs staff in catering, healthcare and education. The roles described below are those which are specific to the prison service.

Prison governor

As prison governor (often referred to as manager these days), your role is to manage the day-to-day running of your establishment. Each establishment may have one or more assistant governors to take on particular areas of responsibility. As a governor or assistant governor you could be involved in many aspects of running your prison. These include security, ensuring that inmates and staff are safe and having plans in place in case of emergencies, dealing with the prison's budget, recruiting and training staff, dealing with disciplinary issues and carrying out inspections. Governors have to ensure that government policies on all aspects of prison life are adhered to. It is the governor who has to talk to the press if something does go wrong. Governors and assistant governors plan how the prison might best be developed to reduce the likelihood of inmates reoffending once they return to society.

Entry, qualifications and training

There are two routes to becoming an assistant governor. Serving prison officers who have been identified as demonstrating great qualities of leadership may be invited to apply to join the National Offender Management Scheme (NOMS) which is an intensive management development programme. Graduates can apply to go straight on to the NOMS, but there are only around 20 places each year, so competition is strong. Your degree subject is not important; it is possessing the right mix of skills that is vital. Graduates go through a series of rigorous selection tests to try to gain a place.

Personal attributes

This is a challenging career. You need excellent leadership skills and self-confidence. You must be able to react quickly and calmly in potentially difficult situations. You must be firm and assertive and yet a good listener too. You need really good administrative and financial skills and must possess the ability to work under pressure.

Prison officer

Prison officers are employed in prisons, detention centres, young offender institutions and remand centres. The work involves supervising prisoners inside the place of detention, escorting them to courts and other prisons and, if relevant, teaching a skill or trade. Officers also deliver programmes that help prisoners address their offending behaviour. Some specialist prison officers are employed as hospital officers, dog handlers, security experts and caterers.

Entry, qualifications and training

Five GCSEs, including maths and English, are required and applicants must pass an aptitude test and an interview. Training is a mixture of time spent at a local prison and residential courses at an officers' training school. In Scotland, the requirement is five standard grades (1, 2 or 3) or equivalent (including maths and English) or three years' experience managing people. A good level of physical fitness is required. NVQs in Custodial Care are available at levels 2 and 3, as is Custodial Healthcare level 3 and Youth Justice levels 3 and 4. There is special training for caterers, dog handlers, physical education instructors and medical staff. An accelerated promotion scheme exists for graduate entrants.

Personal attributes

Officers should be positive thinkers with humanity and common sense; they must be good listeners, assertive, have excellent communication skills and the ability to mix with a wide range of people.

Earnings

In England and Wales, new prison officers start on £18,000 to nearly £28,000. Pay in inner and outer London includes additional allowances. With experience this rises to £29,000. Senior officers earn £31,000 to £33,000. In Scotland, new officers start on £17,000, rising to £23,000 with a few years' experience. Management grades (senior officers, assistant governors and governors) earn from £27,000 to £45,000. The manager of a large prison can earn up to £80,000.

Info

Skills for Justice
www.skillsforjustice.com

Police Service Recruitment
www.policecouldyou.co.uk

Police Service of Northern Ireland
(PSNI)
www.joinpsni.co.uk

PRIVATE INVESTIGATOR

Private investigators work with individuals, businesses, insurance companies, solicitors and other organisations. They are often self-employed, but may be employed by organisations such as law firms or insurance companies. The work is very varied, including tracing missing persons, investigating insurance claims and presenting legal or financial documents to private individuals and to businesses. Private investigators also investigate commercial piracy and fraudulent activities.

Work activities are varied, including interviewing people, carrying out detailed research and surveillance operations.

Entry, qualifications and training

There are no formal entry qualifications, but many private investigators have worked in other security roles – it is normally a second career. A good standard of general education is important. All private investigators must be licensed by the Security Industry Authority (SIA) and the SIA is in the process of developing both the licensing system and appropriate qualifications. The Academy of Professional Investigation runs a level 3 advanced diploma in private investigation. The Academy also offers advice on where you might obtain some training.

Personal attributes

You must have excellent powers of observation and concentration. You need good people skills to be able to talk to people and encourage people to share information with you. You need good research and information-gathering abilities and some knowledge of IT. You should be self-confident, with good business awareness.

Earnings

New entrants earn around £13,000. Private investigators on regular salaries earn between £15,000 and £25,000. It is harder to predict incomes for those who are self-employed, but £20,000 to £25,000 is a reasonable estimate. Top investigators can earn £50,000 to £100,000.

Info

Security Industry Authority (SIA)
0844 892 1025
www.sia.homeoffice.gov.uk

World Association of Professional Investigators (WAPI)
08709 099 970
www.wapi.com

Institute of Professional Investigators (IPI)
0870 330 8622
www.ipi.org.uk

Academy of Professional Investigation (API)
01444 441 111
www.pi-academy.com

Association of British Investigators (ABI)
0871 474 0006
www.theabi.org.uk

PROBATION OFFICER

Probation officers work for local probation trusts, with people who have committed criminal offences. They work with prisoners both while they are serving sentences and after release, to try to ensure that they do not reoffend. They supervise offenders who have community rather than custodial sentences. They interview offenders and try to help them understand the impact and consequences of what they have done. They supervise group activities of various kinds and they prepare reports for courts, magistrates and prison officials.

Probation services officer

Probation services officers work with probation officers. Your work could involve supervising offenders on community projects, helping offenders address some of the issues that led them to offend (drug dependency, lack of a job, family strife, etc). You could also be visiting offenders in prison and helping them to readjust to life after their sentences have been completed.

Entry, qualifications and training

To become a probation officer you must attain the new honours degree in community justice plus the Vocational Qualification (VQ) Level 5 Diploma in Probation Practice while working as a probation services officer (PSO) You can apply to join a local probation trust as an unqualified PSO. Trusts will only recruit PSOs as and when there are vacancies, so you should check their websites to find out about your local situation.

To join a probation trust as a probation service officer you don't necessarily need formal qualifications, but you do need experience of working with people. A background such as youth or community work is very useful. During your first year as a PSO you must pass a level 3 diploma and you will also get plenty of training.

Personal attributes

You need a mature and calm approach to your work. You must have excellent written and spoken communication skills. You must have an understanding approach to people and their problems, but you also need firm confidence to challenge and question behaviour. You must be caring, but also emotionally resilient. You need to be able to work well as part of a team and you must have excellent organisational skills. You have to develop a good understanding of the law and legal processes.

Earnings

PSOs on full-time contracts earn between £19,000 and £26,000. PSOs on temporary contracts earn less than this. Probation officers earn £26,500 to £35,000, more in management roles.

Info

Skills for Justice
www.skillsforjustice.com

Probation Board for Northern Ireland
028 9026 2400
www.pbni.org.uk

Ministry of Justice
020 7210 8500
www.justice.gov.uk

PROJECT MANAGER

'Project manager' is one of those job titles that can leave you feeling perplexed. What industries do project managers work in? What do they do? A project manager can work in any industry and it is his or her job to see that any kind of project is completed according to a client's requirements, within budget and on time. The project manager liaises with all the people working on the project and keeps the client informed of progress or notified of any unforeseen problems. The types of projects managed might include setting up a new department within a business, introducing a new IT system, developing a new market for products, overseeing a construction project, devising a consultation process with a local community or redeveloping a piece of land that has fallen into disuse. These are just a few examples.

Entry, qualifications and training

These may be as varied as the projects themselves, but generally project management is a fairly senior job. Most project managers are graduates and have experience in the sector in which they are managing, eg finance, human resources, engineering, construction or information technology. There are some degree courses in project management, but other useful subjects include business, engineering, accounting, construction, science or technology. Most project managers develop their skills while working and the Association for Project Management offers professional qualifications towards which you can work.

Personal attributes

Being a good leader, able to motivate people from different work teams, is very important. You must be an excellent communicator and have very good problem-solving skills. In fact, you need the knack of anticipating possible problems before they arise. You must be very good at working to deadlines yourself and ensuring that other people do the same. In addition, you need a good knowledge of the particular sector in which you are project managing.

Earnings

Starting salaries are from £27,000 to £50,000 – the variation results from project management being a part of so many industries. Project management is rarely someone's first job. Senior project managers can earn up to £75,000.

Info

Association for Project
Management
0845 458 1944
www.apm.org.uk

Chartered Management Institute
01536 204222
www.managers.org.uk

PSYCHOLOGY

Psychologists work in many different settings, in hospitals and healthcare, in schools and for local education authorities, in industry, in marketing and business, for the police and criminal justice system, and in sport. While these settings may be very different, all psychologists work to measure, understand, predict and assess human behaviour.

Entry, qualifications and training

For most branches of psychology, you must obtain Graduate Basis for Registration (GBR) with the British Psychological Society (BPS). This means completing a three- or four-year degree in psychology, accredited by the BPS, and it is important to check the status of any psychology degree before you begin your studies, if you think you may wish to register as a chartered psychologist. If your undergraduate degree is not in psychology you can start by doing a BPS-approved Conversion Course and sitting a qualifying examination. Consult the BPS website for details of these courses. Further detail on specific qualifications for the different branches of psychology is given in the following sections.

Clinical psychologist

Clinical psychologists work mainly in health and social care settings with clients of all ages who are facing a variety of mental health and emotional problems. Clinical psychologists work as part of a multidisciplinary team devising programmes to help people who are suffering from such conditions as severe anxiety or phobias, depression, addictive behaviour, or behaviours resulting from neurological or physical injury. They assess their clients' mental and emotional states and may offer advice, counselling or therapy.

Entry, qualifications and training

In addition to a BPS accredited degree, clinical psychologists must complete a three-year NHS-funded doctorate programme in clinical psychology. Places on these programmes are highly sought after, so you normally need a First or 2.1 degree plus some relevant work experience. Work as an assistant in a clinical psychology department is most useful, but course providers will give you advice on what work experience is suitable.

Consumer psychologist

Consumer psychologists do not have to be chartered with the BPS. They work in marketing in commercial businesses and other organisations, trying to understand and make use of the psychological basis of the choices that consumers make and why they choose to buy a certain product or service. Much of their work involves interviewing people or organising focus groups. They interpret the results of these interviews and discussions to help marketers understand and exploit trends in consumer behaviour.

Entry, qualifications and training

Most consumer psychologists have a degree either in psychology or in a marketing discipline where the course has covered consumer psychology in some depth. Some consumer psychologists start their career in other roles in marketing departments.

Counselling psychologist

Counselling psychologists work with children and adults of all ages, helping them to deal with difficulties of many kinds. These could include psychological conditions such as anxiety or depression. Problems may be associated with life situations such as domestic violence or bereavement. Sometimes the problems are associated with substance abuse or eating disorders. Counselling psychologists advise their clients on ways of coping with situations and moving on.

Entry, qualifications and training

In addition to the BPS accredited degree, counselling psychologists need to complete a postgraduate qualification in counselling psychology, also approved by the BPS. There is an alternative 'independent route' into this field of psychology. This entails the equivalent of three years' full-time study, supervised work, the submission of a portfolio and an oral examination by the BPS.

Educational psychologist

Educational psychologists work with school students and other young people who are experiencing difficulties in learning and making progress with their education. Students may encounter difficulties because they have a learning disability, a sensory impairment or some emotional problem that is getting in the way. Educational psychologists work with individual students, with parents, teachers and other professionals, to try to find ways round the problem. They may advise students on new ways to learn, encourage them to talk about problems or set up particular programmes of study and activities.

Entry, qualifications and training

In addition to a BPS accredited degree, educational psychologists in England, Wales and Northern Ireland must complete a three-year doctorate in Educational Psychology, in Scotland they must complete a two-year Master's in Educational Psychology plus one year of supervised practice.

Forensic psychologist

Forensic psychologists work mainly in the prison and probation services. The aim of their work is to try to develop interventions that stop offenders from reoffending and help them find ways to change their behaviours. Work may be one-to-one or in groups. They also advise prison governors and other prison and probation staff on what treatment programmes and institutional policies might be most effective in helping reduce offending. They work closely with the court system, with victims and with witnesses. They have to evaluate the programmes they have set up to measure their effectiveness.

Entry, qualifications and training

In addition to a BPS accredited degree, forensic psychologists must complete a Master's degree in forensic psychology (one year full-time, two years part-time) and then undergo two years' supervised practice.

Health psychologist

This is a new and evolving area, and is the practice and application of psychological methods to the study of behaviour relevant to illness and healthcare. Health psychologists work in community, social care and healthcare settings examining the psychological aspects of illness. They help people implement programmes of behaviour that might prevent health problems and they also work with people learning to cope with various aspects of chronic and acute illnesses. At present, only a small number of health psychologists are employed by the NHS.

Entry, qualifications and training

In addition to a BPS accredited degree in psychology, health psychologists must complete a Master's degree in health psychology and two years' supervised work experience.

Occupational psychologist

Occupational psychologists work in organisations of many kinds or for private consultants. They examine how particular work tasks affect the well-being or performance of workers and they also determine which personal characteristics allow someone to perform tasks well. A major part of their work is in designing recruitment tests that will help employers select the most likely candidates to succeed in particular work roles. Occupational psychologists also work with organisations to solve issues of conflict within a work team, or to identify possible new management strategies.

Entry, qualifications and training

In addition to a BPS accredited degree in psychology, occupational psychologists need to complete a Master's degree in occupational psychology plus two years' supervised practice. An alternative route is to undertake three years' supervised practice and study for the BPS Certificate in Occupational Psychology.

Sports and exercise psychologist

Sports psychologists work with sportsmen and women, helping them to improve their performance by examining the psychological aspects of their games and strategies. Sports psychologists teach techniques like relaxation and visualisation, which should help people to perform better. They also undertake research on the general effects of taking part in sport and physical exercise. Sports psychologists are often self-employed, though some are employed by sports teams or by umbrella organisations for particular sports.

Entry, qualifications and training

This is a very new branch of psychology, so there is no formal training route in place yet. Most entrants will have a degree in psychology or in sports science, followed by a Master's degree in sports psychology This is followed by a period of supervised work experience.

Personal attributes

Psychologists have to have excellent interpersonal skills, and be easily able to work with and listen to people who may be very distressed. They have to be good at observing and highly perceptive. In many roles they need good numeracy skills and the ability to write good reports.

Earnings

In the NHS, clinical psychologists and counselling psychologists start on around £22,000 to £27,600. Outside the NHS, salaries vary. Some counselling psychologists are self-employed. Educational psychologists earn £23,000 to £29,000 during training and £31,000 to £42,000 on qualifying. Trainee forensic psychologists start on £19,500 rising to £24,000 after completing training. Occupational psychologists earn between £25,000 and £45,000. Many sports and exercise psychologists are self-employed; earnings to start with are normally £22,000 to £27,000, but much higher with experience and a good reputation. Most experienced psychologists in all branches of the profession earn between £25,000 and £50,000.

Info

British Association for Counselling
and Psychotherapy (BACP)
0870 443 5252
www.bacp.co.uk

British Psychological Society (BPS)
0116 254 9568
www.bps.org.uk

NHS Careers
0845 606 0655
www.nhscareers.nhs.uk

PSYCHOTHERAPIST

Psychotherapy is a generic term within which there are many specialist disciplines. People may practise as psychoanalytic psychotherapists, as cognitive or behavioural psychotherapists, or as counsellors, with varying degrees of training and experience; however, there are plans to introduce greater regulation.

Psychotherapists may work with individuals of any age, couples and families, or groups, resolving problems such as over-shyness, over-aggression, sleeping disorders, separation difficulties, behavioural problems, eating difficulties, self-harm and depression. They work in hospitals, in- and outpatient clinics, child and family consultation centres, GPs' surgeries, special schools for disturbed children, and in private practice.

Entry, qualifications and training

The picture is very different depending on whether you want to go into private practice or work for a recognised public body such as the NHS or HM Prison Service. At present, for private practice there are no specific entry requirements and a wide range of courses of varying quality is available. If you are aiming for salaried employment with a public institution the situation is very different. You must have a degree, preferably in psychology or a healthcare subject. Training that conforms to standards set by the UK Council for Psychotherapy (UKCP) or the British Psychoanalytic Council is normally required. To complicate matters, prospective employers often state which of these they require, so it may well be worth perusing job adverts before you embark on training. The British Association of Counselling and Psychotherapy produces a directory of approved training courses. Approved training courses usually require you to undergo personal therapy as part of your training, and this can prove expensive. Many psychotherapists have worked in other social service, social care or medical professions and take on psychotherapy as a second career.

Personal attributes

You must be a really good listener and able to encourage someone else to talk. You have to be sensitive, patient and calm; able to cope with your clients showing signs of distress. You need to be able to offer understanding and encouragement without becoming overly emotionally involved in your clients' problems. The training and the work can be personally very challenging, so you need emotional resilience. You also need to be well organised and good at working as part of a team.

Earnings

Some psychotherapists are employed by the NHS and they start on a range of £22,000 to £27,000, rising to £32,000 with experience. Many psychotherapists work in private practice and their earnings are linked to what they charge – anything from £30 to £120 per hour; £45 to £60 is the most likely.

Info

The Association of Independent
Psychotherapists
020 7700 1911
www.aip.org.uk

British Association for Counselling
and Psychotherapy (BACP)
01455 883300
www.bacp.co.uk

British Association of
Psychotherapists (BAP)
020 8452 9823
www.bap-psychotherapy.org

The Guild of Psychotherapists
0207 401 3260
www.guildofpsychotherapists.org.uk

UK Council for Psychotherapy
(UKCP)
020 7014 9955
www.psychotherapy.org.uk

PUBLIC RELATIONS OFFICER

As a public relations (PR) officer/executivo/consultant, your main role is to maintain and improve your employer's or client's image with customers, or with the general public. Some PR officers work in-house for a particular company or organisation. Many companies are not large enough or do not choose to employ in-house PR specialists, so many PR professionals work for specialist PR consultancies providing services for a range of clients. Wherever you work, your responsibilities are likely to include a mix of the following: writing brochures, leaflets, press releases, speeches and articles for websites; monitoring the public and media perception of a person, organisation, service or product; organising publicity campaigns and press launches; making presentations; developing and maintaining good relations with the media; and representing your client/company at a wide range of events.

Entry, qualifications and training

This is a very competitive industry and, while not absolutely essential, most entrants are graduates. Degrees in advertising, business, marketing, journalism or public relations are all relevant. The Chartered Institute of Public Relations (CIPR) provides a list of approved degrees. It is possible to join a PR company or department as an administrative assistant and work your way up. Many PR professionals move into a career in PR following on from work in advertising, marketing or journalism. Most of the training is on the job or through a variety of short courses, many run by the CIPR.

Personal attributes

You must be excellent at all aspects of communication, able to write fluently and at the correct level. You must be confident at speaking in public, dealing with awkward questions and building good one-to-one relationships. You have to be a good problem solver and an excellent organiser. You must be able to work as part of a team and to cope with pressure.

Earnings

Trainees earn between £17,000 and £22,000. Experienced PR executives earn between £27,000 and £40,000. Someone running a PR consultancy can earn up to £80,000 to £100,000.

Info

Chartered Institute of Public
Relations (CIPR)
020 7631 6900
www.cipr.co.uk

Skillset Careers
08080 300 900 (England and
Northern Ireland)
0808 100 8094 (Scotland)
0800 121 815 (Wales)
www.skillset.org/careers

PUBLISHING

Publishers produce and sell books of every kind: fiction, biography, travel, cookery, sport, or academic books – name a subject and someone will have published a book about it. Electronic publishing may have had a huge impact on this sector, but many of the roles within publishing remain the same. Most have editorial and production/design departments employing staff in a range of roles. Of course, they will also have sales, marketing and finance departments, but described here are some of those jobs which are specific to publishing.

Book publishing

Editor

Editors liaise with those involved in the design, planning and production of each book. They read and edit the manuscript, prepare it for the typesetter, check the proofs and are responsible for assembling all the various parts, paginated in the correct order, for the printer. There is no automatic promotion system or salary structure. In a small company the only way to move up may be to move out.

The editorial director or managing editor runs a centralised copy-editing department, and commissions and supervises freelance editorial workers.

Commissioning editor

Commissioning editors are responsible both for identifying new authors and new titles likely to be successful and for monitoring the performance of the current titles being published by their company. A commissioning editor's work can include identifying possible future market trends, setting out proposals and costings for new book titles, deciding whether to accept manuscripts and proposals submitted by hopeful authors and overseeing the progress of any book, from the initial idea to the finished product being on sale.

Copy-editor

Copy-editors check the manuscripts submitted by authors and prepare this material for publication. They have to ensure that the text makes sense and that it is in the right 'house style'. Copy-editors work closely with authors, discussing and agreeing necessary changes. Copy-editors need to be alert to any possible legal questions that the text may raise. They also keep commissioning editors informed of progress and problems.

Editorial assistant

Editorial assistants support the whole publishing process in many ways. They often act as personal assistants to commissioning editors or senior copy-editors. They carry out general office duties, such as maintaining databases or filing systems. They are often the contact point on any project for authors, editors, design and production staff, and marketing and sales departments.

Proofreader

Proofreaders check written text after it has been edited, but before it is printed and published. Their role is to check for basic errors such as spelling and typos, but also to check for consistency or continuity. They check that page numbers follow on correctly, that contents and chapter titles match up and that the text follows the 'house style' if there is one.

Entry, qualifications and training

All jobs in editorial are very popular. The most usual career route is to work your way up from editorial assistant through copy-editor and then commissioning editor. It is sometimes possible to join a publisher as a commissioning editor in academic or professional publishing, if you have highly relevant knowledge of particular topics. There is fierce competition for entry-level editorial jobs, so you may well find it useful to do some work-shadowing or voluntary work. This also helps you build up a network of contacts. Editorial work is almost exclusively a graduate career. Degrees in English or publishing are especially useful. If you are interested in a specific area such as scientific publishing, then a degree in a subject relevant to this may also be helpful. Proofreaders often work freelance or on individual contracts, normally working from their own homes.

Personal attributes

All editorial staff need excellent written and spoken communication skills. To be successful you must be able to work to strict deadlines and work well as part of a team. You have to pay close attention to detail and have an eye for good presentation. Commissioning editors must be good negotiators, planners and project managers. Proofreaders may need qualifications in particular fields if they are working in highly specialised technical or scientific texts.

Earnings

Commissioning editors earn between £18,000 and £23,000 to begin with, rising to £30,000 with a few years' experience. Senior commissioning editors earn £45,000 plus. Copy-editors earn between £16,000 and £35,000 if they work in-house. Freelance copy-editors negotiate a fee per contract, often based on an hourly rate. This is around £20 to £30 an hour, but some publishers pay less, or more, than this. Editorial assistants usually start on between £16,500 and £22,000.

Production controller: books

The production controller draws up an accurate specification for the book and invites tenders from typesetters, printers, paper suppliers and binders. When all the estimates have been received, the production controller places orders and ensures that all the production stages are carried out to the required standard and on schedule. Undemanding production work on, for example, leaflets or reprints is often given to a production assistant, who is regarded as a trainee.

Designer: books

(see also Art and Design)

Designers prepare layouts, sketches, specimen pages and dummies, and mark up the manuscripts for the typesetter after they have been edited. All the activities of the design department are managed by the design director. Directors discuss illustrated or complicated technical books with the author and the editor, commission freelance artwork, arrange the in-house preparation of artwork and impose a visual style on the company product.

Entry, training and qualifications

Production and design staff tend to be graduates and will be expected to have a vocational diploma or relevant qualification.

Personal attributes

Production and design professionals will need to be able to work under pressure and to tight deadlines. Being able to work well in a team and to interpret editorial briefs is also a quality expected in this area. Good planning skills are also essential. Production staff will also be expected to negotiate with printers and freelance designers for good deals.

Earnings

For production assistants, starting salaries range from £15,000 to £20,000, rising to an average of around £26,000 after a few years' experience. Senior production staff earn around £30,000.

Indexer: books

Indexers provide a systematic arrangement of the terms appearing in a book, journal or other publication, which could be electronic or paper-based. They also work with page numbers or other locators in order to ensure that the information can be easily found. Indexers are generally employed by publishers or authors. Most are freelances working from home.

Entry, qualifications and training

No formal qualifications are required but a good education, normally to degree level, is necessary, plus subject knowledge in the case of specialist books. Training is by open-learning course leading to accreditation. Registered indexers prove their experience and competence through an assessment procedure and admission to the Register of Indexers.

Personal attributes

An ability to analyse a text and meticulous attention to detail are essential, plus the ability to work to set requirements and time limits.

Earnings

Indexers are usually self-employed and charge either by the hour or a fixed rate for a particular contract. The Society of Indexers can give you advice on what you should charge. They recommend a basic hourly rate of £19.50 per hour for straightforward work, but for more complex indexing work you may well be able to negotiate a much better rate.

Magazines and newspapers

(see also Journalism)

The main career opportunities for those employed by newspaper and magazine publishers, but not on the editorial side, are connected with sales, advertising and production.

Advertisement sales representative: magazines

Commercial magazines depend on advertising revenue for survival. Graduates are often recruited straight from university to sales posts and are trained on the job. Sales staff must know the magazine's readership and build up advantageous contacts with potential advertisers. They spend a lot of time researching, analysing and planning, and need a persuasive manner and numerical skills.

Entry, qualifications and training

Requirements for trainees vary and many sales reps learn through work experience.

Personal attributes

Sales staff need an outgoing personality and good communication skills, and the ability to work under pressure and to meet deadlines.

Earnings

Many advertising reps earn a basic salary of approximately £14,000 and then are expected to earn the rest on commission. Successful advertising sales reps can earn £40,000+.

Design: magazines

The range of work includes cover design, typographical design, layout, design of advertisements and direct mail material. Entrants will need a design qualification. Entrants need to have a good working knowledge of current design software used within the industry.

Production manager: magazines

Production staff are trained in the printing trade. It is their responsibility to see that the magazine is available at point of sale on publication day, and this involves meticulous planning and a tolerance of stress.

Entry, training and qualifications

Production and design staff tend to be graduates and are expected to have a vocational diploma or relevant qualification.

Personal attributes

Production and design professionals need to be able to work under pressure and to tight deadlines. Being able to work well in a team and to interpret editorial briefs is also a quality expected in this area. Good planning skills are also essential.

Earnings

Salaries for new entrants range from £14,500 to £18,000. In London, salaries are a little higher and this is where many jobs are based. Production managers' salaries vary very much according to the range they are producing and how large a team they have to manage, but a general guide is £22,000 to £34,000.

Info

Skillset Careers
08080 300 900 (England and
Northern Ireland)
0808 100 8094 (Scotland)
0800 121 815 (Wales)
www.skillset.org/careers

Book Indexing Postal Tutorials
07708 571548
e-mail: alanindex@tiscali.co.uk

The Booksellers Association
020 7802 0802
www.booksellers.org.uk

Periodicals Training Council (PTC)
020 7404 4166
www.periodicalstrainingcouncil.org

Publishers Association (PA)
020 7691 9191
www.publishers.org.uk

Publishing Training Centre
020 8874 2718
www.train4publishing.co.uk

The Society for Editors and Proofreaders (SfEP)
020 8785 5617
www.sfep.org.uk

Society of Indexers (SI)
www.indexers.org.uk

PURCHASING OFFICER/ INDUSTRIAL BUYER

Purchasing careers exist in all large organisations, whether profit-making or not. Essentially, purchasing and supply management involves identifying the requirements of the company's internal customers and then obtaining the necessary products and services by negotiation and agreement with suppliers. The primary objective is to obtain value for money. This does not always mean achieving the very lowest price – sometimes other commercial considerations are more important. For example, the flexibility and speed of response of the supplier might be the deciding factor, or the need to minimise risk by choosing a vendor with a good business record.

In a manufacturing environment such as a car plant, the purchaser is directly involved in buying components such as wheels, lights and shock absorbers for the production line. In a financial services company, purchases might well be for telecommunications systems, catering services and marketing services, including advertising and design. In retail purchasing the role is slightly different as buyers are more involved in merchandising, selecting product lines that appeal to the consumer and sell quickly.

Entry, qualifications and training

Most companies require a minimum of four or five GCSE passes. Graduates or individuals with A levels usually enter as trainee buyers, working with experienced personnel and continuing their training in the workplace. The minimum requirement for individuals wishing to study for the Foundation Stage of the Chartered Institute of Purchasing and Supply (CIPS) Graduate Diploma is two A levels and three GCSEs (or equivalent). The Certificate in Purchasing and Supply Management is offered to those with no A levels.

Personal attributes

You need good written and spoken communication skills and a high level of numeracy. You have to have the confidence to negotiate firmly and the temperament to take risks at times. You should be able to build good relationships with people and you need good all-round business awareness.

Earnings

New entrants earn between £20,000 and £27,000. With a few years' experience this range increases to £25,000 to £35,000. Senior purchasing managers with large organisations can earn £65,000.

Info

Chartered Institute of Purchasing and Supply (CIPS)
01780 756777
www.cips.org

QUARRYING

Quarrying is opencast mining for clay, sand, limestone, slate and other materials that are just below the layer of topsoil.

Quarry operative

Quarry operatives are involved in the operations connected with this extraction process. Modern quarrying involves using very heavy machinery to excavate, transport, cut and crush the different products, and quarry workers operate this machinery.

Entry, qualifications and training

There are no specific academic entry qualifications, but you must be fit, and having a light goods vehicle (LGV) driving licence or experience of using heavy plant and machinery can be an advantage. If you are between 16 and 24 years old you may be able to do an apprenticeship; availability of these varies according to locality. Some employers will expect you to have four GCSEs to do an apprenticeship; these should include English, maths and technology. The industry offers the chance to do NVQs at levels 2 and 3 in Drilling Operations, Plant Operations and Process Operations. There is also an NVQ level 3 in Working with Explosives, and there are higher-level courses in Sampling. Most of the training is on the job.

Personal attributes

You need to be physically fit and confident in handling highly specialised technical equipment. You should have good numeracy skills for calculating quantities and you must be able to work as part of a team. You should have an acute awareness of health and safety issues.

Earnings

Now entrants earn around £12,000, rising to £18,000 after two or three years' experience. Senior quarry workers earn between £20,000 and £25,000. There are often opportunities to increase earnings with overtime and shift-work payments.

Info

Proskills UK (The Sector Skills Council for the Process and Manufacturing Sector)
01235 833 844
www.proskills.co.uk

Mineral Products Qualifications Council
www.mp-qc.org

Careers in Quarrying
www.careersinquarrying.co.uk

RADIOGRAPHER

Radiographers are healthcare professionals who use different kinds of radiation, such as X-rays or ultrasound, to diagnose or treat injuries and diseases. There are two branches: diagnostic radiography and therapeutic radiography.

As a diagnostic radiographer, you would use highly specialised equipment to produce and interpret images of the body, which could help doctors diagnose the extent of an injury or the progress of a disease. You could also be involved in screening people to check for early signs of conditions such as breast cancer.

As a therapeutic radiographer you would be part of the healthcare team treating patients, many of whom have cancer, using X-rays and other radioactive sources. You would help plan the most appropriate treatment, deliver that treatment and monitor the patient to check what impact your treatment was having on the diseased tissue, but also to check the patient's health.

Entry, qualifications and training

For both branches of the profession, you must take a degree in radiography. You must choose your preferred branch before you start your degree as they are different disciplines. These courses combine academic study with practical placements in radiography departments. You need three A levels, including a science, to get a place on one of these degree courses.

On graduation, entrants are eligible for State Registration with the Health Professions Council (HPC).

Other health professionals or graduates in science or healthcare-related subjects can train through a postgraduate diploma in radiography – though these are fewer in number than the degree course.

Personal attributes

As well as having an interest in science, radiographers should be caring and compassionate but sufficiently level-headed not to get upset when dealing with sick people. They need to be patient and calm when faced with patients who may be frightened or difficult. Good health and reasonable strength are needed for lifting people and heavy equipment. In addition, radiographers should be good humoured, and able to work well in a team and assume responsibility.

Earnings

Newly qualified radiographers are paid between £22,000 and £27,600 (NHS salaries band 5). Specialist radiographers are paid between £25,000 and £33,000 and senior radiographers (described as 'advanced' in the NHS pay scales) are paid £30,000 to £41,000.

Info	
NHS Careers 0345 60 60 655 www.nhscareers.nhs.uk	**Health Learning and Skills** Advice line: 08000 150850 nextstep.direct.gov.uk
Society and College of Radiographers 020 7740 7200 www.sor.org	**Health Professions Council (HPC)** 0207 7840 9812 www.hpc-uk.org

RAILWAY WORK

The rail industry employs many people: drivers, revenue protection inspectors, customer service assistants, signal operators, engineers, fitters, clerical workers, technicians and managers. The last are responsible for the day-to-day running of the railways or are in charge of departments such as planning, engineering, marketing and accounts.

Entry, qualifications and training

Train drivers must be aged 21 or over, with a good general education. Train companies set their own entrance requirements but often use aptitude tests, including tests on train cab simulators. Training takes between 9 and 18 months and includes work towards NVQ level 2 in Rail Transport Operations (Driving). It is likely that a licensing system for train drivers will be introduced in the near future.

Electricians, fitters and mechanics often have experience as technicians or electricians in other sectors before they join the railway. Apprenticeships may be an option for school leavers; those with four or five GCSEs grades A–C, including maths, English and a science, are able to join. All technicians and engineers are put through Personal Track Safety (PTS) training by their employers before they are allowed to work on railway tracks.

Station assistants, booking clerks and other customer service staff need no formal entry qualifications. Engineers and managers normally have a degree in a relevant subject: electrical or mechanical engineering, or business subjects, respectively.

Personal attributes

An interest in railways is a good starting point. Roles such as driving and signal work require good concentration, and safety awareness at all times is essential. Many positions entail a great deal of customer contact or teamwork, so good interpersonal skills are extremely important.

Earnings

Trainee drivers earn around £17,000 to £22,000, and up to £35,000 once training is completed. Trainee fitters/electricians start on £13,000, less for apprentices. After training, earnings are between £17,000 and £20,000. Station staff earn £12,500 to £17,000.

Info

Network Rail
www.networkrail.co.uk

GoSkills (The Sector Skills
Council for Passenger Transport)
01895 817000
www.goskills.org

RECRUITMENT CONSULTANT

The aim of recruitment consultants is to fit people to jobs. Agencies deal with all types of staff, from office and secretarial to highly complex and specialist technical roles. Much of the work involves selling to potential users and matching clients' demands. This includes interviewing prospective job candidates, keeping records of their details and matching them to employers' requirements.

Entry, qualifications and training

Many recruitment consultants have come into the industry after some experience of another job, for example sales, personnel or office work. They are trained either in-house or on courses run by the Recruitment and Employment Confederation (REC). The REC offers two levels of qualification: the Foundation Award, suitable for those in their first year in the industry, and the Certificate in Recruitment Practice for those with more than one year's experience. Both qualifications can be studied by distance learning or at an evening class.

Personal attributes

Recruitment consultants must be able to relate to people at different organisational levels, have good communication skills, work quickly and calmly under pressure and be organised and resilient.

Earnings

Trainees earn a basic salary of around £16,000 to £18,000, plus commission for successful placing. After three years or so, consultants earn between £25,000 and £45,000. In a slow job market it is much harder to achieve the commission part of earnings.

Info

Recruitment and Employment
Confederation (REC)
020 7009 2100
www.rec.uk.com

Chartered Institute of Personnel and
Development (CIPD)
020 8612 6200
www.cipd.co.uk

RELIGIOUS LEADER

Religious leaders work with faith communities and with people who do not subscribe to any religious belief system. As a religious leader your role includes offering spiritual and moral leadership to your followers. Your work encompasses leading groups of people in acts of worship or in specific ceremonies. These might include religious festivals or significant occasions for individuals and families such as births, deaths, marriages, or ceremonies for new members who join a particular faith. The Church of England is the established church in the UK, but as well as other Christian faith groups there are significant numbers of members of other faiths – Buddhism, Islam, Hinduism, Judaism and Sikhism are the largest groups. Your work normally involves pastoral care, visiting people who are sick, who have been bereaved, or who have relationship problems. Religious leaders also talk to those who are having a crisis of faith, or those who want to find out more about a particular belief system. Some faith groups would expect their leaders to go out and actively try to recruit new members, but this would not always be the case. For many religious leaders, part of their work would also include taking part in interfaith discussions or giving advice to government departments, charities and voluntary organisations. Many religious leaders work full- or part-time in hospitals, universities, prisons or for charities, voluntary or faith-based organisations.

Entry, qualifications and training

Each faith has its own particular entry qualifications, but these are usually based on a commitment to and understanding of a particular faith rather than purely academic qualifications. Your best starting point is to check with your own religious leader about how to begin to work towards becoming one yourself. Do remember that religious groups do not have to comply with all the normal equal opportunities legislation, so in some instances it is not possible, for example, for women to become religious leaders. There may be other restrictions. There are many degree courses available in theology, religion and comparative religion, and if this career really interests you, taking such a course could be a useful way for you to explore the subject more deeply.

Personal attributes

A commitment to your own faith and an understanding of the problems that people encounter are essential. The skills mix you might need would vary somewhat not just between different faiths, but between different jobs within that faith. The work of a prison chaplain is quite different from that of someone working in a rural parish, or an inner city area, for example.

Earnings

Pay varies greatly. Some religious leaders are paid a full-time salary and/or are provided with accommodation and other benefits. Many religious leaders have other jobs and do their religious work on a voluntary basis. You need to check with the faith group that interests you exactly what financial benefits may be available.

Info

Board of Deputies of British Jews
020 7543 5400
www.bod.org.uk

Buddhist Society
020 7834 5858
www.thebuddhistsociety.org

Churches Together in Britain and
Ireland
020 7654 7254
www.ctbi.org.uk

Hindu Council UK
020 8432 0400
www.hinducounciluk.org

Ministry in the Church of England
http://www.cofe-ministry.org.uk

Muslim Council of Britain
0845 262 6786
www.mcb.org.uk

Network of Sikh Organizations UK
020 8544 8037
www.nsouk.co.uk

REMOVALS WORK

Removers play a key role when you come to move house – which can be around the corner or on the other side of the world. It is the remover's job to see that all your belongings are professionally packed and transported to their destination. The work may involve packing fragile objects quickly and efficiently, as well as travelling long distances. Some large companies have their own storage facilities, so employees may be involved in ensuring that furniture is stored safely.

Estimators are the technical salespeople in a removals company. They visit customers' homes and estimate the amount of packing space needed, the time it will take and the price.

Entry, qualifications and training

Employees can work towards NVQs for the removals and storage industry. Progression is also possible to supervisory level. A large goods vehicle (LGV) licence would be beneficial, but is not essential when starting out. Estimators should have a good standard of education, with good passes preferably in English, maths, geography and modern languages, hold a full car driving licence and be able to express themselves clearly and persuasively. Training is on the job.

Personal attributes

Removers should be fit and strong. They must be honest and have a sense of responsibility towards other people's possessions. Common sense and the ability to work in a team are important.

Earnings

Earnings and job security are highly dependent on an active property market. Generally, starting salaries are fairly low, £12,000 to £14,000, rising to £16,000 to £19,000 for more experienced staff. Drivers may earn up to £21,000. All employees may earn more for shift work, weekend work, etc.

Info

Skills for Logistics
01908 313360
www.skillsforlogistics.org

British Association of Removers
01923 699480
www.bar.co.uk

RETAILING

We are surrounded by retail stores of many kinds: city shopping centres, local high street stores and large retail parks. Retailers can be small shops specialising in a particular type of product: shoes, car spares or speciality foods, for example. Supermarkets, department stores and discount stores are just some of the other examples of retail outlets.

Retailing offers many different career opportunities. As well as the careers outlined in this section, retailing offers opportunities in distribution management and warehouse work, in finance, in marketing and in human resource management. There are openings at school leaver level (including apprenticeships), through to graduate and senior management opportunities.

Buyer

The merchandise that you find in all kinds of shops – clothes, shoes, food, furniture, electrical goods, jewellery, etc – will have been selected by a retail buyer whose job it is to source the most appropriate goods to sell in retail outlets. As a buyer your role would include finding the right goods at the right price and ensuring that they are available at the right time in your store. You may be the one who has to come up with ideas on new lines that you could sell. You have to work very closely with wholesalers, manufacturers and suppliers at every stage, from negotiating a price and placing an order to monitoring the quality of the supplied products. You have to monitor stock levels to ensure continuous supply and sales levels to confirm that you are choosing the right kinds of goods to sell successfully. Much of your time will be spent visiting suppliers, producers and wholesalers. Buyers work for department stores, chain stores and some smaller independent retailers. In the latter case, you might combine the role of buyer with other management duties.

Entry, qualifications and training

While you don't have to have a degree or HND, many people who get into buying work have higher education qualifications. Useful subjects include supply chain management and business studies. In some cases employers may prefer a degree in a subject closely related to the products you are buying, eg fashion for clothing retailers, information technology for a store that sells computers or food science for food and drink. Some people have worked in other areas of retail such as store management before they move into buying. Training is mostly on the job and there are NVQ level qualifications at levels 2, 3, 4 and 5 towards which you can work.

Personal attributes

You need a broad range of skills, including negotiating, organising and working to deadlines. You need to be able to write reports and also have good numeracy skills when you are negotiating prices. You need to be able to establish relationships with people very quickly and be good at working as part of a team. You need a good understanding and feel for the kinds of products in which you specialise.

Earnings

Assistant buyers earn £12,000 to £20,000. Buyers earn from £21,000 to £45,000 – most earn between £25,000 and £30,000.

Checkout operator

Checkout operators work at the tills in supermarkets and other large retail stores. They scan the prices of all the items customers have purchased, process payments whether by cash, cheque or card, and they may also offer some assistance with packing, eg wrapping delicate items or putting frozen foods into separate bags.

Entry, qualifications and training

No specific qualifications are necessary, though individual stores may request a good standard of education. Training is provided on the job and it is possible to obtain NVQ level 1 in Checkout Operations and NVQ levels 2 and 3 in Customer Service and Sales. Career progression is to supervisory roles.

Personal attributes

You must be polite and friendly and able to talk to people without losing your concentration or slowing down. You need good numeracy skills in order to spot errors. You must have good stamina and be able to work under pressure in a hectic environment.

Earnings

New checkout staff earn around £11,750, rising to £13,000 to £14,000 with some experience. Supervisors earn around £17,000 to £19,000. A few stores include all staff members in profit-sharing schemes.

Display designer/visual merchandiser

Display designers are responsible for shop windows and displays inside stores. These may be to attract customers into a shop, promote a new product or reinforce a company image. Displays are often seasonal or themed. Some designers work to instructions from head office, others create their own designs. The work may include making props, arranging lighting and general care of the display areas. Some shops also employ visual merchandisers who arrange products according to an organisation's display policy.

Entry, qualifications and training

While there are no standard, formal entry qualifications, in practice most entrants have a relevant qualification. There are several three- or four-year degree courses in Design Merchandising Management and Exhibition and Retail Design. There are also some two-year Foundation degrees available in display design or visual merchandising. Other art-based qualifications may be accepted by some employers. A great deal of training is on the job.

Personal attributes

You need real artistic flair and to be good at working with colour and with three-dimensional design. You should be imaginative and practical, able to work as part of a team and able to relate design ideas to commercial impact. You also need good IT skills and preferably to be able to use computer-aided design (CAD).

Earnings

Trainees earn between £11,000 and £14,000, while experienced display designers earn up to £22,000. It is possible for a display manager with a large store to earn more than £35,000.

Retail store manager

Retail store managers work in department stores, in supermarkets and in small, individually owned stores. In a small store they will run the whole operation. In a supermarket they may be responsible for one area, fresh produce or the checkouts, for example. In a department store they may run one or several departments. Managers are responsible for ensuring that everything runs smoothly. They have to organise work rosters, ensure that sales targets are met, that customer service is of a high standard and that sales staff are fully trained.

Entry, qualifications and training

There are several ways to become a retail store manager. Large stores or chains may run graduate management training programmes or programmes open to school leavers with two or three A levels. Experience, however, is often as important as qualifications, and many managers start out as sales assistants and work their way up to management positions.

Sales assistant

There are many opportunities for sales staff in retailing. Your responsibilities and tasks depend on what kind of retail outlet you are working in, as well as your level of experience. In general, sales staff are expected to sort stock, sell goods, ensure these goods are attractively displayed and deal with payments for goods. They also answer customers' queries, give information about products and offer advice. Some sales staff process orders for new stock.

Entry, qualifications and training

While no formal academic qualifications are necessarily needed, GCSEs grades A–C in English and maths are a help, as is some experience of working with people. Training is on the job, and large stores or chain stores may offer some structured training programmes. It is possible to work towards several NVQs at levels 2 and 3 in retail, including Sales, Retail Operations and Customer Service. Many people who start as sales assistants become supervisors for a section of a store, or progress to become store managers.

Personal attributes

You must be polite, friendly and enjoy working with people. You need good basic literacy and numeracy skills and must be reasonably physically fit. Being smart and tidy is important, especially in fashion retailing. If you are interested in management, you have to be well organised, good at solving problems and at leading and motivating other staff.

Earnings

Trainee store managers earn £18,500 to £25,000; the higher rates are more likely if you are on a graduate training scheme. As your career progresses, earnings range from £23,000 to £60,000. Pay depends on the size and type of store. Sales assistants earn between £12,000 and £15,000, but there are often opportunities to move into supervisory or management roles.

Info

Skillsmart Retail
020 7462 5060
www.skillsmartretail.com

ROAD TRANSPORT

(see also Bus/Coach Driver, Heavy Goods Vehicle Driver and Logistics)

Road transport includes passenger transport and road haulage. Passenger transport covers bus and coach travel. Haulage is the transport and distribution of all goods that are carried by road – food and drink, cars, household electrical goods, building materials and much more. While many functions such as administration, financial management, human resources, information technology and marketing are not specific to road transport, there are some particular roles involved. In addition to those described below, passenger transport and haulage firms employ drivers and customer service staff on the passenger side, and drivers and warehouse staff in haulage.

Road haulage load planner

Load planners work to ensure that goods transported throughout the country and to overseas destinations are moved in the most efficient and cost-effective way possible. Load planners decide on the size, type and number of vehicles to be used for any job. They monitor progress as loads are moved, and work out back up plans in case anything goes wrong, such as traffic hold-ups or breakdown of refrigeration equipment. They discuss plans with clients and they may be involved in working out costs. Load planners often use specialised computer software to aid planning, but may have to resort to pen and paper.

Entry, qualifications and training

To start as a trainee you don't always need formal qualifications, though many employers do ask for GCSEs grades A–C, including maths and English. There are sometimes opportunities to do an apprenticeship, in which case you are likely to need three or four GCSEs. A background in transport and distribution is also useful. Most of your training is on the job, and you may be able to work towards NVQ levels 2 and 3 in Distribution and Warehousing Operations.

Road transport manager

Managers work in passenger and goods transport, planning routes, organising schedules, managing staff, liaising with customers and calculating costs. It is the manager's job to ensure that whatever is transported, goods or people, is carried in the safest, most efficient and most cost-effective way. Managers have to ensure that all operations comply with UK and EU legislation on health and safety and employment. They have to know about transporting particular types of load, such as dangerous chemicals, live animals or perishable foods. They are also likely to be involved in training and recruitment of staff.

Entry, qualifications and training

Many managers work their way up from administrative, driving or warehouse posts. Some companies run management training schemes and entry requirements vary, but may be an HND, Foundation degree or degree in a relevant subject. Acceptable subjects include business, logistics, supply chain management and transport. Most training is on the job. Every transport operator has to have at least one employee who has achieved the Certificate of Professional Competence (CPC), so as a trainee manager you would be expected to work towards this.

Personal attributes

Planners and managers need to be logical, well organised and careful in their work. Good IT and numeracy skills are important. They also have to be good communicators, able to manage staff and deal with clients. Managers have to be able to understand and apply relevant legislation. Planners and managers have to be good problem solvers.

Earnings

Trainee planners earn £15,500 to £19,000, rising to £20,000 to £24,000 with experience. Managers earn £20,000 to £24,000 when they are training; £25,000 to £35,000 with experience. In large passenger transport organisations, salaries for senior managers can be £50,000 to £70,000.

Info

GoSkills (The Sector Skills Council
for Passenger Transport)
01895 817000
www.goskills.org

Skills for Logistics
01908 313360
www.skillsforlogistics.org

Chartered Institute of Logistics and
Transport (CILT UK)
01536 740100
www.ciltuk.org.uk

ROOFER

(see Construction Trades)

ROUNDSPERSON

The roundsperson we are all most familiar with is probably the person who delivers milk and other dairy products to people's doorsteps on a daily basis. In fact, working as a roundsperson can involve delivering and selling goods and services of many kinds to private homes and business premises. Examples include doing a sandwich round to businesses, selling ice cream or fast food, and running mobile shops selling many different kinds of goods. Usually, you work for yourself or you operate a franchise for a franchising company.

Entry, qualifications and training

You do not need any formal qualifications to do this work, but some companies set their own entry tests, and you need good basic maths skills for calculating prices and making out bills. You need a full driving licence and many companies prefer applicants to be over 21 years old. If you are selling fast food, you will need a licence to trade from your local Environmental Health Department. You could do a number of relevant NVQs in customer service and sales. If you are employed by a retailer or a franchising company, it usually provides specific training about its own products and services.

Personal attributes

For most of the time you are working on your own, but you have to enjoy and be good at dealing with customers. You must be well organised, with good numeracy skills and usually some computer skills these days. You have to be highly motivated and not mind working some antisocial hours or being out in all weathers.

Earnings

Initial earnings are between £10,000 and £15,000. With experience these can rise to £15,000 to £20,000; there are only a few types of round (milk and sandwiches, for example) where you are likely to receive seasonal tips.

Info

Skillsmart Retail
020 7462 5060
www.skillsmartretail.com

Improve Ltd
0845 644 0448
www.improveltd.co.uk

British Franchise Association
01865 379892
www.thebfa.org

ROYAL AIR FORCE

(see Armed Forces)

ROYAL MARINES

(see Armed Forces)

ROYAL NAVY

(see Armed Forces)

SALES REPRESENTATIVE

A sales representative, often referred to as a 'rep', may work for a manufacturer, wholesale distributor or service industry, persuading potential customers to buy the firm's products and also looking after the needs of existing customers and providing after-sales advice and support. Sales reps sell anything from photocopiers to catering equipment or double glazing. As a 'rep' you are usually assigned a geographical area and travel around it on the firm's behalf.

One distinctive area of work is that of the medical sales rep. Medical sales reps sell drugs and other medical products to GPs and hospitals on behalf of pharmaceutical companies.

Entry, qualifications and training

Requirements for trainees vary, but most firms look for four GCSEs grades A–C or equivalent and in some companies prefer graduates. Medical sales reps nearly always need a degree and most companies prefer this to be in a science-based subject. Sales reps may study for examinations set by such bodies as the Chartered Institute of Marketing (CIM) or the Managing and Marketing Sales Association (MAMSA). Diplomas and certificates are also issued by various trade associations representing particular types of product. Technical sales representatives usually have a degree or equivalent in the relevant subject.

Personal attributes

An outgoing, friendly personality, a manner that inspires confidence and the ability to be persuasive are essential. How 'pushy' you need to be depends on the products you are selling and your employer's attitude. You will have to be resilient, with plenty of stamina to cope with disappointment, and you also need to be well organised and a good time keeper.

Earnings

New entrants earn £18,000 to £26,000, rising to £27,000 to £40,000 with experience. In most cases, salary comprises a basic rate of pay plus on-target earnings (OTE), meaning you have to achieve the sales targets your employer sets. Senior, successful reps can earn £50,000 to £100,000. The highest salaries are paid in the pharmaceuticals sector.

Info

Association of the British
Pharmaceutical Industry
020 7930 3477
www.abpi.org.uk/our-work/careers

Institute of Sales and Marketing
Management (ISMM)
01582 840001
www.ismm.co.uk

Chartered Institute of Marketing
(CIM)
01628 427500
www.cim.co.uk

Managing and Marketing Sales
Association (MAMSA)
www.mamsasbp.com

SCIENTIFIC RESEARCH

Research scientists work in medicine, in physics and in life sciences. They are employed in industry and in academia. The topics and issues they research are extremely wide ranging and are of course determined by the particular field of science in which they work. They may be involved in developing new products, materials or medicines, examining the effects of chemicals on behaviour, or of climate upon plants. Research scientists may be involved in the development of drugs, the study of genetics or stem cell research. In astrophysics they may be tackling questions about the nature of the universe or the structure of asteroids. In whichever scientific specialism researchers work, their main role is to design, carry out and analyse the results of scientific experiments.

Entry, qualifications and training

Scientific research is a graduate-entry profession. While job titles vary, there are basically three levels at which you can get into research. Technician-level posts require an undergraduate degree in a science discipline relevant to the field of research. Research assistants usually need to have a Master's degree in the appropriate area of science, and research associates have usually completed a PhD.

Personal attributes

Regardless of which field of science you enter, you must have a rigorous and questioning approach to whatever you do. You need good numeracy skills and the ability to interpret data accurately. Many posts require good IT skills and/or the ability to work with highly specialised equipment. You need to be able to work on your own and as part of a team. You may well have to negotiate for funds and you have to be an imaginative problem solver with a real fascination for your subject.

Earnings

Typical starting salaries are £17,000 to £20,000 at technician level; £20,000 to £25,000 for research assistant level (usually with an MSc or MPhil); £25,000 to £33,000 at postdoctoral research associate level. Research scientists working in industry or leading a research project or team may earn considerably more than this – in the region of £45,000 to £60,000.

Info

Biotechnology and Biological
Sciences Research Council
(BBSRC)
01793 413 200
www.bbsrc.ac.uk/

Society of Biology
020 7936 5900
www.societyofbiology.org

Engineering and Physical Sciences
Research Council (EPSRC)
01793 444000
www.epsrc.ac.uk

Institute of Mathematics and Its
Applications
01702 354020
www.ima.org.uk

Medical Research Council (MRC)
020 7636 5422
www.mrc.ac.uk

Science and Technology Facilities
Council
01793 442000
www.stfc.ac.uk

SECURITY WORK

Security guards and security officers work for all kinds of organisations and businesses, where buildings, property and people need protection. They work to prevent theft and other criminal activities and to alert the police when the need arises. Typical tasks for security guards and officers include door supervision, checking people who enter a premises to confirm identity, patrolling buildings on foot or monitoring them from a control room, guarding cash and other valuables as they are delivered or removed or when they are in transit, and checking individuals and observing behaviour at airports or other public places. Many security staff begin as security guards and then progress to becoming security officers or supervisors with responsibility for coordinating security arrangements and training other security staff.

Entry, qualifications and training

You don't need formal qualifications, but many employers do ask for a good standard of education including GCSEs in English and maths. You have to pass security checks and your work and personal history is checked for the previous 10 years prior to your seeking employment. Whether you need to be licensed by the Security Industry Authority (SIA) depends on whether you work in-house or for a security contractor. If you work in-house, in other words as an employee of the company for whom you are providing security services, you don't need a licence. If you are employed by an agency or contract company, you do. The training to obtain a licence takes about four days. The SIA is currently looking into licensing all security staff, including in-house employees. Whoever employs you, you may be expected to do training courses in dog handling, first aid, or other specialist skills.

Personal attributes

You need to be polite and helpful, but also able to challenge people assertively when this is appropriate. You should be able to write clear, short reports detailing an incident. You may have to handle technical equipment of various kinds. You should be confident, with a mature attitude to your work, and you must be able to use your initiative. You must be reasonably fit and in many instances you will have to work shifts or do night work.

Earnings

New security staff earn between £12,000 and £16,500 a year. With experience you can earn £21,000 to £23,000.

Info

Security Industry Authority (SIA)
0844 892 1025
www.sia.homeoffice.gov.uk

Skills for Security (Incorporating SITO)
0845 075 0111
www.skillsforsecurity.org.uk

British Security Industry Association (BSIA)
01905 21464
www.bsia.co.uk

Security service personnel

Security service personnel work for the three government security services, MI5, MI6 and Government Communications Headquarters (GCHQ). These services work to protect the UK from a range of serious threats, including terrorism, espionage and serious crime. There is not one typical job in the security services. People may work as surveillance officers watching particular individuals or observing what takes place at particular premises. Others are employed as intelligence officers, gathering, analysing and assessing secret intelligence; perhaps working under cover. The security services also employ linguists to translate information gathered from various sources in the UK and abroad. They also employ computer specialists who can follow information leads found on computers or decode information on seized computers.

Entry, qualifications and training

To work as a surveillance officer you do not necessarily need formal qualifications. Intelligence officers have to be graduates, though the subject does not matter. Linguists must have a degree in languages and a demonstrable ability for learning languages. IT specialists normally have a degree in computer science.

In all cases applicants must fulfil strict nationality criteria and pass rigorous security and background checks. The selection procedure is challenging.

Training for most roles includes an initial induction programme, then a combination of on-the-job training and continuing professional development. Surveillance officers undergo a 10-week training course.

Personal attributes

While specific roles require particular attributes, there are many qualities that are important whatever your role. You must possess absolute integrity and discretion. You must be able to work on your own or as part of a team. You should be a good problem solver and a calm thinker. For many roles you need excellent analytical skills, to be highly observant and have the ability to make decisions and take responsibility.

Earnings

Starting salaries are from £21,000 to £36,000 depending on your role. Salaries for senior staff are from £45,000 to £80,000.

Info

MI5 Careers
www.Mi5careers.gov.uk

SHIPBROKER

Shipbrokers act as go-betweens for ship owners looking for cargo to fill their vessels, and charterers seeking to ship their dry cargo and tanker requirements. The sale and purchase of vessels is also an important service offered to clients. Brokers are paid commission on the contracts arranged. The Baltic Exchange in London is the centre of the chartering market. It is a self-regulated market and the Exchange maintains a register of those seeking employment, which its member companies may consult. Vacancies are also advertised on the website. Additionally, shipbrokers/ship's agents in ports make arrangements when a ship calls for customs clearance – loading and discharging cargoes, meeting crew requirements and so on. Port agents who attend to cargo liners may also be involved in marketing and documenting cargo. In order to maintain contact with the international scene, shipbrokers tend to work long hours and to travel abroad frequently.

Entry, qualifications and training

There are no fixed entry requirements to get into shipbroking, but different companies set their own entry criteria. A few will accept you with GCSEs grades A–C, but it is common for companies to recruit applicants who have at least A levels or their equivalent. Some employers prefer graduates. Any subjects are acceptable, but business studies, modern languages and courses that include modules on transport and/or logistics will be particularly appreciated. A background in administrative work of any kind can also be very useful. There are sometimes opportunities to do an apprenticeship in International Trade and Service (ITAS) and you may also be able to study to NVQ levels 2 and 3 in this subject. You can also work through e-learning and distance-learning courses towards membership of the Institute of Chartered Shipbrokers. The majority of training, however, is provided on the job.

Personal attributes

You have to be very well organised and pay especial interest to being very clear and accurate in what you write and what you say. You should be a good communicator, able to talk to customers, importers and exporters, and good at communicating with people whose first language is not English. You must have good IT skills, and command of any modern language can be really useful. You have to have a good knowledge of geography and to be sensitive when working with people of other cultures.

Earnings

Salaries for new entrants are between £18,000 and £23,000. With a year or two's experience this rises to £26,000 to £35,000. Senior shipbrokers can earn £35,000 to £50,000.

Info

Institute of Chartered Shipbrokers	Institute of Export
0207 623 1111	01733 404400
www.ics.org.uk	www.export.org.uk
British International Freight Association (BIFA)	Skills for Logistics
020 8844 2266	01908 313360
www.bifa.org	www.skillsforlogistics.org

SOCIAL CARE AND SOCIAL WORK

Social care and social work include many careers, all concerned with working with people who need some kind of support. Roles include working with families facing problems, older people who have become ill, young adults involved in substance abuse, adults of all ages with serious physical or learning disabilities, children at risk or people with mental health problems.

Care assistant

Care assistants, also called care workers or social care workers, are employed in many settings with various service users (formerly referred to as 'clients'). The overall job of a care assistant is to help and support people in their daily lives with tasks such as getting up in the morning, bathing and showering, getting dressed, preparing and eating meals, going out shopping or taking part in activities. Some care workers work with clients in their own homes, visiting frail elderly people each day to help them get up and dressed or to go to bed in the evenings. These care workers are usually referred to as domiciliary care workers. Care assistants also work in residential homes for elderly people or for people who have learning disabilities, physical impairments or mental health problems. An important part of the work is also simply to talk to and reassure people.

Entry, qualifications and training

You don't necessarily need formal qualifications, though experience of working with people is a big advantage, especially work in a caring role. Once you are employed you will receive training on the job, including taking part in a 12-week induction programme. There are also several relevant NVQ awards towards which you can work. Before you can work as a care assistant you will have to undergo a Criminal Records Bureau (CRB) check. If you are providing care to people in their own homes you are likely to need a driving licence.

Personal attributes

You need to be caring, compassionate and patient. You need very good communication skills, to be able to listen and to encourage people to communicate with you. You need to be practical and physically fit. You need to be a good problem solver and you must be able to work as part of a team.

Earnings

Earnings start at around £12,000. With experience pay can be £15,000 to £18,000 and there may be some opportunities to earn overtime payments.

Info

Northern Ireland Social Care Council
www.niscc.info

Skills for Care (England)
0113 245 1716
www.skillsforcare.org.uk

Care Council for Wales (CCW)
www.ccwales.org.uk

Scottish Social Services Council (SSSC)
www.sssc.uk.com

General Social Care Council
0845 070 0630
www.gscc.org.uk

Care home managers

Care home managers manage care homes that are registered to provide care. The majority of homes provide care for elderly people who are too unwell or too frail to continue living in their own homes. There are also care homes for adults with learning and physical disabilities. The majority of care homes are in the independent (private) sector, but some are run by local authorities, and many are run by not-for-profit organisations. Care home managers are responsible for all the day-to-day running of the home – everything from seeing that appropriate nursing care is delivered to ensuring that catering and laundry services run well. Care home managers also look at ways to make care more effective, for example by introducing programmes of activities that could help people with dementia to enjoy a better quality of life. Managers also have to respond to complaints and concerns raised by residents or their relatives. They also have to ensure that the home complies with all appropriate legislation and standards. They also have to be business managers – homes are businesses and have to be financially viable – so it is the manager's job to ensure that rooms are occupied and that the home is well marketed and builds links with its local community.

Entry, qualifications and training

This work has become increasingly professionalised in recent years and there are national minimum standards set for qualifications for care home managers. Most care home managers move into this work as a second career. They have either come from a background in nursing or other areas of healthcare, or else they have backgrounds in businesses such as hospitality. Care home managers need to have a relevant degree, healthcare or business qualification. In all cases they should be qualified to NVQ level 4. Exact requirements depend on the type of clients and the level of care a home is registered to provide, eg nursing as well as general daily care. You will have to undergo a Criminal Records Bureau (CRB) check to enter this profession.

Personal attributes

You need a wide range of skills, though the balance of these depends on the size and type of home you manage. You need to be caring and compassionate. You also need to be a good team leader and able to motivate staff. You need good business skills, and to be able to handle budgets and market the home. You need excellent communication skills, to be able to listen sympathetically to a resident and to deal effectively with other healthcare professionals, the media or the wider community.

Earnings

Salaries depend not only on your level of experience, but on the size and type of home you manage and whether your employer is in the independent, public or not-for-profit sector. Generally salaries start at between £20,000 and £30,000, but can reach £40,000 if you work for one of the larger care provider organisations.

Info

Skills for Care
0113 245 1716
www.skillsforcare.org.uk

Care Quality Commission
www.cqc.org.uk

Social work assistant

Social work assistants are part of the social work team. They support qualified social workers who are involved in helping and advising many different clients in the community, in day-care establishments, residential homes, hospitals, schools and their own homes. The work can be varied but might include making contact with clients, booking appointments and following up on enquiries, making routine visits to people to monitor situations, advising clients on what services and resources could be available to them, and conducting routine interviews. A key part of the role is to refer situations to qualified social workers if you have any concerns about a client you have spoken to or visited. Your work is also likely to involve keeping records, attending meetings and updating yourself on changes in social care legislation.

Entry, qualifications and training

While you don't necessarily need formal academic qualifications, many employers expect you to have two or three GCSEs grades A–C. What is most important to employers is whether you have had experience of working with vulnerable people. You may find that your application is strengthened by doing some voluntary work. There are also several full- and part-time BTEC certificate and diploma courses in health and social care. These normally include work placements, so this could also be a way of strengthening your application. You will have to pass a Criminal Records Bureau (CRB) check to do this type of work. Once you have started work, your employer has to provide induction training to approved national standards, and you may also be able to study part-time for further qualifications such as a Foundation degree in health and social care.

Personal attributes

You need excellent communication skills, to be able to listen to and explain things to people who may be coping with high levels of stress. You have to be highly observant, too. You must be calm in tense situations and, while you have to take responsibility, you must be very clear about when to refer a situation to other professionals. You must be well organised, a good administrator and excellent at working as part of a team.

Earnings

New entrants earn between £16,000 and £17,000, more in London. With experience and with further qualifications you can earn £19,000 to £23,000.

Social worker

Social workers are qualified professionals who work in the same settings as social work assistants – a service user's home, schools, hospitals, day centres, residential homes, and specialist units such as drug dependency centres. They may also do outreach work in the wider community. They work within a framework of relevant legislation and increasingly they work as part of multidisciplinary teams with healthcare workers. Each social worker has an allocated caseload to deal with. More than half of qualified social workers work with children and young people. This can include working with young offenders, pupils who have poor school attendance records, or children whose families are in a crisis of some kind.

Much of a social worker's job is to carry out assessments of any service user's situation to see what kind of support they might need, or whether some intervention is required. Can an elderly person continue to cope living in his or her own home, or might he or she be better off in a residential home? Is it appropriate to leave a child with his or her family, or should he or she be placed in care? What treatment programme might help an adult with mental health problems to cope more easily with daily life? These are just a few examples of the kinds of questions that social workers tackle. They have to attend meetings, prepare reports, conduct interviews, monitor progress and review cases on a regular basis.

The majority of social workers are employed by local authorities, but some voluntary and not-for-profit organisations employ their own social workers. Senior social workers are also involved in the purchasing of care packages, the training of staff and the development of strategy.

Entry, qualifications and training

To qualify as a social worker in England you need either a three-year undergraduate or a two-year postgraduate qualification in social work accredited by the General Social Care Council (GSCC). To do an undergraduate degree you normally require five GCSEs and two A levels. It is worth checking with individual course providers because some will accept you without this if you have alternative qualifications or substantial relevant work experience. If you already have a degree then you can apply for a two-year postgraduate Master's course in social work. In all cases your course combines academic study with periods of work placement. If you are interested in social work with children, families and young people, some new initiatives are being developed – a pilot Graduate Recruitment Scheme, aiming to attract high-achieving graduates onto postgraduate social work courses, and a new employment-based training programme for graduates started in 2011.

Once qualified, social workers must register with the GSCC and they must re-register after three years, during which time they must continue learning and professional development. The GSCC has developed three post-qualifying awards towards which social workers can work; these are certificates in specialist and advanced social work. There are five possible areas of study that link into these awards, focusing on mental health, adult social care, children, young people and their families, education practice, and management and leadership.

Personal attributes

Social workers must be patient, understanding and able to empathise with people. They must also have the emotional resilience to cope with distressing situations and clients who are angry, upset or frightened. They must be able to keep calm and assertive when taking decisions that service users may strongly disagree with. They have to be able to take difficult decisions and be responsible for these decisions. Social workers must be able to work alone, but also as part of a social and healthcare team. They must be good organisers and able to manage a demanding caseload.

Earnings

On qualifying you earn between £20,000 and £25,000. Once you have had a few years' experience, salaries range from £26,000 to £40,000.

Info

General Social Care Council
0845 070 0630
www.gscc.org.uk

Skills for Care (England)
0113 245 1716
www.skillsforcare.org.uk

Northern Ireland Social Care Council (NISCC)
www.niscc.info

Care Council for Wales (CCW)
www.ccwales.org.uk

Scottish Social Services Council (SSSC)
www.sssc.uk.com

Speech and language therapy

Speech and language therapists (SLTs) identify, assess and treat people who have communication and/or swallowing disorders. A large proportion of these will be children, but SLTs also help adults who may have communication or swallowing problems caused by disease, accident or psychological trauma. Some SLTs specialise in a particular patient group, for example in the area of severe learning difficulties, hearing impairment or neurological disorders, while others choose more general, broad-based practice. The NHS is the largest employer of SLTs, working in community clinics, hospitals, special schools and homes for the mentally or physically disabled. Some of the larger voluntary organisations also employ SLTs. Often the SLT works closely in a team that may include members of the medical, teaching, therapeutic, psychological and other caring professions.

Entry, qualifications and training

Speech and language therapy is a degree-entry profession. Courses leading to professional qualifications are offered at 15 universities and colleges of higher education throughout the UK. There are a number of two-year postgraduate diploma and Master's courses available to candidates with a relevant degree.

Entry qualifications for courses vary from one institution to another, but the minimum is five GCSEs and two A levels or equivalent. A good balance of language and science is expected. Other equivalent qualifications are considered on merit. All courses will consider applications from mature students (over 21), who are encouraged to apply in the normal way.

Students who successfully pass all academic and clinical components of an accredited course are eligible to obtain a certificate to practise and to enter the professional register of the Royal College of Speech and Language Therapists as full professional members.

Opportunities also exist to work as a speech therapist's assistant. An NVQ in care at level 3 is available.

Personal attributes

It is essential that speech therapists themselves should have clear speech and be able to listen actively In addition, they must have an interest in people as individuals, as well as an enquiring mind, initiative, patience, imagination and a willingness to take responsibility.

Earnings

In the NHS, newly qualified SLTs are paid £22,000 to £27,600. Senior therapists are paid on band 6, from £25,000 to £33,000. Therapists with more management or other special responsibilities are paid on band 7, from just under £30,000 to £41,000.

Info

Royal College of Speech and
Language Therapists
020 7378 1200
www.rcslt.org

NHS Careers
0345 60 60 655
www.nhscareers.nhs.uk

Health Professions Council (HPC)
020 7840 9812
www.hpc-uk.org

SPORT AND EXERCISE

(see also Leisure and Recreation Management, Sports Physiotherapist and Sports Psychologist)

Sport will be much in the public eye in 2012. Not every sporting enthusiastic is destined to become a sports professional, but there are many other jobs associated with sport, for example coaching, training, managing facilities or teaching.

Coach

Coaches help individuals and teams identify areas for improvement in physical fitness levels and for specific sports skills. They also plan and implement training programmes in a wide variety of sports provided by sports centres, clubs, schools, hotels and swimming baths.

Much coaching is done on a voluntary basis; however, there are opportunities for paid work, and many coaches work in a self-employed capacity. Some local authorities employ coaches to offer facilities for local schools at one or more centres in the authority. Such coaches are expected to be able to coach in most of the following sports: badminton, basketball, climbing (on indoor walls), ice skating, squash, swimming, tennis, trampolining and weight training. Increasingly, there is a need for coaches in the summer months to work in outdoor activity centres.

Entry, qualifications and training

Formal academic qualifications are not necessary to become a coach. You need to check the qualifying route with the national governing body for your chosen sport; they will all have their own approved coaching schemes. These vary in length and some are full-time, some part-time, while others can be done via distance learning. The key to qualifying for any of these is to have demonstrable skill in your chosen sport and to be able to show that you have the ability to teach others. There are several degrees available in sports science or sport and exercise. While a degree is not necessary to become a coach, these courses may provide useful background on the psychology of performance. Some of them also offer the opportunity to work towards coaching qualifications in conjunction with studying the academic programme. The various sporting governing bodies have designed qualifications equivalent to NVQs levels 1 to 4. You cannot become an assistant coach until you are aged 16, but beginning as soon as you are able to do so, in the sixth form for example, can be very beneficial.

Personal attributes

In addition to a passion for and understanding of your own sport, you must have excellent communication skills. You must be able to motivate an individual or help a group of players function effectively as a team. You have to be physically fit yourself and aware of the rules and regulations governing your sport. You need lots of enthusiasm, but you must be sensitive enough to work with people of different abilities.

Earnings

Many coaches work part-time and earn £10 to £20 an hour. Full-time work at a basic level pays around £12,000 to £16,000 a year. Senior and experienced coaches may earn £25,000 to £35,000. In professional sport, coaches working with national teams or top athletes and sports stars earn considerably more than this.

Info

Sports Coach UK
www.sportscoachuk.org

Sports Leadership UK
www.bst.org.uk

SkillsActive
08000 933300
www.skillsactive.com

Sport England
www.sportengland.org

Exercise/fitness instructor

There are many different types of exercise that instructors teach to classes or to individual clients. Forms of exercise and well-being instruction include yoga, a combination of exercise, breath control and meditation. Pilates, a form of exercise designed to strengthen core postural muscles, is very popular. Other people prefer very energetic classes, doing fast aerobic exercise that tones up the body and burns calories at the same time. Instructors may also teach aquacise or weight training. Instructors work either at leisure centres or fitness centres, or with individual clients in their own homes. Their job is to ensure that whatever the form of exercise being taught, clients learn to do it correctly so that it is beneficial rather than harmful.

Entry, qualifications and training

Since many different forms of exercise and activity are involved, there is no one entry and training route for everyone. Most instructors or teachers specialise in one or maybe two exercise disciplines. In all cases you need to achieve a level 2 nationally recognised qualification approved by the Register of Exercise Professionals (REP). You also need to obtain a first-aid certificate and you cannot teach unless you have public liability insurance. You can start as an assistant instructor and train while working for professional certificates.

Personal attributes

You have to be physically fit yourself, well able to demonstrate all the techniques you are teaching to others. You have to be a really good communicator, explaining things carefully and realising when people have not caught on. You must be observant and pay attention to detail. You need good organisational skills if you are working at several different locations.

Earnings

Employed instructors earn £13,000 to £18,000. If you work freelance, hourly rates range from £10 to £225 per hour.

Info

Register of Exercise Professionals 020 8686 6464 www.exerciseregister.org	**SkillsActive** Advice line: 08000 933300 www.skillsactive.com
OCR Information Bureau (for information on appropriate qualifications) 024 7685 1509 www.ocr.org.uk	**YMCA Fitness Industry Training** www.ymcafit.org.uk **Active IQ** www.activeiq.co.uk

Outdoor activities instructor

Outdoor activities or outdoor pursuits instructors work at centres providing a range of activities such as hill walking, climbing, abseiling, canoeing, horse riding and sailing. Clients using outdoor activities centres could be people seeking an adventurous holiday combined with an opportunity to learn new skills. Purchasing a day of outdoor activities as a gift for someone has also become very popular. Many businesses send their staff on outdoor activities courses as a method of team building. Sometimes groups of young people identified by social services or other agencies are offered outdoor activities courses to try to help them cope with stress and learn new techniques for dealing with problematic situations. Your work would include planning activities and then briefing participants before you set out. You would check that all equipment to be used is safe and in good working order. During the activity you would explain to participants exactly what to do. You would observe participants to make sure they understood and were doing everything correctly and in accordance with safety procedures. You may have to deal with emergencies – say if someone falls, or a boat capsizes.

Entry, qualifications and training

There is no one specific qualification for this work because so many different activities could be involved. You would normally need experience of and qualifications in one or more of the activities your centre offers. If your work involved instructing children you would have to pass appropriate Criminal Records Board (CRB) checks. Being involved on a voluntary basis with outdoor activities of some kind could also be an advantage.

Personal attributes

You must have good leadership qualities, and be able to motivate and encourage people. Some participants are overenthusiastic and could put themselves or others in danger. Others may be timid and require more help and encouragement. You have to be highly observant, good at anticipating situations and thinking quickly if something goes wrong. You must be an excellent communicator possessed of practical common sense.

Earnings

Junior instructors earn around £12,000 to £14,000. Senior instructors earn £18,000 to £25,000.

Info

Sports Coach UK
www.sportscoachuk.org

SkillsActive
08000 933300
www.skillsactive.com

Institute for Outdoor Learning
01228 564580
www.outdoor-learning.org

Physiotherapist

(see Physiotherapy)

Sports centre manager

Sports and recreation facility managers are responsible for the efficient running of leisure centres, swimming pools, health clubs, sports and leisure facilities at hotels, etc. Managers usually start their career as a recreation assistant and progress through supervisory and assistant manager positions via on-the-job training and professional development.

Entry, qualifications and training

There are two routes into this career. You can either start as a junior or management trainee and work for professional qualifications, or you can do a BTEC qualification, Foundation degree or degree course. The Institute for the Management of Sport and Physical Activity (IMSPA) and the Institute for the Management of Sport and Physical Activity (IMSPA) run relevant certificate and diploma courses that can be studied on a part-time basis. There is also a wide choice of BTEC, Foundation degree and degree courses available in sports and leisure management, leisure studies, sports science and recreation management. Whether you work your way up or join as a graduate trainee, there is a lot of on-the-job training.

Personal attributes

You need excellent interpersonal skills, to be able to motivate staff and to work well with members of the public. You must be well organised, energetic and able to take responsibility.

Earnings

Trainee and assistant managers earn between £14,000 and £17,000. Newly qualified managers earn between £18,000 and £25,000. An experienced manager of a large facility can earn more than £35,000.

Info

SkillsActive
08000 933300
www.skillsactive.com

Institute for the Management of
Sport and Physical Activity (IMSPA)
01509 226474
www.imspa.co.uk

Sports professional

There are opportunities in sport for professional sportspeople and for careers in coaching. Not all sports allow players to be professionals and there are some, such as snooker, where there is room for only a very few professionals. Sports attracting professionals in relatively large numbers are football, cricket, golf, horse racing, rugby (league and union) and tennis.

Sportspeople's careers are generally short but if, during their careers, they have made a name for themselves, there may be opportunities in journalism, broadcasting or consultancy.

Entry, qualifications and training

Professional sportspeople naturally need to be excellent at their sport. Those in team games generally begin by playing for their school, town or county side. In this context, a young player may be noticed by professional selectors. In the case of football, it is not necessary to join a local football league club; apprentices are taken on from all over the country. Because a club apprentice has no guarantee that he or she will ever play for the first side, some clubs allow apprentices time off to obtain academic qualifications.

Personal attributes

As well as talent, professional sportspeople must possess dedication, perseverance and commitment and be highly competitive.

Earnings

Salaries for professionals are often low initially, but the rewards for top performers may be very high. The amount of money earned varies enormously depending upon the sport. Coaches' salaries vary according to whether the work is full- or part-time, what type of work they are doing and the number of hours.

Info

Sport England
ww.sportengland.org

**Talented Athlete Scholarship
Scheme (TASS)**
0191 243 7356
www.tass.gov.uk

SkillsActive
08000 933300
www.skillsactive.com

Swimming pool attendant/lifeguard

Swimming pool attendants and lifeguards work at swimming pools in hotels with leisure facilities, private sports clubs, public swimming pools and local authority leisure centres. Their key responsibility is to ensure the safety of everyone in the pool, watching to make sure no one is getting into difficulty and rescuing and providing first aid to anyone who needs assistance. They also make sure that people are behaving safely and sensibly in the pool. This is very much the lifeguard side of the work. Some swimming pool attendants are also responsible for monitoring the water quality in the pool and checking for levels of chemicals or bacteria. At some facilities, pool attendants may also supervise dry activities such as a gym and fitness suite.

Lifeguards also work as teachers, ensuring that people adhere to safe bathing areas and other rules, monitoring the water for incidents, taking part in rescues, giving first aid and liaising with other authorities such as the police or local coastguard.

Entry, qualifications and training

Formal academic qualifications are not essential for this work. To be a swimming pool attendant or lifeguard you must be aged 16 and to work as a beach lifeguard you must be aged 18. In both cases you must be physically fit and be a good swimmer. To work at a swimming pool you have to have one of the Royal Lifesaving Society (RLSS) lifesaving qualifications – see their website for details. They also offer national qualifications for beach lifeguarding work. All qualifications have to be reviewed every two years, when you must have both your swimming and your first-aid skills checked. Local swimming pools and swimming clubs can provide a lot of helpful information on qualifying.

Personal attributes

Apart from your swimming skills, you must have excellent 'people' skills, be friendly and approachable but also calm, confident and authoritative at times. You should be very observant and good at making quick and very important judgements.

Earnings

Pay starts at £12,000 to £14,000 a year, but in fact many lifeguards and pool attendants work part-time and are paid an hourly rate. Full-time work is more common in large leisure centres, where pool attendants have a wider range of responsibilities and duties.

Info

SkillsActive
08000 933300
www.skillsactive.com

Swimming Teachers Association (STA)
01922 645097
www.sta.co.uk

Royal Lifesaving Society (RLSS)
www.lifesavers.org.uk

Royal National Lifeboat Institute (RNLI)
01202 663553
www.rnli.org.uk/lifeguards

Teacher

(see Teaching)

STATISTICIN

Statisticians design experiments and surveys. They analyse the results of these and use their findings in many different ways. They work for all kinds of organisations, from central and local government, local authorities and the NHS to private industry and commerce in many sectors. Their work varies according to the sector in which they work, but it can include designing experiments to monitor the effectiveness of a new drug, measuring trends in air pollution, predicting the performance of pension plans, or analysing the results of consumer surveys for predicting the future demand for particular products and services. Their work can be concerned with scientific, psychological, social or commercial issues and questions.

Entry, qualifications and training

For most trainee positions you need a good honours degree in a highly numerate discipline, eg maths or economics. If you are working in medical statistics you will probably need a degree or postgraduate qualification in medical or life science. The Civil Service offers a range of training schemes for statisticians with a good honours degree in a numerate subject. Some employers consider applicants with a degree in social science and psychology, particularly if that degree has covered statistical methods in some detail and if work is going to be linked to these specific areas. Training is on the job, though many statisticians work for postgraduate qualifications on a part-time basis.

Personal attributes

In addition to having proven ability with numerical and scientific data, statisticians have to be creative thinkers, good problem solvers and excellent communicators. As a statistician you often need to report your findings and analysis in clear, everyday language to non-mathematical colleagues or clients. You also have to be a good team worker.

Earnings

Trainees earn between £23,000 and £30,000. With a few years' experience salaries rise to £30,000 to £55,000. In general, business and industry pay higher salaries than central and local government and science and medicine.

Info

Royal Statistical Society
020 7638 8998
www.rss.org.uk

SURVEYING

Surveying covers a variety of work in one profession.

Building surveying

Building surveyors carry out structural surveying of properties and report on their condition and valuation. They advise on necessary repairs and maintenance, and prepare plans and specifications for alterations and improvements. Local and central government employ a large proportion of qualified building surveyors, although many are in private practice. Qualifications in this area are available from the Association of Building Engineers (ABE), The Chartered Institute of Building (CIOB) Faculty of Architecture and Surveying (FAS) and the Royal Institution of Chartered Surveyors (RICS).

Commercial/Residential property surveyor

This includes auctioneering, estate agency, valuation and estate management. People working in this area are responsible for the selling or letting, surveying, valuation and management of both urban and rural property. Qualifications in general practice are offered by the ABE, the FAS and the RICS.

Hydrographic surveying

The hydrographer surveys and charts underwater areas such as ports and harbours and offshore areas where drilling for oil takes place. Hydrographic surveying qualifications are offered by the FAS and the RICS.

Land geomatics surveying

The land surveyor measures and charts the earth's physical features so that maps can be drawn. This area of work has become more technical and draws on many disciplines and so the term land geomatics is more widely used now than simply 'land' surveyor. The Royal Institute of Chartered Surveyors (RICS) describes geomatics as the science and study of spatially related information, particularly the collection, interpretation/analysis and presentation of the natural, social and economic geography of the natural and built environments. Geomatics information and analysis is important in a diverse range of sectors, including: construction; property; cartography; offshore engineering and exploration; geographic information systems.

Minerals surveying

Minerals surveyors assist in the design, development and surveying of quarries and underground mines, ensuring safety for the workers as well as optimum profitability for the company extracting the minerals. They also value mineral workings for rating and taxation, and therefore need to be all-rounders with knowledge of geology, the management of mineral workings, taxation and planning legislation. This area of surveying is unique in having its qualifications and duties laid down by law. Minerals surveyors must hold the surveyor's certificate granted on behalf of the Secretary of State for Industry by the Mining Qualifications Board. They must be at least 21 and have at least four years' practical experience (including 2,000 hours underground) in order to sit the exam for this certificate. Further qualifications are provided by the RICS and the FAS.

Planning and development surveying

Surveyors specialising in this area work on a range of projects connected with development, redevelopment and regeneration. They oversee projects such as regenerating a rundown housing area, new developments on brownfield sites or the conservation of rural properties. Their work involves looking at the viability of planning proposals, considering different planning options and monitoring developments that are agreed to ensure that they are adhering to the original proposals and plans.

Quantity surveying

In private practice quantity surveyors work with an architect to draw up design specifications in line with the client's budget. When the finished design is agreed, the quantity surveyor draws up a bill of quantities, detailing the materials and labour that will be needed. Building contractors work on this bill of quantities in preparing their tender for the job; they will use their own quantity surveyors to estimate their costs. Quantity surveyors also monitor costs as the work progresses and is completed. If they train for this work while employed by construction contractors, they usually take the qualification of the RICS. Professional qualifications are also offered by the FAS.

Rural practice surveying

This is often combined with land agency, and concerns the use and development of agricultural land. The qualifying bodies in this area are the FAS and the RICS.

Technical surveying

Technical surveyors, often referred to as surveying technicians, support the work of chartered surveyors. The work includes drawing up plans, estimating costs for projects, and gathering data and information that may form part of plans or reports. The work is often similar to that of a chartered surveyor and includes valuation of land and property and organising the sale of assets. Technical surveyors work in many branches of the profession, including commercial and residential property, rural practice, land geomatics and minerals surveying.

Entry, qualifications and training

The RICS offers a range of qualifications in the different areas of surveying. Normally entrants need three A levels or equivalent for entry into a RICS-approved degree or diploma course. An alternative is undertaking an HND or HNC in a related surveying discipline, which can give advanced entry to those courses. On successful completion of a RICS-approved degree or diploma, graduates enrol onto the Assessment of Professional Competence (APC), which is two years' practical training while in employment, concluding with a RICS professional assessment interview. Various degree backgrounds are valuable for surveying; one-year full-time and two-year part-time postgraduate conversion courses are available.

Technicians need a relevant HNC/HND or NVQ level 4 followed by the Assessment of Technical Competence. This is two years' RICS structured training while working, which concludes with the RICS technical assessment interview. Those who have gained technical membership of the RICS can take a bridging course to become a Chartered Surveyor.

Personal attributes

Logical and orderly thinking, ability in figure work and detailed drawings are called for in this precision work. Communication skills and business acumen are essential. Good oral and written English is an asset, and some areas may require specialised mathematical ability.

Earnings

Newly qualified surveyors earn between £20,000 and £27,000. Experienced surveyors earn between £27,000 and £43,000. Senior Chartered Surveyors working for large companies can earn more than £50,000. Some surveying work, especially general practice, building or quantity surveying, is sensitive to the general economic climate. Salaries may not rise so fast when the property market is sluggish.

Info

Royal Institute of Chartered
Surveyors (RICS)
0870 333 1600
www.rics.org

College of Estate Management
0800 019 9697
www.cem.ac.uk

Asset Skills
Helpline: 08000 567160
www.assetskills.org

The Chartered Institute of Building
(CIOB) Faculty of Architecture and
Surveying (FAS)
www.ciob.org.uk/topics/foaas

The Chartered Institution of Civil
Engineering Surveyors
www.cices.org

Association of Building Engineers
(ABE)
www.abe.org.uk

TAXATION WORK

Those who work in the area of taxation deal with the payment of taxes, which is a source of revenue for public expenditure.

Tax adviser/technician

Tax advisers/technicians work for private firms or independently, offering assistance to other firms/individuals who need guidance through the complications of the tax laws. A tax adviser is able to advise clients on how to plan and present their taxable income so that they legally pay the least tax possible.

Tax technicians work for firms of accountants or solicitors, in clearing banks and for consultancy firms that offer a complete tax service to their clients. However, the largest area of work involves corporate tax in organisations that have their own tax department to prepare corporate tax and VAT returns on behalf of the company.

Entry, qualifications and training

There are two routes into this profession. If you choose direct entry then you apply to become a taxation trainee with a firm of accountants or the tax department of an industrial or commercial or other large organisation. You can then take the Association of Taxation Technicians (ATT) examination. If you pass this you are eligible to take the Chartered Tax Adviser (CTA) examination and become a member of the Chartered Institute of Taxation. You do not need a degree for direct entry, but some applicants do have degrees in business studies, accountancy or mathematics. Accountancy firms and other employers set their own entry requirements, but you must have good numeracy skills. The alternative route into this profession is to qualify first as an accountant, solicitor or barrister and then apply to take the CTA examination. This route is quite popular with graduates.

Personal attributes

You have to be a logical thinker and a good communicator. You need the ability to translate complex financial information into something that is readily understood by someone without a financial background. You also have to be an imaginative problem solver with good business and commercial awareness.

Earnings

Newly qualified tax technicians earn between £27,000 and £37,000. During training, salaries are between £20,000 and £27,000. Tax advisers with a few years' experience or in senior positions can earn £40,000 to £60,000.

Info

Financial Skills Partnership
0845 257 3772
www.directions.org.uk

Chartered Institute of Taxation
0844 579 6700
www.tax.org.uk

Association of Taxation Technicians
(ATT)
020 7235 2544
www.att.org.uk

TaxWorking
www.taxworking.org

Tax inspector

Tax inspectors work for HM Revenue & Customs (HMRC), formed from the merger of the Inland Revenue and HM Customs & Excise. It is the government department responsible, under the direction of the Treasury, for the efficient administration of income tax, tax credits, corporation tax, capital gains tax, petroleum revenue tax, inheritance tax, National Insurance contributions and stamp duties. Inspectors are responsible for the tax affairs of businesses and individuals, ensuring that they pay the right amount at the right time, and helping them to obtain their entitlements and meet their obligations. Inspectors detect and deter non-compliance and encourage voluntary compliance by carrying out enquiry work.

Entry, qualifications and training

If you wish to join HMRC as a trainee tax inspector you need either a good degree (at least 2.1) in any subject, or a professional accountancy qualification. With either of these you can apply to join HMRC's Tax Professionals Development Programme. Competition for places on this scheme is fierce. If you do not have the appropriate qualifications, you can join HMRC as an administrative assistant (GCSEs grades A–C in maths and English), or an administrative officer (five GCSEs grades A–C). HMRC may be prepared to offer you an administrative job without the appropriate GCSEs if you pass an aptitude test. After some experience you can then apply to join the Tax Professionals Development Programme, which lasts four years and includes on-the-job training and further examinations.

Personal attributes

You must be very good at analysing large quantities of information and data. You must be a creative problem solver with an open, enquiring mind. Good written and spoken English, numeracy and IT skills are also essential. You must be a good communicator, calm, fair and able to interpret and apply rules.

Earnings

Graduate trainees on the Tax Professionals Development Programme earn £27,500 with an additional £2,000 for working in London. Having completed the programme, salaries start at £31,000 rising to £44,000 plus with appropriate experience and responsibilities. There is a pay freeze until 2013 for anyone earning more than £21,000.

Info

Her Majesty's Revenue & Customs (HMRC)
www.hmrc.gov.uk

TaxWorking
www.taxworking.org

Civil Service Jobs Online
www.civilservice.gov.uk/jobs

TEACHING

Most formal teaching is done in schools, while lecturing is carried out in universities and other further and higher education establishments.

Lecturer

Further education

Lecturers in this field may teach anyone over the age of 16. The range of subjects taught in further education is diverse and growing rapidly. Most lecturers have a particular expertise but are increasingly expected to teach outside their specialist area. They may work on vocational and/or academic courses. In order to meet the demands of their clients, further education colleges offer courses on a full- or part-time basis. These include evening courses and short courses.

Higher education

Lecturers in universities and other higher education institutions (HEIs) teach mainly undergraduates. As well as teaching, many carry out research, write articles and books, and give outside lectures and broadcasts. Competition is fierce and it is unlikely that a new graduate would be able to enter higher education as a first job.

Entry, qualifications and training

To lecture in further education you must have an NVQ level 3 qualification in the subject(s) you want to teach. You must also have GCSEs in English, maths, and information and communications technology (ICT). After this, you can work part-time towards level 3 and 4 certificate courses or a level 5 diploma. The level 5 diploma confers full teacher status. If you plan to teach on vocational courses, relevant experience in that field is also extremely useful.

To lecture in higher education (HE) you normally need a degree and often a postgraduate degree related to the subject(s) you wish to teach. Sometimes it is possible to do some part-time teaching while you are studying for a postgraduate qualification. On more vocational courses it may be possible to lecture without these qualifications if you have plenty of experience in an appropriate area of business or technology. Many HE institutions also expect you to study part-time for formal qualifications in HE lecturing. Institutions often provide in-house courses on management, curriculum development, IT and administration.

Personal attributes

At all levels you need a compelling and communicable interest in the subject you are teaching. You also need an in-depth knowledge of that subject. You need to be able to plan and develop materials and be a well-organised administrator. You need excellent communication skills, and to be confident when delivering a lecture in a large lecture theatre, but equally good working one-to-one or with small groups of students. If you are working in higher education, you may also need good research skills.

Earnings

In further education, lecturers/teachers are paid between £22,000 and £33,000. Teachers who take on leadership and management roles can earn £40,000 to £50,000 or more. Higher education lecturers on full-time contracts earn between £33,000 and £43,000. Lecturers with considerable management responsibility or other special roles earn £43,000 to £52,000.

Info

University and College Union	Institute for Learning (IfI)
ww.ucu.org.uk	www.ifl.ac.uk

Teacher

Teachers work in all schools in the state and independent sectors. The state sector is by far the larger. The teacher's role is to help pupils acquire particular knowledge and understanding of a subject. Teachers plan lessons, set and mark assignments, help pupils who are having difficulty and maintain a good working atmosphere in the classroom.

Whether teachers cover one or several subjects depends on the age range they train and qualify to teach. The different options are: nursery or early years, teaching pupils aged 3 to 5; primary, teaching pupils aged 5 to 11; secondary, teaching pupils aged 11 to 18; and special educational needs teaching, working with pupils of all ages who have special needs associated with disability, psychological or behavioural issues.

Other work can include supervising pupils in various activities, attending parents' evenings and other functions, and doing all the administrative work and record keeping associated with pupils' assessments and progress.

Entry, qualifications and training

To teach in state schools, you must take the Teacher Qualification course, which gives you Qualified Teacher Status, referred to as QTS. This is not essential to work in the independent sector, but many schools prefer it. There are several types of initial teacher training (ITT), but there are certain criteria you must meet for all of them. You must have GCSEs grade A–C in English and maths. If you are teaching beyond key stages 2/3 your GCSEs must also include a science at grade A–C. You must pass QTS skills tests in English, maths, and information and communications technology (ICT). These tests are computerised and run at more than 40 centres throughout England.

In England and Wales, there are undergraduate, postgraduate, school-based and work-based routes into teacher training, with very similar provision in Northern Ireland. In Scotland, there are undergraduate and postgraduate training pathways.

Personal attributes

Teachers must enjoy working with the age group they teach. They must be excellent communicators and able to motivate and encourage their students. They have to have great self-confidence, be able to handle difficult situations and discuss issues with parents as well as students. They must be able to work under considerable pressure, be well-organised administrators and come up with imaginative solutions to problems.

Earnings

New entrants in England and Wales are paid on a scale of just under £21,000 to just over £30,000. You earn more for taking on extra responsibility or for working in challenging areas.

Info

The Department for Education
www.education.gov.uk

Training and Development Agency for Schools
Teaching information line: 0845 6000 991
www.tda.gov.uk

Department of Education Northern Ireland (DENI)
028 9127 9279
www.deni.gov.uk

Graduate Teacher Training Registry (GTTR)
0871 4680 469
www.gttr.ac.uk

Teach in Scotland
www.teachinginscotland.com

Teacher – English as a Foreign Language (EFL teacher)

Teaching English to people from all over the world and in many different countries is referred to as Teaching English as a Foreign Language (TEFL). Adults and children undertake short English language courses for many reasons – to improve business communication, to increase educational opportunities, to prepare for study in the UK or other English-speaking countries, or simply for social and leisure reasons. There are language centres and schools throughout the UK and in many other countries employing EFL teachers.

Entry, qualifications and training

You do not need to be a qualified teacher to train as an EFL teacher. While this work may be open to anyone with a good level of education and an excellent command of English, it is increasingly becoming a graduate-entry career. A degree in English, a modern language or education is particularly useful. You then study for an appropriate certificated course; this usually amounts to 100 hours, including teaching practice. Suitable courses include the CELTA (Certificate in English Language Teaching to Adults) run by Cambridge University Examinations and the CertTESOL (Trinity College London Certificate in Teaching English to Speakers of Other Languages). Note that to work in some countries you will need Qualified Teacher Status (see Teacher) and you may also need a work permit.

Personal attributes

You need to be confident, imaginative, lively and highly communicative. You have to be able to work with groups of people of all ages, from teenagers upwards, and you also have to have the understanding and patience to work with people of different abilities and varying prior levels of knowledge of English. You have to be able to make classes fun and clear and have the organisational skills to plan your workload. You need to be able to maintain order in a classroom, especially if working with excitable teenagers on their first trip abroad.

Earnings

Based on working full-time in the UK, salaries are between £13,000 and £19,000 a year. However, many jobs are not full time – you are often paid an hourly or monthly rate which equates to the figures above. Much of the work is seasonal too. Working abroad there is an enormous range in salaries, but often accommodation is provided in addition to your salary.

Teaching assistant

Teaching assistants or classroom assistants provide help and support for qualified teachers in the classroom. They can work in any school, but most are employed at primary school level helping younger children with reading, writing and mathematics. They often provide particular support to children with special needs or whose first language is not English. They also help prepare lesson materials.

If a job advertisement describes the post as 'Learning Support Assistant' rather than a classroom or teaching assistant, the work involves supporting an individual child who has particular special needs, such as a sensory impairment, or a physical or psychological disability.

Entry, qualifications and training

At present, this varies from LEA (local education authority) to LEA, though the government does plan to introduce a standard training model. Many LEAs do not ask for any formal qualifications, but some ask for GCSEs in English and mathematics.

Personal attributes

Teaching assistants must be able to build good relationships with children and have a lot of common sense. They should be able to work well as part of a team, and being imaginative and creative is also useful.

Earnings

Teaching assistants are often paid on an hourly rate and this is sometimes close to the minimum wage, though it can be £6.50 to £8 an hour. A lot of the work is part-time and available only during term time.

THEATRE

(see Performing Arts)

THERAPY SPECIALISMS (ARTS-BASED)

There are many different therapists working in the NHS and the independent healthcare sector. Occupational therapy, physiotherapy and speech and language therapy are covered elsewhere. The therapies covered in this section are art, dance, music and drama. They are all based on activities that help people to feel better, gain in confidence and find new ways to express their feelings. While they can be used in many fields of healthcare, they are used a lot in mental health and learning disability, rehabilitation and palliative care settings.

Most arts-based therapists work in hospitals, some in special schools and child guidance clinics, and some in prisons, detention centres and community homes. As posts are often part-time, therapists usually work for more than one institution within an area.

Art therapist

Art therapists use art to treat psychological and emotional disorders. Drawing, painting, modelling and sculpture are among the creative activities employed.

Dance/movement therapist

Dance therapists use movement and dance as a way of helping people to engage creatively in a process of growth and personal integration. Dance movement therapists work with individuals and groups in health, education and social service settings. Their clients include people who are emotionally disturbed or have learning difficulties, and those who want to use this therapy for personal growth.

Drama therapist

Drama therapists work with people of all ages who are experiencing emotional or psychological problems, especially in communicating and understanding their own feelings. Drama therapists help people to express their feelings through role-play and other drama-based exercises. They encourage clients to be creative and to use their imaginations. Drama therapists work closely with psychologists, social workers and other members of the social and healthcare team.

Music therapist

Music therapists help people to express their thoughts and feelings by listening to music, singing, or playing musical instruments. The therapist uses live, improvised music to draw the client into an interactive musical relationship. Therapists work with people of all ages in a wide variety of settings, including special schools, psychiatric hospitals, hospices, day centres and residential homes. Music therapy is used in many clinical areas, including communication disorders, developmental delay, learning disabilities, mental health problems, physical difficulties, emotional problems, challenging behaviour and terminal illness.

Entry, qualifications and training

While each of these four professions has its own requirements, they all follow a very similar pattern. You need a degree relevant to the therapeutic area which interests you, eg art for art therapist, music for music therapist, etc. If you do not have a relevant degree, but you do have a degree in psychology or a background in health or social care, it is worth contacting the relevant professional body for guidance as to the best way into your chosen profession. Once you have graduated you need to take a further course approved by the relevant professional body.

Art therapists then take a diploma or Master's in art therapy approved by the British Association of Art Therapists. Dance/movement therapists need a postgraduate qualification in dance movement. The University of Roehampton and Goldsmiths College both offer this qualification. The main qualification for drama therapists is a postgraduate diploma or Master's course approved by the British Association of Drama Therapists (BADth). Music therapists take a postgraduate diploma course lasting between one and two years. Some courses offer a part-time option.

In all cases, if you wish to work in the NHS or social services departments you have to register with the Health Professions Council (HPC).

Personal attributes

You must have great skill in your own field of art, drama, music or dance and be able to combine this with excellent communication skills. You have to be sensitive, responsive and encouraging. You must be creative and imaginative – if one approach does not work with someone, try something else. You should be able to work with groups or individuals and you should also be able to work closely with other members of healthcare and social service teams.

Earnings

In the NHS, all the various therapy professionals are paid on the same scale. The differences in pay relate to how long you have worked, your level of experience and your responsibilities rather than to the particular therapy specialism in which you practise. Newly qualified therapists are paid on band 5 of the NHS pay scales, which range from just under £22,000 to £27,500. Senior therapists are paid on band 6, from £25,000 to £33,000. Therapists with more management or other special responsibilities are paid on band 7, from just under £30,000 to £41,000. In the independent healthcare sector, salaries for new entrants may be a little higher than those in the NHS, but the gap closes at management level. Working for charitable organisations, as many art therapy professionals do, salaries can be a little lower than in the NHS.

Info

NHS Careers
0345 60 60 655
www.nhscareers.nhs.uk

**British Association of Arts
Therapists (BAAT)**
020 7686 4216
www.baat.org

**British Association of
Dramatherapists (BADth)**
01242 235 515
www.badth.org.uk

Health Professions Council (HPC)
020 7840 9812
www.hpc-uk.org

**Association of Professional Music
Therapists**
020 7837 6100
www.apmt.org

**Health Learning and Skills Advice
Line**
08000 150850
nextstep.direct.gov.uk

Therapy support worker

Therapy support workers, sometimes referred to as assistants, work across the many different health professions allied to medicine. They assist therapists in their work with patients and help patients to carry out the activities that therapists have designed for them. What you might actually be doing varies according to your particular role. With an art therapist, you might be helping prepare materials and equipment as well as working with patients. If you are working with an occupational therapist, you might accompany him or her and a patient on a home visit to see what adaptations to the home might be necessary. If you are working with a physiotherapist, perhaps you will be supervising some exercises, helping a patient get ready for a session in the hydrotherapy pool, or taking a patient's blood pressure. In whatever role you are working, you are likely to have a great deal of contact with patients and work closely with other members of the healthcare team.

Entry, qualifications and training

There are no standard entry requirements, but each hospital and each therapy specialism may set its own requirements. Most will want a minimum of four GCSEs grades A–C; sometimes one of these will need to be a science, for physiotherapy for example, whereas for art therapy an art and design subject would be more usual. Often the most important thing is to have had some experience of working with people. Training is provided on the job, but you may have opportunities to attend short courses and to work towards NVQs.

Personal attributes

While some of these may vary according to which healthcare profession you are supporting, there are many skills and qualities that apply in all situations. You will have to be very good at working with people, understanding, sensitive and good at explaining procedures or treatments. You will need to be good at working as part of a team and you may need to have practical, IT or administrative skills as well.

Earnings

There is considerable variation, but many support staff are paid on NHS bands 3 and 4. This range is from around £15,000 to £18,000 for band 3 posts and £17,500 to £21,000 for band 4 support workers. The NHS Careers website gives more detail on exact salaries.

Info

NHS Careers
0345 60 60 655
www.nhscareers.nhs.uk

TOWN AND COUNTRY PLANNER

Town and country planners are concerned with reconciling the needs of the population for buildings, shopping centres, schools and leisure centres with the necessity of preserving and enhancing the natural and built environment. They collect information about the present use of land and the position of roads and other features, as well as drawing up plans for new schemes. Planners in development control ensure that buildings or developments intended for a particular area are suitable and do not conflict with existing buildings or the surrounding environment. Planners work for local and central government, environmental agencies, and to an increasing extent in private practice. There are also varied opportunities for planning support staff.

Entry, qualifications and training

To become a town planner you must complete a course accredited by the Royal Town Planning Institute (RTPI). You can either do a four-year degree course in town and country planning or a postgraduate diploma course if you already have a degree in surveying or another relevant subject. There is also an option to qualify through a distance-learning course if you are already working in planning but not as a qualified town planner. The RTPI website contains a list of all accredited courses.

Planning support staff normally require GCSE grades A–C in English, maths and perhaps geography and IT. Some employers prefer applicants to have A levels – again geography and IT are particularly useful.

Personal attributes

Town planners and support staff need to have a knowledge of many subjects: economics, sociology, architecture and geography. Planners must be able to work in a team and cooperate with experts in other subjects. Planners need to take advice and opinions from many different people, and therefore need to be able to reconcile the conflicting views of various interest groups. They must be good communicators and have imagination, and an interest in and understanding of both people and the environment.

Earnings

Planning support staff earn £14,000 to £18,000, while newly qualified planners earn between £20,000 and £28,000. Senior planners earn between £30,000 and £40,000. Team leaders and managers earn between £35,000 and £45,000.

Info

Royal Town Planning Institute (RTPI)
020 7929 9494
www.rtpi.org.uk

Local Government Careers
www.lgcareers.com

TRADING STANDARDS OFFICER

Trading standards officers are employed by local authorities and are responsible for enforcing a very wide range of legislation aimed at protecting consumers and traders. Laws relate to food and consumer product safety, credit, descriptions of goods and services, prices, animal health and welfare. While most operations are carried out through random inspections, officers are also required to investigate complaints and, where appropriate, take matters to court.

Entry, qualifications and training

The essential qualification for trading standards officers is the Diploma in Consumer Affairs and Trading Standards (DCATS). The usual way to obtain this qualification is to take a degree in consumer protection or a postgraduate qualification approved by the Trading Standards Institute (TSI); people then apply for trainee trading standards officer posts with a local authority. If you have a lot of previous experience in consumer affairs you may not have to have a degree or postgraduate qualification. Some local authorities may offer sponsorship to applicants interested in doing a degree in consumer protection. Without a degree or relevant experience you can apply for posts as an enforcement officer or consumer adviser in trading standards departments and study for the Foundation Certificate in Consumer Affairs and Trading Standards. The TSI has developed a range of modular courses for trading standards workers at all levels. For all of these you must undergo on-the-job training and submit a portfolio of your work activities.

Personal attributes

You need a broad mix of skills to work in trading standards. You must be a good communicator, confident and persistent, but also patient and tactful at times. You should be able to handle technical equipment and complex technical information. Good IT and numeracy skills and an interest in the law are also important. You should be happy working as an effective member of a team, but also able to work on your own.

Earnings

Trainees earn between £18,000 and £23,500; once qualified, salaries range from £25,000 to £35,000, and £40,000 to £45,000 for management roles. Many trading standards officers move to work with private sector employers or with organisations that look after consumer interests in relation to utilities or the communications industry. These posts are normally paid at equivalent to or higher than management roles in local government trading standards departments.

Info

Trading Standards Institute (TSI) 0845 608 9425 www.tradingstandards.gov.uk	**Local Government Careers** www.lgcareers.com

TRAFFIC WARDEN

Traffic wardens are civilians who work in conjunction with local police forces. They check parking meters and penalise drivers parking on double yellow lines or in other illegal places. They may also be required to do school crossing patrols or traffic control duty, as well as receiving vehicles towed into the police pound and looking out for out-of-date car licences.

Entry, qualifications and training

Each Police Authority sets its own entry requirements, but there is no need to have formal educational qualifications; instead you have to pass a written test, which includes maths and English. Training is on the job, sometimes being supervised by a police officer, and many areas send you on a short, introductory course.

Personal attributes

You need to be calm, confident and possess a degree of common sense to do this work. You should be a good communicator and able to deal with aggression without becoming aggressive yourself.

Earnings

There is some variation between localities, but generally starting pay is between £16,000 and £25,000 – the highest salaries are paid in London. In most cases, you can earn more through shift allowances.

TRAVEL AND TOURISM

(see also Civil Aviation)

Travel and tourism includes many jobs connected with transport, hospitality, recreation management, marketing and administration. There has also been a growth in IT-related jobs linked to travel and tourism as the number of people making their own travel and holiday arrangements via the internet has increased.

Below are some of the key jobs that are specific to the tourism and travel industry.

Resort representative

The role of a resort representative is often very similar to that of a tour manager (see below), but resort representatives are usually based in one centre and work for one tour operator. They have to receive each party of holidaymakers as they arrive at airports and seaports. They accompany them to hotels and run welcome meetings to tell them about tours and activities on offer. They make sure they are available at regular times to deal with queries and in many cases they also accompany parties on tours and trips, or at least take the bookings for these events.

Tour manager

Tour managers (sometimes referred to as tour directors) organise and accompany parties of holidaymakers on a wide variety of tours and excursions. They are often involved in the planning and the marketing of these tours. Another key part of their role is to deal with any problems that holidaymakers have, from losing a passport to being taken ill, or simply wanting further information about a particular activity or destination.

Tourist guide

Tourist guides or couriers accompany groups of tourists on visits to places of interest. These could be castles, museums, art galleries, city centres or places of natural wonder. Your main role as a tour guide is to give detailed and interesting information about these sites. In some cases you will need to have a really good knowledge of your area, as with special-interest tours, where your customers have real knowledge and enthusiasm for art or history, for example.

Entry, qualifications and training

To work as a tour manager, tourist guide or resort representative you do not need formal academic qualifications, although many applicants do have good GCSE results, A levels and a degree in a subject such as education, tourism, geography, history or marketing. Being able to speak the language in the country in which you work is a big advantage. A background in customer care, hospitality or other work in travel and tourism is a big plus for all these jobs.

Personal attributes

You need to have excellent interpersonal skills, being friendly, helpful and calm. You also need excellent organisational skills and to be a tour manager or resort rep you often need good marketing skills too. Tourist guides need to have a genuine interest in the sites and objects they are describing and a flair for conveying information in a lively and informative way.

Earnings

Resort representatives and tour managers earn £12,000 to £16,000, but they get board and lodging in addition to a salary. Some tour managers are self-employed, even though they are allocated work by tour operators. Tourist guides are mostly self-employed and the work is often seasonal or part-time. The Association of Professional Tourist Guides can offer guidance on what fees you should charge.

Info

Institute of Travel and Tourism
0844 4995 651
www.itt.co.uk

International Association of Tour Managers (IATM)
020 7703 9154
www.iatm.co.uk

Association of Professional Tourist Guides
aptg.org.uk

People 1st
www.people1st.co.uk

Tourist information assistant/manager

Tourist information assistants and managers provide information and advice to members of the public about accommodation, leisure activities, amenities, visitor attractions, special events and transport in a particular location and also nationwide. Most tourist information centre staff are employed by local authorities, but some private visitor attractions and organisations such as national parks employ people in this role. Much of the day-to-day work as an assistant is answering questions from visitors to the centres, on the telephone or by e-mail, on all the subjects just listed. Your work is also likely to involve booking events, journeys or accommodation for visitors. Tourist information officers also have many items for sale – books, postcards and gifts – so you will also be selling these items. Part of the job includes collecting appropriate brochures, leaflets and display information for the centre and making sure that they are well displayed and that all information is up to date. As a manager of a centre you have responsibility for choosing and purchasing items to be sold, training and recruiting staff, and ensuring that the centre is presentable, welcoming and efficient.

There are also some opportunities to work with national or regional tourist organisations. In these roles there may be less dealing directly with the public and more involvement with marketing, promotional and publicity work.

Entry, qualifications and training

There are no specific entry requirements for this work, though a good standard of education is important. Many local authorities and other employers expect you to have three or four GCSEs, including maths and English. To join directly as a manager, it may be useful if you have a qualification in marketing, travel and tourism, or business, but this is not essential. Having some background experience in retailing or other jobs working directly with the public is a big advantage for both assistant and manager posts.

Personal attributes

You need to be very good at dealing with people – friendly, approachable and able to give information in a clear and precise way. You should be well organised, and good at sorting and updating information. You need basic computer skills, and some creative flair is useful for organising window or other displays. Working as a manager, you have to be good at motivating people, and good at guessing what products and ideas are likely to do well. All staff must be good at working as part of a team.

Earnings

Assistants start on £17,000 to £19,000; managers earn £20,000 to £30,000, though the latter is only likely in the larger tourist information centres.

Info

Institute of Travel and Tourism
0844 4995 651
www.itt.co.uk

People 1st
0870 060 2550
www.people1st.co.uk

Britain Express
www.britainexpress.com

Travel agent

Travel agents sell tickets for travel by air, land and sea on behalf of transport organizations. They make hotel bookings for individual travellers, business people and holidaymakers. Some travel companies deal only with business travel, and are also involved in arranging conferences and trade fairs. However, travel agents are best known for selling package holidays on behalf of tour operators. Many travel agents will also advise travellers on visas, foreign currency and necessary injections. Travel agents face a lot of competition from people booking their own holidays via the internet, so are having to concentrate on marketing and on services that might give added value to customers. An example of this is developing special-interest packages, eg holidays focused on painting, sailing, horse-riding or ancient history.

Entry, qualifications and training

Modern Apprenticeships and NVQ qualifications are available. No specific qualifications are asked for, but GCSEs in maths, English and geography are an advantage. Computer literacy is becoming increasingly important.

Personal attributes

Travel agents must enjoy dealing with the general public, and have a responsible attitude regarding the accuracy of information given, and good administrative and ICT skills.

Earnings

On the administrative side, earnings start at £13,000 to £16,000. Once you take on more sales work, salaries go up to £15,000 to £25,000. Many sales consultants are also paid commission on holidays or other products sold. Travel agency staff may also get discounts on holidays or flights.

Info

People 1st
0870 060 2550
www.people1st.co.uk

Accredited Travel Professional Scheme
www.itt.co.uk/training_and_
professional_development/ATP_scheme

UNDERTAKER

(see Funeral Director)

UNDERWRITER

(see Insurance)

TOGETHER
WE **CAN** MAKE
A DIFFERENCE

The IAT's purpose is *to advance knowledge and promote excellence in the care and welfare of animals in science* and to enhance the standards and status of those professionally engaged in the care, welfare and use of animals in science.

Job satisfaction in helping to discover new medical drugs and therapies to treat illness, including cancer, diabetes and asthma, and protect the health of people and animals.

Animal technologists work in universities, veterinary colleges, pharmaceutical companies, specialist research organisations and animal breeding companies.

During your career as an animal technologist you will be given:

- Accredited Training and Education

- Continued Professional Development

- Structured Career Pathway and Support

Institute of
Animal Technology

ANIMAL TECHNOLOGY

Animal technology is the specialist profession for those who are responsible for the care and welfare of animals in science (ranging from rats and mice to marmosets, farm animals and fish). Home Office licensed Animal Technologists will also advise on and carry out, scientific procedures in research programmes.

Animal technology is a career that involves the responsible use of animals within the exciting and rapidly evolving scientific environment of a UK bio-medical research centre.

Animal technologists work in universities, veterinary colleges, pharmaceutical companies, specialist research organisations and animal breeding companies.

Animal technologists enjoy the satisfaction of helping to discover new medical drugs and therapies to help understand and treat illness, including cancer, diabetes and asthma, and protect the health of people and animals. We operate to high professional standards, caring for laboratory animals in an expert manner while maintaining the highest scientific and welfare standards.

As animal technologists, we work in close knit teams, with colleagues who share our professional dedication to excellence in the ethical care of laboratory animals.

Our work requires Continuous Professional Development (CPD) or life-long learning to update our knowledge and skills. We study for formal IAT qualifications through workplace training, day release and distance learning.

A structured career path starts with the Level 2 IAT Diploma in Laboratory Science and Technology and we have the opportunity to pursue qualifications through to BSc or Masters level. There are many opportunities for specialisation, promotion and career development.

INDIVIDUAL NARRATIVE

Sally now aged 36, began her career as a trainee animal technologist in 1997 whilst also performing laboratory analysis work. After working in a number of different types of animal research facilities, including academic, government and pharmaceutical organisations, Sally now works as a Supervisor managing 25 staff for a charity funded research body, committed to releasing all research data and models information to the global community.

Sally explains: "My interest in caring for animals has been lifelong and I have taken every opportunity to experience it by working as a volunteer at local vets and stables. I was surprised and pleased to discover a career existed where I could care for animals directly and contribute to discovering information for human and animal health. Animals are fascinating and rewarding to work with on a daily basis. Since I have become a manager I have really enjoyed training new staff because I recognise I can develop someone else's interest and passion for caring for animals. The reward is being able to coach people to have the right approach and I can watch someone handle a rat with kindness and confidence and know I taught them how".

Sally was delighted to find animal technology is a well structured career. "I like to learn new information and approaches and do the best I can. Passing my exams to become a RAnTech (Registered Animal Technologist) was an important step in my career because it recognises my commitment to the animals and their standards of care".

Sally believes animal technology is a good career option for young scientists: "We can specialise if we wish – one of my team is very interested in breeding and another in immunology. I personally enjoy management and training. We are relatively well paid compared to many other animal care jobs but then we are scientifically trained. Medical studies take a long time but it is wonderful knowing that work you are doing now might prove to be an important turning point in treating a disease".

Sally concludes: "The work can be tiring and sometimes repetitive but every job is made more enjoyable by the interaction with the animals. What matters is that we do our job of caring for the animals and working to high scientific standards – the benefits to medical research follow from this".

INTRODUCING THE INSTITUTE OF ANIMAL TECHNOLOGY

The IAT's purpose is *to advance knowledge and promote excellence in the care and welfare of animals in science* and to enhance the standards and status of those professionally engaged in the care, welfare and use of animals in science.

Representing animal technologists both within the UK and Europe, the IAT has over 2300 members made up of individuals and 60 corporate organisations, including the vast majority of the UK's Named Animal Care and Welfare Officers (NACWOs). NACWOs have a legal obligation to be *'actively involved, on a day to day basis, in safeguarding the welfare of the protected animals bred, kept and used at designated establishments'.*

Recognising the importance of learning, both academic and skills based, plus personal development throughout the careers of animal technologists, the IAT supports animal technologists to achieve their full potential. This enables our members to contribute fully to the field of laboratory animal science and technology, animal welfare and UK biomedical science and drug development.

For over sixty years the IAT has awarded qualifications in animal technology and accredited Continuing Professional Development (CPD) for animal technologists and other professionals involved in the care and welfare of laboratory animals.

Education and qualification is a key role of the IAT. The IAT is recognised by QCF (Qualifications and Curriculum Framework) as an Awarding Organisation for its Further Education qualifications in laboratory science technology leading to degree level qualifications and Fellowship (FIAT) of the Institute.

In addition to formal education, the IAT actively and enthusiastically promotes Continuing Professional Development (CPD), enabling animal technologists to keep up to date with the latest in animal husbandry and related scientific advances.

We invite you to view www.iat.org.uk to find out more about the IAT's actitivies and the roles of animal technologists in Biomedical research.

VETERINARY SCIENCE

(see also Animals)

Veterinary science is concerned with the care of animals, including both farm animals and domestic pets.

Veterinary nurse

Veterinary nurses (VNs) assist vets during operations and X-rays, sterilise instruments, look after animals recovering from surgery, and keep the animals and their cages clean. After qualification, the work of a VN can include practice management, staff supervision, teaching and training other nurses or support staff. Some VNs choose to work outside veterinary practice in research establishments, colleges, zoos and breeding or boarding kennels.

Entry, qualifications and training

A nationally recognised Veterinary Nursing Scheme (VNS) is administered by the Royal College of Veterinary Surgeons (RCVS). To train as a VN you must be aged 17 or over and have five GCSEs grades A–C, including English, maths and two science subjects. You must also be employed by a practice registered to offer training. You can get details of practices approved to provide training from the RCVS website or from the British Veterinary Nursing Association (BVNA). If you particularly want to work with horses you can do specialised training as part of your qualification, but you must be working for a practice that takes on equine work.

If you do not have the required GCSEs and are working for an approved practice, you can take a day-release or distance-learning level 2 Certificate for Animal Nursing Assistants. As an alternative to the VNS there are several degree and HND courses available in veterinary nursing. If you consider this route, ensure that the course you choose is approved by the RCVS.

Personal attributes

You have to love animals and be calm, kind and patient when handling them. You have to be able to deal with sad or distressing situations and you must be able to communicate with people as well as their pets. You need to be practical, with an interest in science, and you can't be the least bit squeamish.

Earnings

Trainees earn from £14,000 to £15,000. Qualified VNs earn £17,000 to £22,000. Senior VNs in large practices may earn £25,000. There are sometimes opportunities for overtime through working weekends or evening and night shifts, or for being available to support on-call vets.

Info

Lantra
02476 696996
www.lantra.co.uk

Royal College of Veterinary
Surgeons (RCVS)
020 7222 2001
www.rcvs.org.uk

British Veterinary Nursing
Association (BVNA)
01279 450567
www.bvna.org.uk

British Equine Veterinary
Association (BEVA)
01223 836970
www.beva.org.uk

Veterinary surgeon

Most vets work in private practice, usually starting out as a veterinary assistant and working their way up into a partnership or into their own business. Some specialise in small-animal treatment, including pets such as dogs, cats and birds, while others work with particular kinds of animals, such as farm animals, racehorses or the more exotic zoo animals. Other vets go into research or industry. The Department of Environment, Food and Rural Affairs, for instance, employs a substantial number to work on disease control, monitoring such epidemics as foot and mouth or swine vesicular disease. Others are employed by animal welfare organisations, such as the People's Dispensary for Sick Animals (PDSA), in animal hospitals. Vets are also needed in the food-processing industries, where their job is concerned with checking that conditions are humane and hygienic.

Entry, qualifications and training

A veterinary surgeon must hold a degree from one of the six veterinary schools in the UK. The six universities offering the course set their own entrance requirements but all demand an extremely high standard of A level passes or equivalent. Chemistry is essential, and other useful subjects are physics, maths, biology and zoology. The course lasts five years (six at Cambridge), and covers a formidable amount of academic and practical work, comparable to that needed to be a doctor.

Personal attributes

Vets need to be sympathetic but detached. They must be excellent communicators, explaining to and reassuring pet owners and farmers. Patience, calmness and, later on, a good business sense and problem-solving skills are also important.

Earnings

Newly qualified vets earn around £30,000, but with a few years' experience this rises to £45,000 to £50,000. Senior vets in large practices can earn far more than this – £60,000 to £90,000.

Info

Lantra
02476 696996
www.lantra.co.uk

Royal College of Veterinary Surgeons (RCVS)
020 7222 2001
www.rcvs.org.uk

British Veterinary Nursing Association (BVNA)
01279 408644
www.bvna.org.uk

British Equine Veterinary Association (BEVA)
01638 723555
www.beva.org.uk

WATCH AND CLOCK MAKER/ REPAIRER

Watch and clock makers make timepieces by hand, sometimes to a design of their own.

Repairers receive watches and clocks from customers for servicing and repair. They must be able to examine a timepiece thoroughly for worn-out parts, clean and regulate a watch or clock, and repair or replace faulty parts. The work involves the use of precision tools and electronic equipment. Restoration is carried out on antique clocks and watches.

Entry, qualifications and training

You may be able to get a trainee position without qualifications and gain qualifications part-time. There are also several courses accredited by the British Horological Institute (BHI), including certificates at preliminary, intermediate and final level. You can study for these at the University of Central England in Birmingham and through distance-learning modules. The University of Central England also offers an HND in clock and watch servicing. You may be able to complete courses specialising in restoring and conserving antique clocks and watches. Some local colleges offer part-time courses in clock and watch servicing and repair, and this could be a useful way to get started.

Personal attributes

A real interest in watches, clocks and mechanical devices is a good starting point. You need excellent manual dexterity, to be able to work on intricate, delicate and detailed devices and to maintain a level of careful concentration. You need mathematical skills and you may also need drawing skills. You must be able to deal with clients and customers and, if you work for yourself, you need all the skills of running a business – bookkeeping, marketing your services, managing your own time, etc.

Earnings

Earnings for new entrants are around £15,000. Experienced repairers can earn £25,000 to £30,000 – some of the highest salaries may be paid in restoration and conservation work. If you are self-employed there is a lot of variation in earnings, depending on how much work you do, but £20,000 may be a reasonable average.

Info

Worshipful Company of
Clockmakers
www.clockmakers.org

British Horological Institute (BHI)
www.bhi.co.uk

WATER QUALITY SCIENTIST

Water quality scientists test, analyse, monitor and maintain the quality of drinking water. They also analyse and monitor the water in lakes and rivers and in the ground. They have to ensure that water quality complies with rigorous standards set by legislation. They deal with complaints about quality of drinking water and investigate possible sources of contamination. They also work closely with businesses and other organisations, looking at possible implications for water supply of particular types of development, eg potential sources of pollution and increased demand on supply. They conduct research on water quality and they may be called upon to deal with any emergency such as a total breakdown of supply.

Entry, qualifications and training

You normally need a science degree to do this work. Preferred subjects include chemistry, biology, microbiology and environmental science. It may be possible to get into water science with an HND in a relevant science. Competition in this field is strong because of its link to the environment. Any voluntary work you have done in an environmental science setting will be highly valued, as will any relevant paid work experience in a laboratory. In fact, many people aiming to be water quality scientists work their way up from more junior positions in the industry.

Personal attributes

You need a rigorous and meticulous approach when collecting and analysing samples. You must be a good communicator as you may be dealing with customers, other businesses or representatives of the legislative authorities. You have to be a good problem solver and you should be able to work well as part of a team. You need a genuine interest in the environment.

Earnings

Trainees earn between £18,000 and £23,000. Senior water quality scientists earn £28,000 to £40,000. Technician-level salaries are around £14,000 to £17,000.

Info

Chartered Institution of Water and
Environmental Management
020 7831 3110
www.ciwem.org

Drinking Water Inspectorate (DWI)
020 7944 5956
www.dwi.gov.uk

Environment Agency (EA)
08708 506 506
www.environment-agency.gov.uk

WELFARE ADVICE WORKER

Welfare advice workers are employed by local authorities, by the Citizens Advice Bureau (CAB) and by a wide range of charities and voluntary organisations. Advice workers answer questions and offer confidential advice and practical help (eg help with filling in a form) to members of the public. Some work with specific client groups, rather than the general public, such as students at a college or tenants of a housing association. The work often involves advocacy work, taking up an issue on behalf of a client or dealing with bureaucracy on their behalf. Some advice workers are generalists, offering advice on many different problems; working for the CAB is a good example of this. Other welfare advisers specialise in issues such as debt management, housing questions, consumer concerns, education and career decisions or discrimination of some kind.

Entry, qualifications and training

While there are no formal entry qualifications, many advice workers are graduates in sociology, psychology or similar subjects. They have often had experience of working with people and many advice workers begin their advice careers in a voluntary capacity. There is a variety of part-time courses available at NVQ levels 2, 3 and 4 in advice and guidance work – many people undertake these once they are working in this field.

Personal attributes

You must be very good at listening to people and at explaining documents or rules patiently and carefully. You need good information research skills and good powers of persuasion if your role involves advocacy work of any kind. You need to be well organised and flexible, with good written communication skills.

Earnings

Earnings are from £14,000 to £24,000 – though few posts pay at the top of this range. If you work for a local authority or an academic institution, your starting salary is likely to be higher than if you work for a voluntary body or charity.

Info

Advice UK
020 7469 5700
www.adviceuk.org.uk

National Association of Citizens
Advice Bureaux (NACAB)
www.citizensadvice.org.uk

WINE TRADE

(see also Publican/Licensee and Retailing)

The wine trade has grown and changed significantly in the past two decades, increasing opportunities in wine retailing, buying, importing and marketing. Wine specialists work for supermarkets, for off-licence chains, for specialist wine traders and for the expanding home delivery market. Opportunities exist in retail management, marketing and importing. To work as a wine buyer, you need extensive experience and knowledge. Wine merchants who do not employ their own buyers may use wine brokers who work with growers and select the kinds of wine in which a particular merchant is interested. There are now many English vineyards springing up, creating some further marketing opportunities.

Entry, qualifications and training

On the retail management side, entry requirements vary – some ask for A levels, some prefer graduates. To get into wine brokerage or wine buying, you normally have to have worked in the trade and also completed wine tasting courses. The Wine and Spirit Education Trust (WSET) runs a wide range of courses for professionals as well as amateurs; check the website for further details.

Personal attributes

You need good people skills, whether dealing directly with customers or working with growers from all parts of the world. You need to have a flair for business, good organisational skills and the ability to work as part of a team and to motivate others.

Earnings

Junior managers earn between £15,500 and £19,500. Managers of larger wine and spirit retailers may earn £25,000. Sales staff marketing home delivery wine services earn between £15,000 and £20,000, with possibilities to earn more through commissions on sales. Experienced wine buyers may earn £35,000.

Info

Skillsmart Retail
020 7462 5060
www.skillsmartretail.com

Wine and Spirit Education Trust
(WSET)
020 7089 3800
www.wset.co.uk

WRITER

For writers other than journalists, making a living purely from writing can be very difficult, so many writers, especially before they are established, have other careers as well. There are only a handful of people who become successful fiction writers or writers of really popular non-fiction such as biographies. There are some jobs for writers in residence with theatre companies and regional arts organisations, prisons or university departments, but many of these posts are temporary contracts.

Technical authors write user manuals and instruction books for anything from washing machines to computer software, and there are writers who specialise in writing textbooks and other teaching materials. Technical authors are often on permanent or at least more secure contracts. Many writers of textbooks have other jobs in education.

Entry, qualifications and training

There are no formal entry qualifications, though most writers have a good level of education, especially in English or other subjects where a good command of the language is important. There are many creative writing courses that can teach the technical aspects of writing, but creativity is not something you can learn. If your goal is to work in film, radio or television, it might be worth considering a script-writing course.

Technical authors come from a wide range of academic disciplines, but science, technology and engineering are particularly useful backgrounds. While there are no specific entry requirements for this work, it is very much a graduate profession.

Personal attributes

Being a brilliant communicator of the written word is the key to your success. While creative writers have to have imagination, flair and a way of drawing the reader in, technical authors must be able to make complex material accessible. All writers have to be determined, self-disciplined, highly motivated and able to cope with rejection. Technical authors have to have a very thorough and careful approach to their work.

Earnings

For creative writers the average income is only around £5,000 a year and more than half of all creative writers have additional jobs, many in teaching or lecturing. Technical authors earn between £18,000 and £30,000.

Info

Association of British Science
Writers
0870 770 3361
www.absw.org.uk

Institute of Internal Communication
(IoIC)
01908 313755
www.ioic.org.uk

Creative and Cultural Skills
(The Sector Skills Council for Craft,
Cultural Heritage, Design,
Literature, Music, Performing, and
Visual Arts)
020 7015 1800
www.ccskills.org.uk

The Poetry Society
020 7420 9880
www.poetrysoc.com

Skillset
8080 300 900 (England and Northern
Ireland)
0808 100 8094 (Scotland)
0800 0121 815 (Wales)
www.skillset.org

The Writers' Guild of Great Britain
020 7833 0777
www.writersguild.org.uk

YOUTH WORKER

Youth workers are employed supporting young people aged 13 to 19 – some work may be done with younger people aged 11 and 12 and some services are offered to people up to the age of 25. Youth workers are mostly employed by local authority social services departments or by Connexions services, but some work for charities and other community organisations.

The work of individual advisers depends on their clients' needs. Most of an adviser's time is spent in direct contact with young people. You could be organising activities such as sports or games, mentoring individuals, facilitating discussions or setting up meetings with other agencies. Your clients may have many problems: drug or alcohol abuse, difficult family backgrounds, problems coping with school. As a youth worker you might be based at a youth club or a drop-in centre of some kind. You might also do outreach work, going into the community to identify young people who might be facing difficulties and be in need of support.

Entry, qualifications and training

Since 2010, anyone wishing to become a youth worker must gain a professional qualification in youth work approved by the National Youth Agency (NYA). This can be either a three-year full-time degree course or a one-year postgraduate course, if you have a degree in another subject. Both of these courses are also offered part-time. You can also join a service as a youth support worker and work towards NVQ levels 2 and 3 and then study for a degree part-time. At whatever level you join, much of the training is on the job.

Relevant experience is a really important part of the selection process. You need to have worked either in a paid or voluntary capacity with young people or in the community in some way.

Personal attributes

Youth workers need strong communication and relationship-building skills to engage the trust and respect of young people. They need to be able to listen carefully and respond appropriately; a non-judgemental approach is essential. Youth workers need to empathise with young people's concerns while maintaining professional and emotional detachment. A sense of humour, reliability, flexibility, good time management and team-working skills are also important.

Earnings

Youth support workers earn £15,000 to £17,500; qualified youth workers earn £20,000 to £28,000 – there is some geographical variation.

Info

National Youth Agency (NYA)
www.nya.org.uk

Youth Council for Northern Ireland
028 9064 3882
www.ycni.org

YOUTH OFFENDING TEAM OFFICER

Youth offending team officers (YOTs) work for local authorities. Their work is concerned with trying to stop young people committing crimes or to prevent those who have already committed offences from reoffending. The work is very varied and YOTs work with young offenders right from the stage where they may have to appear in court through to supporting them after they have been released from secure institutions. As a YOT you might have to prepare sentence reports for the courts. You could be supervising young offenders who have received non-custodial sentences, which they must serve in the community. You could be involved in mediation between victims and offenders in restorative justice programmes. Part of your role would be to help young people to get back into education or training or to find work after serving a sentence. Sometimes you would work on a one-to-one basis with your clients, on other occasions you would work with groups. You would also work closely with other agencies, such as those involved in drug rehabilitation programmes.

Entry, qualifications and training

Many YOTs have a background in other relevant work such as social work, the probation service or youth work. Youth offending teams also employ young offending team support workers who work with lower-risk offenders and do not have to have the same background qualifications. The Youth Justice Board website gives further details of specific requirements. Training is through a combination of on-the-job training and short professional development courses. You may also get the opportunity to work towards a Foundation degree in youth justice.

Personal attributes

You need to be a really good communicator, able to be understanding but also clear and assertive. You need to be confident and calm when dealing with clients who might be hostile to you and your ideas. You also need to be good at motivating people. You must be very good at keeping records, managing a caseload and writing clear reports.

Earnings

Qualified YOTs earn from £20,000 to £30,000. Support staff in the team earn £16,000 to £20,000.

Info

Skills for Justice
www.skillsforjustice.com

Youth Justice Board
020 3372 8000
www.yjb.gov.uk

ZOOLOGY

Zoo keeper

(see Animals)

Zoologist

Zoologists work in either research or teaching. Zoologists study the anatomy, physiology, classification, distribution, behaviour and environment of all kinds of creatures, from insects to elephants. When working in zoos they usually coordinate conservation breeding programmes, collection planning and general conservation strategies. A very small number find jobs in industry, mainly in pharmaceutical and animal foodstuff companies. Research zoologists will probably work in one of the many government-backed centres on a variety of projects, including animal behaviour, pest control and the population ecology of birds.

Entry, qualifications and training

A degree in zoology, available at some universities, is needed for a career as a zoologist. Postgraduate training in specialisations such as entomology or nematology is also available.

Personal attributes

Zoologists should have a scientific mind and an interest in research. They should also have keen powers of observation and be patient and confident.

Earnings

New graduates working as research or technical assistants earn around £19,000. Zoologists in research posts earn up to £28,000.

Info

Zoological Society of London
www.zsl.org/science

Index

Index of advertisers